# THE POLITICS OF REAPPORTIONMENT

# THE  POLITICS  OF

PUBLISHED SIMULTANEOUSLY IN GREAT BRITAIN
BY  PRENTICE-HALL  INTERNATIONAL,  LONDON

# REAPPORTIONMENT

EDITED BY MALCOLM E. JEWELL

ATHERTON PRESS 70 FIFTH AVENUE • NEW YORK 11, N.Y.
A DIVISION OF PRENTICE-HALL, INCORPORATED • 1962

THE POLITICS OF REAPPORTIONMENT
*Edited by Malcolm E. Jewell*

*Library of Congress Catalog Card Number: 62-21052*

*Printed in the United States of America   68526*

THE ATHERTON PRESS POLITICAL SCIENCE SERIES

General Editor for American Government and Politics

CORNELIUS P. COTTER

Assistant Staff Director, U.S. Commission on Civil Rights

# FOREWORD

The issue of apportionment is one of the most important problems facing citizens of most of the states. It underlies many of the other problems of state government. Growing judicial concern with apportionment is evidence of a failure of the political process in many states. A political solution to the problem requires better understanding and more accurate information about apportionment, such as this book provides.

*The Politics of Reapportionment* grew out of a National Seminar for Teachers of Politics held in St. Louis in September, 1961, under the auspices of the National Center for Education in Politics (formerly the Citizenship Clearing House).

The seminar was the sixth in a series of annual "national workshops" designed to provide instructors of politics and selected political leaders with an opportunity for extended discussion of substantive issues, research problems, and teaching techniques.

The 1961 seminar was devoted to the timely issue of reapportionment at both the Congressional and state legislative levels. Participants presented essays on the politics of reapportionment in eleven key states. The essays, which had been circulated among the participants in advance, were critically discussed during the seminar sessions. The discussion resulted in a better understanding of the similarities and differences among states and agreement on some of the factors essential to a theory of apportionment politics. Those who participated were impressed with the quality of the studies and with the advantages of such a comparative approach. It was decided to revise the essays, expand the number of studies to include several additional important states, and to publish the collection in The Atherton Press Political Science Series.

The National Center for Education in Politics (NCEP) seeks to encourage college faculty and students to participate in the political life of their communities. Such encouragement means not only stimulating their interest, but providing them with up-to-date, realistic information about politics. To this end, NCEP has sponsored student and faculty conferences through its regional affiliates; offered faculty and student fellowships and internships in government, political parties, and interest groups; and encouraged research and writing in politics. It has sponsored the publication of a number of short volumes on the politics of individual states, and it cooperated in planning a volume on the 1960 national conventions, published by the Eagleton Institute. When it sponsors research and writing in state politics, NCEP accomplishes two objectives: it provides political scientists with the incentive and opportunity to gain first-hand knowledge of the political process, and it helps to fill the wide gap in the current literature of politics available to students at all levels. This book, like earlier studies with which the NCEP has been associated, is designed to supplement the growing interest in comparative state politics.

We wish to acknowledge the contributions of Congressmen Ken Hechler (Democrat, West Virginia) and John J. Rhodes (Republican, Arizona), who participated in the discussions of apportionment during the seminar. Among the political scientists who contributed to the discussions but not to the book were Cornelius P. Cotter, Walter DeVries, Abraham Holtzman, and Robert C. Wood. Thanks are also due the many legislators and other political leaders who supplied information to the authors of the essays. Their contributions were essential to the accuracy of these studies.

Finally, we wish to thank Congressional Quarterly, Inc., for permission to use its maps on Congressional reapportionment.

BERNARD C. HENNESSY
Director
National Center for Education in Politics

*September 1962*

# Contents

# THE POLITICS OF REAPPORTIONMENT

# PART ONE

## Political Patterns in Apportionment

*MALCOLM E. JEWELL*
*University of Kentucky*

A study of legislative apportionment is essential to an understanding of any representative system of government. In the United States the patterns of apportionment have vitally affected the nature of our state and national political institutions, and our political history has been marked by a number of colorful struggles over this issue. Perhaps for these reasons, American political scientists have devoted more attention to apportionment than to many other problems of government. There are numerous descriptive studies of apportionment battles, many statistical compilations illustrating the extent of inequalities, and a variety of ingenious proposals for reform.[1] The

1

1960 census figures, forcing change at the national level and emphasizing inequities at the state level, have renewed professional and public interest in the matter. The recent decision of the Supreme Court has opened new avenues for change and guaranteed renewed battles over apportionment.

Despite the abundance of study and interest, we are far from an understanding of the political causes and consequences of the various apportionment patterns. Since most battles over Congressional and state legislative apportionment are fought out in the states, we must look to the state scenes for an understanding of apportionment. Most of this volume consists of individual case studies of the apportionment problem. This is an exercise in comparative state politics, a field in which systematic study is relatively new. The student who begins to dig below the surface in this field is likely to decide that there are fifty different political systems, offering no basis for comparison. We are interested in developing theories about apportionment and tracing the political patterns that make comparison possible. For that reason we have asked some of the same questions in state after state, and we have tried to summarize the answers in this introductory chapter.

Our search for an understanding of the politics of apportionment may be broken down into four parts:

1. What are the political factors that have caused the various states to follow differing courses in apportionment?

2. What are the political consequences of these differences in apportionment?

3. When a legislature is grappling with any reapportionment problem, what roles are played by the various political groups involved?

4. What are the consequences of transferring this controversy out of the legislative arena?

At the outset we should clarify our use of terms. Technically, "reapportionment" is the reassigning of legislative seats to various counties, cities, or towns; "redistricting" refers to drawing new lines for districts (either encompassing several counties or within a county or city). The difference is merely a mechanical one, and any given change in legislative representation may involve both steps. As a result the terms are often used interchangeably. Since "apportionment" and "reapportionment" are the most commonly used, we will use them here to describe the process as a whole, including redistricting.

There are basic similarities between the apportionment processes for Congress and for state legislatures. Both involve the problem of revising the structure of representation to give full weight to those areas of the states gaining population. Since Congress has made the assignment of seats to the states a nonpolitical chore of the Census Bureau, the political process of Congressional as well as legislative reapportionment is almost exclusively a state function. In both cases the process involves the contending interests of political parties, urban and rural groups, and individual legislators.

It is possible to develop theories about the apportionment process encompassing both Congressional and state legislative levels. Nevertheless, there are profound differences, and these need to be clearly understood at the start. The issue of state legislative reapportionment may be a fundamental source of political conflict in the state. The pattern of legislative apportionment provides the framework for the entire political structure of the state; in some cases, a reapportionment based on population would literally revolutionize state politics. Though Congressional apportionment provides a framework for national politics, it has relatively little impact on the politics of any particular state. For this reason, the conflict over legislative reapportionment may be a continuing one, raging for years in the legislature and in election campaigns. Congressional reapportionment usually becomes an issue in the state only once in a decade or perhaps only once in two or three decades and, once settled, soon fades into the political background. A conflict over legislative reapportionment is generated by groups inside the state; the conflict may remain latent because of the weakness of disadvantaged groups. A conflict over Congressional reapportionment is usually generated by outside forces, by the computations that determine whether a state's Congressional delegation will increase, decrease, or remain the same. Unless there is a change in its size, there is likely to be no issue of Congressional reapportionment. If there is a change, particularly a loss of seats, the pressure for a solution is great.

There is a further difference between Congressional and legislative reapportionment. A change in Congressional districts affects the personal fortunes of congressmen; though they may be influential, they are outsiders and not the determiners of policy in the state legislature. A change in legislative districts affects the personal fortunes of legislators themselves; for that reason, it may easily become the most important issue of a legislative session. This fact makes legislators cautious and reluctant to change the *status quo,* however compelling the legal and political arguments.

All these factors help to explain why Congressional and legislative reapportionment are seldom taken up concurrently by the legislature or passed as a single package, like that approved by the 1961 session of the California Legislature. Likewise, it is rare for one party or group to make concessions on legislative apportionment in return for concessions on Congressional districting; the interests involved in the two situations are not often sufficiently parallel to permit the *quid pro quo* to become a technique of accommodation. In Alabama during the 1961 session, the two issues were joined when urban interests sought in vain to force long-overdue legislative reapportionment by the tactics they pursued in Congressional apportionment, tactics that almost backfired through the loss of an urban Congressional seat. Some state constitutions, as in Illinois and Florida, separate these issues by the timetable they provide for legislative reapportionment.

From the viewpoint of a single state, the stakes—both political and personal—are much higher in state reapportionment, and there is no compulsion from the Census Bureau. For these reasons, our analysis of state reapportionment focuses primarily on the reasons why it has *not* occurred, while our analysis of Congressional reapportionment is devoted more to how it *has* occurred.

## CAUSES OF STATE APPORTIONMENT PATTERNS

Reapportionment is a controversial issue in most states for an obvious reason: an apportionment based on current population distribution would be to the advantage of some important groups and to the disadvantage of others. Consequently, the nature of the apportionment system tells us a great deal about the strength of various political groups in the state. At one extreme, there may be a reapportionment strictly on the basis of population conducted regularly after each census. At the other extreme, the apportionment may bear no relationship to population or may have remained unchanged for many decades, giving certain groups a highly disproportionate legislative voice. There is no single, simple explanation for the variety of patterns in the states. We must examine urban-rural, partisan, and legal factors as the prime determinants of apportionment patterns.

### Urban-Rural Factors

The issue of apportionment cannot, of course, be separated from the trends of population to urban and metropolitan areas. Not only has population grown unevenly, but hundreds of rural counties have lost population in recent years. The more rapid the population changes in a state, the more quickly any apportionment becomes outdated. There is a natural tendency for rapid population changes to induce resistance to reapportionment from the counties lagging in population.

In states where a single metropolitan center has grown large enough to have a majority, or nearly a majority, of a state's population, there is an additional reason to expect an apportionment system out of line with population. Elsewhere in the state citizens will fear state-wide domination by the "big city" or by a single political machine. Long delays in reapportionment or constitutional provisions weighted against population have been designed to prevent a dominant or nearly dominant legislative position for such cities as New York, Providence, Detroit, and Chicago. Often, as in California, other large cities will join with the rural areas to devise restrictions on the representation of a single metropolitan center, such as Los Angeles. The existence of a single metropolitan center which threatens to become dominant intensifies the urban-rural conflict. It must be added that, within the metropolitan areas, there are also significant population shifts occurring. The most heavily populated districts today are usually in the suburban areas, while population has fallen below state averages in some of the central-city districts. As a consequence, there may not be full support for apportionment even in the largest metropolitan areas.

It is misleading to construct any simple formula equating a lag in reapportionment with the speed of population change. There are some states where the urban and metropolitan growth has been slow enough to keep the issue of reapportionment largely dormant. To put it differently, urban groups have not become numerically strong enough to challenge either legislative inertia on reapportionment or constitutional provisions designed for a rural state. Kentucky, Tennessee, and Alabama are examples of states that are more rural than average, that lack a single dominant metropolitan center, and yet that have maintained an apportionment system clearly advantageous to the rural areas.

### Political Factors

The resistance of rural areas to reapportionment is likely to be greater if one political party is preponderantly rural and has a stake in blocking reapportionment. Outside the South, and particularly in the larger industrial states, Republican strength has been greatest in the rural areas and small cities, while Democratic strength since the New Deal has been greatest in the large cities. This familiar fact of recent political history accounts for much of the resistance to reapportionment. In the absence of partisan factors, urban-rural differences may not be acute enough to stimulate such resistance. When one party is largely urban and the other largely rural, party conflict is great enough to ensure a conflict over apportionment. Moreover, in states where the rural areas are largely Republican, the rural legislators can often count on the votes of whatever Republican legislators come from the cities and suburbs in support of the rural position on reapportionment. The normal operation of the single-member district system tends to intensify the urban-rural bipolarization of the two legislative parties. The Republicans carry most of the rural and small-city districts despite large Democratic minorities in some, while the Republican minority in the large cities often goes unrepresented in the legislature. This is even more likely to be true in those states, such as Michigan and Ohio, using at-large legislative districts in the large cities.

Connecticut, Rhode Island, New York, New Jersey, Pennsylvania, Ohio, Illinois, and Michigan are all examples of states with an urban-rural (or metropolitan-versus-nonmetropolitan) bipolarization of partisan strength, and they are all states in which the Republican Party has used its power to establish or maintain constitutional provisions on apportionment that are disadvantageous to the larger cities and to the Democrats. In all these states the constitutional provisions have at times ensured Republican control over one or both houses of the legislature despite a majority of Democratic votes for governor. Malapportionment is not always to blame for divided government. One party may not have state-wide organizational strength and may fail to run strong legislative candidates in all districts. But, when a party fails to elect a legislative majority although the voters have cast a majority of votes for that party's legislative candidates, the apportionment system is usually at fault. Democratic administrations in Connecticut during this century have always had to deal with a Republican majority, and often a large one, in the House, except after the 1958 landslide in which the Democrats gained a three-vote majority. Democratic governors in New York have normally faced a legislature under firm Republican control. During Gov. Mennen Williams' twelve years as Democratic governor of Michigan, his party never had a majority in either legislative branch, though it once had a tie in one house.

The emergence of suburbs as the most rapidly growing population areas in most states has begun to change the political stakes in reapportionment. Though it is an oversimplification to think of all suburbs as Republican, it is true that suburban growth gives the Republican Party a new incentive to support reapportionment, particularly when it is accompanied by population losses in normally Democratic sections of metropolitan centers. This trend also creates a conflict of interest between the rural and suburban bases of Republican support. In New York, Republican administrations during the last two decades have twice carried out reapportionments to take advantage of suburban population gains but have not changed the constitutional system that still discriminates against New York City.

The mushrooming suburbs are a symptom of a more basic problem facing the Republican Party in the North: to elect a governor it must appeal to the urban and suburban voter; for this purpose the rural base of the party is of declining importance. In some states the Republican Party may have to choose between policies designed to maintain a legislative majority through the rural counties and those designed to win an urban majority in the gubernatorial contest. Apportionment is one of the policies in question, and it is an issue on which Republican leaders are likely to become increasingly divided. The Michigan Republican Party is a good example. They were the urban-oriented Republican leaders, concerned about a decade of Democratic gubernatorial control, who took the lead in pressing for a constitutional convention which might, among other things, redesign the apportionment formula to remove some of the rural bias. The opposition, as might be expected, came from the rural Republicans, particularly those whose control of the Senate is assured by the apportionment formula.[2]

Under other conditions, the Democrats may have a stake in maintaining an apportionment system favoring rural areas. This is true in some of the border and Southwestern states where the rural areas have been traditionally Democratic and where rapidly growing suburbs are strongly Republican. Kentucky and Tennessee are examples, although in each the Republicans have traditional strength in certain rural areas. In Maryland the most underrepresented counties are the suburban ones close to Washington, D.C., and these are the areas of greatest Republican gains. In traditionally Democratic Arizona, the Republican members of the legislature come almost entirely from the two largest counties, containing Phoenix and Tucson and their swelling suburbs. Under the present apportionment, Democratic control of the Arizona Senate appears certain as long as Republican strength is limited to these two counties, which have over two-thirds of the state's population but only four of its twenty-eight senators.

Not every state has an urban-rural polarization of party strength. Where this is lacking the parties are less likely to be policy-oriented or distinguishable as liberal and conservative, nor is reapportionment likely to become a partisan issue. This makes up-to-date reapportionment easier and is likely to make the issue a less intensive source of controversy. There may be still other factors that prevent apportionment by population. The restrictions on the population-principle that were developed in California in the 1920's were aimed not at the Democratic Party but at the potentially dominant position of Los Angeles. The more directly a pattern of apportionment serves the interests of a single party, the greater are the obstacles to a change in the pattern. Despite the cross-pressures caused by suburban boom, resistance to reapportionment is likely to be greatest where one party has primarily rural roots while the other is centered in the larger cities.

In one-party states, factions may be an ephemeral and limited substitute for parties. If factions are strong, they may have an important stake in the apportionment system, but they are seldom strong enough and durable enough to influence apportionment as much as parties do in the Northern industrial states. Where factions have any meaning, they often grow out of urban-rural and regional differences. In North Carolina, differences between the coastal and piedmont legislators have contributed to the stalemate over reapportionment that would benefit the more rapidly growing piedmont area. In Florida, though there is no formal factionalism, the northern, rural counties have common interests which help them to maintain a united front against a reapportionment that would benefit the urban counties farther south. In Alabama, though there are no sharply defined factions, issues often arise between urban and rural areas or between the "black belt" and the rest of the state. The sixty-year-old legislative apportionment favors rural areas, especially those in the black belt.[3]

### Legal Factors

Most state constitutions were written many years ago, when the balance of political power in most states was different from what it is today. Since constitutional change is usually difficult and often requires approval of the legislative body constituted by the existing apportionment formula, the constitution must be viewed as one of the important determinants of apportionment patterns.

When the constitution fixes the number of counties or the total number of legislative seats, it limits the flexibility of reapportionment. Most state constitutions require regular reapportionment based on a decennial census. But the constitutions governing only about one-third of the legislative bodies provide that apportionment shall be based solely on population. Frequently an exception is made to the population principle by permitting every county to have at least one member of the legislature; where the number of legislative seats is not much greater than the number of counties, the population principle can be easily eroded. In some states the population principle applies to all but the largest units of government, which are sometimes limited to a certain percentage of the total membership or limited in the sense that no county may have more than one member while the smaller counties are combined into districts. Some states use a scale of apportionment designed to assist smaller counties and handicap larger ones at the same time; the Florida constitution, which assigns at least one House member to each county, gives three to the five largest counties and two to the eighteen next-largest. Where the population principle is followed, the usual technique is to divide the total population by the number of seats to obtain a ratio for figuring how many seats should be assigned each county or group of counties. In some states the population principle is diluted by the use of a weighted ratio; smaller counties need less than a full ratio for one member, while larger ones need more than an additional full ratio to gain more members.[4]

In some state constitutions the population principle is abandoned entirely for one legislative branch. Several states permit each county (or, in Vermont, each city or town), whatever its size, to have one member and no more in one house. In a few states a fixed apportionment, county by county, has been written into the constitution without any provision for change except by constitutional revision.

Some constitutional provisions have only a slightly distorting effect on the population principle, but in most states where the apportionment system permits the most flagrant underrepresentation of urban areas the primary reason is the language of the constitution. Most of these constitutional restrictions on the population principle were adopted decades ago when the spectre of urban domination first began to haunt the rural legislators. In some cases the contrasts in population trends between urban and rural areas have become so sharp in recent years that the constitutional provisions are far more restrictive than was probably ever expected. In Florida, for example, the county was used as the basis for representation, with each county granted one representative and no county permitted more than one senator; no one anticipated that by 1960 the largest county would be three hundred times as populous as the smallest. In some states, however, the restrictions are relatively recent and have often resulted from compromise efforts to end a deadlock over reapportionment by the legislature. The constitutional provision that permits Los Angeles only one out of forty seats in the California Senate was adopted in 1926, after the Legislature proved unwilling to reapportion on the basis of the population principle then in the constitution. Similarly, Michigan voters in 1952 and Illinois voters in 1954 adopted constitutional amendments that fixed apportionments of the state senates and guaranteed the underrepresentation of Detroit and Chicago; they acted after prolonged legislative failure to reapportion under the constitutional provisions based on population.

If the state constitution requires apportionment strictly by population and rapid population changes are occurring in the state, there may be the greatest legislative resistance to reapportionment. The longer the legislature delays, the more pressure there may be for constitutional revision to restrict the population principle. On the other hand, if the constitution requires only limited adjustments to population changes, there may be greater likelihood that this minimal reapportionment will be promptly enacted. In Florida and North Carolina, for example, the legislatures have acted relatively promptly to make the necessary adjust-

ments in apportionment for the lower houses; in both cases each county
has at least one member, and there is a precise constitutional formula
for apportioning the few additional seats to the larger counties.
designated official or board shall act if the legislature fails to apportion

The constitutional feature most likely to produce regular reapportionment is the delegation of the function to an administrative board,
either initially or in the event the legislature fails to act promptly. Arkansas, Arizona, Missouri, Ohio, Alaska, and Hawaii delegate the reapportioning authority for one or both houses to some state official or board
outside the legislature or to local governing bodies under a rigid formula.
Illinois, Michigan, South Dakota, Texas, California, and Oregon provide
that a designated official or board shall act if the legislature fails to
apportion one or both houses within a given period after a census.[5]
On the surface this may appear to be a simple and complete solution to
the apportionment problem.

A more careful look at the states making some use of an official or a
board for apportionment shows that in nearly every case the constitution
limits the application of the population principle. In such states as
Texas, Missouri, and Ohio, the standards that a nonlegislative agent
must follow guarantee considerable underrepresentation of urban centers.
In California, Illinois, and Michigan the provision for nonlegislative
action guarantees apportionment of one house by population while the
apportionment system in the other house ensures urban underrepresentation. Only one state (South Dakota) that uses population as the sole
constitutional standard for both houses also provides for a board to act
if the legislature fails to do so; there, the legislature has avoided board
action by making minor adjustments in apportionment which left the
larger cities underrepresented. In short, constitutional provisions for
board action are usually a guarantee of either limited accommodation
to population trends or of an accommodation limited to only one legislative branch. Provisions to enforce the population principle strictly in
both branches through board action are rare and are unlikely to grow
more numerous.

The Florida constitution contains another type of provision designed
to ensure periodic reapportionment. If the Legislature fails to act at the
time required by the constitution, the governor must call a special session, which is unlimited in duration and which is "mandatorily required
to reapportion." In practice, this provision has had minimum effect,
because the constitution permits only a limited accommodation of apportionment to population changes and because the Legislature has
usually enacted measures that fell short of even this limited accommodation. In 1955 the governor vetoed the only senatorial reapportionment
measure on the ground that it fell short of constitutional requirements.[6]

One aspect of state constitutions that greatly affects the prospects for reapportionment is the provision for constitutional revision. Over half of the states require a three-fifths or two-thirds vote in the legislature for a constitutional amendment, while one-quarter require legislative approval at two successive sessions; the remainder require only one majority approval. Since the legislature operating under an apportionment formula is seldom enthusiastic about an amendment to change the formula, the other avenues of constitutional change become particularly important.

Most state constitutions provide for a method of convening a constitutional convention, and this method of revision has been used even in states lacking such a constitutional provision. Normally, the legislature must vote first on holding a convention. Limited conventions have been used increasingly in recent years; when this is done the legislature has an opportunity to exclude the question of apportionment from consideration. The convention that drew up the New Jersey constitution adopted in 1948 acted under a legislative mandate that excluded the issue of apportionment, because this issue had been blamed for the failure of previous efforts at constitutional revision. In Michigan, however, the issue of apportionment was one of the critical questions that faced the recent constitutional convention. Michigan is one of several states in which the constitution requires the question of calling a convention to be submitted to the voters periodically (the periods ranging from every seven to every twenty years). The Missouri constitutional convention that met in 1943-1944 did not change the apportionment formula but devised a new plan to ensure regular reapportionment of the Senate by state officials and of the House by local officials.[7] One factor inhibiting changes in apportionment by constitutional conventions is that the apportionment of the convention is usually based on that used in one or both legislative branches. On the whole, the convention appears to be an infrequent and unlikely avenue for liberalizing apportionment provisions in the constitution.

A more promising approach to constitutional revision of apportionment is the use of the initiative, but this is permitted by the constitutions of only thirteen states. Four states have used it for apportionment purposes. California (in 1926) and Michigan (in 1952) used it for the compromise plans, already discussed, to guarantee population apportionment in the lower house while assuring underrepresentation of urban areas in the upper house. Arkansas used the technique in 1936 to establish a board to carry out reapportionment (after forty-six years of legislative inaction), and Oregon used the initiative in 1952 to require that the secretary of state reapportion the legislature if the legislature failed to do so (as it had for half a century). In Arkansas, however, the constitutional initiative was used in 1956 to freeze permanently the Senate districts established in 1952.[8] Among the other states where the constitutional initiative could be used are some in which urban areas are seriously underrepresented by constitutional provisions: Arizona, Nevada, and Ohio. The constitutional initiative is the only method of revision that completely bypasses institutions (legislatures or conventions) that are established under the existing apportionment formula.

The statutory initiative may also be used in the fifteen states that permit it and that also make apportionment a legislative rather than an executive responsibility. Colorado used this technique in 1932 to overcome legislative inertia, as did Washington in 1930. The statutory initiative is sometimes subject to legislative revision. After the Colorado initiative, the legislature sought to supersede it with a new act, but the state court voided it because of inequalities. In Washington, however, the legislature succeeded in amending a reapportionment act passed by popular initiative in 1956, the amendments restoring most of the former apportionment.[9]

Constitutional provisions for either constitutional or statutory initiative significantly increase the possibilities for urban areas to overcome inequalities brought about either by constitutional restrictions or by the action or inaction of the legislature. The initiative is available to rural as well as urban political forces, however, and it has been used by them on occasion to add further restrictions to urban representation in the legislature. In two states (California in 1926 and Michigan in 1952) where the voters had a choice of two initiative proposals at one election, they chose the one least advantageous to the urban centers.

## CAUSES OF CONGRESSIONAL REAPPORTIONMENT

Since 1929 the apportionment of Congressional seats among the states has been carried out automatically by the Census Bureau after each decennial census under a mathematical formula established by Congress, and with the total number of House members fixed at 435. Congress did not include in the 1929 law the standards of compactness, contiguity, and equality found in some earlier apportionment acts. Each census has produced a demand in Congress for enlarging the size of the House, but it remains unchanged and unlikely to grow.

### Resistance to Reapportionment

Whether the state legislature will act on Congressional reapportionment depends almost entirely on whether the size of the state's Congressional delegation has been changed. If the state has lost one or more seats, reapportionment is essential to prevent an at-large election for all seats, although in the past legislative stalemate has occasionally produced such an election. If the state has gained one or more congressmen, the legislature is likely to reapportion, though there is less pressure, and the legislature may choose to elect the additional congressmen at-large.

If there is no change in the number of seats assigned to a state, there is not likely to be any legislative action on reapportionment, even though over a period of years gross inequalities in the population of Congressional districts may have developed. There are twelve states that have kept the same number of congressmen continuously since 1930 (excluding states with one member and North Dakota, which prior to 1962 elected two at large). In none of these has there been any reapportionment since 1930, although in some states the last apportionment was based on the 1910 census, and in New Hampshire the last one was in 1881. In some states this leads to major inequalities. For example, Georgia's districts vary from 246,000 to 618,000, and South Dakota's two districts have 159,000 and 494,000.[10] There are five other states that had a stable number of congressmen from 1930 until the 1960 census required a change. Except for West Virginia, which moved a single county to another district in 1951, these states did not make any changes in apportionment until 1961.

There are several reasons why legislatures seldom voluntarily change the boundaries of Congressional districts. The first is a reluctance to disturb the districts of incumbent congressmen. This is more than a form of professional courtesy to fellow politicians. Congressmen who have established considerable seniority in Washington are a distinct asset to the state. Some of them wield considerable influence in the legislature and among the state's political leaders. Voters who have become accustomed to dealing with one congressman may object to being moved into another district. In some of the states it would appear that the district boundaries have been drawn in such a way as to ensure the maximum number of safe districts for both parties. The low level of competition that results seems satisfactory to congressmen and politicians in both parties.

In addition to these factors that might affect the views of all legislators, there are others influencing the dominant group in the legislature. Population trends have made the metropolitan and urban districts disproportionately large in many states. It is natural that the legislature, in which urban areas are usually underrepresented, is generally slow to adjust Congressional districts. Congressional districts that are twenty or thirty years out of date satisfy the dominant groups and the dominant political party in a malapportioned legislature.

Occasionally the legislature will make an unrequired revision in Congressional districts to serve the interests of a dominant political group.

Kentucky was forced to redraw Congressional districts in 1952 after losing one seat. In 1956, when another faction of the Democratic Party was in power, the districts were redrawn to satisfy the interests of that faction. When Washington gained a congressman as a result of the 1950 census, it elected him at-large because the Republican governor vetoed as inequitable a reapportionment plan passed by the 1951 session of the legislature, under Democratic control. In 1957, Democratic control of the state was strong enough to permit redrawing the districts in order to eliminate the at-large congressman and to increase Democratic chances in some areas. When this failed to alter the six-to-one Republican ratio in the Washington Congressional delegation, the next Democratic legislature, in 1959, passed still another revision, affecting only two Congressional districts in an effort to maximize Democratic chances in one of them. This also failed to dislodge a veteran Republican congressman from an otherwise strong Democratic district.

By and large it remains true, however, that when a minority party gains control of the legislature it usually does not try to enact a new Congressional apportionment, unless a recent census has dictated change. There is always the risk that the other party will restore the original apportionment if it regains power, and there is usually pressure from congressmen of both parties to avoid any unnecessary changes in district lines.

### Minimal and Partisan Reapportionment

When the state is gaining or losing Congressional seats, the legislature faces a choice: it may completely revise Congressional districts or it may make minimal changes in a few districts. If the state is gaining a congressman it also has the choice of electing him at-large. Half the states gained or lost congressmen as a result of the 1960 census; few of them carried out a complete revision of Congressional districts. All the reasons already suggested for avoiding voluntary changes in Congressional apportionment serve to persuade the legislators that a required Congressional reapportionment should affect as few districts as possible. The fewer districts changed, the fewer incumbent congressmen have to adjust to a new set of constituents or run against each other. By minimizing changes, the legislators are best able to resist the pressures from urban centers for a greater share of the Congressional seats.

Another, and sometimes contradictory, factor determines the legislature's approach to Congressional reapportionment: the dominant political party seeks to maximize its gains and minimize its losses from reapportionment. Often party interests are served by a reapportionment affecting only a few districts, but in some cases a party in full control of the legislative and executive branches will carry out a full-scale reapportionment. When there is a one-party Congressional delegation and legislature, the motivation of partisan advantage is removed and with it the incentive to make major changes in Congressional districts. Similarly, when no single party controls the governorship and both branches of the legislature, the necessity for compromise dictates minimal changes in Congressional districts, or sometimes an at-large election of additional congressmen. A bipartisan compromise may also be aimed at maintaining as many safe districts for both parties as possible.

A few examples drawn from post-1960 reapportionments will lend substance to these generalizations. The Republican Party had complete control in New York; party strategy dictated extensive revisions in the New York City districts, and the resulting districts, though relatively equal in size, were as oddly shaped and noncompact as any gerrymandered districts seen in the nation in years. The Democrats were in complete control of the California reapportionment process; since the state gained eight congressmen, an extensive revision was necessary, and the Democrats used this opportunity to gain the maximum partisan advantage from the creation of new districts. In Iowa, only one Congressional seat was lost, but the Republican legislature made extensive changes in district boundaries to disperse the remnants of a Democratic district as harmlessly as possible.

In both West Virginia and North Carolina, Democratic legislatures determined to combine the only Republican district with a Democratic one. In both states this purpose was accomplished with relatively few changes in the remaining districts, and as a consequence there were wide variations in the size of the newly formed districts. The Democrats in Maryland, despite their complete legislative and gubernatorial control, faced a difficult problem in maximizing party advantage. The state was gaining a congressman, and the great population gains had come in the suburban counties surrounding Washington and in Baltimore County (not the city); these are among the strongest Republican regions in a Democratic state. The Democratic districts in Baltimore city were below average. The Democrats created the new district by splitting one of the largest partly suburban districts and left the remaining districts unchanged, though two of these were each almost three times as large as the smallest rural Democratic district. This partial reapportionment was challenged by referendum and at least temporarily blocked.

In New Jersey the Democratic governor and the Republican legislature found it possible to compromise in adding a congressman by making a separate district out of a county that had formerly been divided into parts of the two largest districts in the state. Other districts remained unchanged, although they ranged from 255,000 to 585,000 in population.[11] The limited reapportionment appears to have been attractive to both parties because it left unchanged a number of relatively safe Democratic and Republican districts. This seemed to serve Republican interests, even though the smallest districts were Democratic ones (mostly Newark and Jersey City).

In Illinois, where divided government also prevailed, there was prolonged deadlock over the reduction of Congressional districts by one. The major problem resulted from the population trends out of Chicago into the suburban areas of Cook County, trends that the Democrats were reluctant to recognize in reapportionment legislation. The final compromise produced districts in Cook County ranging widely in population; the smaller ones were generally Democratic, but the result was made palatable to both parties by the fact that most seats would be safely Democratic or Republican.

In Ohio, a state with a Democratic governor and a Republican legislature, there appeared to be no possibility of a compromise on reapportionment. Since Ohio was gaining a seat, it was possible to compromise by electing a congressman at-large after efforts to create new districts failed. If either party gains complete legislative-executive control, new districts may be anticipated.

Arkansas illustrates the tendency in a one-party state to make as few changes as possible in Congressional districts. The Arkansas legislature succeeded in reducing six Congressional districts to four by combining four of them into two districts while leaving the other two virtually unchanged, although the two new ones have populations of 518,000 and 575,000, while the old ones have only 360,000 and 333,000.[12]

We have described the Congressional reapportionment problem largely in terms of partisan motivations and the desire to minimize drastic changes in district boundaries. These factors tend to overshadow urban-rural conflicts. One reason is that individual Democratic congressmen have a vested interest in maintaining their urban districts unchanged, even though they may be above average in population. Another factor, of increasing importance, is that many of the urban (in contrast to suburban) districts have actually fallen below the state average. We have already discussed three states—Maryland, New Jersey, and Illinois—where this is true. Massachusetts, Pennsylvania, New York, and Michigan are other states in which there are or have recently been below-average Congressional districts in some of the largest cities (Boston, Philadelphia, New York City, Detroit). While cities, or parts of cities, that are losing population still remain underrepresented in most state legislatures, some of them are overrepresented in Congress. Since these districts are usually Democratic and since overrepresented rural districts in Northern states are usually Republican, both parties in some of the states have reason to prefer a minimum change in Congressional district boundaries. In New York, the Republicans succeeded in increasing suburban representation in Congress at the expense of Democratic city districts; in Illinois and Maryland, Republican efforts in this direction were only partially successful.

In a state dominated by one party, urban-rural conflicts may be clearer. Florida gained four congressmen as a result of the population boom in the metropolitan centers of southern Florida. The rural-dominated Legislature added three districts in some of the largest southern metropolitan areas, and then added a fourth in the rural northern area where there was no significant population gain. The resulting variation in districts is from 237,000 to 660,000.[13]

Reapportionment at the Congressional, as well as the legislative, level can be affected by the legal framework of a state. The statutory initiative could be used to bring about reapportionment and might well be used in states where the Congressional boundaries have long remained unchanged because of a stable number of congressmen. Another instrument of popular control, the referendum, has been used to challenge Congressional reapportionment acts of the legislature. The effect of such a referendum, if successful, is to nullify such acts, forcing the legislature to approve a new apportionment, presumably more in accord with the views of those who instituted the referendum. Almost half the states permit the use of a referendum. This was the method used in 1961 by Maryland suburbanites to challenge the limited reapportionment in that state which left several suburban counties seriously underrepresented. The referendum is often a potent weapon, because a successful petition to place the issue on the ballot keeps the challenged apportionment act from taking effect at the first Congressional election. In Arkansas, the residents of three counties who objected to being put in a certain Congressional district succeeded in their petition campaign; to forestall an at-large election of all congressmen (since the state was losing seats), the legislature passed a new law meeting the demands of these three counties, and the referendum was never held.[14] In California, on the other hand, Republican critics of the Democratic reapportionment were deterred from seeking a referendum by its cost, the large number of required signatures, and the complexity of the issue.

## POLITICAL CONSEQUENCES

## OF STATE MALAPPORTIONMENT

It is abundantly clear that the legislative apportionment systems in many states have left the major urban centers grossly underrepresented. In Connecticut, the four largest cities have 23 per cent of the population and eight out of 279 members in the House. In New Jersey, the five largest counties have 53 per cent of the population and five of twenty-one seats in the Senate. In Florida, the five largest counties have half the population and five of thirty-eight Senate seats. Wayne County has one-third of the population and one-fifth of the seats in the Michigan Senate. Cook County has over half the population and twenty-four of the fifty-eight Senate seats. Los Angeles has almost 40 per cent of the population and one of forty seats in the Senate; the six largest counties have two-thirds of the population and six of forty Senate seats. The statistical details vary, but most of the citizens of metropolitan areas in this country are underrepresented in state legislatures, some of them by large margins. Probably the most comprehensive measurement of inequalities in representation is that prepared by Paul T. David and Ralph Eisenberg, based on the 1960 census figures. Their computations of the value of votes use a value of 100 for persons equitably represented. Their national averages show that the vote of persons in counties of over 500,000 population has a value of only 76, while the vote of those in counties of under 25,000 is valued at 171. The range is somewhat greater in the largest states.[15]

A closer examination of the states shows that it is primarily the growing suburban areas that are underrepresented and that some, though not all, of the districts in the center of metropolitan areas have a population at or below the state average. The study by David and Eisenberg shows that, in most of the twenty-seven largest standard metropolitan statistical areas, the central-city counties are less underrepresented than the suburban counties. Among the counties where the value of the vote is close to the state average are those containing Philadelphia, San Francisco, St. Louis, and New York City. (This is an average of the vote value in the two legislative houses.) The contrast between central city and suburb is sharper if the population variations within the central county are considered, though this is not evident if a single senator represents the county or if house members for a county are elected at-large.

### Legislative Results

What are the legislative consequences of these inequalities? This is one area where more research is necessary. It is easy to provide examples but difficult to find an answer accurate for more than a few states. A legislature dominated by members from the farms, towns, and small cities is not likely to be sympathetic to the needs of the larger cities. Home rule legislation and laws to deal with the specific problems of the larger cities—slum clearance, metropolitan transit, annexation, for example—often fail because of the ignorance and indifference of rural legislators. Urban underrepresentation affects the outcome of votes on labor and welfare legislation and in the South on segregation questions.

Cities are often seriously handicapped by the state legislature in the type of taxes they can levy and the size of tax rates permitted. Perhaps the most direct evidence of discrimination against urban areas lies in the formulas established by state legislatures for the distribution of state aid or of certain proportions of state-collected taxes. When state aid is distributed in greater amounts to counties with lower total assessed property, urban areas sometimes suffer because their *rate* of assessment is generally higher. The distribution of school funds often neglects the needs of urban areas, particularly those growing school districts burdened by heavy construction costs. Probably the most widespread discrimination is in the distribution of some portion of the gasoline tax for road-building. The formula used often favors rural counties because it gives little weight to population, while in some states none of the tax receipts are available to cities for their road needs.[16]

It needs to be said, however, that the picture is not simple. Though there are some issues, notably that of state aid, on which there is a clear conflict between the large metropolitan areas and the rural areas, there are other issues on which the lines are not so clearly drawn. There may be rivalries between the largest cities (such as New York or Chicago) and other urban areas of a state. There is a strong likelihood of differences within metropolitan areas between the central city and the suburbs on such issues as welfare legislation, local taxation, and annexation. Legislators from the rural areas may support those from the suburbs (particularly if both are members of the same party) against the proposals of legislators from the central city. If such voting alignments prevail in the legislature, there may be an alliance between legislators of the most underrepresented and most overrepresented districts. To put it differently, a reapportionment based strictly on population would help the suburban areas more than the urban and might handicap the largest cities in solving some of their problems. Such a reapportionment would help the legislature in dealing with the problems of an urban society by increasing the proportion of legislators familiar with such problems, but it would not guarantee any easier agreement in the legislature on the solution of these problems.

## Impact on State Politics

Perhaps the most significant feature of malapportionment is its impact on the political structure of a state, a point foreshadowed in our analysis of the causes of apportionment patterns. There is no doubt that the apportionment system has aided the Republican Party in many Northern states and, in recent years, has helped the Democratic Party in border and Southwestern states. The impact of the apportionment system on politics is most evident in those competitive two-party states where one party has been able to maintain control over one or both branches of the legislature despite the popular majorities won by the other party, guaranteeing divided government. Divided government during Democratic administrations, due largely to the apportionment system, has been the rule in recent decades in many of the Northeastern and Midwestern industrial states. In some of the Northern states, one of two factors may tend to decrease the Republican advantage from malapportionment: the growth of suburbs often means that Republican districts become underrepresented, and the use of at-large elections in metropolitan counties of some states usually gives the Democrats some advantage.

In states where the dominant position of one party is being challenged by the minority party, malapportionment is seldom the only explanation for divided government, but it can be an important contributory factor, making it difficult for a party that scores a breakthrough in the gubernatorial race to capture the legislature as well.[17] This is most evident in some of the states where the Republicans have been making recent efforts to challenge Democratic control, for example, Maryland, Arizona, and New Mexico. Republican growth has been greatest in the booming suburban districts of these states, while the overrepresented rural areas are traditionally Democratic.

Any apportionment system that serves the interests of a dominant majority party undermines the prospects for two-party competition in a state. Malapportionment may have further impact if it causes the rural *wing* of the minority party to be overrepresented in the legislature. In most states today a party must make some appeal to the urban vote if it hopes to compete in gubernatorial elections. If the party's legislative record is made primarily by rural legislators (who have little personal interest in reapportionment), it is not likely to be one that will form the basis for a strong gubernatorial campaign. This is the problem of the minority Republican Party in Kentucky; its legislative voice is primarily rural, and its urban and suburban voters usually lack legislative representation, owing both to the single-member district system and to malapportionment. A minority party can even be handicapped by overrepresentation. In Rhode Island the apportionment system usually assures small-town, Republican control of the Senate; these Republicans make a conservative record that handicaps the party's generally hopeless struggle for gubernatorial victory in a heavily urban state. Moreover, Republican senators gain enough patronage from their strategic position that they have little incentive to make a record conducive to Republican victories.[18] Malapportionment encourages divided, irresponsible government; it frustrates minority efforts at complete electoral victory; it fosters government by patronage and political deals. All these features undermine a viable two-party system in the states.

Particularly in a state where one party is dominant, the apportionment system can affect the balance of power in a party. Factionalism is sometimes along urban-rural or regional lines, and overrepresentation of rural areas or one section of the state in the legislature strengthens the hand of one faction, not only in legislative matters but in such questions as patronage and state aid that may be of immediate interest to a political faction. The Long organization in Louisiana was originally established on a rural foundation, and the apportionment system gave it an advantage. In a state like Florida, one gubernatorial candidate frequently is particularly strong in urban areas; if successful in the primary election, he faces inevitable difficulties in dealing with a rural legislature. For years, rural elements have usually dominated the Florida Legislature, organizing and running it to serve their interests and to frustrate strong gubernatorial leadership.[19] The formation of an urban faction that has continuity and a deeper basis than personal loyalties is handicapped by the inability of any such faction to control the Legislature.

The apportionment system has a more direct effect on the party when the composition of state party committees or conventions is linked by law to legislative apportionment; in such cases, rural control of the legislature would guarantee rural control of the party organs. Among such states are South Carolina, Louisiana, and Texas. State party organs in the South sometimes play an important role, such as determining whether the national party's presidential candidate will appear on the state party ticket. The apportionment system may even affect the nomination of a party's candidates. The county-unit system that applies to state-wide primaries in Georgia (and has recently been challenged by the courts) provides that the winner is the candidate with the largest number of county-unit votes. The unit vote of each county is cast as a whole for the primary winner there, and the number of unit votes is twice the number of representatives that the county has in the legislature. This system at least reduces the likelihood of divided government by giving the rural areas an advantage in the gubernatorial race as well as in the legislature. Maryland has a similar system with unit votes based on seats in the legislature, which is apportioned to favor rural areas, and with a party convention acting like an electoral college to ratify the voters' decisions as interpreted through the county-unit formula.[20]

## CONSEQUENCES OF MALAPPORTIONMENT IN CONGRESS

It is more difficult to demonstrate the impact of malapportionment on the decisions made by Congress. A careful analysis of the population statistics and political proclivities of 435 Congressional districts would be necessary to show whether certain groups or one political party has an advantage. Frequent restudy would be necessary to take account of population and political trends in the country. The apportionment of Congress is the result of decisions, and indecision, by fifty state legislatures, often acting with differing motives and conflicting political objectives. It is safe to say that neither urban nor rural groups have an advantage resulting from malapportionment of Congressional seats that is comparable to the advantage rural areas have in certain states and that neither national party has the advantage enjoyed by one or the other party in some states. The textbook answer with regard to Congress is that equal representation of states in the Senate and apportionment of House seats by rural legislatures give rural groups an advantage in both houses. This traditional answer deserves careful examination.

## Who is Underrepresented?

The growing urbanization of this country has affected the nature of representation in the Senate. According to the 1960 census, thirty-nine states have a population more than 50 per cent urban, and in half of the states more than half the population lives in standard metropolitan statistical areas. In all but the most completely rural states the senators must be sensitive to urban opinions. In such states as New York, Pennsylvania, Ohio, Illinois, and California, the major urban centers are so important that the senators are likely to be oriented predominantly to urban interests, though each of these states has a number of representatives from districts containing small towns and farms. This is the factor that has made the Senate in recent years appear more liberal than the House on labor, welfare, and economic issues.

One of the difficulties of appraising House apportionment is that the districts cannot be neatly divided into metropolitan, urban, suburban, or rural. Even if the Congressional districts in a state were equal in population, the urban residents could be effectively underrepresented if the major cities were each swallowed up in a predominantly rural district. This might be largely the consequence of geography and not the result of malapportionment by the state legislature. The growth of cities and suburbs increases the likelihood that urban areas will dominate urban-rural districts, and this fact helps to offset the fact that, in the absence of reapportionment, urban growth means that the gap between the size of urban and rural districts will grow. Similarly, districts that encompass urban and suburban areas are growing more heavily suburban, and this tends to offset the trend toward purely suburban districts becoming substantially more populous than purely urban ones. With these qualifications in mind, the political scientist should be cautious about asserting gross differences in urban and rural apportionment or about trying to measure precisely the degree of malapportionment. In some states, the ratio between a few of the largest and smallest districts is as much as two-to-one or occasionally three-to-one, but the enormous discrepancies found in state legislative apportionment are absent.

The Congressional Quarterly, in a study of the Congressional districts existing in 1960 (based on the census of that year), concluded that the suburban voters were substantially underrepresented but that urban voters, as a whole, were only slightly disadvantaged. There were 126 urban districts (primarily those containing the central cities of metropolitan areas); in these the relative value of the vote was 95 (based on a national average of 100). There were sixty suburban districts (in the heavily populated areas around central cities); here the value of the vote was seventy-five. In the remaining districts, loosely described as rural, the value of the vote was 112. The suburban voter was underrepresented and the rural voter overrepresented in all sections of the country. The urban voter was overrepresented in the Northeast and in the West, but underrepresented slightly in the Midwest and substantially in the South. The Congressional Quarterly estimated that an "ideal" reapportionment would provide a net gain of seven urban seats and twenty surburban seats, with twenty-seven taken from rural areas.[21]

Another way of illustrating statistically the consequences of malapportionment is to examine the smallest and largest districts. After the 1950 census the average Congressional district was about 348,000; after the 1960 census it was about 412,000. During the 1950's nearly all the districts below 275,000 (based on 1950 figures) were completely outside metropolitan areas. Few of these districts were affected by post-1960 reapportionments. By 1962 most of the districts under 300,000 population (based on 1960 figures) continued to be those outside metropolitan areas, but there were several such districts in the metropolitan areas of New Jersey, Maryland, Illinois, and Michigan—all states where there was only limited reapportionment.[22]

During the 1950's four-fifths of the districts over 450,000 were completely or largely in metropolitan areas, some of them primarily urban and some primarily suburban. By 1962 three-fourths of the districts over 500,000 were completely or largely metropolitan. Very few of the oversize districts of the 1950's were much affected by reapportionment after 1960. The metropolitan districts that joined the oversize ranks in the 1960's were almost always ones that had grown rapidly during the preceding decade and were changed little or not at all by reapportionment legislation. The suburbs constituted an increasingly important part of these districts. Oversize rural districts fell into two categories. About half were districts unaffected by reapportionment and usually containing one large urban center; the rest were the victims of inequitable reapportionments, in several cases because two districts were combined into one.

### Partisan Advantage

What effect has malapportionment had on the political makeup of Congress? Any complete answer to this question would require a probing of the intricacies of gerrymandering. If the answer is based only on the relative size of Democratic and Republican districts, the political consequences of malapportionment are less than might be expected. The pattern can perhaps be examined most accurately in the large states where both parties win at least a few Congressional seats. New York, Pennsylvania, Illinois, and Ohio all had Congressional reapportionments carried out after the 1950 census by Republican legislatures (although Illinois and Ohio had Democratic governors). In none of these states was there any clear pattern of discrimination in the *size* of districts. There was little difference in average population between districts won consistently from 1952 to 1960 by the Democrats and those won by the Republicans; in Illinois the Democratic districts were actually slightly smaller, while the greatest contrast, New York, gave the Republicans a moderate advantage. The largest districts included both Democratic urban districts and Republican suburban districts. In Michigan, however, the 1951 apportionment passed by a Republican Legislature (with a Democratic governor) created districts numerically favorable to the Republicans. The five consistently Democratic districts (all in Wayne County) averaged about 115,000 larger than the ten consistently Republican districts.

Across the country the weighting of Congressional apportionment to favor rural areas does not provide as much of an advantage to the Republican Party as might be expected. During the 1950's there were twenty-five districts over 450,000 and forty-nine districts under 275,000 (based on the 1950 census). Two of the larger and six of the smaller were not won by a single party in four or five of the Congressional elections, 1952-1960, and can be classified as marginal districts. Of the remaining large districts, seven were Southern Democratic, seven Northern Democratic, and nine Republican; of the small districts, seventeen were Southern Democratic, six Northern Democratic, and twenty Republican. The distribution of Southern Congressional seats has had little effect on partisan competitive advantage (with a few exceptions in such states as Tennessee and Texas). Of all seats won by Northern Democrats in at least four out of five elections, 6 per cent were in large districts and 5 per cent in small; of those won by Republicans, 6 per cent were in large districts and 12 per cent in small. Since, outside the South, there are more small rural districts that are Republican than Democratic, there seems to have been a slight Republican advantage from the apportionment pattern of the 1950's.

The reapportionment bills passed in 1961 and 1962 were bipartisan compromises in a number of the larger states. There were a few examples of reapportionment bills clearly benefiting one party—the Republicans in New York and the Democrats in California, for example. Despite the example of New York, recent trends in Northern politics suggest that the Democrats will seldom be so outnumbered in state legislatures in the foreseeable future as they have frequently been in the past in Northern states. Closer two-party competition decreases the likelihood of flagrant gerrymandering by either party. In the South, however, Democratic control of the legislatures remains strong and usually overwhelming. Republican Congressional districts in the South include several metropolitan counties that are underrepresented: Dallas, Texas (in a district with a population of 951,527); Arlington, Virginia; Tampa, Florida—the number is likely to grow. Congressional reapportionment across the country usually lags behind population trends, sometimes far behind. In the past this lag has been a handicap primarily to the Democratic Party. The population growth in Republican urban and suburban districts, both North and South, and the shrinkage of some Democratic urban districts mean that the reapportionment lag will handicap the Republicans as much as or more than the Democrats. At the moment, during this period of transition, it appears that Democratic and Republican advantages from malapportionment roughly balance.

## Effect on Policy

The impact of malapportionment on Congress is not only a matter of parties but of policies. The population migration into metropolitan centers is being reflected only gradually in Congressional apportionment. Consequently, the House of Representatives is less sensitive to the needs of cities and particularly metropolitan areas than it would be under an equitable apportionment system. There is no certainty, however, that urban representatives will be "liberal" and rural representatives "conservative." Both Northern Republicans and Southern Democrats representing the large cities may represent primarily their higher-income constituents. In recent years there has been a tendency for Southern Democrats from metropolitan districts to be slightly less conservative than their rural colleagues.[23] If labor unions were stronger and the potential of the Negro vote were more fully realized in Southern metropolitan areas, there would probably be a more significant contrast between the voting patterns of metropolitan and rural congressmen in the South, provided there were sufficient competition in Congressional primaries.

A number of the most liberal Republican congressmen come from metropolitan areas, but so do a number of the most conservative Republicans. The place of a Republican congressman's voting record on a liberal-conservative continuum appears to be determined more by the two-party balance in the Congressional district than by its urban or rural nature. An examination of districts won by Republican congressmen continuously from 1952 through 1960 shows that there are a higher proportion of liberals or party mavericks in the districts where the Republican presidential margin was less than 55 per cent in 1960 and less than 60 per cent in either 1956 or 1952. Among these marginal districts the proportion of Republican liberals was not lower in rural areas but was actually slightly higher than in metropolitan areas. In the secure Republican districts, there was a high proportion of conservatives, equally high in metropolitan and in rural districts. Republican metropolitan districts appear more likely to produce liberal Republicans only in the sense that they include a higher proportion of marginal districts; 42 per cent of Republican metropolitan districts and only 16 per cent of Republican rural districts are marginal.[24]

## ROLES IN THE REAPPORTIONMENT STRUGGLE

The concept of *role,* one of the most useful tools devised in recent years for analysis of the legislative process, is best suited to bring into focus the struggles in various legislative bodies over Congressional and state reapportionment. The role played by a legislator is the pattern of behavior that he associates with his status as a member of the legislature. The role that he assumes may result from his understanding of the norms established by fellow legislators, the customs and habits of the legislative body, or from the expectations of persons outside the legislature: constituents, pressure groups, perhaps the governor. Research has shown that legislators hold various concepts of their roles, that the role concepts of a single legislator may change under varying circumstances, and that these role concepts directly affect his behavior in the legislature.[25]

We are interested both in the concepts held by legislators of their role in reapportionment conflicts and in the role played by three groups outside the legislature: congressmen, the governor, and pressure groups. In this area, the research remains to be done; the author knows of no studies probing role concepts in the reapportionment controversy. Extensive interviewing along these lines might shed considerable light on the successes and failures of struggles for reapportionment. The studies in this volume and earlier studies provide enough clues, however, to enable us to speculate about role concepts and, in so doing, to provide a framework for the case studies that follow.

The Legislator

At the start of this chapter we emphasized the contrasts between Congressional and legislative reapportionment. At the heart of this contrast is the difference in the roles played by the legislator. When legislative reapportionment is the issue, the legislator sees his own political future at stake, sees himself as the possible victim of such proposed legislation. His role is motivated primarily by the desire for political self-preservation. This motivation is absent when the issue is Congressional reapportionment, and he can view it with greater detachment.

There are probably some differences in the role concepts of various legislators concerning apportionment, but there is enough similarity in the pattern from state to state to suggest that most legislators recognize a set of norms as standard in most legislatures. It appears to be universally true that legislators do not see themselves as human computers, bound only to translate the census returns into districts of near-perfect equality.

In Congressional reapportionment battles, one of the most widely accepted norms is that the majority is entitled to redistrict in such a way as to maximize party advantage. Though blatant examples of gerrymandering and population inequality will evoke loud protests from the minority, members of both parties recognize that the majority has certain prerogatives in reapportionment. In a competitive, two-party state, most legislators view this as a party issue and are more inclined than usual to support a party position. The New York reapportionment of 1961 illustrates this, although there were a few legislators breaking party ranks for local reasons. Particularly in states dominated by a single party, the legislator may seek to advance either regional or urban-versus-rural interests. This is one reason why rural legislatures have been so slow to change Congressional apportionment patterns favorable to rural interests. Conflicts between party interests and local interests are settled in a variety of ways, but usually loyalty to party appears to be the strongest force. In North Carolina, where there were regional differences over reapportionment, eastern legislators were able to force a consolidation of districts in the western part of the state because this might eliminate the one Republican congressman. In Illinois and Pennsylvania, Democratic Party leaders trying to avoid the loss of seats in Chicago and Philadelphia were able to keep rural Democratic legislators in line while they negotiated with Republican leaders over a compromise.

One of the most widely accepted norms in the politics of reapportionment is that sitting congressmen should be disturbed as little as possible. This means that two incumbent congressmen should not be forced to run against each other if it can be avoided and also that district boundaries should be changed as little as possible. This motivation may conflict with the desire of the majority to maximize party advantage, but legislators often seem to perceive party advantage in terms of the interests of the party's congressmen. Moreover, party advantage, and in fact the advantage of both parties, may consist of leaving unchanged as many districts safe for both parties as is possible. We might define the legislator's perception of his role in reapportionment as that of disturbing the *status quo* as little as possible. The *status quo* serves the immediate and tangible interests of incumbent congressmen (perhaps with accumulated seniority) and those of one or even both parties. The only argument for change is the need for population equality, and to most legislators—even those from underrepresented areas—this argument appears highly theoretical and devoid of practical advantage.

The legislator's role in legislative apportionment is, of course, a far more personal one. He resists not only changes that would endanger his re-election but those that would adversely affect his colleagues. The desire to prevent political injury to fellow legislators becomes the most important argument for the *status quo* when the proposed change in apportionment is not sufficiently drastic to endanger legislative control by a party or region. When reapportionment does occur, this concern for individuals is likely to dictate the nature and extent of change. The following description of the 1955 legislative reapportionment in Illinois describes the attitude of legislators in most states:

> From the beginning, all the legislative committees involved in redistricting placed primary consideration on people, notably sitting senators and representatives, rather than on abstractions like area, population, contiguity, or ethnic characteristics. Influential members all agreed that there was no point in chipping out districts that satisfied the constitutional requirement but did not satisfy the members, if it was possible to satisfy both the members and the constitution. There were innumerable combinations that would satisfy the constitution, and the more practical approach was to try to satisfy the members first.[26]

Another fundamental principle under which legislators usually operate is that each house should be free to conduct its own reapportionment, at least if this does not involve any fundamental change in the apportionment pattern. This cooperative arrangement does not necessarily break down when the two houses are controlled by different factions or parties. The conservative-dominated Texas Senate in 1961 accepted the House apportionment plan designed to strengthen liberal control in the House.

If personal considerations are more important in legislative reapportionment, loyalty to party or region is somewhat less so. These do not conflict in the case of a legislator whose party and locality benefit from the *status quo*. The legislator whose city or county stands to gain from reapportionment may still oppose it if the boundaries of his own district will be changed. The legislator in a district scheduled to lose seats has a close personal identity of interest with his district, and this combined interest is likely to override partisan factors. In a state where the constitutional or statutory apportionment regularly handicaps the urban-based party, that party must win rural seats if it is ever to win a legislative majority. If it succeeds, legislators from those rural districts, whose tenure is thus made insecure, are likely to break party ranks and vote against any reapportionment that would hurt their districts.

Rural legislators seem to be more concerned with what their districts stand to lose from reapportionment than urban legislators are with possible gains. If the reapportionment plan under consideration is a limited one, legislators whose district or party stands to gain are often reluctant to press for action because the probable alienation of fellow legislators (possibly endangering their proposed bills) is too high a price to pay for the limited gains to be anticipated. If a major reapportionment, perhaps involving constitutional change, is suggested, the threat to vested partisan and local interests is usually great enough to inspire the most vigorous opposition.

The attitude of legislative leaders is fundamentally the same as that of rank-and-file legislators, but where legislative leadership is strong they are in a strategic position to protect their own interests, and those of such political allies as congressmen. In North Carolina's 1961 Congressional redistricting the legislative leaders played a key role as they sought to protect the districts including their home counties. Legislative leaders in Washington who were adversely affected by the 1956 reapportionment by initiative were in a strong position to effect legislative amendment of the apportionment plan.[27]

## The Congressman

A Congressional reapportionment is an acid test of a congressman's political strength among fellow politicians. There seems to be considerable variety here. Some congressmen have built personal organizations, and others work closely with party leaders and legislators; some are almost inviolate because of the power that derives from seniority, while others are expendable. Letters, telephone calls, even personal trips to the state may be anticipated from the congressmen. A good example of a congressman's influence is the success of Clarence Brown of Ohio in preventing any alteration in his district during the 1961 session of the legislature. In states where there is danger that deadlock will force an at-large election for all seats, the incumbent congressmen, who have the most to lose, are sure to be as active as possible in the controversy. In

1962, Massachusetts congressmen played a key role in breaking the deadlock in that state. Once a plan has been developed to eliminate a Congressional district, all congressmen unaffected by the plan are likely to work for its support; rural Alabama congressmen lobbied vigorously in person and by proxy in support of an unsuccessful plan to eliminate the Birmingham district.[28] Congressmen may work to increase the margin of electoral safety in their districts; in Pennsylvania this motive produced bipartisan cooperation among congressmen from the Pittsburgh area.

## The Governor

For a number of reasons, the role of governors in reapportionment controversies varies from state to state. In some states the governor is traditionally much stronger in legislative leadership than in others. Some governors have a party majority in the legislature, others face an opposition legislature, while others operate in a one-party state where there is no party discipline. The personalities and abilities of individual governors vary. Within this pattern of variety, the governor's role seems to be more clearly defined, and more positive, when the issue is Congressional than when it is legislative reapportionment. If it is true, as we have suggested, that party loyalties are more binding on the question of Congressional reapportionment, this helps to explain why the governor, as party leader, plays a significant role.

There seems to be no doubt that the governor was instrumental in achieving New York's recent Congressional reapportionment; he called a special session to consider the Republican plan and used his powers of persuasion to bring a few disgruntled Republican legislators into line. The Democratic governors in Illinois and Pennsylvania played major roles in the involved negotiations with Republican leaders that resulted in compromises. Gov. Edmund Brown's role in California's reapportionment, though apparently less important, was significant on some occasions.

In one-party states, the factor of party loyalty is absent, but strong gubernatorial leadership may be customary. In Kentucky, the governor took the initiative in proposing a Congressional reapportionment plan and encountered little difficulty in securing its enactment by the 1962 legislature. His predecessors had been just as successful in effecting reapportionment in 1952 and 1956. The North Carolina governor appears to have been influential but not decisive in the 1961 Congressional reapportionment. During the 1961 struggle over reapportionment in Alabama, the governor was frequently in conflict with the legislature, but was able to win a partial victory because he used the veto power boldly and had a small but determined band of supporters in the legislature. The governor and some urban legislators originally hoped to force revision of legislative apportionment in connection with redrawing Congressional boundaries to eliminate one district. This effort failed, and the rural, black-belt legislators succeeded in passing a Congressional redistricting bill to divide up the Birmingham district. The governor returned the bill to the legislature with an executive amendment proposing instead that primaries be held in the nine existing districts with an at-large run-off primary to eliminate one of the nine winners. The governor's amendment would have been rejected but for a ninety-six-hour filibuster by his supporters that used up the remaining time fixed by the constitution for the legislative session. Then, at a later special session, the legislators accepted a plan based on the governor's proposal.[29]

Since most legislative bodies usually have a strong built-in resistance to their own reapportionment, the governor might be expected to play a vigorous role in initiating either constitutional or statutory reapportionment. The governor usually has a large urban constituency; many of his problems of legislative leadership derive from the rural bias of legislative representation. Yet the governor seldom perceives his role in legislative reapportionment to be a forceful one. He may give lip service to the need for reapportionment, but he seldom makes it a major item in his legislative program or concentrates the power of the governor's office in its behalf. The primary reason for this caution is that governors are usually reluctant to jeopardize other parts of their program by demanding a reapportionment measure likely to alienate the legislators by threatening their personal and political interests.

In a state where the apportionment system encourages divided government, a Democratic governor (such as Michael DiSalle in Ohio) knows he cannot win approval for reapportionment from a Republican legislature; he is likely to avoid the issue because it would only alienate Republicans whose votes he needs on other issues. A governor who leads a party majority in the legislature is better able to take the initiative on reapportionment, as Gov. William Stratton did in 1953 when he pushed the constitutional apportionment compromise through the Illinois legislature.[30] Governors in two-party states, however, seldom have firm control over their legislative party. In California, where party discipline is weak and sectionalism is strong, Gov. Edmund Brown in 1960 opposed an initiated plan for Senate reapportionment largely because it jeopardized other parts of his program, notably a water-resources plan that had sharpened sectional differences. The governor of Washington played no role in the 1957 legislative effort to revise a reapportionment plan adopted by initiative, but he refused to veto the legislative amendment to the initiative because he did not want to destroy his rapport with the legislature.[31]

In the South, where party conflict is muted, the other factors are unchanged; legislators have a personal stake in the *status quo* and represent largely rural districts. In both Tennessee and Kentucky the governor is a strong legislative leader, but his strength is based in considerable part on rural support, which he shows no inclination to jeopardize. What happens when a Southern governor who owes his support more to the city voter is elected? He still must face a rural legislature, and he is usually more interested in enacting a legislative program than in long-range change through reapportionment. Gov. Terry Sanford of North Carolina was very interested in a bold educational program, for which he needed rural votes; he supported reapportionment in principle, but not with pressure. Gov. Leroy Collins of Florida, on the other hand, gave high priority to a fundamental change in apportionment and failed to achieve his objective. His failure seemed to prove the wisdom of other, more cautious, governors, because his campaign cost him considerable support from the rural legislature for other aspects of his program.[32]

The governor's role in reapportionment is a cautious one, usually not through choice but through necessity, the necessity of achieving immediate legislative victories and postponing the campaign for reforms that offer the theoretical possibility of strengthening the governor's position. As the authors of a study on Florida apportionment point out, especially where there is little party or factional cohesion to unite the governor and a legislative majority, "the reapportionment question can produce more intense conflict between the governor and the legislature than almost any other. Furthermore, the tensions built up by this conflict can very easily spill over into other issues, causing antagonisms which may completely destroy the effectiveness of that executive leadership which is so vital in contemporary government at all levels." [33]

### Pressure Groups

Pressure groups seldom play as important a role in reapportionment controversies as they do in many other issues. One explanation for this lies in the attitude of legislators toward "outside" interference in reapportionment. The attitude of two Illinois legislators, quoted by Steiner and Gove in their study of legislative politics, is probably typical of the views held by most legislators: "I don't think it's up to the committee on constitutional revision [a nonlegislative group] or any newspaper to redistrict the state. It's up to the legislature, according to the mandate of the people." "Outsiders shouldn't stick their noses in and tell this committee how to reapportion the state." [34] In other words, legislators have certain notions of the proper role for pressure groups: they have a right to lobby concerning bills that affect them directly, but the question of reapportionment is primarily the concern of legislators.

There is least reason to expect pressure group activity when minor adjustments in legislative apportionment are under consideration. The risk of alienating legislators outweighs the relatively minor gains that pressure groups might hope to achieve.[35] The account of Texas reapportionment, however, suggests some activity by individual lobbyists on behalf of legislators affected by proposed apportionment plans. Congressional apportionment presents a similar pattern of behavior: often the proposed changes are too limited to affect the interests of pressure groups, while an effort by a group to effect more drastic changes might alienate the congressmen concerned.

Fundamental changes in legislative apportionment should be of interest to pressure groups because they could change the entire political environment in a state. Pressure groups satisfied with the *status quo* need not take the initiative; their role can be purely defensive.[36] They are groups with an urban base that have an interest in changing the apportionment pattern, and these groups often seem passive. Their reasoning is probably similar to that of the urban-based governor. As long as the legislature is under rural control, these urban pressure groups need rural votes to win any part of their legislative program. From this short-run viewpoint, it is not good tactics to sponsor reapportionment plans. In Tennessee, at least, the strongest pressure for change has come from the elected officials of the major cities. In a number of states, most notably in Washington, the League of Women Voters has taken the initiative among pressure groups in seeking constitutional or statutory reapportionment.[37] Perhaps the League has less of a vested interest in maintaining rapport with rural legislators. Minorities, such as Negro groups, sometimes seek to increase the chances of their members being elected by trying to influence the drawing of districts, as in California, or trying to abolish county-wide, at-large elections for the legislature, as in Ohio. They do not often appear to be as concerned about the larger issues of urban-rural representation.

Pressure-group activity is most evident in the largest industrial states where labor is strong, where it is usually closely allied to the Democratic Party, and where the existing apportionment pattern often frustrates the Democratic-labor majority. In both California and Michigan, labor unions played major roles in the initiative campaigns for apportionment by population (in 1948 and 1952), and in both cases business and farm groups were successful in defeating their efforts. In both states there has been a continuing struggle over apportionment involving most major pressure groups. Urban pressure groups have much greater opportunities to act in states like these, where they can bypass the legislature through the use of the initiative. In Washington, however, labor failed to play a role in the 1956 campaign for reapportionment by initiative because its efforts were concentrated on defeating a "right-to-work" proposal at the polls.[38] Labor's interest in the New York apportionment system is strong, as evidenced by the authorship of the New York chapter in this volume. In that state, however, lack of the initiative process forces labor to deal with Republican majorities in the Legislature.

The lobbyist for major urban interest groups today is a skilled professional, accustomed to dealing in immediate political realities and unwilling to sacrifice his present bargaining position for problematic long-term advantages. He has developed personal contacts with legislators, both urban and rural, that he does not want to jeopardize, and he recognizes acute legislative sensitivity on the issue of apportionment. Consequently urban pressure groups are willing to gamble on a reapportionment campaign only in states where they are strong and where the stakes are high.

## A NEW ARENA FOR THE CONFLICT: THE COURTS

E. E. Schattschneider has asserted that "private conflicts are taken into the public arena precisely because someone wants to make certain that the power ratio among the private interests most immediately involved shall not prevail." [39] The legislature does not merely ratify and record the balance of power among contending groups, because some groups that lack private economic power have political power that can be exploited in the legislature. There is not, however, only one public arena. Private groups contend over which public arena should be used to settle their differences. A group that cannot win its point in the city council or the county commission shifts its demands to the legislature. During the last three decades groups seeking economic reform and welfare legislation, once defeated in state legislatures, have turned to Congress, while business interests have advanced the cause of state rights because they felt their political power was stronger in the state legislature. The Negro, so often rebuffed in Congress, in the state legislature, and in the Southern voting registrar's office, has turned to the courts.

The urban citizen who is trying to bring about reapportionment, particularly at the state level, recognizes that his political power is least in the malapportioned legislature. To what other arena can he turn? He might turn to the governor or to gubernatorial candidates, because in most states a governor cannot win election, or re-election, without considerable urban strength. We have examined the limitations to this approach: the governor may not want to jeopardize other parts of his program, and he may be unable to force legislative action. He may seek constitutional revision, but this normally requires legislative approval. A constitutional convention offers one route to reapportionment, recently tried in Michigan, but in some states (such as New Jersey) political leaders have excluded the issue of apportionment to avoid jeopardizing other goals of constitutional reform. Moreover, the apportionment of the convention normally is based on that of the legislature. In thirteen states, the urban voter may use the constitutional initiative to bypass completely both legislature and convention. This is the only political tool designed to break the vicious circle of constitutionally imposed mal-apportionment. These states and a few others have the less powerful statutory initiative. If the urban voter has a majority, the initiative should be a powerful tool in his hands. Experience has shown, however, that urban voters outside the major metropolitan centers, and in sur-prisingly large numbers within them, are often unenthusiastic about initiated proposals for reapportionment. Moreover, the great majority of states make no provision for either constitutional or statutory ini-tiative.

In some states the urban citizens have not exhausted all promising avenues for restoring majority rule to the legislature. In other states these avenues are few or have proved to be dead ends. The one remaining approach is the courts. Here the urban voter hopes to have an advan-tage not based on numbers but on the language of the national and sometimes the state constitutions.

## A Negative Judicial Role

Traditionally the courts have played only a negative role in the apportionment conflicts. They have occasionally invalidated legislative apportionment statutes that conflicted with state constitutions, but, in-stead of forcing the legislature to enact a substitute, the courts have usually permitted resurrection of the prior (and usually less equitable) apportionment. State courts have regularly rejected appeals to force legislative action, even when the state constitution *requires* periodic re-apportionment. The increasing use of executive officers or commissions to conduct reapportionments in place of the legislature or in the event of legislative inaction opens the way to a more important judicial role, since these groups are subject to mandamus action.[40]

In the absence of effective judicial remedies at the state level, urban citizens in recent years have turned to the federal courts. In the famous case of *Colegrove* v. *Green* (1946), involving an inequitable pattern of Congressional districts in Illinois, the U.S. Supreme Court appeared to close the door to relief in the federal courts. Speaking for the majority, Justice Frankfurter declared that the area of apportionment was one that the courts had traditionally, and properly, refused to enter because of its "peculiarly political nature." "It is hostile to a democratic system to involve the judiciary in the politics of the people." The issue must be left to Congress and the state legislatures.[41]

Although Frankfurter's opinion appeared to leave no room for doubt or vacillation, it was a four-to-three decision, and subsequent developments suggested that the issue might be reopened in the courts. In several apportionment cases lower federal courts granted judicial relief, and the Supreme Court continued to expand its supervision of voting rights in the states. In 1956 a federal district court in Hawaii, in an opinion urging reversal of traditional judicial attitudes toward reapportionment, ordered at-large elections for the territorial legislature, which had not been reapportioned since 1901.[42] Congress then acted to update the apportionment. Similarly, a federal district court in Minnesota accepted jurisdiction of a case challenging the legislative apportionment in that state, unchanged since 1913. The court announced it would defer a decision until the next legislative session, and the legislature promptly enacted a new apportionment law substantially better than the old one.[43]

The Supreme Court, in its decisions of recent years on desegregation and Negro voting rights, has proved that the Fifteenth Amendment and the "equal-protection" clause of the Fourteenth Amendment can be powerful weapons for citizens unable to gain equal treatment from state legislatures. The Constitution prohibits racial discrimination; but does it also prohibit geographic discrimination in voting? The federal court in Hawaii had said: "Any distinction between racial and geographic discrimination is artificial and unrealistic. Both should be abolished." [44] In the case of *Gomillion* v. *Lightfoot* (1960), the Court invalidated an Alabama statute changing the municipal boundaries in Tuskegee to exclude certain voters, but it acted because the legislation was clearly designed to disenfranchise *Negro* voters.[45]

Within the last few years a number of cases have been filed in state courts and federal district courts challenging legislative apportionment systems, usually on the ground that they violated the equal-protection clause of the Fourteenth Amendment.[46] As subsequent chapters show, when *Baker* v. *Carr* was decided, cases were pending in the courts of several states, and in a matter of weeks old cases were reopened and new ones were initiated in a number of others.

### *Baker* v. *Carr*

The Supreme Court's decision in the Tennessee apportionment case, *Baker* v. *Carr,* announced on March 26, 1962, was a landmark in the apportionment controversy in this country.[47] It settled one important question: the federal courts *will* hear cases in which citizens claim that the pattern of legislative apportionment is a denial of equal protection under the Fourteenth Amendment. But the decision left many unanswered questions about its scope, standards of equality in apportionment, and the nature of judicial remedies. In the immediate wake of the

Court's decision, there has been no legislative stampede to correct apportionment inequities and head off judicial action. Consequently, we may anticipate several years of litigation before the full impact of this decision becomes clear. At the moment, the importance of *Baker* v. *Carr* lies in the fact that it has given urban citizens the choice of a new arena in which to battle for equal apportionment. This has undoubtedly strengthened the hand of urban interests in the legislative arena, where the major battles will continue to be fought. How much the balance of power shifts in the legislatures depends largely on the answers to questions that must still be settled in the courts.

The majority opinion in *Baker* v. *Carr*, written by Justice Brennan, did not answer any more questions than necessary. The opinion did not deal with the merits of the case, and it did not provide any guides to the lower courts. Justice Brennan held: "(a) that the court possessed jurisdiction of the subject matter; (b) that a justiciable cause of action is stated upon which the appellants would be entitled to appropriate relief; and (c) because the appellees raise the issue before this Court, that the appellants have standing to challenge the Tennessee apportionment statutes." [48]

One key to the decision lies in the definition of a "political question," which is pertinent to the justiciability of the case. Justice Frankfurter, in *Colegrove* v. *Green,* had defined apportionment as a political question, which the Court would not decide. In his dissent to *Baker* v. *Carr,* Frankfurter described what he meant by this term: the court should avoid decisions when there are no standards for judicial judgment, when the issues at stake are policy matters traditionally fought out in nonjudicial forums, and particularly when the questions concern the structure and organization of political institutions in the states. [49] Justice Brennan, speaking for the Court, defined "political question" somewhat differently: it includes those cases in which there is a constitutional commitment of an issue to a coordinate branch of government, where there are no judicially discoverable or manageable standards for resolving the question without a prior nonjudicial policy determination, or where an unusual need exists for unquestioning adherence to a policy decision already made. Brennan concluded that these standards do not apply to the state apportionment controversy. [50]

The conflict between majority and minority opinions is not merely over definitions. Justice Frankfurter argued not only that apportionment has traditionally been a nonjudicial issue but also that patterns of apportionment not fully based on population have been traditional and widespread in our national and state governments. Consequently, he denied that apportionment by population is "the basic principle of representative government." He asserted that the Court was asked in this case "to choose among competing bases of representation—ultimately, really, among competing theories of political philosophy—in order to establish an appropriate frame of government for the State of Tennessee and thereby for all the States of the Union." [51]

It is important to note that Justice Brennan's opinion did not assert that apportionment must be based on population. At most, the decision suggested that some systems of apportionment might constitute an abridgement of the equal-protection clause. Justices Clark and Douglas in concurring opinions discussed a variety of issues that Justice Brennan had carefully avoided, but even they did not provide clear standards for the lower courts. Clark, though wishing to settle the case on its merits, denied that the equal-protection clause requires mathematical equality. Douglas asserted that the basic question is the extent to which a state may weight the vote of one person more heavily than it does another's; he did not answer that question but remarked that universal equality is not the test of "equal protection." Justice Stewart, in a brief concurring opinion, tried to neutralize the effect of the other concurring opinions by emphasizing the limited scope of the Court's decision.[52]

## Unanswered Questions

One of the most important questions that remains to be answered about the *Baker* v. *Carr* decision concerns its scope. Will the courts pass judgment on all types of Congressional and legislative malapportionment, or only a few? This decision applied to state legislatures. Will the courts be equally willing to intervene in Congressional redistricting controversies? In principle there seems to be no difference between the two. In both cases, it is the action, or inaction, of state legislative bodies that is in question. The Court would not be challenging any political decisions made by Congress (which Justice Brennan indicated the Court was reluctant to do), although the Court might decide that judicial intervention was unnecessary because Congress has the power to set standards for Congressional districts and has done so in the past.[53] On the other hand, the Constitution can be interpreted as providing a popular base for the House of Representatives; this would provide an additional reason for judicial intervention.[54]

Will the courts intervene to force reapportionment in states that have either a constitutional or statutory initiative? To understand why the existence of the initiative might make a difference, we must look first at Justice Frankfurter's argument against judicial intervention. In *Colegrove* v. *Green,* he argued that the remedy for malapportionment is "to secure State legislatures that will apportion properly." In his dissent to *Baker* v. *Carr* he said that "relief must come through an aroused public conscience that sears the conscience of the people's representatives." [55]

Implicit in the traditional judicial assertion that apportionment is a political question is the belief that the people can and should settle the question themselves by electing representatives who will reapportion. The obvious fallacy in this argument is that a malapportioned legislature is not likely to be responsive to the urban majority of voters who can elect only a minority of legislators. Unless the voters can bypass the legislature through the use of the initiative, the majority of voters are powerless. Likewise, they are powerless to achieve reapportionment through constitutional amendment (which the legislature must approve) unless the constitutional initiative exists. Lawyers who argued the Tennessee case on behalf of urban voters emphasized that Tennessee does not have the initiative. It is not apparent whether the Court considers this factor important; Brennan's decision made no mention of it, except in summarizing the appellants' argument. Justice Clark, however, in his concurring opinion, said that he would not consider judicial intervention "were any other relief available to the people of Tennessee," and he emphasized the absence of the initiative and referendum in that state.[56]

The absence of the initiative provides a strong argument to the advocates of judicial intervention, but the presence of the initiative does not necessarily destroy the case for judicial intervention. The equal-protection clause applies to minorities as well as majorities; in fact it was designed for and has been applied to minority groups on most occasions. In some states (like Oklahoma) that have the initiative, only a minority of the citizens may live in the large urban communities that are underrepresented. Even in a state as urbanized as California the residents of one or two metropolitan centers may be seriously underrepresented and unable to gain enough allies among residents of cities less discriminated against to win an initiative fight at the polls. If the courts provide relief only to states that lack the initiative, it will indicate that Frankfurter's concept of a political question continues to have some effect and that judicial action is possible only where a political solution satisfactory to the *majority* is impossible.[57]

Legislative malapportionment can result from constitutional provision, legislation, or prolonged legislative inaction. There is no difference in their effect; any one of them may lead to great inequalities in representation. But there may be differences in the judicial interpretation of each. The Justices who concurred in *Baker* v. *Carr* emphasized that an apportionment system did not necessarily have to guarantee mathematical equality in voting. They said that the equal-protection clause prohibits "invidious discrimination." Clark said that "there must be some rational design to a State's districting." [58]

If these are the standards that the courts use in applying the equal-protection clause to apportionment inequities, the form of malapportionment most vulnerable to judicial attack is likely to be that (such as in Tennessee) resulting from decades of legislative inaction. Such a pattern obviously has no clear purpose; it does not serve to balance one house against the other or to guarantee each county a minimum of representation. Justice Clark emphasized the "topsy-turvy" nature of apportionment in Tennessee and the fact that there were great inequalities even among rural counties of approximately equal size. Though Justice Harlan in his dissent suggested that legislative refusal to accommodate representation to the growth of urban population might be quite rational, malapportionment by inaction seems to be the most vulnerable to the charge of irrationality.[59] Likewise, Congressional malapportionment will probably be attacked most successfully in those states where it results from the failure to make periodic and comprehensive reapportionments.

Statutory malapportionment often results when a legislature yields reluctantly to the pressures for reapportionment and corrects the inequities only partially. This results in a more "rational" apportionment and usually eliminates the most "invidious" discrimination, leaving the courts less reason to object. Recent statutory malapportionment is perhaps most likely to be tested in the courts in cases where a legislature has reapportioned in compliance with, or in order to head off, a court decision nullifying an outdated pattern of apportionment. It is likely that, in such cases, a rural-dominated legislature would try to make as few changes as possible in the existing apportionment. What standards will the courts set? How small an adjustment in apportionment can the legislatures get away with? The courts will be forced to deal with these questions and to translate "equal protection of the law" into precise terms.

The Tennessee case provided the first answers to these questions. Following the Supreme Court decision in *Baker* v. *Carr,* the legislature reapportioned both houses, raising the representation of the metropolitan counties from about one-half to about three-fourths of the number to which they would be entitled by a population standard. The three-judge federal court overruled the apportionment because it was "devoid of any standard or rational plan" with regard to the Senate and permitted some inequalities in the House.[60]

A related question involves political gerrymandering. If equal protection of the law does not require mathematical equality in voting, does approximate equality of districts completely satisfy the requirements of equal protection? Is there any constitutional protection available for voters in a political party who are underrepresented because district lines are distorted, either in order to dissipate their voting strength or to concentrate it in one district and waste votes? It would seem likely that the courts would try to avoid involvement in such an issue. It would be a highly "political" question, involving the court directly in partisan battles; there are no clear standards for objective, impartial districting; and it is often difficult to prove discrimination or even to accurately determine the results of gerrymandering. But a case can be made that flagrant gerrymandering, if it is successful in altering the political balance in a state or a Congressional delegation, unreasonably deprives voters of effective representation and leaves them no political recourse. *Gomillion* v. *Lightfoot* showed how sensitive the Court is to the manipulation of political boundaries for the purpose of disenfranchising Negroes.[61] If a Southern legislature or city should change the boundaries of legislative districts or city wards in order to split up strongly Negro voting units and perhaps prevent the election of Negro legislators or city councilmen, it is conceivable that the Court might intervene. If it did so, this might open the way to judicial review of gerrymandering.

The most intriguing and perhaps the most important question with regard to the Court's decision is whether it applies to malapportionment resulting from the provisions of state constitutions. It is true, of course, that state constitutions are not exempt from the equal-protection clause. But it may be difficult to show that constitutional provisions for apportionment are irrational and inconsistent. Some such provisions are designed to ensure every county at least one representative in one branch of the legislature. Some serve the purpose of preventing a single metropolitan area from dominating the state legislature. Several constitutions guarantee a balance between urban control of one house and rural control of the other; in some cases this compromise has been designed to assure periodic reapportionment, at least of the popular-based house. Such patterns of apportionment are familiar, widespread, traditional, consistent, and rational; they are often woven into the political fabric of the state, as well as rooted in its constitutional base. But these provisions frequently *guarantee* inequalities far greater than those resulting solely from legislative inaction or statutory law. Where malapportionment significantly changes the balance of power in a state it is usually the result primarily of the state constitution.

It may be argued that such constitutional provisions are a relic of the past and that, where the constitutional initiative is lacking, the majority of voters are unable to force legislative action on an apportionment amendment. In such states as Michigan, however, the constitutional provisions are compromises adopted by the voters in recent years. In other states, such as California and Florida, the voters have rejected constitutional amendments in recent years, either because of rural and small-city fear of big-city dominance or because of opposition to a compromise by both the most urban and the most rural elements.

In the months immediately following the *Baker* v. *Carr* decision, the Supreme Court remanded to the state courts cases challenging the apportionment provisions of the Michigan and New York constitutions. In so doing, the Court ruled only that these cases, like the Tennessee case, presented a justiciable cause of action. It did not provide any clues about its attitude toward state constitutional provisions that guarantee inequitable apportionment. Jutsice Harlan dissented in both cases, criticizing the absence of guide lines for the lower courts. He particularly noted in the Michigan case that the issue involved a constitutional provision adopted by popular vote only a decade ago.[62]

Other federal and state courts have struck down constitutional provisions. In the Georgia case the three-judge federal court ruled invalid an apportionment based in part on state constitutional requirements.[63] A circuit judge in Maryland, acting under the guidance of the state Court of Appeals, ruled invalid the state constitutional provisions for apportionment of the lower house.[64] A state judge in Mississippi also invalidated an apportionment based on constitutional requirements.[65] Yet in Alabama, where the apportionment was sixty years out of date, the three-judge federal court held that the requirements of the equal-protection clause would be met if the legislature complied with the state constitution, even though that document contains provisions placing significant limits on the population principle in apportionment.[66]

A major unanswered question pertaining to state constitutions is whether the equal-protection clause requires that *both* houses of the legislature be apportioned by population. This is important because a number of state constitutions require apportionment by population in one house, but give some weight, and often considerable weight, to area in the other house. Moreover, there is already pressure in some states, such as Alabama and Tennessee, to amend the constitution to place apportionment in one house largely or completely on an area basis. This question is directly involved in the Michigan case remanded by the Supreme Court to the state court. In the Georgia case, the three-judge federal court decided that the Supreme Court action in the Michigan case did not represent an "authoritative decision" requiring that *both* houses be apportioned by population, and the court ruled that at least one house in Georgia must be so apportioned.[67] Shortly thereafter, the three-judge federal court in Tennessee ruled that at least one house in that state must be apportioned strictly by population.[68] The state circuit judge in Maryland ruled that one house must be apportioned by population but that the other might be based on area and argued that this arrangement "protects the minorities" and "helps to protect the republican form of government guaranteed to the States" by the U.S. Constitution.[69] This latter point of his decision was appealed and upheld by the state Court of Appeals. This fundamental question will remain unsettled until the Supreme Court has decided it, and its decision will be of far-reaching importance.[70]

If the courts decide to permit most inequalities of apportionment that derive from state constitutions, they will be tolerating massive inequalities in certain states and perhaps encouraging rural groups to campaign for additional constitutional limitations on the population principle. If the courts permit "federal" plans that ensure apportionment by population in only one house, they will be encouraging divided government and political deadlock in the states. If the courts challenge only those constitutional restrictions that have been approved, or not disapproved, by a relatively recent popular vote, the courts will face serious difficulties in interpreting the meaning of popular votes. If the courts accept some constitutional restrictions but not others, they cannot avoid setting some precise standards for apportionment. Finally, if the courts tolerate constitutional inequalities in apportionment, even if explicitly or implicitly approved by the voters, they will be denying equal protection of the law to urban and suburban *minorities.*

One area of uncertainty involves the sanctions that the courts might employ, the levers that would be necessary to force legislative action. Justice Brennan, speaking for the Court, naturally did not suggest specific remedies but expressed certainty that "the District Court will be able to fashion relief if violations of constitutional rights are found." Justice Douglas suggested that a judicial determination that reapportionment was necessary might be enough to spur legislative action, as occurred in Minnesota. Justice Clark, on the other hand, implied that the courts might frame at least provisional apportionment plans.[71]

Most of the federal and state courts that acted in the months following *Baker* v. *Carr* to implement that decision gave the legislature a specific period of time in which to carry out a reapportionment, and in most cases the governors of those states convened special sessions to meet the deadlines set by the courts. What steps would a court take if the legislative session ended in deadlock or produced an apportionment plan that did satisfy the court? In Tennessee the court gave the next session of the legislature a chance to devise a better plan than that first enacted. In a number of other states (including Alabama, Oklahoma, Wisconsin, and Mississippi) the courts warned that they would prepare, directly or through a court-appointed master, a specific reapportionment plan and direct that it be put into effect. These steps seemed more likely than an order for at-large elections, which the courts seemed to recognize would be unwieldy.[72]

The problem of judicial sanctions would be more difficult if the courts invalidated constitutional provisions for apportionment. If the voters rejected an amendment to base apportionment more nearly on population, would the courts still insist on a change? If the legislature submitted an amendment offering only limited accommodation to the population principle and the voters approved it, would the court accept this verdict? If the legislature or the voters proved unwilling to change the state constitution, what standards would a court use in providing a new pattern of apportionment?

The decision in *Baker* v. *Carr* has left most of the questions unanswered, not only because a majority of the Court refused to deal with the merits of the case, but also because the Tennessee situation presented such an extreme example of "invidious discrimination." The apportionment was sixty years out of date, it violated the state constitution instead of resulting from it, and it was not subject to change by the majority of voters in the absence of the initiative. Many of the serious apportionment problems in this country exist in states where the apportionment is not so capricious, and the legal case there must be argued on different grounds.

In the last analysis, apportionment bills and constitutional amendments are going to continue to be written primarily by the state legislatures, where they will be subject to all the same pressures that have existed in the past. But no legislature will in the future be unmindful of the courts. The decision in *Baker* v. *Carr* has added a new factor to the legislative situation. How important that factor is, how much rural legislators will have to bend to the will of the courts, depends in large part on the answers given by the courts to the questions we have raised. Few legislative bodies are likely to make major changes in apportionment until the nature of judicial intervention has been more fully determined and more clearly articulated.

One critical question that the courts must settle is whether the equal-protection clause applies to a minority of voters who are discriminated against by an apportionment system that has the clear support of a majority of voters. Beyond that, the courts will have to set some standards for apportionment. The issue will probably arise when constitutional or statutory apportionment provisions that set relatively small limits on the principle of population equality are challenged in the courts. Individual justices of the Supreme Court have denied that absolute equality is necessary, but the courts cannot escape a precise answer to Justice Douglas' question: to what extent may a state weight one person's vote more heavily than another's? If the Supreme Court does not lay down some clear and consistent standards, the lower courts are likely to provide an inconsistent pattern of decisions that will fit Justice Clark's description of the Tennessee apportionment: "a crazy quilt without rational basis."

# Notes

1 A description of some of the best recent works on Congressional and legislative apportionment is to be found in the "Bibliographic Note."

2 Many of the examples in this chapter are drawn from the case studies in this volume, for which no citations are given in footnotes.

3 See the section on Alabama in *Compendium on Legislative Apportionment* (2nd ed.; New York: National Municipal League, 1962).

4 For a more detailed analysis of constitutional limitations, see Malcolm E. Jewell, "Constitutional Provisions for State Legislative Apportionment," *Western Political Quarterly*, VIII (1955), 271-279.

5 Gordon E. Baker, *State Constitutions: Reapportionment* (New York: National Municipal League, 1960), p. 31; Hugh A. Bone, "States Attempting to Comply with Reapportionment Requirements," *Law and Contemporary Problems*, XVII (1952), 387-416.

6 William C. Havard and Loren P. Beth, *Representative Government and Reapportionment: A Case Study of Florida* (Gainesville, Fla.: Public Administration Clearing Service, University of Florida, 1960), pp. 12 f., 32, 37-39.

7 Victor D. Brannon, "Missouri's Apportionment Key," *National Municipal Review*, XXXV (1946), 177-182.

8 Baker, *op. cit.*, pp. 47-50.

9 *Loc. cit.* Note, however, that courts in Massachusetts and Missouri have held that the initiative is not applicable to legislative apportionment. Lashley G. Harvey, "Reapportionments of State Legislatures—Legal Requirements," *Law and Contemporary Problems*, XVII (1952), 373.

10 The statistics in this chapter for Congressional districts existing in 1960 are from *Congressional District Data Book* (Washington: U.S. Department of Commerce, Bureau of the Census, 1961). Information on the number of seats assigned to each state after each census since 1790 is to be found in the *Congressional Directory*.

11 *Congressional Quarterly Weekly Report*, XIX (1961), pp. 857 f. Statistics in this chapter for districts created in 1961 or 1962 are drawn from the excellent detailed analyses in the *Congressional Quarterly Weekly Reports* and are used by permission of the Congressional Quarterly.

12 *Ibid.*, pp. 1739 f.

13 *Ibid.*, pp. 954-956.

14 *Ibid.*, pp. 681-683, 1040, 1739 f.

15 Paul T. David and Ralph Eisenberg, *Devaluation of the Urban and Suburban Vote* (Charlottesville, Va.: Bureau of Public Administration, University of Virginia, 1961), pp. 8-16.

[16] For a more extensive discussion, see Gordon E. Baker, *Rural Versus Urban Political Power* (New York: Random House, 1955), pp. 27-39.

[17] See Malcolm E. Jewell, *The State Legislature: Politics and Practice* (New York: Random House, 1962), pp. 24-26.

[18] Duane Lockard, *New England State Politics* (Princeton: Princeton University Press, 1959), pp. 177-190.

[19] Loren P. Beth and William C. Havard, "Committee Stacking and Political Power in Florida," *Journal of Politics*, XXIII (1961), 57-83.

[20] Baker, *Rural Versus Urban Political Power, op. cit.*, pp. 22 f.; William C. Cornelius, "The County Unit System of Georgia: Facts and Prospects," *Western Political Quarterly*, XIV (1961), 942-960.

[21] *Congressional Quarterly Weekly Report*, XX (1962), pp. 153-169. Used with permission of the Congressional Quarterly. The Congressional Quarterly classifies districts according to the largest population group—urban, suburban, or rural—in each. With a few exceptions, it defines as urban all those living in the central city or cities in the "urbanized areas" so classified by the 1960 census. Suburban population is that living in what the Census Bureau calls the "urban fringe," the closely settled areas contiguous to central cities. All other areas, though perhaps containing cities up to 50,000 population, are defined as "rural." No method of classifying Congressional districts is perfect, and it should be noted that this system classifies as rural certain districts that would not normally be placed in that category. Such districts may have as little as 34 per cent rural population if the remaining population is evenly divided between urban and suburban. Moreover, it does not distinguish between a completely rural district and a rural district encompassing a metropolitan area such as Montgomery, Alabama, or Madison, Wisconsin.

[22] These statistics are based on: *Congressional District Data Book, op. cit.*

[23] The measurements of liberalism and conservatism are based on the figures of the Congressional Quarterly, which were used with its permission. Metropolitan congressmen are those from districts where a majority of persons live in either the central cities or the urban fringe of the 213 "urbanized areas" so defined by the Census Bureau, that is, where a majority live in the "urban" and "suburban" areas as defined by the Congressional Quarterly. All other districts are defined arbitrarily as rural. The median scores of congressmen on the Congressional Quarterly's "party-unity" and "conservative-coalition" scales were used for the years 1959-1961. The first measures how often a congressman voted with his party on roll calls where a majority of the two parties were opposed; the second measures how often he supported the "conservative coalition" on roll calls when a majority of Southern Democrats and Republicans opposed a majority of Northern Democrats. We are assuming that these two categories of roll calls are a rough measure of "liberalism" and "conservatism." The congressmen popularly assumed to be most liberal and conservative generally appear on the opposite ends of these scales. See *Congressional Quarterly Almanac*, XVII (1961), pp. 638-652.

[24] The same definition of metropolitan and rural districts referred to in the preceding footnote is used. The Congressional Quarterly's "party-unity" and "larger-federal-role" scales were used for the years 1959-1961. The first measures a congressman's support for his party when the two parties are opposed; the second measures his vote on several relatively important roll calls concerning an increased role for the federal government in a variety of fields. See *Congressional Quarterly Almanac*, XVII (1961), pp. 631-641.

[25] For more careful definitions of role concepts and examples of their use in research, see John C. Wahlke *et al.*, "American State Legislators' Role Orientations Toward Pressure Groups," *Journal of Politics*, XXII (1960), 203-227, and Ralph K. Huitt, "The Congressional Committee: A Case Study," *American Political Science Review*, XLVIII (1954), 340-365.

[26] Gilbert Y. Steiner and Samuel K. Gove, *Legislative Politics in Illinois* (Urbana: University of Illinois Press, 1960), p. 97.

[27] Baker, *The Politics of Reapportionment in Washington State* (New York: Holt, Rinehart, and Winston, 1960), pp. 8 f. (Second edition in new format by McGraw-Hill.)

28 *Congressional Quarterly Weekly Report,* XIX (1961), pp. 1549, 1563, 1635.

29 *Loc. cit.*

30 Russell E. Olson, "Illinois Faces Redistricting," *National Municipal Review,* XLIII (1954), 343-348.

31 Baker, *The Politics of Reapportionment in Washington State, op. cit.,* p. 13.

32 Havard and Beth, *Representative Government and Reapportionment, op. cit.,* pp. 33-52.

33 *Ibid.,* p. 32.

34 Steiner and Gove, *op. cit.,* pp. 98 f.

35 The account of legislative apportionment in Illinois indicates that pressure groups in that state held this view and also accepted the legislators' belief that the actual delineation of districts was a legislative prerogative. *Ibid.,* pp. 99-102.

36 Nevertheless, a prohibitionist group in Kentucky, in a presession questionnaire to legislators, sought a commitment from them to oppose reapportionment, obviously in the belief that urban legislators were less sympathetic to its cause.

37 Baker, *The Politics of Reapportionment in Washington State, op. cit., passim.*

38 *Ibid.,* pp. 5 f.

39 E. E. Schattschneider, *The Semisovereign People* (New York: Holt, Rinehart, and Winston, 1960), p. 38.

40 See Anthony Lewis, "Legislative Apportionment and the Federal Courts," *Harvard Law Review,* LXXI (1958), 1057-1098, and Baker, *State Constitutions: Reapportionment, op. cit.,* pp. 50-55.

41 *Colegrove v. Green,* 328 U.S. 549, at 552-554, 556.

42 *Dyer v. Kazuhisa Abe,* 138 F. Supp. 220.

43 *Magraw v. Donovan,* 163 F. Supp. 184.

44 *Dyer v. Kazuhisa Abe, op. cit.,* 236.

45 *Gomillion v. Lightfoot,* 364 U.S. 339.

46 For a careful analysis of court cases preceding *Baker* v. *Carr,* see James E. Larson, *Reapportionment and the Courts* (University, Alabama: Bureau of Public Administration, University of Alabama, 1962).

47 *Baker v. Carr,* 369 U.S. 186.

48 *Ibid.,* 197 f.

49 *Ibid.,* 277 f., 289.

50 *Ibid.,* 217.

51 *Ibid.,* 300.

52 *Ibid.,* 242-245, 258, 265 f.

53 Note Justice Frankfurter's argument that the Constitution has given Congress "exclusive authority to secure fair representation by the States in the popular House and left to that House determination whether states have fulfilled their responsibility." *Colegrove* v. *Green, op. cit.,* 554.

54 Since the *Baker* v. *Carr* decision, suits have been filed in several states challenging existing Congressional districts.

55 *Colegrove v. Green, op. cit.,* 556; *Baker v. Carr, op. cit.,* 270.

56 *Baker v. Carr, op. cit.,* 258 f.

57 The three-judge federal court, in nullifying the apportionment system in Georgia, noted that the state had no initiative provision in its constitution. *Toombs* v. *Fortson,* 30 *U.S. Law Week* 2606. One of the states where a three-judge federal court has ordered reapportionment, however, is Oklahoma, which has the constitutional initiative.

58 *Baker v. Carr, op. cit.,* 244, 258.

59 *Ibid.,* 254-256, 336.

60 *Baker v. Carr,* 31 *U.S. Law Week* 2003.

61 *Gomillion v. Lightfoot, op. cit.*

62 *Scholle v. Hare,* 369 U.S. 429; *WMCA, Inc.* v. *Simon,* 30 *U.S. Law Week* 3383.

63 *Toombs v. Fortson, loc. cit.*

64 *Maryland Committee for Fair Representation* v. *Tawes,* 30 *U.S. Law Week* 2522 f., 2587.

[65] *Fortner* v. *Barnette.*

[66] *Sims* v. *Frink, 30 U.S. Law Week* 2512.

[67] *Toombs* v. *Fortson, loc. cit.*

[68] *Baker* v. *Carr, 31 U.S. Law Week* 2003.

[69] *Maryland Committee for Fair Representation* v. *Tawes, op. cit.,* 2587.

[70] On July 27, U.S. Supreme Court Justice Potter Stewart set the stage for a decision by the highest court on the question of whether the Fourteenth Amendment requires that both houses be apportioned by population. He stayed a decision by the Michigan Supreme Court which had invalidated that state's senatorial apportionment. Stewart stressed that the case presented issues not previously decided by the U.S. Supreme Court. Though not ruling on the merits of the case, Stewart indicated his own belief that the state constitution could use some basis other than population alone for apportionment of one house.

[71] *Baker* v. *Carr,* 369 U.S. 198, 250, 260.

[72] Most recently, the federal court in Alabama became the first to order a specific apportionment put into effect, and state officials complied with the order. The court ordered put into immediate effect House and Senate apportionments passed by the legislature for adoption four years hence, and it invalidated an alternative Senate plan based on area and passed as a constitutional amendment. The Michigan Supreme Court had ordered at-large Senate elections if the legislature failed to reapportion in a month, and the harshness of this remedy was apparently one reason why U.S. Supreme Court Justice Stewart stayed the decision. The Kansas Supreme Court on July 30 stayed a lower court order for at-large elections and gave the legislature a chance to act in the 1963 session.

# PART TWO

# Rural Control of the Legislature
# Through Apportionment

*INTRODUCTION*

Rural control of one or both branches of the legislature is a familiar feature of American state government. The case studies that follow could be duplicated in state after state. In all these examples except Colorado and Kentucky the malapportionment results in large part from constitutional provisions. Many of these are of long standing; some, as in California and Texas, were adopted after years of legislative inertia. California is the clearest example of one apportionment pattern familiar in American politics: the preservation of rural control in one house and apportionment by population in the other.

The apportionment system used in the California Senate reflects the strength of regionalism in the state and the fear of state-wide control by a single metropolitan region (Los Angeles). Malapportionment serves conservative interests but is not at present a tool of control by a single party. Nor does the malapportionment in Colorado, more moderate than in many states, serve the interests of a single party. Both parties have urban as well as rural roots. Denver's legislative voice is only slightly weakened by the apportionment system and is strengthened by the unity resulting from its at-large elections. The legislative disadvantage of the suburban counties surrounding Denver, however, is becoming increasingly apparent.

In Florida, malapportionment is the foundation upon which rural control of the state is built and authority exercised by the enormously powerful clique of legislators from small towns. This control is of direct and immediate benefit to the rural areas in terms of legislation. Rural dominance is being challenged by urban elements in the Democratic Party, but the influence of these groups in gubernatorial politics is undermined by the personal, fractionized nature of Florida politics. Malapportionment is a potential handicap to the growing suburban wing of the Republican Party in Florida.

In North Carolina and Kentucky, the urban-rural conflict is muted because urban and suburban growth has been slower. Though both are rural states, the legislative majority is disproportionately rural. In both states reapportionment has potentially important implications for the Republican Party, though that party is still shackled to its traditional rural base. Both states have strong governorships, and the governor is thus a potential source of leadership when he comes to realize the increasing importance of urban votes.

Texas is part of the familiar pattern of rural control and underrepresentation of booming metropolitan areas. But it is also a state where factional politics often dominate the legislature and where reapportionment (within constitutional limitations) has become a tool of the dominant faction.

In most of these states there have been recent campaigns for reapportionment, none of them successful. As urban groups and political forces with an urban base become numerically strong, well organized, and aware of their stake in reapportionment, they may succeed in changing the apportionment systems. If they do, the balance of power could be changed, in some cases drastically, in every one of these states.

# 1

## The California Senate

SECTIONAL CONFLICT AND *VOX POPULI*

*GORDON E. BAKER*
*University of California, Santa Barbara*

Traditionally fond of superlatives, Californians as late as 1962 could claim the questionable distinction of having the most unrepresentative upper house of any legislature in the fifty states.[1] A clear majority of the California Senate is elected by approximately 10 per cent of the state's population. Los Angeles County's 6,038,771 inhabitants receive the same Senate representation as 14,294 in a Sierra Nevada mountain district, while the six most populous counties (containing 65 per cent of the state's inhabitants) elect 15 per cent of California's senators.

### BACKGROUND

It was not always so. The constitution of 1879 had provided for eighty Assembly and forty senatorial districts to be established on a population basis, with decennial reapportionment assigned as a legislative duty. This system worked well enough until 1910, when antagonisms intensified between northern and southern sections and rural and urban areas of California. After the 1920 census the Legislature failed to adjust districts for either house. To resolve this impasse, two separate groups sponsored initiative campaigns in 1926 aimed at amending the constitution. The first proposal, pressed by interests from rural areas and the San Francisco region, was advertised as a "compromise" solution and was mislabeled the "Federal Plan," with a purported analogy to the structure of the United States Congress.[2] The eighty-member lower house was to continue on a population basis, with enforced decennial redistricting. But the Senate of forty seats would shift drastically to a system whereby most counties would send one senator each, with only the sparsely settled counties combined into districts (a maximum of three counties in any dis-

51

trict). Although all large urban counties stood to lose from the change, those outside Los Angeles were willing to accept a reduction in representation [3] in exchange for a plan clearly giving northern California, with a majority of the counties, permanent control of the Senate. In retaliation, groups from Los Angeles initiated their own measure to enforce the existing population standard for both houses. In November 1926 the electorate defeated this latter proposal, but ratified the northern-sponsored "Federal Plan."

Critics of the California Senate have pressed for change periodically since adoption of the 1926 amendment. In 1928 it survived a state-wide referendum by a large majority, with only Los Angeles and San Francisco counties showing more votes cast against it. Two decades later, in 1948, an initiative campaign, backed primarily by the State Federation of Labor, attempted to move in the direction of a population standard, but with any single county limited to a maximum of ten seats. This move aroused a formidable array of opposition, including many urban business groups, the state Chamber of Commerce, and virtually all newspapers. A well-financed and emotion-laden campaign depicted the proposal as dangerous and virtually subversive and, according to Prof. Thomas Barclay, "gave meager support for the dogma that man is a rational being." [4] Under such circumstances, the initiative was overwhelmingly defeated, failing to carry a single county. The fact that a large majority of urban voters cast "no" ballots caused one close observer to wonder at this "amazing spectacle of a people approving their own disfranchisement." [5]

This defeat did not quiet perennial criticism of the amount of power wielded by senators representing an ever-decreasing portion of the state's citizenry. Dissenters from the *status quo* could point to several extreme disparities. By the 1950's, California's ten most populous counties contained over three-fourths of the state population, but elected only one-fourth the senators. At the other end of the scale, the ten least populous districts also comprised one-fourth of the upper house but represented less than 3 per cent of the people. In terms of legislative power these extremes carried a built-in potential for minority veto. For example, measures requiring a two-thirds vote of both houses (such as the state budget and constitutional amendments) could be blocked by fourteen senators representing as few as 5 per cent of the people. The internal organization of the upper house likewise reflected these disparities, especially in the sectional alignment, as the smaller group of southern California senators held a distinct minority of committee chairmanships and places on standing committees.

Each session of the Legislature revealed substantial differences in social, economic, and political outlook between the area-based Senate and the population-based Assembly. The conflict was not a partisan one, for party lines in California do not correspond to rural-urban or sectional differences. The following summary illustrates some of the major policy questions persistently at issue:

> Despite similarity between urban and rural partisan political senti-ment, certain urban groups and related farm groups feel that they have very difficult sledding in the rurally dominated upper house. During the decade 1935-46, for example, Assembly bills regulating wages and hours and working conditions, particularly of women, children and farm labor, were killed in the Senate. In the last decade many Assem-bly bills providing improved or expanded health and welfare benefits were defeated in a Senate committee or on the floor. Until 1958 [*sic,* 1959], this was also true of bills creating a fair employment practices commission. In rebuttal, excepting only the farm labor issue, it could also be fairly stated that the Senate has approved such welfare meas-ures, but frequently—say critics—too little and too late.[6]

During the 1950's, opponents of rural and northern domination of the upper house continued to propose constitutional modification through the Legislature, but without success. One scheme defeated in the 1953 session would have allocated twenty senators to the ten southern counties and twenty to the less populous section comprising forty-eight northern counties.

This general approach toward a sectional split was revived in the summer of 1959 by some twenty-eight community organizations and city governments in and near Los Angeles. Another initiative campaign, led by Frank G. Bonelli, chairman of the Los Angeles County Board of Super-visors, eventually materialized. The primary impetus for this new re-apportionment drive apparently stemmed from the recent legislative fate of a "possessory-interest" tax bill. County and city governments, especially in the Los Angeles region, had urged passage in Sacramento of a measure which would allow local governments to continue taxing private defense contractors' possessory interest in inventory and other personal property owned by the federal government. The bill passed the urban-based As-sembly but went down to defeat in the Senate. The result, according to Bonelli and his associates, was a loss of more than $200,000,000 in assessed valuation from the tax rolls of Los Angeles County alone. Defenders of the Senate's action answered that the measure's passage might have en-couraged defense industries to move elsewhere. In any event, the battle lines on this and other issues were forming. By the summer of 1960 a sufficient number of signatures (420,402 were needed) had qualified Senate reapportionment once again for the ballot.

## THE INITIATIVE CAMPAIGN OF 1960

Known popularly as the "Bonelli Plan" or the "20-20 Plan," the proposed amendment would have initially divided Senate membership in half. Within each section, the most populous counties were assigned additional strength. Los Angeles County would receive a total of seven senators, and three other southern counties, two each; all remaining counties, large and small, in the region considered south retained their senators. In the north, the three most populous counties in the San Francisco Bay area would each receive two senators. The three next most populous northern counties would each retain its present one senator, while the remaining northern counties (including some fairly populous ones) would lose strength by being combined into larger districts than before.

On the November ballot, reapportionment was designated as Proposition 15. Though there was a variety of arguments advanced on both sides of the issue, the state's water problem was a recurring major theme. On the same ballot as the reapportionment initiative was Proposition 1, the $1,750,000,000 California Water Resources Development Act. This was a legislative compromise plan to divert surplus northern water to the thirsty southland. The legislative struggle over the issue had been bitter and persisted into the 1960 election, where, as a bond measure, it required ratification by the voters before going into effect. Several opponents of reapportionment charged that the presence of Proposition 15 on the same ballot endangered the water proposal by arousing northern reluctance to authorize a plan, the execution of which might be subject to a differently constituted state Senate. In answer, some sponsors of reapportionment contended that increased political power for that section most in need of the water was necessary whether water bonds passed or failed. Southern Californians, they asserted, would ultimately pay the greatest share of water bonds and should have a more adequate voice in the Senate for future decisions on details of the water program.

Both major parties in California experienced some internal sectional divisions over the reapportionment plan. While state-wide party organizations observed an official neutrality on the controversial issue, much of the leadership in both parties announced their opposition, and many local units outside the southern metropolitan areas followed suit. The argument against Proposition 15 printed in the official voters' pamphlet was signed by both the president of the California Democratic Council and the outgoing president of the Republican State Central Committee.

The only state-wide political figure prominently in favor of Proposition 15 was former governor Goodwin J. Knight (Republican), who ruefully recalled over television some of his own troubles as chief executive vis-à-vis rural power in the Senate. On the other hand, Knight's Democratic successor, Edmund G. Brown, publicly urged defeat of the reapportionment plan, stating: "If Proposition 15 passes, we could have a sectional war in this state. I don't know how many lame-duck senators we'd have, but we will come to a dead stop in California in 1961 and 1962." [7]

While observing that urban areas were entitled to more Senate representation, the Governor urged a more broadly conceived solution than the Bonelli Plan. He also promised that defeat of the reapportionment initiative would result in his asking the 1961 session of the Legislature to authorize a "blue-ribbon" commission to study the whole problem of representation in the Senate.

In order to understand the position of most party leaders and of state officeholders on Senate reapportionment, it is necessary to keep in mind several facets of California's unique political situation. Prior to 1934 the Republican Party held a large majority of both registered voters and state offices. Although the registration lead thereafter shifted markedly in favor of the Democrats, the Republicans were able for years to maintain their hold on most state positions with only occasional exceptions. Though the Democrats held a majority of the Assembly from 1937 to 1943, it was a badly split party, one which was unable to capture the Senate. Party lines were extremely loose, and sectionalism was strong. The system of cross-filing, which allowed candidates to file (without party identification) in the primaries of all parties, gave an enormous advantage to incumbents. Since most incumbents in the early 1930's were Republicans, they were able to maintain a high survival rate in the face of a substantial lead in Democratic registration. Campaigns tended to stress nonpartisanship and to soft-pedal issues and programs. While sectional and urban-rural antagonisms were frequently pronounced, they did not correspond closely to partisan divisions. Neither party was essentially urban-based or rural-based, southern or northern in orientation.

During the 1950's the situation changed in several respects, with the skillful organization of the once-disunited Democrats and the modification, and later the abolition, of cross-filing. This shift reached its culmination in 1958, with the Democrats sweeping both houses of the Legislature and most state-wide offices. Governor Brown won by a margin of more than one million votes. Just as spectacular was the Democratic superiority of twenty-eight to twelve in the once-Republican Senate. Most of this change in Senate strength, over a period of four years, had taken place in mountain and other nonmetropolitan districts, where the rise in Democratic organization had coincided with the availability of an unusually able group of younger and generally liberal party candidates.

Given these circumstances, it is hardly surprising that 1960 found Governor Brown and other state-wide Democratic leaders hostile to a plan which would eliminate several of the party's most prominent senators. The 1959 legislative session had been a highly successful one for the Governor, and he could see nothing but trouble ahead in 1961 if the senators were diverted from legislative business by a 120-day wake for those members of the club not likely to return again. These facts would explain the Democrats' opposition even without the complication of the water bond issue on which Governor Brown had staked his prestige.

The coolness of most leading Republicans toward Senate reapportionment is at first glance less understandable. Since the party's strength was largely in suburban areas, one might expect a possible GOP gain in Senate seats from the districts Proposition 15 would add to metropolitan counties. Indeed, Supervisor Bonelli, a Democrat, was able to convince a number of individual Republicans in Los Angeles that at least some of that county's proposed seven districts would inevitably be Republican. But Republicans had their own sectional divisions and, in addition, many in all areas balked at the extent of the proposed changes. The reallocation of the forty Senate seats was sufficiently drastic to create some uncertainty as to what the electoral results might be. Moreover, the ballot measure provided that the 1961 Legislature would draw the new boundaries for single-member districts in those counties allocated more than one senator. In 1960 the Democrats held both houses by comfortable margins and were expected to retain their control in the November election; thus Democrats would be in a position to gerrymander part of the Senate as well as Assembly and Congressional districts. Finally, Republican incumbents in the Legislature are influential in party circles, and they were no more anxious for a change than were Democratic incumbents. Even senators from populous metropolitan areas were not eager to share power and patronage in their counties with anyone else.

Most economic interest groups also opposed Senate reapportionment in 1960. The negative attitudes of farm organizations, manufacturing associations, and the California Chamber of Commerce were not surprising, since such groups had been similarly aligned in previous apportionment battles. But this time organized labor, sponsor of the defeated reapportionment initiative in 1948, was split sectionally and, except in parts of the southern area, was not active in favor of the proposed Senate change. The state AFL-CIO took an officially neutral position, while the organization's executive officer announced personal opposition to the "20-20" plan. This apparent shift of position in a period of a dozen years can be attributed in large part to the changed composition of the Senate by 1960. It was overwhelmingly Democratic and moderately liberal. Though labor had some grievances with the upper house, they were far fewer and less serious than in the past. Moreover, like other major groups with active lobbyists at the state capitol, labor must have been naturally reluctant to antagonize virtually all sitting senators by backing a ballot measure that was anathema to incumbents.

Proposition 15 received more support in the Los Angeles region (especially from small suburban newspapers) than did the unsuccessful initiative of 1948. Several civic groups, including the Los Angeles Chamber of Commerce, backed the Bonelli Plan. Yet even the metropolitan community was typically divided, with many important economic groups and the most influential daily press in opposition. Outside Los Angeles, suspicion of the state's most populous city and county was strong, with heavy adverse sentiment in the remaining southern (as well as northern) counties. In view of these circumstances, the defeat of Proposition 15 in the November election came as no surprise. The state-wide margin against the measure was nearly two to one, with Los Angeles the only county showing a favorable vote (1,155,308 to 925,996).

## THE "BLUE-RIBBON" COMMISSION

At Governor Brown's request, the 1961 session of the Legislature authorized the creation of a nine-member reapportionment study commission, composed of two legislators from each house and five public members to be named by the governor. Though this legislation swept through both houses without opposition, it did not indicate any great legislative enthusiasm for Senate reapportionment. According to the enabling act, the new study group's job was to "ascertain, study and analyze all facts relating to representation in the State Senate, including but not limited to, proposals designed to modify the present federal plan of apportionment by increasing the representation of extremely heavily populated counties without destroying or rendering ineffective the tested principles of equitable representation for all geographic areas of the state." [8]

Members of the commission appointed by the Governor and the legislative leaders included a majority from the Los Angeles and San Francisco areas, among them Supervisor Bonelli, leading proponent of the recently defeated initiative, and Assemblyman Jesse Unruh, Democratic majority leader—both from Los Angeles.

During November and December 1961, the nine-member group held seven hearings in representative sections of the state—San Diego, Eureka, Chico, Fresno, Los Angeles, Palm Springs, and San Francisco. Both private individuals and spokesmen for organizations and governmental units were invited to appear. Except for the meetings in Los Angeles and San Diego, the Commission found little demand for a change in Senate representation. Indeed, at hearings outside the metropolitan area, some spokesmen even insisted that, if any change were made, it should be in a more rural direction, with each of the fifty-eight counties allocated a senator. The Los Angeles and San Diego hearings brought forth many advocates of more representation for metropolitan areas in general and southern California in particular.

Although Governor Brown had expressed the hope that the commission would start its survey "without any preconceptions at all and work toward what it believes will provide the maximum benefit to California," [9] there were certain political realities which obviously limited the discretion of the study group. In the first place, the commission was to report its findings and recommendations to the Governor and the Legislature by February 10, 1962, so that any proposals could be considered by the lawmakers as part of a special session concurrent with the thirty-day budget session. Consequently, the blue-ribbon group would necessarily give weight to legislative reaction. Since any proposed constitutional amendment stemming from the Legislature requires a two-thirds vote of both houses, the difficulty of obtaining such support, especially in the Senate, could scarcely be ignored. At the same time, if the commission displayed excessive caution, this would probably arouse another initiative campaign. Indeed, Supervisor Bonelli was on hand to remind his commission colleagues that he and others were ready to start circulating petitions if necessary.

After studying the stormy background of Senate reapportionment in California, as well as the variety of representative systems in other states, the commission was able to accept certain general principles. There was agreement that some change was needed. Yet the need for acceptance by the Legislature and ratification by the voters and the failure of the initiative campaigns of 1948 and 1960 seemed to dictate the wisdom of starting with the existing district pattern and adding to it where needed. This would necessitate some enlargement of the Senate, but this seemed preferable to the risks involved in reshuffling the forty seats.

After considering several possible formulas which would add seats to more populous counties, the study group eventually agreed on a proposal to submit with its report. It was clear that the commission was carefully aiming at legislative acceptance, for the recommendations were modest in scope. These included retention of the existing forty-district pattern for the Senate, except that a county exceeding 1,500,000 population would receive an additional senator for each additional increment or any part thereof. However, no county could have over 10 per cent of the entire Senate membership. The Legislature would create single-member districts of approximately equal population in counties with more than one senator, with decennial redistricting provided.[10]

Since Los Angeles County was the only one with sufficient population in 1960 for an increase, it would have a total of four senators out of forty-three. One or two other counties might reach the 1,500,000 population mark by 1970, for an added seat each. Los Angeles would not receive a fifth senator until the Senate reached a total of fifty, probably not until at least 1990. The reason given by the commission for holding the initial increase to Los Angeles was that little demand for added Senate strength had been heard from other counties, with the possible exception of San Diego.

In explaining its recommendations, the commission concentrated on the work load of senators from rapidly growing metropolitan areas, particularly the sheer impossibility of any single senator adequately representing the interests of more than 6,000,000 people in Los Angeles. For example, it was physically impossible for one senator to serve on more than a handful of the important standing committees where the bulk of legislative business takes place. This "work-load" rationale was the one most likely to have an impression on the lawmakers, for even senators otherwise opposed to a change had admitted the existence of this problem in regard to Los Angeles.

A unanimous report had been the hope of Commission Chairman Charles Wellman, who persuaded all nine members, with a wide diversity of viewpoints, to sign the report, with the opportunity of adding "concurring opinions." Three members added separate statements. Supervisor Donnenwirth indicated in a footnote his belief that a maximum of three senators should be the limit for any county. Senator Rattigan appended a lengthy concurring statement in which he took exception to some of the reasoning advanced by the commission, though he agreed on the workload argument. He concurred in the recommendations "because they are limited and self-limiting" and because the alternative might be another drastic initiative proposal. "In other words, a virtue of the Commission's proposal is that we could do worse—and we very well might." Finally, in answer to critics of the Senate, Rattigan pointed to several rural senators with metropolitan backgrounds and contended that "the Senate membership is rather more urban-minded, and more capable of understanding urban problems, than is suggested by its familiar identification as a dynasty of hayseeds." [11] Senator Rattigan also indicated that his concurrence did not commit him in any way to future legislative consideration of Senate reapportionment.

Supervisor Bonelli's concurring statement more nearly approached a dissenting opinion. He insisted that the limitation on Los Angeles County was too severe and that a sound reapportionment should provide additional representation for all heavily populated areas, rather than for just one county. "By signing this report and thus indicating my concurrence with it I have intended to alert the people of the State of California to the drastic need for reapportionment of the Senate and to enable the Legislature to consider the question at the 1962 Special Session." [12]

## THE 1962 SESSION AND ITS AFTERMATH

Governor Brown strongly endorsed the report of the blue-ribbon commission and included its recommendations on the call for the special session. He asked the Legislature to approve the commission's proposed constitutional amendment for submission to the voters in the November general election. This would require fifty-four votes in the Assembly and twenty-seven in the Senate. Most observers felt that the proposal could get through the lower house, but were less optimistic about the upper chamber. Several rural and mountain senators expressed either disapproval or doubts, while no solid endorsements could be found from others. Neither of the senators who had been members of the study commission moved to push the legislation, and early in the session Senate leaders expressed serious doubts about chances of passage. Finally, in mid-March, the upper house held an extraordinary one-and-one-half hour closed caucus on the issue and decided to wait to see what happened in the Assembly before acting.

In the lower house, Jesse Unruh, who had served on the blue-ribbon commission, had become speaker. Since the Senate would make no move, Unruh introduced the commission's proposal in the Assembly. But the plan encountered some coolness there because it benefited only Los Angeles. It was also under fire from many southern California spokesmen, including Bonelli. In order to overcome the objections, Speaker Unruh amended his bill to include an additional senator each for the five next most populous counties, two in the south and three in the north; Los Angeles would have the same total of four recommended in the original bill. By late in March this gained added support in the Assembly and, after barely failing to carry on a first attempt, finally secured the necessary two-thirds margin by one vote. Unruh's prestige—and the Governor's— had been on the line, and the Speaker had had to exert all his considerable influence and power to salvage the narrow victory, one which clearly could not be duplicated in the upper house. Conceivably, Unruh may have felt that Assembly passage of a stronger measure could prod the Senate into accepting the more moderate commission plan.

The Senate, however, was in no mood to pass any reapportionment during that session. The Assembly-passed measure died a quiet death in committee. Then the Senate passed a bill appropriating $100,000 for a thirteen-member commission to study the reapportionment problem and report back at the 1964 session. This proposal met overwhelming defeat in the Assembly, with Speaker Unruh asserting: "We have had study after study . . . . It is now a problem that the people must decide." [13] On April 13, the 1962 special session adjourned. The conservative *Los Angeles Times* editorialized: "There is an intimation of the death wish in the hearts of the senators at Sacramento when they reject almost casually the proposals for reapportioning their house." [14] Governor Brown expressed this reaction: "I am disappointed. There must be a reapportionment of the State Senate. Los Angeles County with its 6,500,000 residents needs more than one senator. If there is no initiative, I will propose reapportionment of the Senate in January." [15]

By this time an initiative campaign was already under way in southern California. At Bonelli's urging, a seven-member strategy group in Los Angeles had been formed. In addition to Bonelli and Mayor Samuel Yorty of Los Angeles City, the committee consisted of the president of the Los Angeles Chamber of Commerce; the executive secretary of the county Federation of Labor (AFL-CIO); the president of the county division of the League of California Cities; and two prominent women, one Democrat, and one Republican. In addition, support was readily found from various leaders in Orange and San Diego counties. On April 16, Bonelli and two others flew to Sacramento to file the new reapportionment initiative. The attorney general gave the prospective measure the title of "Senate Reapportionment," and within a few days petitions were in circulation. Proponents had until June 28, 1962, to obtain the necessary 420,-402 valid signatures, and they succeeded in doing so.

The new initiative measure provided for a Senate of fifty members. The existing forty districts were retained, except that counties having a 1960 population of 600,000 or more were to be divided into two or more senatorial districts. Counties with populations in excess of 1,200,000 (only Los Angeles qualified) would receive two senatorial districts, plus one additional district for each additional 1,000,000 people. The result was that the ten added Senate seats would be distributed as follows: five more to Los Angeles County (for a total of six) and one more each to San Diego and Orange counties in the south and to Alameda, San Francisco, and Santa Clara counties in the north. The 1963 Legislature was required to fix boundaries for multidistrict counties. After the 1970 census and each subsequent decennial federal census the Legislature would reapportion senatorial districts on the basis of "population, geographic area and economic affinity," but no county could have more than six senators and no district could contain more than three counties. In the event of legislative inaction, the redistricting would be done by the Reapportionment Commission (five state executive officers) which since 1926 had been potentially in reserve but never used for Assembly or Congressional redistricting.

As the latest reapportionment initiative campaign took shape, there was a widespread feeling that its chances for success were much better than the two previous efforts. For one thing, the proposal was far more moderate, in that it did not change any existing districts. Moreover, in contrast to the 1960 initiative, it was not likely to draw criticism as a section-based scheme. For the first time in many years, the major metropolitan communities of southern California displayed an apparent united front that involved figures from both parties as well as from a diversity of economic groups. A considerable amount of newspaper support was assured. When Bonelli filed the initiative, the *Los Angeles Herald-Examiner* published a strong endorsement and appealed for volunteers to circulate petitions. The *Los Angeles Times* was editorially concerned about reapportionment as never before, as were other newspapers in the Los Angeles-San Diego area. At least a good share of this shift in attitude by a largely conservative press was due to its awareness that the Senate had changed markedly in both partisan control and political outlook. As Senator Rattigan expressed it: "Many of those who once defended the *status quo* are now less interested in doing so—the *status quo* itself having vitally changed." [16]

Whether the 1962 initiative could get sufficient support in northern-urban California was less clear. While three counties in the San Francisco Bay area would double their Senate representation, this was not necessarily an incentive for supporting a plan from which Los Angeles was the largest beneficiary. Moreover, historical accidents in the evolution of California's county lines had bequeathed to the Bay area nine counties which already had eight and one-half senators. At the same time, the new initiative was sufficiently moderate that it seemed unlikely to draw from any area the kind of intensive organized attack which earlier attempts had suffered.

By the spring of 1962 the plan for a modified Senate seemed to have a fair chance of success in the November election. The "Federal Plan" had originated from a ballot measure and might well be changed in the same way. Indeed, after the events of the special session of 1962, it seemed unlikely that the Senate itself would ever consent to any meaningful reapportionment. Urban leaders pressing for a Senate revision could be thankful that one heritage of the "progressive era," the initiative process, allowed them to circumvent the Legislature in proposing a change in that institution. But the possibility of success here—whether in 1962 or in some future election—depends first upon convincing a majority of California's urban dwellers that they can trust themselves with a greater share of representative strength.

# Notes

1 George B. Merry, "Minority Rule: Challenge to Democracy," *Christian Science Monitor*, October 2, 1958.

2 While this northern proposal provided for a lower house based on population and an upper house based on area, the term "federal" is otherwise inappropriate. All states are unitary rather than federal in internal make-up; counties are merely legal agents created by the state.

3 The San Francisco Chamber of Commerce contributed $25,000 to finance the campaign, even though the city would be reduced from seven senators to one! See Thomas Barclay, "Reapportionment in California," *Pacific Historical Review* (June, 1936), pp. 97 f.

4 "The Reapportionment Struggle in California in 1948," *Western Political Quarterly*, IV (1951), 317.

5 Carey McWilliams, *California, The Great Exception* (New York: A. A. Wyn, 1949), pp. 97 f.

6 *Compendium on Legislative Apportionment*, s.v. "California" (New York: National Municipal League, 1960).

7 *Santa Barbara News-Press*, October 28, 1960.

8 Senate leader Hugh Burns, Fresno Democrat, who introduced the bill creating the study commission, stated: "I am not indicating at all, in any sense of the word, that there is anything wrong [with the *status quo*]." *Los Angeles Times*, May 31, 1961, p. 23.

9 *Loc. cit.*

10 *Report of the State of California Study Commission on Senate Reapportionment* (Sacramento: February 1962), p. 3.

11 *Ibid.*, pp. 50, 53, 56.

12 *Ibid.*, p. 47.

13 *Los Angeles Times*, April 14, 1962, p. 13.

14 *Los Angeles Times*, April 13, 1962.

15 *Los Angeles Times*, April 13, 1962, p. 1.

16 *Report of the State of California Study Commission on Senate Reapportionment*, *op. cit.*, p. 54.

# 2

## Colorado

### A MATTER OF BALANCE

*WILLIAM P. IRWIN*
*Western Reserve University*

Just over a century ago, at a time when eastern Colorado was still a part of the Kansas and Nebraska territories and tempers were short over issues of Free Soil and mining-camp government, the *Rocky Mountain News* took occasion to observe that a politician is a person who, "buoyant by putrefaction, rises as he rots." Time has moderated the opinion, even in the *Rocky Mountain News,* but the Colorado public still tends to be wary of politicians and their enthusiasms.

The attitude is not one of dour distrust of all things political; it could hardly be in a state which elected a Populist governor in 1896 and was host to strong movements of Grangers, Populists, Greenbackers, Free Silverites, and Progressives. In fact, none of these groups has wholly disappeared except in name, to this day. But neither are Coloradans politically capricious nor indifferent. Not since William Jennings Bryan has the spark of hero worship been struck, and few political bosses worthy of the name have boasted any success. The key, rather, has been balance—a two-party balance, but in the midst of political experiment and diversity.

Since 1896 Colorado has been almost precisely divided, Democratic and Republican, in cumulative vote for presidents, governors, and United States senators. Since 1928 the Republicans have controlled the state legislature seven times, the Democrats six, and it has been divided on four occasions. The split ticket has become to the parties a haunting symbol of the popular limitations that are put on their power and responsibility. Rarely is one party able to capture all the state's executive offices, and occasionally, as in 1956, the voters have elected a governor of one party and a lieutenant governor of the other.

Any discussion of legislative apportionment in Colorado must proceed against this curious background of political balance and diversity, for it immediately tempers the normal assumptions regarding partisan advantage and rural-urban conflict which elsewhere may wholly dominate the apportionment process.

## A MATTER OF STATISTICS

The Colorado constitution contains six basic and essentially innocent provisions for legislative apportionment. Paraphrased, but in the familiar categorical manner, they are:

(1) The General Assembly shall apportion itself (but an apportionment may be referred to, or initiated by, the electorate); (2) at five-year intervals, following each federal decennial census as well as each state census, to be taken in each year ending in the number five; (3) "according to ratios to be fixed by law." (4) The Senate shall have a maximum of thirty-five members, the House of Representatives, sixty-five. (5) Legislative districts shall be contiguous and "compact as may be." (6) No county shall be divided in forming legislative districts.

The force of the several provisions has varied considerably and sometimes unexpectedly, as in other states; in some instances the significance of one or another of them—for example, the prohibition against dividing counties when districting—has become apparent only through long experience. For the moment, however, it is enough to survey the immediate consequences of these constitutional provisions as they relate to the current apportionment act and recent population trends.

Colorado is divided into sixty-three counties, including the constitutional City and County of Denver, the joint city-county government of which operates within a single jurisdiction. Populations vary radically among the counties, from a high of 493,887 in Denver (1960) to only 208 in Hinsdale County and 424 in Mineral, both tucked away in the San Juan Range in the southwest quarter of the state. Since the Apportionment Act of 1953, which is still in force, the counties have been grouped into twenty-five senatorial and thirty-five representative districts, each composed of one or more whole counties as the constitution prescribes. Fourteen senators, two-fifths of the whole number, are elected in four multimember districts, and forty-one representatives, almost two-thirds of the House, come from eleven such districts—a circumstance of major significance which is discussed at length below.

Colorado is one of only nine states which employ population figures alone as the basis of apportionment in both houses. Without elaboration, the constitution states simply that apportionment shall occur "according to ratios to be fixed by law," a provision which offers considerable leeway for political artifice. In fact, however, the ratios established have not been unduly complex or obscure. The most thorough reapportionment measure in the history of the state was an initiated act approved at the polls in 1932. It provided for one senator per district for the first 17,000 of population and another for each additional 35,000 persons or fraction over 32,000; one representative for the first 8,000 people and another for each additional 19,000 or fraction over 17,000. It is evident that a significant, if not radical, rural bias was introduced into both houses by means of the low first apportionment ratio, a bias that has been a fundamental element of legislative apportionment in Colorado throughout its history. The Apportionment Act of 1953 was essentially a modification of the initiated measure of two decades earlier. It fixed ratios of one senator for the first 19,000 persons and one more for each additional 50,000 or fraction over 48,000; one representative for the first 8,000 and another for each additional 25,500 or fraction over 22,400. The consequences of this last, and current, act may be noted in greater detail.

The counties of Colorado may be divided, somewhat arbitrarily, into four categories by population: (1) Denver, (2) suburban, (3) urban, and (4) rural. The suburban counties are Adams, Arapahoe, Jefferson, and Elbert,[1] all adjacent to, or near, Denver. Only El Paso, Pueblo, and Boulder counties, which include the cities of Colorado Springs, Pueblo, and Boulder, are classified as urban. The rural counties are the remaining fifty-five in the state.[2]

On the basis of 1950 population figures, the apportionment of 1953 (which became effective at the election of 1954) had none of the startling disparities which characterize some other states. As Table 1 indicates, Denver and its suburbs were allotted representation in almost identical ratios, although neither was apportioned representation equal to its population. The value of the popular vote[3] in the metropolitan area as a whole, which in 1950 had 42.9 per cent of Colorado's population, was only .78. The urban counties of El Paso, Pueblo, and Boulder, it will be noted, fared only slightly better. In the rural constituencies, on the other hand, the combined population of which was roughly equal to that of the Denver metropolitan area, the value of the average vote cast for a state legislator was 1.29, or roughly two-thirds again the value of its metropolitan counterpart. The extremes of representation under the 1953 act occurred, in the Senate, in the suburban district of Arapahoe and Elbert counties, given a vote value of .68, and in the mountain constituency composed of Chaffee, Park, Gilpin, Clear Creek, Douglas, and Teller counties, in which the vote value was 1.95, almost three times as great. In the House, suburban Jefferson County was assigned a vote value of .73, whereas a vote cast in the plains district of Cheyenne and Lincoln counties was rated at 2.18, nearly three times as large.

In the interval between 1950 and 1960, Colorado experienced some

## TABLE 1

### LEGISLATIVE STRENGTH OF MAJOR CATEGORIES OF
### COLORADO COUNTIES

| | 1950-1953 | | | | 1960-1963 | | | |
| | Population, 1950 | Pct. of state population, 1950 | Pct. members of legislature, 1953 | Vote value, 1953 | Population, 1960 | Pct. of state population, 1960 | Pct. members of legislature, 1960-1963 | Vote value, 1960 |
|---|---|---|---|---|---|---|---|---|
| Denver | 415,786 | 31.4 | 25.0 | .78 | 493,887 | 28.2 | 25.0 | .87 |
| Suburban* | 152,523 | 11.5 | 9.0 | .77 | 364,950 | 20.8 | 9.0 | .43 |
| Metro-politan (Denver plus suburban) | 568,309 | 42.9 | 34.0 | .78 | 855,129 | 48.8 | 34.0 | .69 |
| Urban | 213,007 | 16.1 | 14.0 | .88 | 336,703 | 19.2 | 14.0 | .74 |
| Rural | 543,773 | 41.0 | 52.0 | 1.29 | 562,115 | 32.0 | 52.0 | 1.62 |
| | 1,325,089 | 100.0 | 100.0 | | 1,753,947 | 100.0 | 100.0 | |

* Includes Elbert County, with approximately 4,000 population, as part of a senatorial district with Arapahoe County.

remarkable population changes. While the population of the state as a whole grew during the decade by 31.5 per cent, the entire increase occurred in fewer than half the counties and overwhelmingly in the metropolitan and urban areas. The Denver metropolitan area, ranked third in rate of growth in the United States in 1960, increased by 50.5 per cent. The three Denver suburban counties of Arapahoe, Jefferson, and Adams grew by 116.5, 129.2, and 197.7 per cent, respectively, and the urban counties of El Paso, Pueblo, and Boulder experienced increases of 30 per cent or more. In the same period, however, thirty-six of the state's sixty-three counties lost population, in extreme instances by more than 30 per cent! The effects of these population changes are evident in Table 1. Although the city of Denver grew at a rate of 18.2 per cent, it did not keep pace with Colorado as a whole. It emerged at the end of the decade, therefore, with relatively *greater* influence per constituent in the General Assembly than it had had in 1954, the value of its popular vote having risen from .78 to .87. On the other hand, the suburban counties suffered a radical setback in relative legislative authority, a condition that has been common throughout the United States. The value of their vote fell from .77 to .43. Although the category of rural counties includes some, such as Weld, Larimer and Mesa, which had sharp urban population increases, the countervailing loss in others resulted in a deceptive but statistically useful appearance of stability. Again in keeping with national trends, the rural constituencies improved their relative influence in the legislature, the average value of their vote having risen from 1.29 to 1.62.

The full impact of the complex population changes in the state is best illustrated, however, by the inequities in representation that were produced among particular constituencies in the short interval between the Apportionment Act of 1953 and the census of 1960. In the Senate, the value of the vote had dropped to .39 in suburban Jefferson County, .42 in Adams, and .43 in Arapahoe, while it had swelled to 2.87 and 2.50 in two thinly populated Great Plains districts. Thus, by 1960, the value of a vote cast for a senator in Kit Carson, Cheyenne, Lincoln, or Kiowa counties was more than seven times that in Jefferson County. The disparity was even greater in the House of Representatives. Jefferson County, again, had the lowest vote value, .42; at the other extreme, in Huerfano County, a rural constituency in the south of the state, the vote had risen to a value of 3.43, eight times its counterpart in the new housing developments of Jefferson County.

There is no evidence that the lure of Colorado, which was popularly discovered only after World War II, has in any way begun to fade. Population projections through 1963 indicate that the inequalities of legislative apportionment which had developed by 1960 will continue to be magnified with each passing year. The principal fault of the General Assembly when reapportioning Colorado in 1953 was its inability, or perhaps unwillingness, to anticipate the population boom along the Rocky Mountain front. It remains to be seen what praise or blame it must bear in the current decade. For its part, the Forty-Third General Assembly adjourned *sine die* in mid-February 1962 without having taken action. The fact is that the members were by no means uniformly stricken with their plight, and the public, even the urban public, had expressed no great indignation on the subject.

## A SKIRMISH IN THE LEGISLATURE

Evidence of population growth and its impact on legislative apportionment had been the subject of discussion for some years in the late 1950's. The census figures of 1960 came as no surprise to most Coloradans, who had watched various other growth indicators with a feeling of some economic satisfaction; in fact, the count was a disappointment to some of the more self-conscious cities and towns.

In the first session of the Forty-Third General Assembly, in 1961, some consideration was given to reapportionment, but action was deferred to the following year. The determination of the legislature to perform its constitutional chores was apparent, nonetheless, in passage during the first session of House Joint Resolution No. 24. Opening with the words, "whereas the Forty-Third General Assembly is required by constitutional mandate to reapportion the General Assembly at the Second Regular Session convening in January 1962," the resolution directed the Legislative Council to begin study of the problem. A committee of the Legislative Council, together with its staff, toiled throughout the summer and fall and, on November 30, 1961, more than a month before the second session opened, submitted its recommendations. The substance of its proposals, introduced as Senate Bill No. 28 and House Bill No. 14, and given primary consideration during the session, were as follows.

Apportionment ratios called for one senator for the first 22,000 of population, another for the next 80,000, and still others for each additional 60,000; one representative for the first 8,682 constituents, a second for the next 42,000, a third and a fourth for the next 50,000 each, and still others for each additional 26,400 persons. If the ratios were unusually complex, however, their effect was not.

Senatorial districts were to be reduced from twenty-five to twenty-three, involving only minor boundary changes, and the suburban counties of Adams, Arapahoe, and Jefferson were to gain an additional senator each, while one was to be taken from rural Weld County. In the House, Adams, Arapahoe, and Jefferson were again assigned another representative each, while three other constituencies, including urban Pueblo County, were to lose one. Minor boundary changes were to preserve the existing thirty-five House districts.

As introduced, the Legislative Council proposal would have overcome the worst inequities of the old apportionment. The curious ratios would have had the effect of penalizing the rapidly growing urban and suburban areas without seriously weakening the city of Denver. The metropolitan areas of Denver, Pueblo, and Colorado Springs, with 63.3 per cent of the state's population in 1960, would have controlled precisely 50 per cent of the members of the legislature. The value of the vote in the Denver metropolitan area would have been .82 and in the rural districts reduced slightly to 1.45.

The bill was lost, along with perhaps a dozen others, in sharp skirmishing throughout the legislative session. The support and opposition which the bills received are of more than passing interest. As might be expected, legislators from the rural constituencies in both political parties almost uniformly approved it, while opposition centered for the most part in the Denver metropolitan area and Pueblo. The Republican members from urban Colorado Springs sided throughout the session with their rural colleagues. Various proposed amendments to the bill in both houses which would have increased representation in the urban and suburban areas outside Denver did not receive the wholehearted support of the Denver members. Relations between Denver and its suburbs and between Denver and Colorado Springs have not been altogether cordial on a number of issues, and an unusual community of interest has been reached between the city and some of the liberal Democratic legislators in the rural areas, a fact examined further below.

In the Senate the bill was dramatically amended late in the session to reduce the number of Denver senators by half while doubling their number in the suburbs. The effect of the amended measure would have been to smother Denver's influence in the Senate and to open the way for a "federal" Senate apportionment. Sponsored by rural Republicans, although reported from the committee of the whole, the amendment was carried by a large majority, including five rural Democrats and the entire Republican delegation, one of whom was from Denver. It was opposed by all Democrats from Denver, the suburban counties, and Pueblo, as well as by the Democratic president *pro tem* and the majority floor leader, both from rural constituencies. In the final vote on the amended bill, the lone Denver Republican shifted to the opposition.

The result of the Senate amendment, as anticipated by its sponsors, was to kill the measure altogether. The suburban members were given the difficult and unrealistic choice of supporting the amendment, thereby incurring the wrath of Denver, or appearing to oppose increased suburban representation in the Senate. It is not surprising, therefore, that they divided on party lines. Quite predictably, when the amended bill reached the House, it was shelved by the Rules Committee. Thus refusing to consider the Senate version, the House wearily defeated the unamended Legislative Council proposal in a straight party vote.

The legislative session of 1962 was only the first skirmish in the apportionment contest in Colorado. After it adjourned, two groups were successful in petition campaigns to put radically different constitutional amendments on the ballot for a vote in November. A "federal" plan, basing apportionment on population in one house but more on area in the other, was supported by the Chamber of Commerce, the Cattlemen's Association, and the Farm Bureau. A proposal for basing representation in both houses on population was supported by the AFL-CIO, the Colorado Education Association, and the League of Women Voters. The fact that there were two conflicting proposals increased the difficulties of passing either.

It seems almost certain that, if the voters reject both plans, the General Assembly will act to reapportion at its next session in 1963. The elements of the problem will not be greatly altered at that time, however, if they are altered at all. For the simple fact is that there are at least two major obstacles to reapportionment in Colorado, as in any other state:

the law and the men who make the law. It may be worthwhile to look more closely at some aspects of the character of both.

## THE CASE FOR GUY POE

The constitutional provision that the legislature "shall revise and adjust the apportionment for senators and representatives . . . according to ratios to be fixed by law" is not, of course, unique. The required ratios are not embedded in the constitution, as is the case in some other states, but are established without hindrance by the legislature itself, a fact which gives considerable flexibility to legislative action. To the public, nevertheless, the provision is abstruse and easily misunderstood: although Colorado is generally (and not incorrectly) classified among states whose legislatures are apportioned according to population, for practical purposes its constitution neither requires nor suggests that this be the case. For, in the absence of any standard or even indication of equality of representation, the General Assembly is constitutionally free to apportion itself in any way of which it is *politically* capable. It is not difficult, of course, to devise ratios to fit almost any preconceived apportionment scheme.

Under the circumstances it is remarkable that apportionment ratios have not been greatly abused, a fact which testifies to the partisan balance which has characterized most of the history of Colorado politics. But it caused no great surprise when the most seriously considered apportionment measure of the 1962 session, the Legislative Council proposal, was introduced, providing for one representative per district for the first 8,682 of population, a second for the next 42,000, and so on through additional varied ratios. It was evident to the members of both parties in the legislature and not a few interested observers that the unusual number of 8,682 was precisely the population, in 1960, of the third smallest and third most overrepresented House district in the state. Nor did anyone concerned fail to note that the district was held, as it had been for some years, by the majority caucus chairman, who was at the same time chairman of the Rules Committee, member of the Education, Local Government, and Agriculture and Livestock committees, and a member, too, of the Apportionment Committee of the Legislative Council!

But even these considerations faded into insignificance for the more-than-casual observer with the further appreciation that Rep. Guy Poe was—to be sure—rural, but a rural liberal Democrat and member of the board of the Rocky Mountain Farmers Union who on more than one occasion had given invaluable support, both in and out of the legislature, to his urban, professional, and labor associates. And, if the reader will be patient, it may be added that Poe was not only beloved among Democrats but respected among Republicans and represented one of the more inflexible districts, bounded as it was (and may indeed remain) on *two* sides by the state of Nebraska and on each of its two other sides by safe Republican districts!

As already noted, the measure died in the Forty-Third General Assembly. It ought, perhaps, to be added that the two districts which had populations of less than 8,682 could both have been enlarged without endangering the political lives of their incumbents, one of whom was also a liberal Democrat, the speaker of the House, and a member of the Rules Committee, as well as being the most probable Democratic nominee for Congress in 1962 in the Third Congressional District, and the other of whom was a conservative Republican whose membership on the Appropriations, Business Affairs, and Labor and Employment Relations committees was considered critical by his party colleagues. Each man, it should be noted, embodied certain requirements of partisan responsibility which could not be sacrificed to the more remote and somewhat vague principles of equal apportionment.

## THE CASE FOR MULTIMEMBER DISTRICTS

Perhaps the most interesting of all the constitutional provisions for legislative apportionment in Colorado is the prohibition against dividing counties when creating districts. Inevitably, it has led to extensive use of multimember districts. Since 1953, when the present boundaries were established, fourteen of the thirty-five senators have been elected at-large in such multimember districts and forty-one—almost two-thirds—of the sixty-five representatives. Denver County—which is coterminous with the city of Denver—alone presently elects eight senators and seventeen representatives, all at-large.

Not surprisingly, there is a strong tendency for one party to dominate such constituencies. Thus in the Forty-Third General Assembly, concluded in 1962, Denver County was represented by seven Democratic senators and but one Republican, fourteen Democratic representatives and only three Republicans. In occasional recent elections the Democratic Party has swept all or all but one of the twenty-one House and Senate seats available in Denver.[4] Republicans, on the other hand, have consistently controlled the two Senate and three House seats in El Paso County (Colorado Springs), while immediately adjacent Pueblo County, which is dominated by the industrial city of Pueblo, is habitually represented by four Democratic House members and two Democratic senators. In some of the smaller multimember districts, one-party control has been virtually unshakeable for years.

The consequences of multimember districting have been far-reaching. The urban, industrial counties of Denver, Pueblo, and Adams alone (among sixty-three counties) have had a combined total of twenty-three representatives and eleven senators since the Apportionment Act of 1953, or approximately one-third of the membership of each house of the General Assembly. Inasmuch as the Democratic Party has been able to control an overwhelming majority of these seats in recent years (ten of the eleven Senate seats and from twenty to all of the twenty-three available in the House through the last three elections), an urban and Democratic leverage is brought to bear on the General Assembly which goes some distance toward compensating for the rural, Republican bias created by the apportionment ratios. There is no question that in Denver, which on occasion has voted Republican in both state-wide and mayoral [5] elections, the Republican Party could increase its representation substantially in the legislature if the city were districted.

Two other and related consequences of the use of multimember districts are also evident, particularly in Denver, which is an unusual, if not unique, example of urban politics. It is apparent that there is a strong impulse toward increased discipline in the dominant political party in a large multimember district in both its electoral and legislative behavior. The result in Colorado has been an additional, but perhaps unmeasurable, increment of urban and Democratic influence in state politics. The normal presumption of Democratic success in Denver elections for the state legislature has put a high premium on party nomination, not unlike that in one-party areas of the United States. Despite the fact that Colorado has a direct primary system, the Denver County Democratic leadership has been able, with few exceptions, to control nominations through effective use of a preprimary convention designation system which is as old in Colorado as the primary itself.[6] Because the leadership has been liberal and labor-oriented in recent years, party nominees have generally tended to reflect these attitudes. In the recently concluded Forty-Third General Assembly, for example, sixteen of the twenty-one Denver Democrats in the two houses were strongly liberal, four were of moderate disposition, and one may be classified a conservative.

During the course of a campaign, this sense of party discipline is imparted to, or assumed by, the Democratic candidates for the legislature in Denver, who tend to campaign for and with one another and to make common cause with respect to the party platform. Because it is difficult for each of twenty-one candidates of the same party, running at large in the same constituency for identical office, to finance his own campaign, campaign funds are normally raised and expended on behalf of all the candidates by the party's Central Committee. Newspaper, radio, and billboard advertising is bought for the entire ticket, radio and television broadcasts are made with all candidates present, and occasionally joint public appearances are arranged.

The culminating and most significant aspect of this Democratic Party discipline in Denver is its extension into the legislature. Although no study of party or platform voting in the Colorado legislature has been made, it is a matter of common observation in both political parties that the Denver Democrats, with occasional obvious exceptions, tend to vote as a bloc. A survey of the Senate and House *Journals* of the 1961-1962 General Assembly, for example, reveals that typically six, and often all, of the seven Democratic senators were united on roll-call measures, while in the House the core tended to vary between ten and thirteen, with only one consistent dissenter.

At times the tension of such discipline (as moderate as it is by some standards) breaks through the surface of party harmony. In 1958, for example, the Denver County Democratic Assembly took the unusual course of denying a primary ballot position to an incumbent senator for the express reason that he had too often broken ranks on party measures, an action which caused some consternation both in and out of Denver. A similar effort was made in 1960 to purge an incumbent representative, the failure of which, however, lent some strength to his independence and reputation for martyrdom.

It is interesting to note that the effects of the multimember district on the Republican Party in Denver have inclined to the contrary. It may be speculated that Republican and Democratic temperaments vary; but there appear to be other, less obscure, reasons why such is the case. The chronic minority position of Republican members of the General Assembly from Denver and perhaps, too, the expectation of defeat among Republican legislative candidates (in spite of the ability of the Republican Party to win some other city-wide elections) have tended to weaken both electoral and legislative discipline among them. The party has not been able to hold the rein as effectively on its candidates as have the Democrats, or to mount a similar unified campaign. In 1958, when a "right-to-work" campaign was being conducted in the state, two Republican candidates for the House of Representatives took public stands against the proposed constitutional amendment in opposition to both formal and active support for the measure by the Denver Republican leadership. While both candidates were defeated in a Democratic sweep, one ran near the top of his slate. In the legislature, too, the Republicans from Denver have been irregulars, most of whom, in recent General Assemblies, could be classified as moderates or liberals.

None of these observations, of course, has been lost on the Republican Party or, for that matter, on rural, conservative Democrats. From time to time efforts have been made to amend the constitution to permit districting within a county, often in association with a "federal plan" of apportionment. In 1954 the voters defeated by a substantial margin a proposed amendment providing for both county districting and a modified "federal plan," under which existing senatorial districts were to be frozen and representative districts based on equal populations. In 1957 a Governor's Commission on Legislative Apportionment took extensive testimony throughout the state; although it was dissolved without making formal recommendations, it was apparently disposed toward both the "federal plan" and county districting. In the 1961 and 1962 sessions of the legislature a number of proposals were made toward one or both ends, including a recommendation of the Legislative Council for a constitutional amendment, to have been submitted to the electorate in November 1962, providing that "a county . . . may be divided . . . in the formation of districts if it contains sufficient population within itself to form two or more districts." The resolution, of course, failed, although there is a strong probability that the matter will be raised again by Republicans in the future.

## THE FURTHER CASE FOR RESTRAINT

From time to time efforts have been made to devise alternate machinery for reapportionment when the legislature fails to act, or, more stringently, to remove the initiative for apportionment from the General Assembly altogether. In 1953 a House concurrent resolution, which died in committee, would have given alternate jurisdiction to a commission composed of the lieutenant governor, the attorney general, the secretary of state, the state controller, and the commissioner of education. In 1954 a constitutional amendment was defeated at the polls which provided that the chief justice of the Supreme Court of Colorado would appoint a commission to reapportion when the legislature was delinquent. Two years later, in 1956, an identically worded resolution died in House committee. Still another constitutional amendment, defeated in 1956, would have given the original initiative for reapportionment to the Supreme Court; and in 1957 a Senate concurrent resolution was lost in committee which stipulated that reapportionment would be carried out by a five-man committee appointed by the Supreme Court.

Since adoption of the Colorado constitution in 1876, when the state entered the Union, sixteen five-year apportionment periods have elapsed. No reapportionment has occurred at the odd intervals for the sufficient reason that no state census has ever been taken. Federal enumerations have been followed by reapportionment only in 1881, 1901, 1913, 1932, and 1953; in only three of these instances did the General Assembly fully discharge its constitutional responsibilities. In 1913, for reasons lost to time, the members cut up the electoral pie with sporting abandon, having recorded no legal ratios as the constitution demands. And in 1932 the legislature was relieved of its burden entirely when an initiated apportionment measure was approved by the voters, the only one ever to survive a referendum.

The constitutional maximum of thirty-five senators and sixty-five representatives was reached as long ago as the Apportionment Act of 1901. The result of the provision has been, of course, to reduce the available alternatives for apportionment, although the difficulty has been partially overcome by use of the multimember district. The sparse population of the rural areas, isolated in pockets by the barriers of mountains and arid land, has dictated the creation of large districts, difficult for campaigning. Such considerations have lent weight to the demand that rural districts be restricted to manageable geographic areas by pegging the ratio of population to the first senator or representative at a low figure. The inevitable result has been to further justify the rural bias of the General Assembly.

On occasion it has been suggested that the state be divided entirely into large, multimember districts as a means of adding flexibility to the constitutional limitation on numbers of legislators, and, indeed, a bill to this effect was introduced in the legislative session of 1962. At times in the past, too, attempts have been made to increase the size of the General Assembly, such as that of the Legislative Council in 1962, which proposed to enlarge the Senate to thirty-nine members and the House of Representatives to seventy-three.

Unlike the record in many other states, the constitutional condition that legislative districts be compact and contiguous has never been seriously violated, in part, perhaps, because of sparsity of population in the rural areas, but more obviously because of the prohibition against dividing counties. Topographically, some of the districts are nightmares, however; for, except as a cartographer's projection, Colorado is hardly a compact or even contiguous economy. Although three-fourths of its population is gathered at the eastern foot of the Front Range of the Rocky Mountains, the remainder is flung out in remote communities on the high plains or strung like beads through the high valleys and along the river bottoms of the western mountains. Blizzards on the plains and mountain passes closed for the winter in the midst of fall campaigning are accepted as unavoidable obstacles to reapportionment planning on the continental divide.

## A LEGISLATIVE PROFILE

Several years ago, Professors Steiner and Gove suggested that there are four obstacles to reapportionment by legislatures themselves:

1. Individual preservation, the desire of each legislator to be in a "safe" district;

2. Mutual preservation, the willingness of members to cooperate with each other in protecting incumbents against potential challengers;

3. Political party preservation, the desire of the leaders of each political party organization to maximize its strength in the legislature;

4. Bloc preservation, the desire of members of voting blocs—whether based on geographic, economic, or ideological cohesion—to retain existing personnel and strength. Such blocs are often bipartisan, and their membership is relatively small.[7]

Of these, the authors concluded that personal preservation was the greatest obstacle of all. It would be difficult and possibly absurd to single out one or another obstacle as having been decisive in the recent activities of the Colorado General Assembly. Each factor merges into the other, and their influence upon any legislator may be wholly mixed and even unperceived. The case of Rep. Guy Poe, cited above, illustrates not only the existence of the several obstacles, but perhaps their reasonableness and persuasiveness as well. To choose only one among them, it may be asked if sufficient attention has been paid to the impact which the various models of legislative apportionment have on the organization and responsible behavior of political parties. Happily, the question will not be answered here; but it may be worthwhile to analyze briefly the curiously complex balance which characterized the partisan and ideological composition of one state legislature at the moment of an apportionment contest.

In the Forty-Third General Assembly, as Table 2 indicates, the Democrats had nominal majorities of 19-16 in the Senate and 33-32 in the House. The figures probably have greater significance than would be the case in most other states. The remarkable balance between Republicans and Democrats in Colorado history has inclined both parties toward somewhat more disciplined behavior than is generally true among nonindustrial states. Moreover, the uncommon unity among Denver Democrats in recent years has frequently produced a unified reaction among rural Republicans, a circumstance which has often hardened (but sometimes sundered) party lines. The final vote on House Bill No. 14, the Legislative Council reapportionment measure, is a case in point: while reasons for their actions were certainly varied, no member broke caucus in the straight party division which occurred, although five minority members subsequently changed their votes for the record. But there are other and perhaps more fundamental matters to be considered.

## TABLE 2

### IDEOLOGICAL COMPOSITION OF THE COLORADO LEGISLATURE, 1961-1962

**Senate 35**

| Democrats 19 | | | | | | | | | Republicans 16 | | | | | | | | |
|---|---|---|---|---|---|---|---|---|---|---|---|---|---|---|---|---|---|
| Urban 9 | | | Suburban 2 | | | Rural 8 | | | Urban 4 | | | Suburban 1 | | | Rural 11 | | |
| Lib | Mod | Con | Lib | Mod | Con | Lib | Mod | Con | Lib | Mod | Con | Lib | Mod | Con | Lib | Mod | Con |
| 8 | 1 | 0 | 1 | 1 | 0 | 0 | 4 | 4 | 0 | 1 | 3 | 0 | 0 | 1 | 1 | 2 | 8 |

**House 65**

| Democrats 33 | | | | | | | | | Republicans 32 | | | | | | | | |
|---|---|---|---|---|---|---|---|---|---|---|---|---|---|---|---|---|---|
| Urban 18 | | | Suburban 3 | | | Rural 12 | | | Urban 8 | | | Suburban 3 | | | Rural 21 | | |
| Lib | Mod | Con | Lib | Mod | Con | Lib | Mod | Con | Lib | Mod | Con | Lib | Mod | Con | Lib | Mod | Con |
| 12 | 4 | 2 | 1 | 2 | 0 | 5 | 5 | 2 | 2 | 3 | 3 | 1 | 0 | 2 | 1 | 1 | 19 |

(Legend: Lib—liberal; Mod—moderate; Con—conservative.)

A glance at Table 2 will give an indication of the predicament of the suburban areas. Not only are their representatives few—three in the Senate, six in the House—but they are currently almost precisely divided by party and by liberal-conservative orientation. Unaccustomed to working in harness except in occasional opposition to Denver and often (if justifiably) strident in their demands for greater representation in the anticipated reapportionment, the suburban legislators were unable to get a sympathetic hearing in the legislative session of 1962 from either the Denver or rural members. An amendment to House Bill No. 14, offered by a representative from suburban Arapahoe County, for example, would have increased suburban representation substantially, but partly at the expense of Denver; it was overwhelmingly defeated by the combined Denver and rural members. Thirteen of the seventeen votes cast for the hapless measure came from the Denver suburbs and the heavily urbanized counties of El Paso, Boulder, and Weld.

The rural-urban division in the Forty-Third General Assembly provides a better indication of basic attitudes toward apportionment than does party identification. While the election of 1962 may change the partisan balance in the legislature in 1963, it will not alter present rural-urban proportions. Thus in the new session, as in the last, the rural legislators will control the Senate and House with majorities of 19-16 and 33-32, even in the unlikely event that the urban and suburban members can achieve unity.

But even the representation of rural and urban interests is no safe standard for judgment of Colorado legislative behavior. The residues of Populism on the high plains and in the hard-rock and coal-mining communities, the historic radicalism of the dry-land wheat farmers, and the presence of large Latin American and southeastern European populations in southern Colorado, all tend to temper the conservatism of much of the rural areas. On the other hand, conservatism, rural at its edges, is centered in the towns and cities of Colorado Springs, Boulder, Fort Collins, Greeley, Fort Morgan, and Glenwood Springs.

A final glance at Table 2, transient as its figures may be, will perhaps impart the sense of balance which characterizes the whole of Colorado politics. There were few in the Forty-Third General Assembly who could be consistently called urban conservatives or rural liberals. That there were some, however, was in keeping with a minor but dramatic tradition in Colorado that has made it one of the more sensitive and interesting political creations of the Union.

# Notes

1 Elbert County is included in the suburban category because, with Arapahoe County, it composes a senatorial district.

2 The "rural" category, which includes Weld, Larimer, Mesa, and others with large populations, is not entirely satisfactory. The inclusion of counties of mixed character does not significantly affect the meaning of the figures in Table 1, however.

3 The "value of the vote" measure used here and in Table 1 is a modification of a measure devised by Paul T. David and presented in Paul T. David and Ralph Eisenberg, *Devaluation of the Urban and Suburban Vote* (Charlottesville: University of Virginia, Bureau of Public Administration, 1961), pp. 7 *et seq.* The value of a popular vote will vary inversely with the number of constituents (or voters) represented by each legislator. If, for example, the average number of constituents per legislator in a state is 10,000, the value of a popular vote in a district of 20,000 will be only 0.5, or one-half the average value, whereas a vote in a district of only 5,000 persons will have a value of 2.0, or twice the average.

4 Four of the eight Denver senators are elected every two years for a term of four years.

5 Denver city elections are by law nonpartisan, but the central committees of both parties are invariably, but informally, active in support of "their" candidates.

6 Half a century ago, Colorado pioneered the system of preprimary designation in which the office-seeker must receive at least 20 per cent of the votes of a party assembly (convention) to be listed, in order of assembly ranking, on the primary ballot. It is possible, also, to reach the primary ballot by petition, but the option is not often used.

7 Gilbert Y. Steiner and Samuel K. Gove, *The Legislature Redistricts Illinois* (Urbana: University of Illinois Press, 1956), p. 7.

# 3

# Florida

## POLITICS AND THE "PORK CHOPPERS"

*HUGH DOUGLAS PRICE*
*Syracuse University*

Florida today he would be hard put to recognize Miami, but he would
Jennings Bryan peddled real estate in Miami. When it comes to problems of legislative apportionment, superlatives are as much in order as
in dealing with climate, oranges, or missiles. If Bryan were to return to
Florida has been described in superlatives since the days when William
find the state Legislature little changed, except in individual members,
from the 1920's.[1]

## POPULATION AND THE CONSTITUTION

From 1950 to 1960 Florida was the fastest-growing state in the
Union. It was also the state with the least representative legislature of
any in the Union. There are a handful of states with somewhat less
representative senates but fairly acceptable houses and a few others with
less representative lower houses but fairly acceptable senates. In compos-
ite ranking, however, Florida stands alone: in *both* House and Senate
the ratio of largest to smallest population per member is on the order
of 100-to-1, and in *both* House and Senate a majority of the members
are elected from areas with less than 15 per cent of the state's 1960
population.

Over much of the past decade legislative apportionment has been
the dominant issue of Florida state politics, rivaling even the question
of school desegregation (with which it is indirectly connected). There
were special sessions of the Legislature (costing the state $300,000), court
fights by members losing their seats, proposed constitutional amend-

ments, gubernatorial vetoes of token reapportionment measures, stirring editorial demands for action or the "secession" of south Florida, and the emergence of a Senate "Pork Chop Gang" determined to oppose any threat to small-county control of that body.[2] At the end of the decade the Senate remained unchanged from its 1945 apportionment, which had been based more or less on the 1940 census figures. The House had obeyed the constitutional requirement for decennial reapportionment, but this involved only a shift of two of its ninety-five seats.

Florida's apportionment problems are the unhappy result of three main factors. First, the constitutional provisions are awkward and relatively inflexible, although neither House nor Senate is established on a basis of one legislator per county. Both houses are supposed to reflect population, but only to a modest degree and by using the county as the basic unit. In the House, which has more members than there are counties, every county has one seat, but an additional one or two seats go to the larger counties. In the Senate, which has less members than there are counties, no county gets more than one seat, but the smaller counties (where contiguous) are supposed to be grouped together so that all districts shall be "as nearly equal in population as practicable."

The second factor contributing to the problem has been the state's fantastic and highly uneven population growth. While the population of many north Florida counties has been static or even declining, a number of south Florida counties have been doubling, tripling, or even quadrupling their population within a decade. (Thus Broward County, the fastest-growing metropolitan area in the country, increased 297.9 per cent from 1950 to 1960.) The problem is not that of a single metropolis versus the rest of the state. Dade County (Miami) is by far the largest, but it contains only about one-fifth the state population. Yet there is a clear trend toward increasing concentration of the population in a relatively few of the sixty-seven counties. Thus, by 1960 the five most populous counties contained a majority of the state population. But four of the five are in south Florida, which now has the votes to dominate any state-wide election. This is a bitter pill for north Florida politicians, long accustomed to dominating state politics.

The third and decisive difficulty has been the resort, especially by small-county senators, to attitudes of intransigence and parochial self-interest. The twenty-two state senators constituting the Pork Chop Gang have come to regard the Senate as their private club, to be used as they see fit. To date they have carried on highly effective guerrilla warfare against reapportionment. The struggle has gone on at two different but related levels. First, there has been a continuing debate over the constitutional provisions themselves: ten proposed constitutional amendments have been voted by the Legislature since 1915, but only one was approved at the polls (in 1924). The small-county senators want a "federal" Senate with sixty-seven senators. To get this, which would give them a perpetual strangle hold on the state, they are willing to make the lower house represent population somewhat more directly. At a second level, however, the small-county bloc in the Senate continues to ignore the existing constitutional article on apportionment. More recently they have indicated that they will accept a very modest change in Senate districts, but only in return for a serious weakening of the existing constitutional provision (which they have blithely ignored since reapportionment came due in 1955).

## "CREEPING REAPPORTIONMENT" IN THE HOUSE

Since the politics and the legal provisions for apportionment differ considerably between the two houses, it may be useful to look first at the lower house. Since 1924, apportionment of the House has been almost—but not quite—frozen. A constitutional amendment of that year provided that the five most populous counties should each have three representatives, the eighteen next most populous counties each have two representatives, and the remaining counties (currently forty-four) each have one representative. With sixty-seven counties, this results in a ninety-five-member lower house. What is more important, this system freezes absolutely, regardless of total population, the percentage of seats going collectively to the "big five" counties, the "middle eighteen," and the "little forty-four."

How to reapportion the House, then, involves no exercise of legislative discretion or judgment; the process is completely determined. Indeed, with so automatic a formula the process might well have been delegated to an administrative agency, thus removing any temptation to "play politics." As it is, not only must the Legislature itself pass a bill to carry out the change, but it waits until five years *after* the federal census before taking up the apportionment question. (It was formerly done after the middecade state census, since discontinued.) The Legislature has conveniently failed to shift the reapportionment date forward, thus delaying such changes as are made by an unnecessary five years.

Despite all the handicaps, the House has come to be the relatively more representative chamber. But this is so, not because the system is particularly equitable, but rather because the situation in the Senate happens to be even worse. By 1960 the extremes of House representation were represented by Gilchrist County, which had one seat for 2,868 people, and Dade County, which had three seats for 935,047 people. When and if reapportionment is carried out on the basis of the 1960 figures (it will be due in 1965), the average population per legislator for the "big five" counties will be 166,457; for the "middle eighteen" it will be 57,897; and for the "little forty-four" it will be 14,261. That the representative character of the House has deteriorated over the years is clearly evident in the following table showing the seats and percentage of population in each of the three size categories of counties:

TABLE 1

HOUSE APPORTIONMENT: DISCRIMINATION BETWEEN
SIZE CATEGORIES

| County size category | Permanent House seats | | Percentage of state population | |
| --- | --- | --- | --- | --- |
| | No. | Per cent | 1930 | 1960* |
| Big Five | 15 | 15.8 | 39.9 | 50.4 |
| Middle Eighteen | 36 | 37.9 | 35.1 | 36.9 |
| Little Forty-four | 44 | 46.3 | 25.0 | 12.7 |
| Total | 95 | 100.0 | 100.0 | 100.0 |

* Reapportionment on 1960 figures not yet in effect.

None of the changes in population *between* the three categories, whether gains of the "big five" or losses of the "little forty-four," are in any way considered under the current provision.

In addition to the sharp discrimination between the three categories there is further discrimination by the equal treatment of increasingly unequal populations *within* each of the categories. These also have increased over time:

TABLE 2

HOUSE APPORTIONMENT: DISCRIMINATION WITHIN
SIZE CATEGORIES

| County size category | Ratio of largest county to smallest county within the same size category | |
| --- | --- | --- |
| | As of 1930 | As of 1960* |
| Within Big Five | 2.5 | 2.8 |
| Within Middle Eighteen | 3.6 | 6.2 |
| Within Little Forty-four | 5.9 | 12.6 |

* Reapportionment on 1960 figures not yet in effect.

The size categories are so broad and the differences in size within the categories so great that "reapportionment" of the House seldom involves more than a switch of two or perhaps three seats. Thus the 1955 reapportionment, based on the 1950 census, involved two counties moving up to the "middle eighteen" grouping and two others dropping from it to the "little forty-four." The 1960 figures indicate, for the first time since the system was adopted, a change in the "big five," with Broward County displacing Polk (which has slipped to eighth rank). Two south Florida counties are also due for promotion to the "middle eighteen" category, displacing two north Florida counties. All told, this will involve a shift of only three of the ninety-five seats.

On the whole, south Florida is at less of a disadvantage in the House than in the Senate. This is partly because of the round of new county creations, mostly in south Florida, during the 1920's boom. (This brought added House, but not Senate, seats.) Another reason is that the more-or-less automatic nature of such reapportionment as does take place in the House manages to reflect, however feebly, actual population growth. If one defines south Florida to include the peninsula up to and including Marion County (Ocala), then this area includes 73.5 per cent of the 1960 state population. North Florida, with barely one-fourth of the state population, still elects nineteen of the thirty-eight state senators and forty-five of the ninety-five House members.

## PORK CHOPPERS AND PARALYSIS: THE STATE SENATE

The state Senate has been a much stronger bastion of small-county control than has the House. Reapportionment of the Senate under the existing provisions *could* be much more substantial than the minor changes called for in the lower house. But the criteria for establishing districts in the Senate are not as definite as in the House. The rural-oriented Pork Chop Gang which currently controls a majority of Senate seats has taken advantage of this to oppose any major readjustment of the existing thirty-eight districts and to severely limit any proposals for creating additional districts in urban south Florida.[3]

The constitution currently provides for thirty-eight senators to be elected from individual districts which are "to be as nearly equal in population as practicable, but no county shall be divided in making such apportionment, and each district shall have one Senator. . . ." Any multicounty district must involve contiguous counties. Prohibiting any county from having more than one senator is obviously a major limitation. As a result, Dade County (Miami), with one-fifth of the population, elects only one of the thirty-eight senators (who has the distinction of representing the third largest legislative district in the United

States). But even within this limitation much more could be done to make the Senate more representative. That almost nothing has been done is a tribute, of sorts, to the political power of the small-county bloc.

In practice, the small-county bloc has ignored the requirements of the constitution, has maintained tiny "rotten-borough" districts dating from before 1900, and has yielded only minor concessions to the very largest of the south Florida urban centers. Recent proposed concessions have usually been for a bargain requiring a new seat for some medium-sized north Florida county if a new seat were to be established in south Florida. The last Senate reapportionment was a relatively minor one, accomplished in 1945 (on the basis of the 1940 population) and then only after a fifty-three-day special session of the Legislature. Reapportionment was due again in 1955, but the only plans the Senate would pass were so out-of-line with the constitutional requirement or with a population basis that they have been either vetoed by the governor (in the case of legislation) or turned down by the voters (in the case of constitutional amendments).

At present there are twenty single-county districts, ten two-county districts, five three-county districts, and only three four-county districts. But the grouping of counties into districts indicates a greater concern for maintaining the *status quo* than for carrying out the constitutional mandate. Thus, for example, the twenty single-county districts do *not* go to the twenty most populous counties! Tiny Jefferson County, with 9,543 people, is a full Senate district, whereas fast-growing Manatee (69,168) and Sarasota (76,895) counties are lumped with yet a third county to form a district with 158,657 population. And Brevard County (111,435) has been able to put a man in orbit—it includes Cape Canaveral —but has yet to get its own man into the state Senate, where it shares a district with Seminole County (54,947).

The inequities in the Senate result, in part, from the limiting of the largest counties to one senator each. They also result from systematic discrimination against south Florida by the dominant small-county bloc, as is indicated in Table 3.

Thus, a majority of all north Florida districts have *less* than 50,000, whereas a majority of all south Florida districts have *over* 100,000. Or, to look at the two areas which should—under the existing constitutional provision—"exchange" their status, five of the six single-county districts with less than 50,000 are in north Florida, whereas four of the six multi-county districts with over 75,000 are in south Florida.

The small-county bloc has ignored the obvious intent of the apportionment article[4] for a variety of reasons, the most important of which is that they have discovered that they can "get away with it." State-wide public opinion is of little or no concern to the rural Pork

TABLE 3

CONTRAST IN SENATE REPRESENTATION, NORTH
AND SOUTH FLORIDA

Number of Senate districts, 1961

| Total district population (1960) | North Florida | | South Florida | | |
|---|---|---|---|---|---|
| | Single-county | Multi-county | Single-county | Multi-county | Total |
| under 10,000 | 1 | — | — | — | 1 |
| 10-25,000 | 1 | 3 | — | 1 | 5 |
| 25-50,000 | 3 | 5 | 1 | 3 | 12 |
| 50-75,000 | 2 | — | 2 | — | 4 |
| 75-100,000 | — | 2 | — | 1 | 3 |
| 100-250,000 | 1 | — | 3 | 3 | 7 |
| over 250,000 | 1 | — | 5 | — | 6 |
| Total | 9 | 10 | 11 | 8 | 38 |

Choppers, and the governor's power to summon a special session to deal with reapportionment proves to be an empty weapon. There is no provision in Florida for legislation by initiative or for proposing constitutional amendments by initiative, and the small-county bloc sees to it that no such "dangerous" loopholes are established. Finally, even a constitutional convention would be no threat, since the current constitution provides that delegates to such a convention be elected on the basis of existing legislative apportionment!

The only possible chink in the armor of the small-county bloc would seem to lie in the possibility of court enforcement of the existing provision for Senate apportionment. And they have sought to close off this possibility by offering a limited adjustment of Senate districts in return for a major rewording of the constitutional criteria for assigning districts. The proposed constitutional amendments of 1942, 1944, 1948, and 1952 (all defeated by the electorate) involved no change in the criteria but did provide for a slight increase—usually from thirty-eight to forty—in the number of seats.

Beginning in 1955, however, the small-county bloc, while refusing to carry out the existing provisions, has proposed a series of changes in the constitutional criteria. Most of the proposed amendments have called for a slightly more "popular" House, but a Senate based more or less on geographic area. Thus the 1956 proposal called for a pure-and-simple "federal" system, with one senator for each county. The proposed constitutional revision of 1958, which the Florida Supreme Court ruled off the ballot, called for an increase in Senate seats but a major weakening of the apportionment criteria. The 1959 amendment followed similar lines, but added a crucial provision that no multicounty Senate district should include more than three counties. After its defeat, the 1961 Legislature proposed yet another variation, which might be termed "creeping federalism," or a "quasifederal" system. It would provide a district for every county with 50,000 or more population (now or later) and put a limit of three on the number of small counties to be joined into a multicounty district. It is to be voted on in November 1962. Details of the various proposals affecting the Senate passed by the Legislature since 1940 are summarized in Table 4, below.

TABLE 4

PROPOSED CHANGES IN CONSTITUTIONAL BASIS OF
FLORIDA SENATE, 1940-1962

| Year of vote | Change Senate seats from 38 to | Change criteria for assigning seats to | Outcome at election |
|---|---|---|---|
| 1942 | 40 | (no change) | Defeated |
| 1944 | 41 | (no change) | Defeated |
| 1948 | 40 | (no change) | Defeated |
| 1952 | 40 | (no change) | Defeated |
| 1956* | 67 | One seat per county, on "federal" basis | Defeated |
| 1958* | 45 | "Population and such other pertinent factors" as Legislature determines | Ruled off ballot by courts |
| 1959* (special election) | 44 | "Population, geographic area, and economic affinity" and no more than three counties to a district | Defeated |
| 1962* | 45 (more later) | One seat for each county with 50,000 population; no more than three counties to a district | ? |

* Also involved some expansion of the lower house.

## URBAN-RURAL CONFLICT: TRUTH AND CONSEQUENCES

The extent of urban underrepresentation in Florida should, by now, be clear. Does it make a political difference? It certainly does, and it is one of the basic facts of life to anyone familiar with Florida politics. Its importance is well known to every lobbyist in the state (the six most influential have been termed "country horses," [5] perhaps because they pull so much weight with the small-county legislators), as well as to the small-county bloc who are determined to maintain the existing system. Some of the most obvious effects of the apportionment situation involve the structure of influence within the House and Senate, apportionment of state taxes and expenditures, treatment of state-wide (including urban) policy questions, apportionment of Congressional districts, and tension between the governor and Legislature.

The style of operation of the House and Senate combines personalized politics (minimizing party, faction, or issues) and a hierarchical influence-structure. Small-county legislators usually designate one of their own men for election as president of the Senate and another as speaker of the House. These positions are rotated each biennium, but virtually always to small-county men (there was an exception in the House in 1955). The presiding officers, in turn, exercise powers comparable to those of the speaker of the national House of Representatives in the days of "Czar" Cannon, that is to say, they name all committee members and designate all committee chairmen. As a result, the urban legislators, few in number to begin with, find themselves at an almost hopeless disadvantage. In the House, for example, Havard and Beth have shown that they are especially likely to be assigned to special "dog-house" committees of little importance, such as the "Aeronautics Committee." [6]

From their positions of power the small-county men have dictated fantastic concessions in regard to distribution of taxes and allocation of state expenditures. One recent survey concluded that the small counties represented by the twenty-two senators of the Pork Chop Gang currently "pay only 14 per cent of the state's taxes and get back 27 per cent of the state's benefits." [7] Some taxes are even distributed among the sixty-seven counties on an equal basis! This, for example, is the case with the share of state race-track revenue returned to the counties.

For some of the smaller counties, the state largess is so great that local taxes are almost unnecessary. Thus the amount of racing revenue returned amounts to only 20 cents per person per year for Dade County, but runs as high as $61.07 per person in one of the smallest counties. The race-track fund alone can account for the bigger part of a small county's general and school funds. For counties of under 10,000, the racing fund accounts, on the average, for 42.99 per cent of county school funds (the high was 87.26 per cent) and for 30.36 per cent of county general funds (the high was 64.76 per cent).[8] This almost incredible form of allocation was satisfactory to the racing interests, since it provided a politically impregnable basis for legal race-track betting.

Another major effect of small-county domination in the Legislature is to transfer most state-wide policy questions into lobbying campaigns focusing on the "rotten-borough" representatives. The small-county crowd keeps a firm grip on the so-called "killer" committees (the key committees in which major bills can be killed), with results such as the following:

> In the 1959 session of the legislature, these "killer" committees killed legislation before it reached the floor, which would have provided the following: central purchasing, chancellor for the state university system, regulation of unethical business practices, urban renewal, state control of unclaimed bank accounts, regulation of billboards on highways, aid to libraries, integrity in government, and provisions for less costly purchase of highway rights-of-way.[9]

The other side of the coin is that many pieces of legislation are so tailored as to appeal to a majority of legislators drawn mainly from small-county members and representing a minority of the state population. This has generally been the case with the more extreme measures intended to preserve segregation, a matter of much greater concern to north than to south Florida. It is also a pattern which occurs in a variety of economic policy issues. In a recent session, for example, the lobby for the small loan companies (which operate almost entirely in urban areas) rounded up enough small-county support to pass a law increasing the maximum "small loan" from $300 to $600, even though the proposal was opposed by most urban legislators.

Since Congressional districts are drawn by the state Legislature, rural favoritism appears there also, but to a much slighter degree than in apportionment of the state Legislature. Since Florida has gained additional seats in Congress in each recent census, new districts could be created in the fast-growing areas without taking seats away from the more static areas.[10] And, perhaps more important, Congress is not seen as an arena for direct rural-versus-urban or north-versus-south Florida conflict. Thus the 1961 Legislature assigned three of the state's additional four seats to south Florida. Of course, on population south Florida should have got all four. As it now stands, the three north Florida districts other than Duval County (Jacksonville) have a 1960 population of 857,773; the three extreme south Florida districts have 1,643,313.

The major aberration of the 1961 Congressional redistricting (which had to be carried out to avoid having the additional seats elected at-large, with south Florida playing the dominant role) was the carving out of a rural north Florida district of less than 250,000 population.[11] This was intended to benefit the area represented by the chairman of the Senate Committee on Reapportionment. He and his north Florida colleagues displayed a near total lack of interest in how the other three additional seats should be fitted into the state pattern. As long as north Florida received its additional (undeserved) seat, they did not care about the rest. As one of them commented, in regard to the other districts he felt like Rhett Butler saying goodbye to Scarlet O'Hara ("Frankly, my dear, I don't give a damn.").

## EFFORTS AT CHANGE: RETROSPECT AND PROSPECT

Prospects of achieving a change in the apportionment picture via political pressure have dimmed, but the Supreme Court's 1962 decision has heightened hopes for judicial intervention. The high tide of political pressure for a fairly extensive change of the state Senate came in the first year of LeRoy Collins' one and one-half terms (1955-1961) as governor. Not surprisingly, this brought on a period of heightened sectionalism in state politics and of bitter conflict between an urban-oriented governor and the rural-dominated Legislature. Despite the deep involvement of the Governor, up to 1962 the political process had yielded no solution to the problem. The Legislature continued to ignore the existing constitutional provisions as they relate to the Senate; the voters continued to turn down proposed amendments advanced by the small-county men.

Events preceding Collins' election as governor had laid the grounds for conflict with the Legislature. In 1952 Dan McCarty, a south Florida moderate, won the Democratic primary for governor, but died soon after the inauguration. As it happens, Florida elects no lieutenant governor, and the powers of "acting" governor pass to the president of the Senate. In 1953 this was Charley Johns, a leader of the north Florida Pork Choppers.[12] He quickly discharged most of the key McCarty appointees and reversed many of the policies for which McCarty had campaigned. In the 1954 Democratic primary, for the remaining two years of the McCarty term, south Florida voters rallied to support Collins, an urban-oriented state senator from Tallahassee. Collins won, although his home county and one adjoining county were the only ones he carried in the whole of north Florida. Thus Collins was governor and Johns was back in the Senate with his small-county friends when the Legislature was due for reapportionment in 1955.

After his election Collins had appointed a citizens' committee on reapportionment (as he had for a number of other problem areas). It brought in a moderate recommendation to adopt a sliding-scale formula for the House, with progressively larger increments of population required for a county to receive additional members. For the Senate it recommended that, in addition to the thirty-eight districts, one additional senator be elected by a county for each major fraction of 300,000 population over its initial 300,000. The Legislature, however, paid little or no attention to the recommendations. It enacted a proposed constitutional amendment expanding the size of the House, but adopting a sixty-seven-senator "federal" plan for the Senate. This would be subject to voter approval in the November 1956 election.

Governor Collins, however, pressed the Legislature to reapportion under the existing provisions. When it failed to do so, he used his constitutional power to summon a special reapportionment session. The special session, which met in the summer of 1955, produced much ill will but only one piece of legislation: a bill providing for the minor reapportionment, according to formula, of the lower house. In regard to the Senate, however, there was a complete stalemate. Neither side perceived that the complicated existing criteria indicated a specific apportionment pattern. The small-county bloc refused to do more than adjust districts to permit Bay County (in north Florida) and Monroe County (Key West, in south Florida) to become single-county districts. The Governor and his supporters continued to press for single-county districts for Sarasota and Manatee counties (both in south Florida and both with strong Republican organizations) as well as for Bay and Monroe.

In an address to a joint session, the Governor managed to alienate members of the small-county bloc yet further by threatening to appeal over their heads to the people:

> There can be only one recourse then for me, and those who fight with us in every corner of Florida, and that is to take the issue to the people in the elections next spring. The people will become aroused. I predict the organization throughout Florida of citizens groups crusading for fair representation. Candidates for all elective offices, statewide and local, will be required to take an open stand for fair representation or for the status quo . . . .[13]

The trouble with this, as with Mr. Justice Frankfurter's confidence in appeals to enlighted conscience, is that the constituents of the small-county bloc are delighted with their favored status. Far from facing local committees for "fair representation," the Pork Choppers returned home to find solid support for holding the line against reapportionment. The only people who became "aroused" were those urban residents who have almost no voice in the Legislature anyway.

But in another sense the Governor's tactics did "arouse" many of his opponents within the Legislature. The usual pattern of low-temperature bargaining between governor and legislators was disrupted. Collins would have run into strong opposition from the Pork Chop Gang on most of his program in any event. But his refusal to "play the game" in regard to reapportionment, in addition to his defeat of Senator Johns in 1954, gave added cause for intransigent opposition. Some observers suggest that if the Governor had gone all the way—vetoing local bills, halting road construction in certain areas, cutting off patronage—he might have won. But this was not the Collins style of politics.

In the 1956 Democratic primaries Governor Collins won an unprecedented majority vote in the first primary.[14] But most of his antagonists in the small-county bloc fared equally well! In the November general election the sixty-seven-senator plan was narrowly defeated (288,-575 to 287,662), with most of the south Florida urban counties heavily opposed. This set the stage for another round of apportionment battles, with essentially the same cast of characters.

The 1957 and 1959 sessions of the Legislature put forward new "compromise" apportionment plans, the key provisions of which are indicated in Table 4, above. The 1957 proposal was to be voted on as part of a general constitutional revision. The various articles were to be linked on the ballot so that voter rejection of any one article, such as that on apportionment, would result in defeat of the whole project. This aspect of the process was, however, declared an improper procedure by the Florida Supreme Court, and the proposals were ruled off the ballot.

The 1959 proposal was designated an "emergency measure" to be voted on at a special 1959 election. This would have had the effect of settling the issue, one way or the other, so that there would be no apportionment measure pending during the crucial 1960 Democratic gubernatorial primaries. In retrospect, it appears that Collins might have been wise to oppose the special election; by carrying the issue over to 1960 he would have improved the chances for nomination of an urban-oriented candidate (he was not eligible to succeed himself). Although Collins indicated his acceptance of the 1959 proposal, it was defeated in a light vote (177,955 to 146,601). In general, the "gold-coast" counties of the lower east coast turned in the heaviest majorities against it.

The special election had, however, nicely removed reapportionment from the pressing issues of the 1960 primaries, thereby opening the way to the governorship for a nonurban candidate. South Florida had a surplus of contenders, including John McCarty (brother of the former governor), Ted David (who had been the pro-Collins speaker of the House in 1955), and Doyle Carlton (a south Florida state senator and son of a former governor). Other major candidates included Haydon Burns (mayor of Jacksonville) and Ferris Bryant (a conservative former speaker of the House who had been an unsuccessful candidate in 1956).[15] Collins endorsed Carlton, who faced Bryant in a run-off primary. Carlton, who proved to be a rather colorless campaigner, failed to crystallize really solid urban support. As a result, Bryant, who had the enthusiastic support of the small-county bloc, was nominated and elected. Supporters of

genuine reapportionment would no longer be able to count on gubernatorial support.

In 1961 the Legislature, no longer under pressure from the governor, followed its usual pattern: failure to carry out the Senate reapportionment due since 1955 and submission to the voters of another
"stacked" proposal. This time the proposal was more sophisticated; it
aimed at guaranteeing small-county control of the Senate without saying
so quite as clearly as had the previous proposed amendments. The existing criteria would remain but would be rendered largely inoperative by
two additional stipulations. First, a seat would be provided (on a "federal" basis) for every county with 50,000 or more population. Second,
no multicounty district would contain more than three counties. The
latter provision would constitute a major safeguard against the extensive
reapportionment due under the current provisions.

This proposal is to be voted on in November 1962. As expected,
Governor Bryant has praised it in strong terms. At a news conference
after the Supreme Court's decision in the Tennessee case Bryant stated:

> The situation (in Tennessee) is quite different from Florida, which
> has been vigorous in its responsibilities in this field.
> The proposal that will be before the people is a vast improvement
> over the present formula . . . . I believe the voters will approve it if
> they are not misled by false hope . . . .
> To defeat the new plan now would give the small counties every
> tool they need to come back and adopt the past apportionment.

This statement does more credit to the Governor's political acumen than
to his training at Harvard Law School; the Tennessee and Florida cases
are quite similar, the Florida Legislature has been sadly negligent in its
responsibilities, the proposal is no improvement, informed opinion is
that it has little or no chance of adoption, since it was proposed by the
small-county bloc it can hardly be a threat to their position, court intervention is a new "tool" not previously available.

The next step in Florida now seems to depend upon judicial action.
A suit filed in Federal District Court in Miami asking that the Legislature be held illegally constituted had been dismissed in 1959 but was
reactivated after the 1962 Supreme Court decision. In addition, a detailed computer analysis of the full import of the existing constitutional
provisions for the Senate has finally been carried out and is expected
to furnish grounds for a more direct challenge to the existing form of
the Senate.

This renewed legal activity has given fresh impetus to political opposition to the pending constitutional amendment. The Florida League
of Women Voters, leading Republican spokesmen, and many south
Florida newspapers have already indicated their opposition to the proposal. The state attorney general asked that the courts delay any pos-

sible action on pending apportionment suits until after the November, 1962, election. But events were to move to a more rapid climax.

On July 23, 1962, a three-judge federal court in Miami held that the existing apportionment was "null, void and inoperative" and warned that the court itself would reapportion the state if the Legislature failed to do so. It also held that the proposed amendment did not meet the standards of equal protection and set an August 13 deadline to consider what further steps might be taken.

Governor Bryant, shifting his ground to adjust to the new situation, called the Legislature into special session. Although regretting the judiciary's intervention, the Governor presented his own proposal for reapportionment; this called for a sweeping expansion of the lower house to 144 seats (apportioned among the counties on a strict population basis) coupled with a modest change in the Senate, from thirty-eight to forty-five seats. But his proposals ran into trouble. Many legislators felt that a constitutional amendment, rather than just a statute, was necessary. And the small-county bloc talked angrily of the need for an investigation of the federal judiciary and of the virtues of a sixty-seven–senator plan.

After ten days of maneuver, the two houses finally agreed on a proposed constitutional amendment. If acceptable to the courts and approved by the voters in November, it would provide for a House of 135 members, with the additional forty seats going to the larger counties. The Senate would be expanded to forty-six members, but still with no county electing more than one senator. All proposals to realign the existing thirty-eight Senate districts on a population basis or to provide for an additional senator for counties with over 400,000 population were voted down.

Under the proposal, the lower house would reflect population rather closely. The Senate, however, would remain something of a small-county citadel. Whether the courts would regard this as invidious discrimination remained to be seen. Whatever the final outcome, it appeared that the end of an era was near.

The long-range outcome remains very much in doubt. Although the small-county bloc has grown increasingly confident of its ability to thwart political pressures for reapportionment (and has even been able to neutralize, for a time, the governorship), it has been unsuccessful in its efforts to buttress its legal position. Advocates of more than token reapportionment have failed to sway the Legislature and are currently lacking in influence with the Governor, but they would seem to have a better case than in most states for successful court intervention. Meanwhile Florida remains, as Anthony Lewis of *The New York Times* recently noted, "possibly the most astounding situation" in the country with respect to apportionment.

# Notes

1 For a comprehensive history of the problem in Florida see William C. Havard and Loren P. Beth, *Representative Government and Reapportionment: A Case Study of Florida* (Gainesville: University of Florida, Public Administration Clearing Service, 1960).

2 The term "pork chopper" seems to derive from a narrower usage in trade-union jargon suggesting one who benefits from preferential place at the expense of the commonweal. Cf. Harold Wentworth and Stuart B. Flexner, *Dictionary of American Slang* (New York: Thomas Y. Crowell, 1960), s.v. "Pork Chopper."

3 An increase in the number of districts, with no one county to have more than one senator, would actually reduce the representation of the very largest counties still more. They support an expansion because the new districts would supposedly go to major urban counties in the 75,000-to-150,000 class, and this would serve to weaken the hold of the dominant small-county bloc. Dade County's one senator would be in a stronger position in a Senate of forty-five members in which such counties had senators than in one with thirty-eight members in which they did not.

4 Until recently all sides to the dispute have assumed that the criteria for the Senate, unlike those for the House, were not really operational. Actually there is a "one best way" to apportion the Senate in accord with the existing criteria. With recent advances in operations research it would be relatively easy to analyze all the possible combinations and determine which one results in thirty-eight districts as nearly equal as practicable, but with only contiguous counties joined into multicounty districts (and no more than one senator for any one county). Should the Supreme Court decide to make existing state constitutional provisions enforceable in the courts, this point may prove of considerable significance.

5 See Paul Douglas, "Lobbying at Tallahassee," *Florida Trend*, IV (1961), No. 1, 14-16. The six operate, in part jointly, from the Cherokee Hotel in Tallahassee.

6 Loren Beth and William Havard, "Committee Stacking and Political Power in Florida," *Journal of Politics*, XXIII (1961), 57-83.

7 V. M. Newton, Jr., *Crusade for Democracy* (Ames, Iowa: Iowa State University Press, 1961), p. 122. Newton, managing editor of the *Tampa Tribune*, has done much to expose the operations of the Pork Choppers.

8 A proposal to write the existing provisions into the constitution was on the ballot in 1960, but failed. These figures are from John M. DeGrove and Wylie Kilpatrick, *Constitutional Amendments of 1960* (Gainesville: University of Florida, Public Administration Clearing Service, 1960), pp. 18, 21.

9 Newton, *op. cit.*, p. 129.

10 In game-theory terms, the state Legislature is a "zero-sum" problem, whereas the addition of more Congressional seats is not.

11 The area which should have received the additional district is the fast-growing Palm Beach-Broward County area of the lower east coast, which had 660,345 population in 1960 and is likely to reach a million by the end of the decade. A desire to minimize Republican opportunities for gains (they hold only one of the eight old districts) may have contributed to the very low priority accorded this area. Growth in Republican strength throughout most of south Florida is so general that relatively little could be achieved by gerrymandering.

12 Johns represented a tiny two-county district (the 1960 population was 18,489) in which the main industry is the state penitentiary. A sizable part of the population is, of course, nonvoting convicts.

13 Quoted in Havard and Beth, *Representative Government* . . . , *op. cit.,* p. 62.

14 For evidence of the sharpening of sectional feeling see the map in H. D. Price, *The Negro and Southern Politics* (New York: New York University Press, 1957), p. 101. At page 105 there is a map of the existing Senate districts, which indicates those with particularly small district populations.

15 The more-or-less standard technique of running for governor is to acquire a following and reputation through a good showing in one campaign, as a sort of "warm-up" for an all-out bid four years later. Thus Ferris Bryant, the winner in 1960, was a respectable "also-ran" in 1956, and several of the candidates in 1960 doubtless had their eyes on 1964.

# 4

## North Carolina

### PEOPLE OR PINE TREES *

*PRESTON W. EDSALL*
*North Carolina State College*

"Someday we will stop giving pine trees equal representation with people." This prophecy by Sen. Hubert B. Humphrey of Greensboro was not fulfilled in 1961. Indeed, the apportionment provisions of the North Carolina constitution seem to protect pine trees and ignore people. For a century and a quarter, the constitution has provided a House of 120 members and a Senate of fifty. The constitution allots to each county (now 100 in number) one representative in the House and directs the distribution of the remaining seats to the more populous counties under a rule so precise as to eliminate discretion. Senate districts contiguous in territory and as nearly equal as possible in population are likewise required. The General Assembly is directed to accomplish House reapportionment and Senate redistricting after each national census. These

\* Since January 1955, the author has been engaged in a comprehensive study of legislative politics and processes in North Carolina. In 1959-1960, he was assisted in this work by a grant from the Social Science Research Council, and much of the research providing background for the events of 1961 was done during that year. Many of the happenings described in the following pages he personally witnessed, but, whenever possible, quotations attributed to actors in these events have been drawn from printed sources. Especially useful have been various studies prepared by John Sanders, assistant director of the Institute of Government of the University of North Carolina. These include articles on legislative representation appearing in the February, November, and December 1961 issues of *Popular Government* and two processed documents, one containing data on, and the other maps of, *North Carolina Congressional Districts, State Senatorial Districts,* and *Apportionment of the State House of Representatives.* Mr. Sanders also supplied numerous special maps and tables during the legislative session. Unfortunately the *House Journal* for the 1961 General Assembly had not appeared when this study was completed, but the *Senate Journal* has been available. The author has relied to a great extent on his own notes and on many personal interviews.

obligations confronted the 1961 biennial session, and experience suggested that it would have trouble meeting them.

Reapportioning and redistricting the General Assembly seats had twice been skipped for whole decades—1931 to 1941 and 1951 to 1961—and the legislation adopted in 1941 had made only minimal changes in the state Senate. To understand the course of events since 1950, it is necessary to look at North Carolina's peculiar brand of sectionalism and to appraise the present status of urban-rural relations in a state some 60 per cent rural.

## SECTIONALISM AND GROWING URBANISM

North Carolina is divided into three geographical areas: the east, the piedmont, and the mountains.[1] The east consists of the Outer Banks, the tidewater, and the coastal plain stretching some 180 miles inward from Cape Hatteras. Predominantly agricultural, this area is developing some industry, is lined with beach resorts, and at Wilmington and Morehead City is driving hard to capture an appropriate share of waterborne commerce. In this whole area are only three cities of more than 30,000. Of the forty-three counties in the geopolitical east, seven gained more in population than the state average, seventeen gained less, and nineteen showed absolute losses. Only in Brunswick and Sampson counties does the Republican Party have much strength.

The piedmont, extending from the fall line to the mountains, includes thirty-two counties. Here, twenty-seven gained in population, eleven of them by more than the average. The area contains six of the state's seven cities over 60,000 in population: Durham (Durham County), Raleigh (Wake County), High Point and Greensboro (Guilford County), Winston-Salem (Forsyth County), and Charlotte (Mecklenburg County). The population figures of the last three exceed 100,000, the largest being Charlotte, with 201,000. It is in this area that the most rapid industrial development has taken place. Republicans have long battled Democrats successfully, or with occasional success, in a band of counties extending eastward through Randolph in the central piedmont. Their strength is growing elsewhere, especially in the urban counties. Democrats in these counties feel that their eastern colleagues, who have few Republicans to battle, do not comprehend the nature of their problem.

The mountains westward, a scenic vacation-land, is slowly developing industrially but still relies on other sources of income. Of its twenty-five counties, only three gained population in excess of the state average, whereas fifteen suffered absolute losses. Here, the Republican Party fights on equal or better terms with the Democrats. The area has found increasing economic and political ties with the east, and, in the matter of legislative representation, these ties were also close with piedmont counties of static or declining population.

There has been a rapid growth in North Carolina's cities in recent years, especially in the piedmont. Even so, only eight of the state's 100 counties had over one-fiftieth of the 1960 population (91,123), and only eight others had in excess of 70,000 people. Forty counties having populations under 25,000 controlled 33.3 per cent of the House and 17.9 per cent of the Senate. Almost precisely the same degree of Senate control (18.1 per cent) went to counties of over 100,000 population, but they had only 19.2 per cent of the House. The relative population ratios of the two groups of counties is 12.5 per cent to 30.6 per cent.[2]

Except in the matter of representation, no deep-seated urban-rural split yet exists in North Carolina. Reasons for this are many: education is treated as basically a state-wide function; a modern optional-charter plan, state-wide in character, accompanied by a custom which allows a county's representatives to get special local-government legislation easily, permits urban areas most of the advantages of home rule; and thus far the small-county-dominated General Assembly has kept out of the property tax field and has enacted much forward-looking legislation designed to aid cities in meeting new problems. Perhaps a good word should be said for hurricanes! These major disasters make the coastal counties of the east friendly to legislation also desired by cities. Organized labor has very little representation at Raleigh, support for labor legislation has been divided, and the urban representatives have produced their share of antiunion votes.

## FAILURE IN THE FIFTIES

Failure to reapportion and redistrict in the 1950's was not caused by lack of effort. The 1950 census results apparently made mandatory a shift of two House seats from one eastern and one piedmont county to two piedmont counties. Bills designed to accomplish these transfers appeared in every regular session from 1951 to 1959 but died either in committee or on the floor—twice in the House and once in the Senate.

Legislation to redistrict the Senate in conformity with the existing provisions of the constitution also got nowhere. Every session through that of 1957 witnessed the introduction of at least one bill designed to carry out recommendations originally made by an interuniversity committee which studied the problem in 1951. Piedmont representatives usually sponsored the bill, with some assistance from populous counties outside the area. Committee reports were always unfavorable. No floor action occurred.

During the period covered by these fruitless proceedings, there was a constant show of activity, much of which substituted study for deeds, but which, in balance, produced some valuable ideas. Two commissions studied the problem of apportionment: a Commission on Legislative Representation, created in 1955 under the chairmanship of Dean Carroll T. Weathers of the Wake Forest Law School, and a Constitutional Commission, established in 1957 and chaired by Victor S. Bryant. Both groups recommended the use of commissions or individual officials to handle reapportionment, removing this burden from the legislature. These proposals did not meet with legislative approval. On several occasions during the 1950's there were efforts made to amend the constitution by providing that no county should have more than one senator. Although this plan was defeated by the voters in 1954, it was adopted by the Senate in 1957 and again in 1959, but killed in the House both times. Another suggestion that stirred interest in the legislature was the "federal" plan of basing representation on population in one house and giving the counties equal apportionment in the other. Proposals to give each county one seat in either a smaller House or a larger Senate were defeated in 1957. Other proposals which gave greater weight to population in both houses (including the suggestions of the two commissions) generally included an increase in the number of members, but this concession to legislative sensitivities did not result in passage of the measures. The net result of a decade of discussion and study was to bring to public attention a wide sample of the techniques being used in other states. None won both legislative and public approval.

## HOUSE REAPPORTIONMENT

The General Assembly of 1961, like its predecessors beginning with 1943, was composed as follows: [3]

|        | East  | Piedmont | Mountains |
|--------|-------|----------|-----------|
| Senate | 20.17 | 20.99    | 8.84      |
| House  | 47.00 | 46.00    | 27.00     |

The Republican Party held only fifteen House seats, eleven from mountain counties and four from the piedmont. Republicans also held two Senate seats, their normal quota. Hence the General Assembly showed a typical Democratic dominance.

Almost without objection, the legislators performed their exact responsibility to reapportion the lower house. They also submitted to the voters a constitutional amendment to make House reapportionment an automatic ministerial function of the speaker in future decades. In light of the failures of the 1950's, these results may seem surprising, and several explanations may be offered for them. Only four seats were involved, and except for the loss of one by mountainous Buncombe County, the shifting was intrasectional. The growing piedmont thus gained only one seat, while the east held its own; consequently there was no significant change in the political balance. Furthermore both political parties were committed to reapportionment by their 1960 platforms and the statements of their gubernatorial nominees and many of their legislative candidates. The presiding officers of the two houses, the committees they appointed, and some outstanding opponents of Senate redistricting, such as Sen. Lindsay Warren, favored House reapportionment. What is more, automatic House reapportionment had long been a favorite idea with Warren, and he readily allied himself with Rep. Ed Kemp of Guilford to introduce identical automatic reapportionment bills in their respective houses.

## REDISTRICTING FAILS: THE SENATE

Reapportionment of the House had proved easy; redistricting the Senate proved impossible. Why? First, the General Assembly has never felt obligated to obey the constitutional directive that "each Senate District shall contain, as near as may be, an equal number of inhabitants." To accomplish such equality would require that each district elect the same number of senators and would appear to require either twenty-five two-member or fifty one-member districts. Instead, the state has had combinations of two-member and one-member districts ever since the adoption of the present constitution. This means that in seventeen of the state's thirty-three districts the people vote for two candidates. In computing the number of citizens represented by each of the two senators, it is customary to divide his constituent population by two and use this figure in arguing the fairness of the representation. The justice of this procedure seems open to serious question.

Second, a predominantly rural legislature is not likely to be hasty in shifting Senate seats from rural areas to the few large counties. This reluctance is strengthened by an unusual practice affecting the choice of senators: the Democrats in nearly all multiple-county senatorial districts and the Republicans in some have formal rotation agreements, providing in each case a fixed order in which counties shall have the sole privilege of nominating a senator. Though almost always purely intraparty arrangements, these rotation agreements have enjoyed statutory recognition since 1911 [4] and appear to have been adhered to rigidly. Their effect is to guarantee to nearly every county in the state a senator at regular intervals. Senators serving by virtue of rotation agreements and representatives whose counties could scarcely hope to elect senators without them are understandably unwilling to support redistricting legislation that would upset these arrangements.

Third, among many Democrats in and out of the legislature there was fear that the Republican Party would gain from the kind of redistricting the constitution directed. Presidential margins had become close, and in 1960 the relatively unknown Republican gubernatorial candidate ran close in half the counties, actually carrying twenty-six, and reducing normal Democratic margins from 300,000 to 121,000. Democratic Congressional majorities, which had surpassed 400,000 in 1952 and 1956, in 1960 shrank to 271,495. State Senate and House races were similarly closer as the Republicans overcame the 1958 catastrophe which had reduced their legislative strength to five.

No redistricting bill was ready for introduction when the 1961 session opened, but Sen. Claude Currie, whose concern over legislative representation was of long standing, presented a resolution directing the appropriate legislative committees to "commence immediately to study the subject of senatorial redistricting and to hold public hearings thereon." [5] Shortly after that Lieutenant Governor Philpott named Currie chairman of the Committee on Election Laws and Legislative Representation and gave him a committee which, as events showed, was divided 7-to-6 on the issue of real or token redistricting. Among the six was Sen. Lindsay Warren and it was he, in the end, who led the resistance.

Political mathematics made necessary the drafting of a bill capable of attracting twenty-six Senate and sixty-one House votes, and the measure introduced by Senator Currie on March 3 appeared to have accomplished this. By leaving nineteen districts untouched, there were potentially twenty-eight senators and sixty-four representatives whose personal situations would remain the same; in addition, at least four more senators and thirteen representatives were from districts benefiting by the bill. Support in the Senate was, however, known to be far less than these figures indicated. Senate supporters claimed twenty-one sure votes and several others likely to come their way.

Senator Currie made no pretense that his bill achieved equal representation but maintained that it improved the situation and offered a reasonable adjustment of opposing positions. One-fiftieth of the state's population was 91,123. Seven districts came within 3,000 of this figure. Nine more were within 10,000. However, three districts fell 30,000 below and eight rose above the average by 28,000 to 57,000. Guilford, Forsyth, and Mecklenburg counties each received a second senator, though Mecklenburg was technically entitled to three.

A public hearing on March 22 brought forthright arguments for the bill from Dean Weathers and Victor S. Bryant, whose labors have already been noted, and from representatives of civic organizations. Mrs.

Neal Austin, state president of the League of Women Voters, argued that industrial leaders contemplating establishing in the state regarded good government as one important factor and would avoid inadequately represented industrial centers. One by one the Democratic leaders who appeared urged that the passage of the Currie bill was vital to the party's future. Irving S. Carlyle warned: "If the General Assembly fails to do its duty, the blame will rest squarely and entirely . . . on the Democratic Party. If the Democratic Party is unwilling or unable to shoulder the responsibility for redistricting, then sooner or later—and it may be sooner than we expect—the people of North Carolina will look to the Republican Party to carry out that mandate." Throughout the hearing, committee opponents of the measure remained silent, except for the tapping of Lindsay Warren's cane.

A week later the Currie bill, amended in certain minor particulars in hope of winning critically needed support, was reported favorably on motion of one of its opponents and, on April 5, was debated on the Senate floor.[6] Both sides had prepared well for the day. The debate was long and bitter, the parliamentary tactics both heavy-handed and clever, and the result foregone. Supporters left no argument unstated; even the growing spectre of *Baker* v. *Carr* appeared and the infinitely more frightening goblin, a Republican governor.

Opponents of the bill had their spectre, too: big-city bosses, big-county rule. Sen. Clarence Stone of Rockingham County, who had made the rafters ring with his demand for another representative for his county in 1955, advanced the most singular argument this author has yet to hear: if the large counties lacked representation in the Senate, they made it up by their large share in the administrative branch!

Sen. Lindsay Warren attacked the Currie bill and certain piedmont Democrats with equal fervor. He wanted rule neither by the small nor the large counties; present representation was fair. "I brush aside the constitutional argument," he declared. Did members want a North Carolina in which a group of piedmont counties would control the Senate? This is the goal to which the population formula would lead. To begin to shift to the urban piedmont counties, where Republicanism was on the rise, Senate seats now held by the strongly Democratic east, where the 1960 state and national victories had been won, would start the Democratic Party toward defeat. This would be not only unfair but also unwise.

Warren's attack drew response from Sen. Hubert Humphrey of Guilford County, who defended the Democratic leadership in the piedmont and called upon his colleagues to "rise above sectionalism and say we truly . . . believe in the People." Failure to act would make the 1961

General Assembly the most remiss in the state's history. "Someday we will stop giving pine trees equal representation with people."

Pine trees or people? This issue was sharpened almost immediately when Sen. Frank Banzet introduced a comprehensive amendment undoing such real changes as the Currie bill contained. Gone were the additional senators for the three largest counties. Efforts to send Banzet's amendment to committee failed, as did efforts to postpone consideration and to adjourn, and the amendment was adopted 32-to-17. Numbered among the dissenters were five small-county senators, including one of the two Republicans, and twelve from urban and industrial counties, ten of which were piedmont districts. On April 6, the Banzet-amended Currie bill passed the Senate, whence it went to its graveyard in the House Committee on Senatorial Districts.

In addition to redistricting failures, Senate rotation agreements compounded Democratic troubles. The sensitive spots were the Tenth District in the east and the Twenty-fifth District in the piedmont. In the four-county, two-senator Tenth, Cumberland County (which Governor Sanford had served in 1953) had far outgrown the other three, and yet it had to share a seat alternately with Brunswick; in the three-county, two-senator Twenty-fifth District, Catawba had passed Iredell in population but was committed to alternating with smaller Lincoln, while Iredell had a senator every time. On behalf of Catawba, Sen. William B. Shuford and Rep. Henry J. Hill introduced corrective legislation, as did Sen. Hector McGeachy for Cumberland. Both Senate bills were defeated 23-to-24 on June 7 after having won favorable committee reports. The House bill joined others that never emerged from committee.

Now rotation agreements are supposed to promote party harmony; when they fail to do so the time for top-level intervention has arrived. Evidence over several years indicated a need for reform; hence Governor Sanford took the position that state law should require the automatic review of rotation agreements after every census. Sen. Wills Hancock then introduced a bill to require the renewal, amendment, or renegotiation of existing agreements and the filing of certified copies of the new versions with the State Board of Elections by December 1, 1963. Agreements not so certified were to be abrogated, and procedure was outlined for their replacement by the board not later than February 1, 1964. Such agreements would then remain in force until 1973. The Hancock bill went to the Calendar Committee, which had been set up to handle late session proposals, and a more limited committee substitute resulted.

Argument over this committee substitute was lively. Sen. Luther Hamilton, a former Superior Court judge, expressed surprise that there was legislation on the books giving sanction to rotation agreements and indicated grave doubt that such legislation could stand a constitutional test, a viewpoint shared by many others. Putting aside any doubts, the Senate amended the bill further and sent it to the House, where the Calendar Committee killed it with an unfavorable report.

## PROPOSED CONSTITUTIONAL AMENDMENTS

While the emasculated Currie bill languished in the House, efforts were made in the Senate to resolve the apportionment issue by constitutional amendment. Proposals to limit all counties (or all but the three largest) to two senators each were beaten by the rural bloc, and the Senate once again passed a constitutional amendment to limit any county to a maximum of one senator. Opposition came largely from piedmont Democrats. Like the Currie bill, this constitutional amendment died in the House committee.

Two small groups in the House also sought means to solve the total problem of legislative representation. The hard core of the groups consisted of representatives from counties certain to lose seats in 1963 or disadvantaged by the Senate rotation system. Their proposals, all of which involved amending the constitution, ranged all the way from almost total adoption of area (county) representation to a considerable expansion of popular representation. Most of their suggestions showed the influence of other and earlier proposals.

Only one of these plans emerged from committee. It provided for ten more Senate seats to be distributed among existing districts, with no county to receive more than two senators but with three multicounty districts allotted three each. The House would be increased to 150 seats, with fifty of them assigned to the twenty-eight largest counties. Geographic, population, and area interests were to guide future redistricting, which was to be the responsibility of the legislative leaders, subject to legislative alteration. The bill was evidently something of a grab bag, but it won a favorable committee report, only to be tabled in the House by a vote of 65-to-45.

On June 12, when it had become apparent that the Senate problem would remain unsolved, Governor Sanford announced that legislation to create a senatorial redistricting study commission would be introduced and that he hoped the proposal would receive widespread support. Two days later, Sen. Stewart Warren introduced a joint resolution creating a nine-member commission to study the redistricting problem and to consider whether a constitutional amendment was needed. The commission was to work with thoroughness and dispatch and report to the Governor "as soon as possible." The resolution did not gain the support the Governor had asked. Opponents quickly inserted two amendments, one increasing the commission to eleven members and the other directing that the commission's report be made to the 1963 General Assembly— a means of avoiding a special session call. Interpreted by the supporters of the original Currie bill as a device to avoid immediate responsibility by restudying an already exhausted subject and viewed as somewhat dangerous by those who favored the *status quo,* the resolution went down to defeat on second reading on June 19 by a vote of 18-to-27. Obviously, the Senate saw little to gain from another study-commission fiasco.

## APPRAISAL AND PROSPECT

General Assembly members left Raleigh on June 22 with their most difficult political problem still unsolved. When they return in February 1963, or perhaps earlier, their choices may lie between voluntary and court-compelled redistricting. A brief examination of the relevant facts seems essential:

The distribution of House seats conforms precisely to the provisions of the state constitution. Wide discrepancies exist between counties in terms of population and representation, which vary in population from 4,520 to 272,111. Expressed in terms of relative representation, the greatest spread is 8.40 to 0.47.

The Senate situation is quite different. Not only are state constitutional requirements openly unfulfilled, but discrepancies are great. Table 1 demonstrates this by showing the actual 1960 population and the relative representation under the present law following the 1940, 1950, and 1960 censuses. Evidently, the 1962 situation is much worse than that created in 1941, which was far from the constitutional rule itself. These facts alone appear to bring the matter within the ruling in *Baker* v. *Carr.*

How much freedom of choice will the General Assembly have in solving its problems? Would a constitutional amendment limiting a county to one or to two senators irrespective of its population conform to the equal-protection clause of the Fourteenth Amendment? Could a plan to place the Senate and most of the House on an area plan of representation meet the test? The reasonable courses seem two in number. Either the present provisions of the North Carolina constitution should be carried out, or some such plan as was suggested in the amendment defeated in the House in 1961 should be adopted; perhaps the first course will have to be adopted, whatever the hope for the second.

Politically, either approach is now possible. Objections to increasing the size of either or both houses are somewhat less valid than before, because the 1963 General Assembly will meet in a new and ample Legislative Building. May leadership in the coming session be expected

TABLE 1

RELATIVE REPRESENTATION, SENATE DISTRICTS

| District No. | No. of senators | 1941 act | 1950 census | 1960 census | 1960 population |
|---|---|---|---|---|---|
| 1 | 2 | 1.30 | 1.41 | 1.58 | 115,058 |
| 2 | 2 | 1.37 | 1.54 | 1.77 | 102,711 |
| 3 | 1 | .87 | .97 | 1.16 | 78,465 |
| 4 | 2 | 1.35 | 1.48 | 1.60 | 56,591 |
| 5 | 1 | 1.16 | 1.27 | 1.30 | 69,942 |
| 6 | 2 | 1.04 | 1.11 | 1.23 | 147,473 |
| 7 | 2 | 1.03 | .86 | .71 | 255,441 |
| 8 | 2 | 1.16 | 1.25 | 1.25 | 144,995 |
| 9 | 2 | .93 | .94 | 1.02 | 178,533 |
| 10 | 2 | .95 | .83 | .74 | 246,550 |
| 11 | 1 | .92 | .93 | 1.02 | 89,102 |
| 12 | 2 | 1.06 | 1.10 | 1.13 | 162,822 |
| 13 | 2 | .93 | .88 | .82 | 222,428 |
| 14 | 2 | 1.06 | 1.03 | 1.06 | 171,499 |
| 15 | 1 | .90 | .95 | 1.01 | 89,541 |
| 16 | 1 | .88 | .77 | .71 | 128,644 |
| 17 | 1 | .46 | .43 | .37 | 246,520 |
| 18 | 2 | 1.10 | 1.12 | 1.11 | 162,286 |
| 19 | 2 | 1.42 | 1.53 | 1.64 | 110,505 |
| 20 | 1 | .47 | .41 | .33 | 272,111 |
| 21 | 2 | 1.11 | 1.17 | 1.47 | 150,954 |
| 22 | 1 | .56 | .56 | .48 | 189,428 |
| 23 | 1 | 1.10 | 1.21 | 1.29 | 70,519 |
| 24 | 1 | .90 | .98 | 1.07 | 84,801 |
| 25 | 2 | 1.13 | 1.12 | 1.10 | 164,531 |
| 26 | 1 | .81 | .73 | .71 | 127,074 |
| 27 | 2 | 1.11 | 1.19 | 1.30 | 137,881 |
| 28 | 1 | .81 | .79 | .77 | 117,878 |
| 29 | 1 | 1.45 | 1.68 | 2.02 | 45,031 |
| 30 | 1 | 1.03 | 1.24 | 1.59 | 57,140 |
| 31 | 1 | .65 | .65 | .70 | 130,074 |
| 32 | 2 | 1.36 | 1.42 | 1.50 | 121,421 |
| 33 | 1 | 1.19 | 1.42 | 1.76 | 51,615 |

of Governor Sanford, who in 1953 voted for the one-senator limitation?
In 1961 he threw weight behind House reapportionment and the Warren-
Kemp constitutional amendment for automatic House reapportionment.
The Governor also pronounced Senator Currie's bill satisfactory shortly
before it was debated, but he simultaneously pointed out that redistricting was the proper province of the Senate. Senator Currie commented
later that he knew of no action the Governor had taken to support the
bill. There is strong reason to believe that, once the Banzet version of

the Currie bill passed the Senate, the Sanford administration made some effort to get it through the House. The simple truth appears to be that the Governor was so deeply involved in the garnering of support for his "quality education" program that he gave limited attention to redistricting, a matter likely to bring him into controversy with legislators whose votes he needed. Late in the session he encouraged the introduction of the previously mentioned study-commission bill. In refraining from major activity in support of redistricting, the Governor behaved as his predecessors had done; that is to say, he supported the principle of updating legislative representation but reserved his pressure for ventures to which he assigned higher priority.

In 1963, however, Sanford may be expected to make legislative representation a major consideration. He recently expressed confidence that "the matter will be taken care of in the next Legislature." If Governor Sanford does assume the lead, he will find strong allies in the General Assembly, among leading citizens of both political parties, and in the daily press. Perhaps he could even have the support of the North Carolina courts. The state Supreme Court ruled years ago that legislative representation is a political matter under the state constitution; [7] today, in light of *Baker* v. *Carr,* it might rule otherwise.

# Notes

[1] The division of the counties of the state into the three areas involves several border-line cases. The assignment made here differs somewhat, for obvious reasons, from that used in the chapter on Congressional redistricting.

[2] *Congressional Quarterly Weekly Report,* XX (1962), 176.

[3] Decimals take account of Senate rotation arrangements in districts crossing sectional lines.

[4] *Public Laws of 1911,* ch. 192.

[5] SR 4 (same as HR 2), ratified Feb. 10, 1961. *Session Laws,* Res. 2.

[6] For following paragraphs see *Senate Journal,* pp. 180 f., 183 f., and daily press.

[7] *Leonard* v. *Maxwell, Commissioner of Revenue,* 216 N.C. 89, 3 S.E. (2d) 316, June 1939.

# 5

# Kentucky
## A LATENT ISSUE

*MALCOLM E. JEWELL*
*University of Kentucky*

The legislative halls of Kentucky have not witnessed a battle over state reapportionment since 1942. Political oratory across the state in recent years has touched almost every issue except this one. Though the Louisville press occasionally reminds the voters of that city that their votes count for less than they should in the legislature, no one seems to listen. Reapportionment is not a major issue today in Kentucky. In fact, however, the apportionment system is an inseparable part of the political pattern of Kentucky, and any significant change in apportionment would alter the balance of political power. Moreover, as Kentucky becomes more urban and less rural, this issue is growing in importance. The issue of reapportionment is not dead, but dormant, and it is being gradually awakened in response to the recent decision of the U.S. Supreme Court.

## THE LEGAL FRAMEWORK

Legislative malapportionment in Kentucky is primarily the result of legislative inaction rather than constitutional restriction. The constitution provides for reapportionment by the legislature every ten years, but does not provide any machinery to ensure it. The constitution requires that senatorial apportionment be by population. For House districts it provides: "Not more than two counties shall be joined together to form a representative district: Provided, in so doing the principle requiring every district to be as nearly equal in population as may be shall not be violated." [1] Though the constitutional language is obviously not a model of clarity, the Kentucky Court of Appeals in 1907 said that more than two counties *could* be placed in a representative district.[2] Under the

111

present apportionment, there are no House districts containing more than two counties, but this custom would have to be broken to accomplish any significant change in the apportionment pattern. The constitution also sets the number of senators at thirty-eight and the number of representatives at 100. Kentucky has 120 counties.

The last reapportionment was in 1942. It gave Jefferson County (containing Louisville) five senatorial districts, established four single-county districts, and provided twenty-nine multicounty districts ranging from two to seven counties. The House has nine counties with more than one representative district (ranging from two to eleven), thirty-one single-county districts, and forty two-county districts. Each Senate and House district has a single member. The districts that were created in 1942 were far from equal by 1940 census standards; Senate districts ranged from 57,000 to 93,000, and House districts from 15,000 to 48,000. Since that time over two-thirds of Kentucky's counties have lost population, while the two largest counties, Jefferson and Fayette, have gained about 60 per cent in population. At present, the smallest Senate district is 45,000, the largest single-county district is 132,000, and the largest district in Jefferson County is estimated at almost 290,000. In the House, the smallest district is 11,000, the largest single-county district is 68,000, and the largest district in Jefferson County is almost 140,000. Not only the range in size but the average variance of districts is greater in the House than in the Senate, largely because the legislature has limited any House district to two counties.

## URBAN-RURAL IMPLICATIONS

It is easy to show that the metropolitan centers are discriminated against in Kentucky, but it is more difficult to prove how much actual importance this has. There is no single dominant metropolis comparable to New York or Chicago. Jefferson County, containing Louisville, is by far the largest, with one-fifth the state's population. The seven other counties containing cities of over 25,000 have another one-fifth of the population. As long as the larger urban centers represent a minority in the state, the urban-rural differences are unlikely to provide a focal point for conflict. But the shift of population to urban centers, particularly Louisville, is rapid enough so that the apportionment distortions will grow rapidly and the possibilities of political conflict will increase.

The rapidly growing metropolitan areas of Jefferson and Fayette counties (Louisville and Lexington) are most clearly discriminated against in apportionment. Together they have 24 per cent of the population, 16 per cent of the senators, and 13 per cent of the representatives. Some but not all of the other counties containing cities over 25,000 are handicapped by the apportionment. The rigidity of county boundaries makes some of these counties too large for one member and too small for two, and this is also the case with several of the larger rural counties. The apportionment can also be measured in terms of overrepresentation of the smallest districts, particularly in the House. Thirteen members from the smallest House districts represent 6 per cent of the population; thirteen from Jefferson and Fayette counties represent 24 per cent. It is possible for counties with 42 per cent of the state's population to elect a majority of senators, while 34 per cent can elect a majority of representatives.

Though rural areas are overrepresented in the legislature, the governor cannot ignore the needs of metropolitan areas. Kentucky has traditionally had a governor who exercised strong influence in legislative affairs. While he cannot dictate a program, a Democratic governor can usually depend on strong support from one faction of his party and often from most of the party. Under some conditions he can also win Republican support. Factional divisions among Democrats are not based primarily on urban-rural differences. Though the Chandler administration (1955-1959) differed sharply with Louisville legislators, the cause was no more profound than the Louisville Democratic organization's support of Chandler's opponents. Consequently, legislative voting is most likely to follow a factional and/or party line, when there is any pattern at all, rather than an urban-rural line. Since the state is still quite rural and the metropolitan areas in particular remain a minority, the exact size of the representation held by large cities is less important than in more urbanized states.

Even when issues arise that particularly affect the large cities, their representatives do not always take a united stand. On the important question of annexation, for example, representatives of the suburbs are most likely to oppose the city interests. In recent years, legislators from Jefferson County have been divided on such issues as city and county wage taxes, the power of local school boards to raise the school tax, and the extension of the sewer system in the county. These divisions sometimes, but not always, follow party lines. It should be noted that in Kentucky, as in most other states, the suburbs rather than the cities are most severely underrepresented.

Despite rural domination of the legislature, it is often true that a bill which serves urban interests will pass if there is substantial urban agreement concerning it and if the governor supports it. Most legislation that vitally affects city-dwellers creates controversy in the cities, however. Rural legislators are often apathetic concerning urban problems, and these may remain unsolved unless the governor can be persuaded to lend his weight to a specific piece of urban legislation. The present formula for distribution of state education funds indicates the legislature's concern with the admittedly serious problems of rural school districts which are often losing population and sometimes located in depressed areas. There has been little legislative effort to cope with the problems of school construction in the urban districts with mushrooming population. Two cents of the gasoline tax goes into a fund for rural roads, without any comparable allocation for urban road needs. Urban-rural conflicts in Kentucky do not dominate the legislature, but they are likely to become more evident as the population and problems of metropolitan areas continue to increase.

## PARTISAN IMPLICATIONS

On the surface the present apportionment does not appear to discriminate greatly against either political party. A comparison of the number of legislative seats held and votes polled by each party is meaningless because of the large proportion of uncontested seats (55 to 60 per cent in recent years). Since both parties have both urban and rural sources of strength, neither is directly handicapped by an apportionment system favoring rural areas. The solid core of Republican strength lies in nine Senate districts and nineteen House districts, most of them rural, won quite consistently in recent years.[3] The average of these nine Senate districts is 5,800 smaller than the Senate average, while these nineteen House districts average 4,700 less than the average House district. In 1942, under this apportionment, Republican districts, particularly in the Senate, were larger than average in population, but most of them (outside metropolitan areas) have lost population since then. Today the apportionment system appears to give the Republicans a slight advantage if only the consistently Republican districts are considered.

On the other hand, underrepresentation of urban counties hurts the Republican Party because much of the potential Republican vote lies there. There are about twenty House districts where the Republicans consistently run candidates and usually lose, but when the party is strong enough to elect a governor it often wins a number of these seats. These twenty competitive districts, half of them in Jefferson County, average 10,700 more than the average House district. In the 1961 elections the Republican Party captured local offices in Jefferson County, including most of the legislative seats. If the Republican revival there is not short-lived, the party will have a greater stake in reapportionment. In Jefferson County the added seats should be in areas where the Republicans are either dominant or on equal footing with the Democrats.

Another important consequence of the present apportionment is that it affects the balance of power *within* the two parties. The Republican gubernatorial and presidential strength comes particularly from certain rural counties in the mountains and from the metropolitan suburbs. The Republicans in the legislature, primarily rural in most sessions, are unsympathetic to urban needs and make a record that is no asset to the party in its effort to capture a greater proportion of the urban vote. Meanwhile, population continues to decline in most rural counties and to grow in the urban centers. The apportionment system helps to perpetuate the Republican Party's status as a minority because it makes the legislative party predominantly rural and because it helps to deprive the occasional Republican governor of a party majority in the legislature.

The rural wing of the Democratic Party obviously benefits from the apportionment, but this is less significant because factionalism in the party does not follow urban-rural lines. It is impossible to prove that the present apportionment consistently serves the interests of either faction. Moreover, a gubernatorial candidate of either faction must make some appeal to urban as well as rural voters. Factionalism in Democratic politics does not have a significant socioeconomic base. It is a system of constantly changing personal coalitions.

## THE SOURCES OF APATHY

There are a number of reasons why legislative reapportionment in Kentucky has not been a lively issue in recent years. In a few words, those groups that benefit by the *status quo* are conscious of their advantage, while other groups see no immediate advantage in pressing for change. Any significant reapportionment would be politically upsetting to most members now serving in the legislature. Their districts would be changed, they would sometimes have to run against other incumbents, and in most rural areas they would face criticism from their constituents if they supported a reduction in rural representation.

Since legislators react instinctively against reapportionment, any such action in Kentucky would surely require the strong support of the governor. The last such apportionment was initiated in 1942 by the governor, who called a special session for that purpose. Press accounts at the time indicated that all the pressure of the governor's office was required to bring about passage of the governor's reapportionment plan. The governor appeared personally on the House floor and talked to the legislators while the measure was being passed by a narrow margin. Governors in recent years have been unwilling to invest so much of their political resources to bring about reapportionment. They have been unwilling to jeopardize other parts of their programs by seriously proposing legislative reapportionment. Any Kentucky governor depends on the votes of numerous rural legislators for enactment of his program, and nothing would alienate them more surely than a reapportionment program.

The administration proposed, and succeeded in enacting, a Congressional redistricting measure in 1962. It was necessitated by the loss of one seat; otherwise, it would never have been suggested. The administration's bill made minimum adjustments in district boundaries, alienated the minimum number of congressmen and legislators, and even satisfied most Republicans. It combined the districts of two congressmen whom the administration judged to be the most expendable. Though some legislators in the combined districts made efforts to substitute another plan, the administration had relatively little difficulty in passing its measure without amendment in the legislature. The administration gave no hint that it even considered proposing a legislative apportionment act to accompany Congressional redistricting.

Since the present apportionment discriminates against the cities, there should be protests by urban legislators. Most urban Democrats in the present legislature are loyal to the administration and have followed its lead. Democrats from Jefferson County might be expected to lead a drive for reapportionment. However, a reapportionment that gave Jefferson County an equal voice in the legislature would benefit Republicans more than Democrats. The largest senatorial district in Jefferson County, three times the size of the next largest, is consistently Republican. The two largest House districts in the county are about 140,000 and 132,000; the others range from 24,000 to 55,000. Of the two largest House districts, one is consistently Republican and one is a "swing district"; with one exception the smallest districts in the county are usually Democratic. The suburban parts of the county are most underrepresented and the Republicans in Jefferson County have the greatest stake in reapportionment.

Republican legislators from Jefferson County made reapportionment one of their campaign themes, but it was not included among the planks of a platform adopted by the party's legislators at the start of the session. One reapportionment bill introduced by a Republican would have given Jefferson County its proportionate share of Senate and House seats, but the bill never emerged from committee and created little stir. There was no evidence that rural Republicans were interested in supporting a reapportionment that would have cost their counties representation in the legislature. Republicans said little in public about the issue, for three reasons: their own party was not united; as a minority, they had little hope of success; and they did not want to jeopardize other measures in which they were interested.

In some states, reapportionment has been an issue in constitutional revision. In 1960 Kentucky voters narrowly defeated a proposal for a limited constitutional convention, and another such proposal has started through the legislative mill. Although reapportionment might be considered in such a convention (since the legislative article of the constitution is one of the sections open for revision), little has been said about such a possibility. One reason is that, despite the ambiguity of the constitution, malapportionment results primarily from legislative inaction and not constitutional provision. The constitution could, of course, be amended to provide alternatives to the legislature as the reapportioning agent. In all likelihood apportionment would not be a significant issue in a constitutional convention because other reforms have priority, and the supporters of constitutional revision do not want to alienate rural voters by even mentioning the issue.

## THE COURTS—A SPUR TO ACTION?

The Supreme Court's decision on apportionment did not bring any immediate or powerful response in Kentucky, but there soon were indications that it might be the catalyst that would spur a revision of legislative districts.

The decision came a few days after adjournment of the regular biennial session of the legislature. The governor, Bert Combs, said early in April that he did not plan to call a special session. He said that the problem in Kentucky was not urgent and was less acute than in many states; parenthetically, he noted that the urban areas had been well represented in the executive branch. Obviously the Governor did not welcome revival of an issue that might create problems in the 1963 gubernatorial primary. He was willing to have the issue studied in order to provide guidance for his successor and the 1964 session of the legislature. The Governor recognized, however, that if there were further court decisions "the situation could change overnight."

Pressure for swifter action soon came from several sources. The Kentucky Municipal League urged that reapportionment be undertaken quickly, and threats of a court suit came from Republican leaders in Jefferson County and from the Kentucky Civil Liberties Union. Although the Governor made it clear that he still preferred to delay the issue, he took several steps toward reapportionment, presumably in response to these pressures. On May 2, the Governor initiated a suit in the state courts to clarify the ambiguities in the state constitution with regard to apportionment. In mid-June, he met with interested individuals to explore the question of reapportionment. Those groups that had already taken a public stand in favor of reapportionment urged a special session, but the mood of legislators attending the meeting was not at all one of urgency. The Governor then turned the problem over to a specially appointed bipartisan committee.

On June 26, the City of Louisville brought a suit in federal court asking that the 1942 apportionment be held unconstitutional and that the governor be required to call a special session of the legislature to deal with reapportionment. The mayor of Louisville and the Jefferson County judge, both Republicans, obviously believed that this would be the most effective way of bringing about a special session, possibly before the case was heard in court.

In the first months after the Supreme Court's decision, it was evident that reapportionment would come in Kentucky, though perhaps not until the judiciary had intervened. The prospects for action were enhanced by the nature of the state constitution and by the fact that reapportionment in Kentucky would have no immediate and revolutionary effect on state politics. Yet the ultimate effect of a comprehensive and equitable reapportionment in the state could be a far-reaching one with profound political implications.

# Notes

[1] Section 33.

[2] *Ragland* v. *Anderson*, 125 Ky. 141 (1907).

[3] For a more detailed description, see Malcolm E. Jewell, "Party and Primary Competition in Kentucky State Legislative Races," *Kentucky Law Journal*, XLVIII (1960), 517-535.

# 6

## Texas

FACTIONS IN A ONE-PARTY SETTING

*H. DICKEN CHERRY*
*Baylor University*

On the surface, the story of the 1961 legislative reapportionment in Texas appears to be simply the familiar one of a rapidly growing urban population confronting a constitution written by rural people and subsequently amended by rural legislators to protect rural interests. This is part of the story in Texas, but only its beginning. The present constitutional provisions permit, in fact ensure, some adjustment in apportionment to population trends. Since Texas is a one-party state, partisan factors are missing from the reapportionment process. In the limited reapportionment conducted in 1961, a dominant legislative faction played the role of a majority party in seeking to minimize injury to its members, though the uncertain base of Texas factions makes it as difficult for a faction as for a party to use reapportionment to strengthen its legislative majority.

## THE CONSTITUTIONAL BACKGROUND

The Texas constitution provides for a Senate of thirty-one members and a House with a maximum of 150 members (maximum reached in 1921). The House is apportioned according to total population, the Senate according to qualified voters. If a county has sufficient population to entitle it to one or more representatives, it is made a House district.[1] If it does not have the required population, it is joined with one or more contiguous counties to form a district.[2] If a county has excess population (e.g., more than enough for two representatives but not enough for a third), it is made a district for electing those two and, in addition,

120

is joined with one or more contiguous counties to form a "floterial district" which elects the additional representative. The constitution prohibits any county, regardless of number of qualified voters, from having more than one senator.

During the thirty-year period 1921-1951 the Legislature did not reapportion, but it did substantially alter the framework within which redistricting now takes place when it passed and the voters ratified two amendments to the apportionment sections of the constitution. The sponsors of these amendments presented each of them as the solution to the problem of ensuring redistricting promptly each decade. The theory of the 1936 amendment was that redistricting could be assured if the constitution ensured continued rural domination of the House as it already did in the case of the Senate. Accordingly, this amendment provides that no county may have more than seven representatives (which would have required a population of about 300,000 in 1936) until its population reaches 700,000, and it may then have one additional representative for each 100,000 population over 700,000. Despite this amendment, no redistricting occurred in 1941. In 1948 an amendment with a different approach was adopted. It provides for a five-member ex-officio board to redistrict both legislative branches if the first Legislature following each decennial census fails to do so.

A look at population statistics since 1920 affords considerable insight into the machinations and hesitations of the Texas Legislature on the issue of redistricting during the 1930's and 1940's. As late as 1920 two-thirds of the state's population of 4,700,000 was rural. During the next two decades, rural population showed a net increase but declined to only 54 per cent of the total. Since 1940 rural population has exhibited a net loss. From 1940 to 1950, while the urban population was increasing 58.4 per cent, the rural was decreasing 11.6 per cent. A total of 146 counties out of 254 lost population during the 1940's. In forty-eight of them the loss was greater than 20 per cent. This trend continued during the fifties. While the urban population was increasing 2,300,000 or 48.5 per cent, the rural population was declining by nearly half a million. No less than 143 counties sustained losses during the 1950-1960 decade. Nearly all of the gain was accounted for by twenty counties, and of those twenty the "Big Four," which include Dallas, Fort Worth, Houston, and San Antonio, now contain 3,500,000 of Texas' 9,500,000 people.

At present the legislative representation of only these four largest counties is arbitrarily limited by Texas' constitutional provisions. Only one other county has sufficient population to be seriously considered for a senator of its own. No other county has sufficient population to have reached seven representatives. The application of the constitution to the Big Four requires them to have less than one-fourth of the members of the House and about one-eighth of those of the Senate, although they have over one-third of the state's population.

Because the Texas Legislature now has an ex-officio redistricting board hanging over it, there is no problem in Texas of obtaining prompt redistricting after each census. Texas' reapportionment problem is, therefore, not that of Tennessee and some other states where legislatures fail to act; it is rather that in Texas equitable representation is unconstitutional. With the four largest conunties limited to one senator each, the Legislature is prohibited from drawing district lines that would allow the upper chamber to reflect the bulk of the increase in population. Senate redistricting therefore characteristically involves only the shuffling of a few counties in a few districts to add to the least populous districts. This is what took place with regard to the Senate in 1961. On the other hand, redistricting of the House characteristically involves much more far-reaching changes, as it did in 1961.

## THE INTERESTS IN 1961

Very few individuals or groups outside the Legislature itself took an active part in the 1961 redistricting activity. Public interest was practically nonexistent. The AFL-CIO was strongly in favor of the bill written by the House Committee on Congressional and Legislative Districts, but this could hardly account for passage of the bill. Other powerful lobbies took no recognizable stand. These included the Texas Manufacturers Association, the Chambers of Commerce, the Texas State Teachers Association, farm groups, and the corporation lobbyists. The strongest among the pressure groups have supreme confidence in their ability to determine elections regardless of where district lines are drawn. The weaker ones do not want to alienate the good will of leading legislators, which is their stock in trade. Independent professional lobbyists did all they could as individuals, however, against portions of the committee bill which injured their individual House friends.

Two interests, however, bulked much larger in the redistricting battle than all others. One of these was "personal interests." The House members who intended to run again naturally did not want their districts changed. Those whose districts had lost population were aware that change was inevitable and had already decided which of alternative additions they would prefer. Obviously, these personal interests tend to be mutually exclusive; in the final decision a choice which favors one member is at the expense of another. What interest determined these final decisions in the Fifty-Seventh Legislature? What interest overrode all others in conflict with it? The answer is: that of the dominant House faction.

Every regularly elected member of the Texas House is a Democrat. However, the political philosophies of the members run from left of Sen. Ralph Yarborough to right of Sen. John Tower. The dominance of one all-embracing party means that there is a complete absence of party responsibility in Texas government. The responsibility of Texas' elected officials to the public and to groups is personal. This is true of legislators as well, but in the legislative process a single individual is ineffective if he must operate in an unorganized, unstructured assembly. Therefore, the Texas legislator, especially the House member, who has to display no party loyalty to get elected, exhibits quite consistent loyalty to the faction with which he aligns himself *within* the legislative body. In the Texas House the event which serves as the device for dividing members into relatively fixed alignments is the election of the speaker.

After minor candidates for speaker had withdrawn, the showdown in the 1961 speaker's race was between James Turman and Wade Spilman. The former is what the Texas press and public generally call a "liberal"; the latter a "conservative." Turman won by an 83-to-66 vote, indicating that in the elections of 1960 the "liberals" had apparently won control of the House for the first time in some dozen years. In order to avoid the ideological baggage which goes with the terms "liberal" and "conservative," those who voted for Turman will be called "Turmocrats" in this paper and those who voted for Spilman will be called "Spilicans." These House factions play the same role and exhibit as much cohesion as the parties labeled Democratic and Republican in the U.S. Congress. A study of roll-call votes on a dozen major bills where a switch in less than twenty votes would have reversed the result shows that at least 70 per cent of the Turmocrats never failed to vote together. On only three occasions did the Spilicans drop below 70 per cent in solidarity. These factions hit highs of 88 and 89 per cent, respectively. These major bills included such diverse subjects as a general sales tax, a pension plan for police and firemen, inspection of out-of-state milk, civil jury reform, legislative redistricting, escheat of abandoned property, and operation of REA cooperatives in areas annexed by cities.

The urban-rural conflict which dominates legislative politics in many states does not correlate very closely with the factional division in Texas' Fifty-Seventh Legislature. Of the large city delegations, San Antonio was for Turman, Dallas was for Spilman, Houston was 5-to-3 for Spilman, and Fort Worth was 4-to-3 for Spilman.[3] In the medium-sized cities (districts populous enough to have more than one representative) Turman got nineteen votes and Spilman fifteen. A regional analysis excluding the cities shows that a majority of the south Texas members were for Spilman (who comes from that region), a majority of east Texas was with Turman (his region), a bare majority of central Texas members were with Turman, and a majority of west Texas favored Spilman. However, there were far too many exceptions to these generalizations to allow the conclusion that this division is geographically clear-cut.

In terms of legislative voting behavior the fact of a member's being a Turmocrat or a Spilican was more indicative of how he would vote on most matters, including reapportionment, than was the fact that he was from a certain region or that he had a rural or urban constituency. In a traditional analysis, urban members would have been expected to be *for* the milk bill, yet the Spilican members from Houston and Dallas voted to recommit it. In some states the REA bill would be expected to exhibit a rural-urban split—yet San Antonio, which is Turmocrat, was solidly for it; Dallas, which is Spilican, was solidly against; Fort Worth, which is 4-to-3 Spilican, was 4-to-3 against; and Houston, which is 5-to-3 Spilican, was 8-to-1 against. Being a Turmocrat or a Spilican would seem to be more a matter of ideological disposition or predisposition than of geography or population density. Hence, a piece of legislation such as the REA bill is perceived not so much as a rural-versus-urban issue as it is that of "socialistic" cooperatives versus private enterprise. An example of factionalism prevailing even over urban self-interest in 1961 was the solid vote of the Dallas delegation against the redistricting bill by which its own county was to gain two seats! These Dallas members were all Spilicans, and for them the decisive characteristic of the redistricting bill was, as we shall see presently, that it was the work of Turmocrats.

## THE TECHNIQUES

The only formal technique available for redistricting in Texas is a statute. The mastery of this technique to serve the Turmocrat cause can properly be called gerrymandering. The actual writing of the statute involved was the responsibility of the Committee on Congressional and Legislative Districts. This committee, like all those of the House, is appointed by the speaker. It is usually a sort of limbo to which the speaker condemns unfriendy members. In the Fifty-Seventh Legislature, however, this twenty-one-member committee was composed of nineteen Turmocrats and two Spilicans.

For the purpose of holding hearings, the committee divided itself into five regional subcommittees with the chairman, a potential successor to the speaker, presiding over each subcommittee. Every member of the House was invited to appear before one of these subcommittees. Each member was assured that the committee would avoid, wherever possible, putting two incumbent members in the same district. Each member was also asked whether he expected to run for re-election. This testimony, together with U.S. census figures on population by counties, constituted the raw material for what eventually became H.B. 349.

The committee made its report in the form of H.B. 349 on May 4. This bill, together with Senate amendments regarding Senate districts, survived all efforts to defeat or amend it. Its severest test came on May 8, when Rep. Menton J. Murray (Spilican from Harlingen) offered a complete rewrite of the bill. Murray's substitute was designed to gain Spilican support and also pick up the votes of enough disgruntled Turmocrats to form a majority. The substitute failed 64-to-73. Of the members for, fifty-four were Spilicans and ten were Turmocrats. The sixty-eight Turmocrats against were joined by only five Spilicans. After the Spilicans lost this battle their hope shifted to the Senate, which is overwhelmingly "pro-Spilican." However, the Senate abided by the long-standing custom of the Legislature that neither house will meddle in the internal affairs of the other. Accordingly, the Senate not only did not change the House districts but appended its proposal for new Senate districts as an amendment to the House bill. The final hope of the Spilicans was that the House would refuse to concur on the ground that the Senate amendments were not germane to the original bill. When this question was raised as a point of order, the Speaker overruled it. The House then voted 80-to-55 to concur, and the bill was sent to the governor, who signed it into law.

## OUTCOME

The new law, which goes into effect with the 1962 primaries, reduced the number of House districts from 105 to 94. (With the total membership fixed at 150 and the populous counties gaining seats, the result is fewer districts with the multiple-member districts having seats added to their delegations.) It made some kind of change in 48 of the 105 districts with which it began. Of these changes, twenty-four represented clear-cut gains or losses in the districts' voting strength in the House. Eleven districts gained: eight counties gained one or more representatives and three became separate districts for the first time. Thirteen districts lost: their new district lines enclose two incumbents. Three of these were so completely disassembled that the counties making up each of them were awarded to three or more new districts. The new apportionment reflects the geographic shift in Texas' population. If anything, it slightly overcompensates for the shift in population from the north and east toward the south and west.

In order to meet the requirements of the constitution, H.B. 349 necessarily discriminated against the big metropolitan counties. Nevertheless, Houston had gained sufficient population to earn its county four new members, and Dallas gained two. Below the Big Four, there are sixteen counties which have sufficient population to entitle them to one or more representatives. However, their representation is based on multiples of 54,000, rather than of 100,000. None of them will have any incentive to support a change in the present system until and unless its number of representatives reaches seven.

## PROSPECTS

What results are to be expected from the new law in terms of House factions? First, it should be noted that the House committee could not, or at least did not, do much to determine which districts would gain members. Population dictated this, and the factional affiliation of the additional members had to be left to fate. On the other hand, the distribution of the districts suffering losses was almost fully within the control of the committee. Of the thirteen new districts which would pit two present members of the House against one another, the districts are drawn in such a way as to produce the following factional prospects: In three new districts Spilicans will be opposing each other. In three districts Turmocrats will be running against Spilicans, but the districts are composed predominantly of the Turmocrats' old district. In four districts Turmocrats who intend to run again will be in districts which include Turmocrats who will not run for re-election. Two districts will find Turmocrats who voted consistently with the Turmocrat faction throughout the session given an advantage in opposing two who deserted the faction immediately after the vote for speaker. Only in a district which had to be cut from two representatives to one will two loyal Turmocrats have to face each other. These results suggest that the redistricting committee protected the political future of Turmocrats in every instance in which it could possibly do so.

In any other state, this gerrymandering which reduces the Spilican (conservative) strength and the awarding of additional seats to urban areas could be expected to produce a new House with an even more comfortable majority for the Turmocrats (liberals). However, many Texas cities are unlike those in other states. Dallas, which gains two members, is consistently conservative. Houston, which gains four, fluctuates violently from extreme liberal to extreme conservative. Austin and Corpus Christi, which gain one each, are consistently liberal. El Paso and Amarillo, which gain one each, presently have delegations which are evenly divided. Hence, one can note the successful gerrymandering in H.B. 349, but cannot predict whether it will achieve the factional results intended.

What would be the likely effect on Texas government if the House in the Fifty-Eighth Legislature were to have an increased number of liberal members? The probable answer is, "divided government, Texas style." The 1961 Senate usually voted about 24-to-7 against House bills which were strongly backed by Turmocrats. Further, the Lieutenant Governor, who was in his sixth consecutive term, used his vast powers as presiding officer to block passage of Turmocrat measures. No drastic change in the Senate could be anticipated from the redistricting bill, but 1962 does hold the slimmest of chances that a more liberal House may be matched by a more liberal Senate. Stranger things have happened in Texas politics, but the odds are that the Fifty-Eighth Legislature will be another in which the House and Senate reach many an impasse and which will be able to enact few major pieces of legislation.[4]

Another prospect to be anticipated from this and future reapportionments has to do with techniques of campaigning for House seats. The 1961 bill—and presumably also its successors—takes the members subtracted from multiple-county districts and adds them to multiple-member counties. It was noted earlier that members from such counties must all run county-wide. This introduces the prospect that a dominant local intraparty organization could unite behind a slate in the Democratic primary and win all of the seats in the county's delegation even though it did not have strength in all sections of the county. In Texas' three largest cities the practice is already established of running two slates, rather clearly identified as liberal and conservative, in the Democratic primary. The fourth largest city, Fort Worth, is moving toward this practice. Other cities may join the ranks as they become major cities. The practice correlates directly with a city's size. The success of this slate technique has been impressive. Results of the last two elections show the following: In Dallas all the members of the conservative slate were elected each time. In Houston all members of the liberal slate won in 1958, and all but one of the conservative slate won in 1960. In San Antonio all but one of the conservative slate won in 1958, and all but one of the liberal slate won in 1960.

If this trend continues and spreads it will signal the end of the tradition of rigidly individualistic, almost atomistic, campaigning for state representative posts. For the candidates of the future it will mean that they cannot expect to be elected unless they are on one of the slates. For the voter in the Democratic primary it will mean a narrowing of his choice to two candidates for each House seat, but it will provide him with more reliable indicators than in the past about the kind of legislative performance to expect of each candidate. For the Democratic Party of Texas, which has been split into factions in major state-wide races and in party conventions for more than a dozen years, it will mean two sets of established big-city organizations, which will add permanency and continuity to the factions. For the Republican Party in Texas this solidification of Democratic factions will be either the worst or best thing that has ever happened. Since this trend can be expected to give the voters clear-cut choices in the Democratic primary, there would seem to be little place for a third organization. Further, since the Democrats have run-off primaries when needed, it would appear that Republican candidates would have little chance in general elections. (In 1961, two Republicans were elected to the Texas House in special elections that required no run-off and hence were decided by pluralities, but they are given almost no chance to be re-elected over a single Democratic nominee.) On the other hand, the trend could work to the advantage of the Republican Party in two possible ways: (1) With functioning conservative organizations in existence in major urban centers, the Republicans have an opportunity to capture operating organizations intact and thus save themselves the task of building them. (2) If feelings between the two Democratic factions become more bitter as the factions crystallize into permanent organizations, the Republicans might organize to attract general election votes from conservatives who did not get their way in the Democratic primaries and would rather vote for a Republican than for a nominee of the rival Democratic faction.

Another prospect suggested by the results of the 1961 reapportionment is that Texas may drift unconsciously into the so-called federal plan which other states have deliberately chosen in structuring their bicameral legislatures. Texas' population growth between 1950 and 1960 raised the unweighted base of House apportionment from 51,000 per representative to 64,000. At the present growth rate (25 per cent per decade) the raw base will reach 100,000 with the 1980 census. But that is the arbitrarily high base fixed by the constitution to discriminate against cities. Continued strict adherence to the constitution beyond 1980 could result in overrepresentation of the cities in the House. At the same time, the constitutional limitation of no more than one senator per county would have compounded their underrepresentation in the Senate. This would be a variation of the "federal plan" unique to Texas, but a recognizable variation nonetheless.

A further prospect is suggested by this. It is difficult to imagine the spirit and intent of the present constitution being destroyed by the growth and urbanization of population without some movement toward constitutional revision. No amendment to the apportionment section is presently in sight, and the movement of the League of Women Voters for a completely new constitution has failed to get broad support in spite of a decade of persistent effort. However, as more people become aware of the future results of applying the present apportionment formula, a change is likely. It is most likely to be in the direction of fixing an absolute maximum number of House seats permitted to any one county.

Regardless of whether the constitution is changed or what the changes are, the politics of Texas reapportionment is likely to remain basically unchanged. Whatever the constitutional framework within which they work, democratic legislative bodies operate by majorities and minorities. The more dependable the majority, the more efficient is the legislative process. When a given majority participates in redistricting —a step that can materially influence future majorities—it can be expected to maximize gains and minimize losses to its own loyal members. In a two-party setting the majorities and minorities bear party labels, and partisan redistricting is a practice which the public recognizes and perhaps even accepts. In Texas the mechanics are much the same, but the participants bear no labels for the public at large to recognize. The outcome of House elections in census years and of the speaker's election following therefrom will continue to be of prime importance in determining the outcome of redistricting. And through it all the voter will remain unaware of the added significance of his vote in census years, unmindful of the speaker's race and which speaker candidate each representative candidate supports, and uninformed (except in the big cities, with their slate system) as to the all-important factional affiliation of the candidate he chooses.

# Notes

1 In multiple-member districts each candidate runs county-wide against all others who have filed for the same ballot "place" ("Place One," "Place Two," etc.).

2 No county is ever divided to make a House or Senate district. Hence, district lines always run along county boundaries.

3 One of Turman's votes from San Antonio and two of his three votes from Houston were cast by members who had run on "conservative" slates in their respective cities. The San Antonio member was dean of the House. All three are well-known personalities who led their slates and might better be called "moderates" on the basis of their legislative voting records. They joined the Turmocrat majority on the vote for speaker but did not do so on as many votes during the remainder of the session as did many of their colleagues.

4 The 1962 primary results in fact indicated that in 1963 the Senate would become somewhat more liberal and the House somewhat more conservative.

# PART THREE

# Congressional Reapportionment
# and Partisan Deadlock

*INTRODUCTION*

There is always resistance to changing Congressional districts—from the incumbent congressmen, their constituents, and often from the state's dominant political forces. In two-party states, a single party controlling the executive and legislative branches has both the means and the incentive to accomplish major changes. But when the control of government is divided in a two-party state, the outlook is for deadlock, and compromise is not easily achieved. Following the 1960 census, Illinois, Pennsylvania, and Ohio faced the necessity of Congressional reapportionment. Illinois was losing one seat, Pennsylvania was losing three, while Ohio faced the happier prospect of gain-

131

ing a seat. All three states had Democratic governors. The Republicans
had narrow legislative majorities in Illinois, held half the seats in the
Pennsylvania Senate, and had more substantial legislative control in
Ohio. In short, all three states had divided government.

The case studies of Illinois and Pennsylvania are remarkably similar.
Party discipline was strong in both. The task of accommodating party
interests was complicated by serious population losses in the Democratic
strongholds, Chicago and Philadelphia, and corresponding gains in the
largely Republican suburbs. The Democrats tried to minimize their
losses by extending urban Congressional districts into the suburbs, but
not far enough to jeopardize Democratic majorities. In both states it
proved relatively easy to make adjustments outside the cities, in declining
rural areas.

Both parties in the two states weighed the risks of gambling on
at-large elections. Both practiced "brinkmanship," and as a result the
regular legislative sessions ended with reapportionment unaccomplished.
There were strong pressures for a solution, including those from incumbent congressmen, and the special sessions produced compromises
that fell short of comprehensive reapportionment. The compromise in
Illinois was something of a Democratic victory, perhaps because that
party evidenced stronger organizational unity. The Democrats had to
concede more in Pennsylvania, partly as a result of Democratic setbacks
in local elections in which the party's reapportionment plan had become
an issue.

In Ohio, the problem was considerably simpler, since the state was
gaining a seat. With a divided government, there was no real prospect of
comprehensive reapportionment. A Republican effort to divide the largest Congressional district in the state fell victim to Democratic opposition and the personal interests of congressmen and legislators. The new
congressman will, as a result, be elected at-large.

Partisan deadlock also prevented change in the legislative apportionment system, in which both Ohio parties had vested interests. The
Republican Party, with its strong rural base, effectively defended the
constitutional provision assuring each county one representative, while
the Democratic Party opposed any change in the at-large elections in
metropolitan centers, at least in those with normal Democratic majorities.

Partisan deadlock over Congressional reapportionment in the wake
of the 1960 census was evident in other states. The Republican-dominated
Legislature in Michigan carved out a single new Republican district in
the underrepresented Detroit suburbs, but the Democratic governor
vetoed the bill, leaving the new congressman to be elected at-large. Massachusetts came closer than any other state to the brink of an at-large

election. After House Speaker John W. McCormack failed in his Congressional effort to restore the seat lost by Massachusetts, the Democratic legislature and Republican governor finally accepted a plan endorsed by most of the state's congressmen, who had the most to lose in an at-large election.

# 7

## Equilibrium in Illinois
### FRUSTRATION AND ACCOMMODATION OF THE PARTIES

*DAVID W. MINAR*
*Northwestern University*

Like many other states, Illinois found reapportionment a source of considerable political trouble in 1961. Illinois, indeed, has a history of apportionment difficulties, for reasons obviously rooted in the geographic, social, and political make-up of the state. The legislature was not reapportioned at all between 1901 and 1955. The state was the source of the *Colegrove* v. *Green* dispute,[1] and in 1954 it experienced a keen battle over a constitutional amendment providing for redistricting of the General Assembly. It elected a congressman-at-large from 1942 to 1946 because of the problems involved in redistricting. The 1961 legislative sessions added another chapter to this history of acute partisan reapportionment struggle in its handling of the problem of reconstituting the state's Congressional districts. When 1960 census returns indicated that Illinois' Congressional delegation would be reduced from twenty-five to twenty-four, the state faced the prospect of redistricting in 1961 or electing all its congressmen at-large in 1962. The 1954 General Assembly apportionment amendment had provided that election districts for the state House of Representatives not be redrawn until 1963; thus, that even more onerous political task was fortunately disentangled from the job of Congressional reapportionment in the 1961 legislative session.

### POLITICAL BACKGROUND TO 1961

The 1961 reapportionment process can perhaps best be understood against the background of political balance and frequent deadlock characteristic of Illinois in recent years. In many respects the state is an interesting example of the political operation of closely matched social forces, perhaps most dramatically illustrated in the fact that largely urban Cook County (which includes Chicago) is the home of 51 per cent of the people of the state. This is not to suggest that the balance of political power in Illinois is the product of a simple Cook County–down-state division. Parts of Cook County (most of the suburban areas) are heavily Republican, whereas some down-state areas, particularly in the St. Louis metropolitan sphere and parts of the far-south "delta," are often Democratic. But in general terms the political condition of the state is one of near-equilibrium, reflected in the relatively equal command of elective office by the two major parties. Control of state-wide offices, the state legislature, and the Congressional delegation has tended to swing from one party to the other, though with significant long-run Republican preponderance. Similarly, Illinois has sometimes gone Republican and sometimes Democratic in presidential elections. In 1960, President Kennedy won the state by a scant 10,000 votes. In the same election Democratic candidates won contests for United States senator, governor, and five out of six other state-wide executive offices, while the Republicans won a narrow majority of seats in both houses of the General Assembly.

Political balance was doubtless part of both cause and effect of the legislative apportionment arrangements worked out in the early 1950's and written into the Illinois constitution in 1954. Despite the standard constitutional requirement of decennial reapportionment, the districts in use until 1955 were those established in 1901; by midcentury they were, of course, grossly disproportionate in population, with Chicago and the rest of Cook County underrepresented in both houses.[2] Though we will deal with it only briefly here, the achievement of a new basis of apportionment for the Illinois legislature in 1954 is interesting both as a case in itself and as a factor in conditioning the Illinois political system for the handling of the Congressional problem in 1961.[3]

As usual in such situations, the main impediment to reapportionment before 1954 had been a legislature anxious to maintain the *status quo* on which many of its members depended for their political lives. Years of attempts at statutory change had simply been buried, in large part under down-state fears of giving Cook County its proper share of seats. Constitutional apportionment reform had been further inhibited by amendment procedures that required extraordinary referendum majorities of a size impossible to attain for the purpose. One of the major breakthroughs for legislative reapportionment came with the passage in 1950 of a "Gateway Amendment" reducing the size of popular majorities required for constitutional revision. The movement for the "Gateway" united those interested in reapportionment with others whose main interests lay in constitutional reform of the state's judicial and financial structures, in combined strength sufficient to accomplish their common goal.

Complete revision of the constitutional basis of legislative reapportionment followed ratification of the Gateway Amendment within five years. In the process, of course, the Assembly had to be persuaded to submit and the voting public to approve a reapportionment amendment. The persuasion of the legislature seems to have been largely the work of Gov. William G. Stratton, a down-state Republican. The successful referendum campaign drew support from a variety of interests, including segments of organized business, labor, and agriculture, all the Chicago daily press, and elements in both political parties, spearheaded by a bipartisan group of prominent citizens. In 1955, the General Assembly, now threatened by the constitutional contingency of reapportionment by commission if it did not act, redrew Assembly election districts as directed by the new amendment. This task was accomplished only through a tortuous process of negotiation and accommodation.

The nature and operation of the scheme adopted in Illinois in 1954 illustrate the limits of reapportionment politics in a large, divided, and politically balanced state. The interests of no important party, group, or section were ignored. Perhaps the extraordinary thing is that the change could be made at all; that it was is a tribute to the extremely intricate mechanisms of democratic politics. The result, however, is a governmental process so structured as to ensure in the future a high degree of balance and often deadlock and policy frustration.

The amendment established a "federal plan" for the General Assembly: a Senate substantially representative of areas and a House representative of population. Representation in the Senate is drawn from fifty-eight districts electing one senator each. The constitution specified apportionment of districts among areas of the state, Chicago having eighteen, Cook County outside Chicago six, and the remainder of the state thirty-four. It also provides that "all Senate districts shall be formed of contiguous and compact territory. In their formation, area shall be the prime consideration." [4] The district boundaries established in the 1955 legislative session are presumably permanent; the constitution does not require or even mention Senate reapportionment.

Representation in the House is drawn from fifty-nine districts, each electing three members for two-year terms by a system of cumulative voting. The amendment specified apportionment of seats in 1955 among areas and directed apportionment thereafter as follows: "In redistricting subsequent to the 1960 census, and thereafter, the fifty-nine representative districts shall be divided among (1) that part of Cook County that is within the present corporate limits of the City of Chicago, (2) that part of Cook County that is outside such corporate limits, and (3) the remaining one hundred and one counties of the state, as nearly as may be, as the population of each of these three divisions bears to the total population of the state." [5] Outside Cook County, districts must be "bounded by county lines" unless a county is entitled to more than one representative, and no district may contain less than four-fifths of the "representative ratio." If reapportionment is not accomplished by the legislature in specified years, the governor is required to appoint a commission of ten, five each from lists of ten submitted by the state central committees of the two major parties.[6] Final certification of the commission's plan requires the concurrence of seven members. If the commission fails to certify a plan within four months, all members of the House are elected at-large for the next session.

Party divisions in the Assembly since reapportionment have been relatively close and shifting. The Senate has been controlled by the Republicans by margins of eighteen, ten, and four votes in successive sessions. The House was Republican by eleven votes in 1957, Democratic by five in 1959, and Republican by one, though organized by the Democrats, in 1961. In the election of 1960, it should be recalled, a Democrat was elected governor by a popular vote of landslide proportions, and control of the state government thus divided between the two parties. The tendency toward narrow party margins in the House is reinforced by the cumulative voting system which in effect ensures minority representation from all districts.[7]

The foregoing perhaps suggests a purely structural interpretation of Illinois politics, but no such theoretical purity is intended. Policy, for example the policy problem of Congressional redistricting, is the outcome of interplay of social forces, formal structures, political organizations, and individual behavior. The structures of Illinois politics are what they are because of the traditions and social shape of the state. They do, in turn, impose constraints and restraints on the policy processes and hence on policy itself. In combination with other factors they constitute the political setting within which the reapportionment task of 1961 was worked out. The nature and effects of some of the specific organizational and behavioral factors in the process will be apparent in the analysis of Congressional reapportionment that follows.

## THE REGULAR LEGISLATIVE SESSION:

## REAPPORTIONMENT FRUSTRATED

For several reasons, the 1961 Illinois legislature met in a particularly high-charged political atmosphere. The very narrow Kennedy victory in Illinois had been followed by charges and countercharges of election fraud which heightened the partisan tension ordinarily generated in a presidential year. Though the Democratic candidate beat the incumbent Republican governor by a substantial margin and Democrats won the United States Senate seat and all but one of the state-wide elective executive offices, both houses of the General Assembly were nearly evenly divided by party. The Democrats, despite their November victories, were in somewhat less than perfect condition: concerned about their reputation as "boss-dominated," somewhat nervous about relationships between Gov. Otto Kerner and Chicago Mayor Richard Daley (the acknowledged Democratic leader of the state), and as always plagued with incipient factional struggle, especially along Chicago–down-state and liberal-organization lines. The Illinois Republican Party was deeply rent after November, divided by bitterness over the Stratton campaign and by a three-way rivalry for leadership between those led by Secretary of State Charles Carpentier (an easy winner in November), the remnants of the Stratton group, and some prominent "amateurs" who aspired to guide the party out of the wilderness. In the circumstances, it is extraordinary that party lines held as firmly as they did in the legislative session.

The session itself was bitterly partisan from its very start. Republicans organized the Senate by 31-27 straight party-line votes. Organization of the House, however, proved more difficult. Though Republicans outnumbered Democrats 89-88, they lost the speakership through defection of three of their members who held patronage jobs in the Democratically controlled Chicago Metropolitan Sanitary District. The contest for the speakership precipitated a wild first-day scene in which the Secretary of State, presiding, adjourned the House before it was organized and the Democrats stayed in session to hear the message of the outgoing Republican governor. Despite Republican threats to hold up organization (and Kerner's inauguration) indefinitely if necessary, they finally yielded and Paul Powell, a Democratic down-stater who in 1959 had, with Republican help, beaten a Daley-sponsored candidate for speaker, reassumed the office with solid Democratic and slight but sufficient Republican support. With the speakership go considerable control over the flow of House business and the power to appoint committees.

Anger over loss of the speakership stayed with the Republicans throughout the session. It rendered more difficult agreement on a number of important items included in the new Governor's program, the most vital of which were revenue measures. The state faced a serious deficit prospect, and available reserves were depleted about the time the Kerner administration took office. To remedy the situation, the Governor urged submission to the voters of a new revenue article (almost inevitably the prelude to an income tax), a half-cent increase in state sales tax, broadening of the sales-tax base, and an increase in the corporation franchise tax. Mayor Daley added a plea for a half-cent increase in the sales tax permitted Illinois municipalities. Of these proposals, only the state sales tax increase and broadening were accepted by the legislature, the former only by the defection of four politically vulnerable Republicans who broke ranks despite a caucus decision. The Governor announced before adjournment that he would call a special session, probably in the fall, to reconsider the revenue question. In this political and legislative setting the regular session of the General Assembly considered, but failed to pass, a Congressional reapportionment act. At that point the practical alternatives were reapportionment in an autumn special session or election of all twenty-four congressmen at-large.

A review of the attempt to reapportion in the regular session will help to clarify what was at stake and what happened to inhibit solution of the problem. The participants in the struggle seem to have been principally motivated by (1) partisan advantage and (2) as much respect as possible for the presumptive right of any incumbent to retain his seat. The practical effects of these principles are sometimes countervailing, but this alone does not seem sufficient to explain the difficulties of reaching accommodation.

The political demography of the situation is pertinent. The Illinois Congressional delegation elected in 1960 included fourteen Democrats, of whom ten were from Cook County, and eleven Republicans, of whom three represented Cook County or partly Cook County districts. By 1960 Illinois districts ranged in size from 235,202 (First, William L. Dawson, D., Chicago south side), to 905,761 (Thirteenth, Marguerite Stitt Church, R., north Cook County suburbs plus Lake County). This disparity in size is largely the result of radical population shifts. Between 1950 and 1960 most of the State's 1,300,000 population gain had concentrated in Cook County suburban and other northern Illinois Republican strongholds.[8] Meanwhile, Chicago and down-state districts had tended either to lose population or to make only slight gains. To cite the extremes, Representative Dawson's district had lost 88,152 residents in the decade while Mrs. Church's had gained 439,697. In terms of population proportions, Chicago was entitled to 8.3 seats, the Cook County suburbs to 3.7, and the other 101 counties to twelve seats after the 1960 count.

Each party entered the reapportionment process with fairly firm ideas of its own goals. The Democrats sought to preserve as many safe Chicago districts as possible. They advocated that the state's lost seat be made up by combining two down-state Republican districts (Nineteenth and Twentieth) into one. They would then have remedied some of the population imbalance between city and suburban districts by extending the boundaries of the former into the latter, but probably not far enough to endanger Democratic control. The Republicans demanded that the number of Chicago districts be cut from ten to eight, that two down-state Democratic districts be combined, that the northern Illinois areas of rising population and Republican propensity gain seats, and that the suburbs not be contaminated by combination with Chicago areas. Along with these major changes went minor boundary revisions in both plans.

The parties, starting from these positions, were expected to reach some mutually acceptable accommodation during the course of the legislative session. The basic strategy was to have a Republican plan passed by the Senate and a Democratic plan passed by the House, and both then sent to a conference committee of ten. The conference was set up by a resolution adopted eleven days before the end of the session.

Given the population distribution and the firm Republican control of the Senate, it was anticipated that the Democratic sacrifice would have to be the greater. As time went on, speculation as to what the Democrats would give up began to take shape. Prominently mentioned as subjects for sacrifice were Rep. Peter Mack (Twenty-first, down-state)—whose district might, it was thought, be combined with the Twenty-third (Shipley, D.)—and Roman Pucinski (D., Eleventh), whose Chicago district might be dissolved. In the nether world of political rumor various rewards were anticipated for the prospective district-losers: organization slating for U.S. senator or a federal judgeship for Mack, a high federal executive appointment for Pucinski. Measured against the final outcome of the apportionment process, these rumors appear to have been fairly accurate.

Apparently the conference did not seriously attempt to resolve the conflict until the final two days of the session, one of these, July 1, falling after the clocks were stopped. By this time the Assembly was laboring under a burden of fatigue and partisan pique, the sales tax dispute not being settled until July 1. The reapportionment conference committee met in the afternoon and evening of July 1, with neither party willing to budge from its basic proposal. Anticipated Democratic concessions were not forthcoming. It is said that several telephone conversations with Mayor Daley produced only his demand that Democrats hold firm for ten Chicago districts. The Republicans, especially those from down-state, sensing that an at-large election would be to their advantage, refused to give in. Incumbent congressmen of both parties, including at least four actually present in Springfield at the time, were said to be urging that some basis for redistricting be found. The regular session was finally adjourned at midnight on Saturday, July 1, without final reapportionment action.

Review of the case suggests two explanations for the failure to reach a decision. One is the context of partisanship which rendered compromise difficult. The other is the failure of the mechanics of the legislative process, particularly their failure to provide time for solution. The Illinois legislature, typically for such bodies, works at a very leisurely pace in the early months of the session and reaches most important decisions in the final days. In the present case the bargaining process apparently was scarcely even begun earlier. The system for reaching accommodation may simply not have been put in motion soon enough to permit decision. It seems reasonable to suppose that a longer period of bargaining would have produced a decision; pressures on both sides for solution were substantial, and even a sharply divided legislature is an institution accustomed to reaching satisfying agreement. A contextual factor in the explanation of the Assembly's delay is that reapportionment was probably not only a game in itself but also part of the other games the legislature was playing, that is, it was being used as a bargaining token. It was variously rumored, for example, that the Democrats would make reapportionment concessions in exchange for concessions on one or another of the revenue issues. If this was the case, it is no surprise that efforts at solution of the reapportionment problem itself were held back so long that the mechanics of the decision-making process could not accommodate it.

## THE SPECIAL SESSION:

### REAPPORTIONMENT ACCOMPLISHED

Though the Governor continued to express some reluctance to do so, it was probably inevitable that he would include reapportionment on his call for the fall special session. The pressures for solution from nearly all sides, but especially from his own party, were strong. As things happened, it became increasingly clear that a comprehensive alteration of the revenue structure in the fall would be impossible, and reapportionment loomed larger as the main piece of legislative business. On September 26, he announced that the session would convene on October 10 and outlined the major problems to be specified in the call. These included reapportionment, a half-cent increase in the service occupational tax, a rise in the corporation franchise tax, state reimbursement of the Chicago Transit Authority for transportation of school children, addition of eighteen judges each to the Cook County Superior Court and Chicago Municipal Court, an additional appropriation for a Revenue Study Commission, and several minor items. All of the important items involved either hold-overs from, or revisions of, actions taken by the regular session.

Meanwhile, public speculation and private discussion on the reapportionment problem continued. Party leaders from both sides conferred and occasionally made brave statements about their indifference to the whole matter, and the Governor applied what pressure he could for

prenegotiated solution. A bipartisan committee of legislators, congressmen, and other party leaders apparently met some success, at least in
narrowing the area of disagreement. By the time the special session convened, however, there was not the measure of understanding between
the parties many had hoped for. During the period between sessions maps
were developed by both the Better Government Association, a Republican-oriented group, and the Independent Voters of Illinois, a liberal-
Democratic group, but neither appears to have had appreciable influence on the outcome.

The atmosphere of the special session was much like that of the
regular, with partisan feeling still running high and with little enthusiasm for the work at hand apparent. The session dragged on for six
weeks, finally adjourning the day before Thanksgiving. At various times
even up to the final days it appeared that nothing would be accomplished
on the Governor's priority items. Less than two weeks after the session
began, the Governor fired an uncharacteristic news-conference blast at
the Republican legislators, charging them with "circus clown antics,"
accusing them of playing "political roulette" with the welfare of the
citizens, and demanding a "positive, constructive approach" to the state's
problems. Shortly thereafter (though not necessarily because of it) a
Senate committee sharply questioned and rejected two Kerner appointees
to the newly established FEPC on grounds of dubious prior political af-
filiations. Thus in many respects the obstacles to reapportionment seemed
insurmountable. It should be noted at this point that even the rules
were stacked against it, for, to be effective in time for the 1962 primaries,
reapportionment legislation had to carry an emergency clause requiring
passage by two-thirds majority. Nevertheless, by its adjournment the
special session had seen not only the reapportionment problem settled
but also acceptance of most of the Governor's other major items, including the service occupation tax, Superior Court judgeships, and revenue
study funds.[9]

The mechanics of the special session were much like those of the
regular one, with the notable exception that the special session produced
positive results. Again, contradictory bills were passed in the two houses,
and the problem was sent to conference, where the real work of accommodation was carried out. One conference committee reported its inability to agree and was replaced before a second reached a satisfactory
solution, and even in the final few hours, as agreement was being patched
together, it repeatedly threatened to fall apart. When the leadership
groups had finally agreed, however, the compromise bill passed easily,
48-5 in the Senate, 141-29 in the House. All dissenting votes in the Senate
and all but three in the House were cast by Republicans.[10]

In general terms, three factors would seem to account for the success of reapportionment in the special session. One of these is that reapportionment did become the major item of business and therefore was not allowed to be caught in the machinery or to languish for want of attention. Though even the special session worked at a leisurely pace, its main focus was reapportionment; in effect the end of the session waited on the conclusion of the reapportionment struggle.

A second factor was the mounting sense of public pressure for action. Though such pressure is hard to measure, there is no doubt that it was felt to a greater or lesser degree by members of both parties. In ordinary circumstances the Illinois legislature is neither highly visible nor highly responsive to the people; in this case the public distaste for inaction and "political arrogance," complemented by a vociferous press, was, though not overwhelming, at least apparent.

A third factor was the hazard of the alternative to reapportionment, election at-large. It is difficult to judge the probabilities in such an election with any certainty, but at best it would have been expensive, confusing to voters, and risky for candidates and parties. Some politicians predicted that primaries would find more than one hundred candidates on each party ballot, and many supposed that one party or the other would sweep the delegation. The latter result would have deprived the state of the services of many respected, prominent, high-seniority congressmen. Probably some incumbents with state-wide reputations, for example, Mrs. Church and Rep. Noah Mason, would fare well in an at-large election; others, especially those from Cook County who are identified as "ethnics"—for example, Representatives Dawson (a Negro), Pucinski, Kluczynski, Libonati, and Rostenkowski, all Democrats, and Derwinski, a Republican—would be at a distinct disadvantage. At the party level, the Democrats would benefit from tighter unity and organization and their ability to turn out the Chicago vote. On the other hand, Republicans presumably would gain from the normal "midterm" effect in 1962 and from the presence at the head of their ticket of a well-known name, Sen. Everett McKinley Dirksen, as a candidate for re-election. (At the close of the special session the Democratic opponent for Dirksen had not yet been chosen by party slate-makers.)

Most observers thought the Republicans somewhat safer in an at-large situation. However, the variables were uncertain. Democrats dominated state-wide total Congressional votes in 1958 and 1960; Governor Kerner won the state by more than 500,000 and Sen. Paul Douglas by more than 400,000 in 1960. Yet, simple predictions were impossible; with few exceptions, incumbent congressmen of both parties pressed for districting. The imponderabilities of election at-large for both candidates and parties probably helped drive political leaders to agreement.

It is both impossible and unnecessary to go into detail here on the

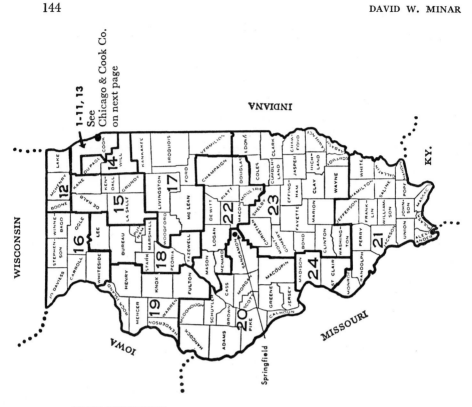

NEW DISTRICTS

CURRENT DISTRICTS

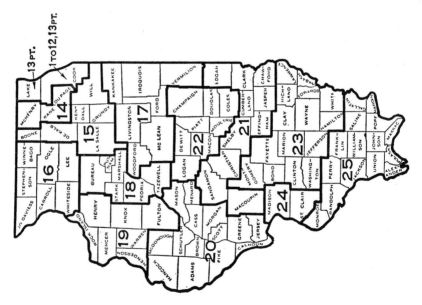

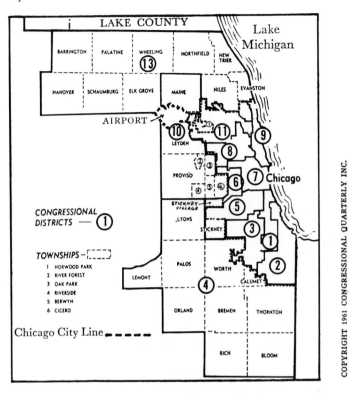

CHICAGO & COOK COUNTY

Assembly's reapportionment solution, but a few comments will illustrate its general political characteristics. The mean population of the twenty-four new districts is about 420,000, and the range is from 268,000 (Sixth, Democratic Chicago west side) to 520,000 (Tenth, Republican western Cook County suburbs).[11] Interestingly, the two extreme districts are contiguous. Down-state, aside from minor boundary shifts that for the most part magnified pre-existing party dominance, the major change came in the combination of parts of Representative Mack's Democratic district with parts of the Republican district of Rep. Paul Findley, in such fashion as to include the home communities of both in the new Twentieth. The new district is probably Republican, though neither incumbent was happy with the outcome. Lake, McHenry, and Boone counties in the state's northwest corner were combined to make a new, heavily Republican district.

The major problems arose, of course, in Cook County. Here, the first step was the combination of the districts of Democrats Sidney Yates and Edward Finnegan, with the agreement of both incumbents. Until the Democrats slated Yates to oppose Dirksen for the Senate seat in 1962, it was understood that Finnegan, a freshman congressman, would yield and go to the Superior Court bench. Including this district, the Democrats had eight Chicago seats in the safe or probably safe category and the Republicans three safe in the suburbs. The disposition of the twelfth Cook County seat was the final and most difficult question. It was solved by creation of a "swing" district (Eleventh) in northwest Chicago, including in it, along with some traditionally Democratic city area, a Republican ward and one suburban township. The composition of this district was the main subject of the final and crucial committee negotiations, the problem being what constituted a swing district. The only sitting member resident in the area is Roman Pucinski (D.), a young and notably vigorous campaigner.

Thus, on the basis of recent electoral performance, the new districting pattern seems likely to yield eleven Republicans and eleven Democrats, with two districts questionable. The even division of seats between Cook County and the rest of the state seems equitable. By the standard of equal population, however, the Chicago-suburban distribution is subject to question, with nine seats almost entirely based in city territory and three outside. One suburban district, the Thirteenth, includes one Chicago ward. The three suburban districts all retain populations over 500,000, about 60,000 more than the largest city district and almost twice the size of the smallest. Furthermore, the largest districts are those most likely to grow in the next decade.

## CONCLUSIONS

Though estimates of the probable party composition of the new Congressional delegation vary, observers, the newspapers, and many Republican politicians concede that the Democrats gave up much less than might have been expected.[12] The major explanation would seem to lie in their greater cohesion and more effective organization. In the course of the reapportionment process they seemed better able to unite on both tactics and goals; indeed, Democrats complained of the difficulty of finding Republicans with whom they could make authoritative agreements. By comparison, the power structure of the Democratic Party is well-defined and understood. The reward for party unity in this case was high. After the session ended, the newspapers quoted Republicans in such comments as: "You've got to hand it to 'em. They don't panic. They're real pros at this business." And "Republicans gave the ball game away every time." [13]

During the entire reapportionment struggle there was little evidence of important overt involvement by interest groups outside the parties, legislators, and incumbent congressmen. Two reasons may be suggested for this. One is that reapportionment has come to be regarded as a uniquely legislative and political function. The other is that the impact of reapportionment on "private" interests is so generalized and indirect that the problem does not often trigger group action. What small group interest in reapportionment there was in the present case was confined chiefly to those primarily motivated by abstract "good-government" aims and by those closely tied to one or the other political party.

The 1961 Congressional reapportionment process in Illinois illustrates many of the mechanisms that might be expected in a political setting of two-party competition. The principal forces at work were partisan, and the balance of the system dictated action, but action of the sort least likely to upset the political equilibrium. The structures of state politics proved able, but only with difficulty, to accommodate the conflict and produce a satisfying, if not optimal, solution. What advantage could be gained went to those who were best equipped in organization and leadership to operate within the confines of the game. But the outcome was one of accommodation. In summary it may be said that the story exemplifies both the frustrations of political deadlock and the ways a well-balanced political system can overcome them.

# Notes

[1] 328 U.S. 549 (1946).

[2] After the 1950 census the legislative districts (from each of which three representatives and one senator were elected) ranged in population from under 40,000 to over 700,000.

[3] For an excellent account of the 1954-1955 legislative reapportionment process see Gilbert Y. Steiner and Samuel K. Gove, *Legislative Politics in Illinois* (Urbana: University of Illinois Press, 1960), chaps. 4 f.

[4] *Illinois Constitution*, article IV, sec. 6.

[5] *Ibid.*, sec. 7.

[6] *Ibid.*, sec. 8.

[7] "In the twenty-nine legislative sessions since 1902, involving a total of 1,496 district elections, in only twenty-four instances (a mere 1.6 per cent) has one party captured all three seats . . . ." Austin Ranney, *Illinois Politics* (New York: New York University Press, 1960), p. 21.

[8] The last Congressional apportionment was made in 1951, when the state also lost one seat. The map was not extensively revised at that time; the lost seat was taken care of by combination of two down-state districts.

[9] Of the fourteen items on the Governor's call, ten were passed by the Assembly. Of the four rejected, one was regarded by the administration as a politically advantageous "throw-away" from the start.

[10] Dissenting votes in the Senate were cast by one Cook County suburban Republican (who publicly protested the inclusion of his home community in a city district) and four down-state Republicans, at least one of whom had Congressional ambitions destroyed by the apportionment. Of the twenty-six Republicans in the House who cast dissenting votes, twelve represent down-state districts, eleven Cook County suburbs, and three Chicago. The three Democratic dissenters all represent Assembly districts within or partially within Representative Mack's old Congressional district.

[11] The Cook County district population figures are estimates which vary somewhat from source to source.

[12] Some gloomy Republicans have predicted party distribution of the new seats as high as 14-10 in favor of the Democrats, a net loss of one Republican.

[13] *Chicago Sun-Times,* November 26, 1961, p. 18; November 23, 1961, p. 4.

148

# 8

## Pennsylvania

### THE LIMITS OF POWER IN A DIVIDED GOVERNMENT *

*EDWARD F. COOKE*
*University of Pittsburgh*

*WILLIAM J. KEEFE*
*Chatham College*

Possibly no question thrust before state legislatures is inherently more troublesome, more likely to arouse discontent, or more susceptible to hard bargaining than legislation to redistrict the state. It is not surprising, then, to learn that anyone who was to have much to do with Congressional redistricting legislation in Pennsylvania viewed the 1961 session with misgivings. And there were good grounds for such feeling, for, as the legislature set out to carve new districts from old, it faced several persistent and irksome conditions.

1. The state's leisurely rate of population growth was the most obvious fact. Unless Congress were to enlarge the membership of its lower house, Pennsylvania would lose three seats, dropping from thirty to twenty-seven.

2. Pennsylvania had been without an effective political majority since 1954, when the Democrats had captured the governorship for the first time in twenty years. Their 1954 victory did not extend to the Senate, which remained under Republican control. Again, in 1958, the Democrats won the governorship and the House, but lost the Senate. And finally, in 1960, they won

* The authors wish to thank Thomas Adams, a fellow of the National Center for Education in Politics working in the office of the Pennsylvania Democratic State Committee, and their colleagues J. Dale Chastain and Albert J. Ossman of Chatham College and Morris Ogul of the University of Pittsburgh for their critical advice and suggestions.

149

the House but could only gain an even split (25-25) in the Senate. Between 1954 and 1961, Pennsylvania state government was conducted under circumstances common to many Northern states where Democrats win the governor's chair and Republicans win one or both houses of the legislature. Politics during this interval consisted as usual of negotiations, artful compromise, and occasional sleight of hand.

3. A close look at the 1960 census of population revealed an embarrassing fact. The arsenal of Democratic strength in the state, Philadelphia, had lost 3.3 per cent of its population during the past decade, while the state as a whole increased by 7.8 per cent. This fact had to be viewed against another hard statistic: Philadelphia had produced a 331,544 margin for John F. Kennedy in the 1960 election, an accomplishment that more than neutralized the heavy rural and small-town Republican vote, and Pennsylvania had given its thirty-two electoral votes to the Democratic candidate. The state's prominent Democrats, including the governor, found it difficult to forget this fact; the state's prominent Republicans, including the state chairman, were not in a mood to ignore it.

4. The state legislature, though formally charged with Congressional redistricting, was itself a notably unrepresentative institution. The Senate was last redistricted in 1921. The House, redistricted in 1953, was only slightly more representative, since the equality principle has been emasculated by the constitutional provision that each county be accorded at least one representative. Despite pious declarations in their platforms, neither party was anxious to reapportion the General Assembly. Rural Republicans and in particular big-city Democrats looked askance at the matter, for both would lose seats. The big gainers in an equitable reapportionment act would be the suburban areas, and rural Republicans in Pennsylvania are sometimes as chary of their colleagues who live on the outskirts of the big cities as they are of the Democrats who live within.

5. There were few signs of creative altruism among either party's Congressional delegation. One Democrat, Francis E. Walter, of Easton, dropped early hints that he might retire at the end of the current session, thereby helping to relieve the congestion, but no one was wagering on it. The Democratic floor leader of the Pennsylvania House, Stephen McCann, put the problem succinctly: "Show me three congressmen who are willing to give up their seats."

6. The possibilities of stalemate were realized from the outset.

The Republican Party could not hope to pass its own redistricting bill, and it was unlikely that the Democrats could push their version through a fifty-member Senate divided equally between the parties. (A majority of the membership, or twenty-six votes, is required for the passage of bills.)

## THE SETTING

The record of the General Assembly in the passage of Congresssional redistricting acts has not been distinguished by excessive delays or by intense partisanship; ordinarily it has done the job with dispatch. One reason for this is that until 1931 Pennsylvania had the pleasant task of adding districts. Since that time the problem has been to eliminate districts—two in 1931, one in 1941, three in 1951, and again three after the 1960 census. In addition, past control of the redistricting machinery by the Republican Party diminished the likelihood of protracted negotiations. In 1941-1942, however, the Democrats held a majority in the House and were able to prolong deliberations until a compromise measure was formulated; this act provided for thirty-two districts and one congressman-at-large. On assuming full control of the legislature and the governorship in 1943, the Republicans passed a new and (to them) more favorable redistricting act. The 1951 act, also passed by Republican majorities, eliminated one Democratic district in northeastern Pennsylvania and two marginal districts in western Pennsylvania.[1]

Although Pennsylvania legislators are apparently no less partisan than those of other states, previous Congressional redistricting acts have not been marked by conspicuous gerrymandering. The state's geography, its uneven population distribution, and the willingness of its politicians to live with conventional arrangements have tended to constrict the majority's opportunity to shape districts in the party interest. Table 1 furnishes certain evidence on this point.

Since the 1931 reapportionment act, the difference between the percentage of seats won and the Republican proportion of the two-party vote has averaged about four per cent. In the usual election, the Republicans have picked up one more seat than the number to which their vote would entitle them. In landslide years, such as 1946, the Republicans tend to win most of the marginal districts, thereby increasing their representation substantially without a commensurate increase in vote. It is possible, as in 1954 and 1960, for the Republicans to obtain more than a majority of the seats with less than a majority of the two-party vote. Nonetheless, Table 1 shows that the parties are fairly evenly balanced, a condition which leaders in both parties sought to obfuscate during the public debates of 1961.

TABLE 1

PARTY PROPORTION OF TWO-PARTY VOTE FOR CONGRESSMEN
AND NUMBER OF SEATS WON, 1932-1960

| | Republican | | | Democratic | | |
|---|---|---|---|---|---|---|
| Year | No. seats | Per cent seats | Per cent 2-party vote | No. seats | Per cent seats | Per cent 2-party vote |
| 1932 | 22 | 65 | 54 | 12 | 35 | 46 |
| 1934 | 11 | 32 | 48 | 23 | 68 | 52 |
| 1936 | 7 | 21 | 44 | 27 | 79 | 56 |
| 1938 | 20 | 59 | 53 | 14 | 41 | 47 |
| 1940 | 15 | 44 | 48 | 19 | 56 | 52 |
| 1942 | 19 | 58 | 53 | 14 | 42 | 47 |
| 1944 | 18 | 55 | 49 | 15 | 45 | 51 |
| 1946 | 28 | 85 | 58 | 5 | 15 | 42 |
| 1948 | 18 | 54 | 51 | 15 | 46 | 49 |
| 1950 | 20 | 61 | 52 | 13 | 39 | 48 |
| 1952 | 19 | 63 | 52 | 11 | 37 | 48 |
| 1954 | 16 | 53 | 49 | 14 | 47 | 51 |
| 1956 | 17 | 57 | 53 | 13 | 43 | 47 |
| 1958 | 14 | 47 | 49 | 16 | 53 | 51 |
| 1960 | 16 | 53 | 48 | 14 | 47 | 52 |

Although the vote-seat ratio shows that the Democrats have been consistently disadvantaged, an equitable redistricting would not automatically improve their position. Indeed, the negative differential between seats and votes for the Democrats might increase. Since 1931, a majority of the overpopulated districts have been won by Republicans, while the underpopulated districts have ordinarily (up to the 1950's) been divided about equally between the parties. Covering the period 1931-1960, Table 2 marks off the most extreme instances of inequality of population—districts with a plus or minus 15 per cent of the ratio. It shows that the most overpopulated districts have been Republican. In 1960, at the other extreme, there were eight Democratic and four Republican districts that were at least 15 per cent under the population ratio for the state; five of the eight Democratic districts were in Philadelphia.

Table 3 relates population data to types of Congressional districts. The principal beneficiaries of malapportionment over the 1931-1960 period have been rural and urban-industrial districts. During the decade 1950-1960, population movement from city to suburb led to significant

TABLE 2

PARTY REPRESENTATION IN OVER- AND UNDERPOPULATED
CONGRESSIONAL DISTRICTS, 1931-1960

| Year | Republican +15 −15 | | Marginal* +15 −15 | | Democrats +15 −15 | | Total districts +15 and −15 | Total number districts |
|------|------|------|------|------|------|------|------|------|
| 1931 | 1 | 3 | 2 | 1 | 1 | 2 | 10 | 34 |
| 1942 | 3 | 2 | 0 | 0 | 0 | 2 | 7 | 32 |
| 1943 | 4 | 4 | 1 | 0 | 1 | 1 | 11 | 33 |
| 1951 | 2 | 2 | 0 | 0 | 1 | 2 | 7 | 30 |
| 1960 | 4 | 4 | 0 | 2 | 0 | 8 | 18 | 30 |

* A marginal district is defined as one having a 55-45 per-cent vote distribution and a history during the life of the districting act of being carried at least twice by each party.

underrepresentation of suburbs and overrepresentation of cities. In 1960, no Congressional district classified as "urban-industrial" was underrepresented; nine were overrepresented. The First District in Philadelphia, for example, was 158,469 under the average for the state (419,236), while neighboring suburban Delaware County was 133,918 over the ratio.

TABLE 3

OVERREPRESENTATION AND UNDERREPRESENTATION OF
CONGRESSIONAL DISTRICTS, ACCORDING TO
RURAL-URBAN CHARACTERISTICS *

| Year | Rural +15% −15% | | Semirural +15% −15% | | Suburban +15% −15% | | Urban-Industrial +15% −15% | |
|------|------|------|------|------|------|------|------|------|
| 1931 | 1 | 3 | 1 | 0 | 0 | 1 | 2 | 2 |
| 1942 | 2 | 1 | 0 | 0 | 0 | 0 | 1 | 3 |
| 1943 | 0 | 4 | 4 | 0 | 0 | 0 | 2 | 1 |
| 1951 | 1 | 2 | 1 | 0 | 1 | 0 | 0 | 2 |
| 1960 | 0 | 2 | 1 | 3 | 3 | 0 | 0 | 9 |

* Rural districts are those whose population is classified by the Census Bureau as over 40 per cent rural, usually open country; semirural have between 40 and 60 per cent rural populations, usually industrial cities surrounded by rural counties; suburban are densely populated fringe areas on the periphery of metropolitan centers; and urban-industrial districts are those in which the population exceeds 60 per cent urban with an industrial economic base.

From a geographical standpoint, the most extreme cases of malapportionment in 1960 occurred in eastern Pennsylvania. Each of the four suburban Congressional districts around Philadelphia had populations in excess of 100,000 over the average for the state, and all returned Republicans to Congress. Moreover, the six counties comprising these four districts had, in the 1952-1960 interval, an average Republican registration of 71 per cent and average Republican vote of 61 per cent; in 1960 they contributed 22 per cent of the total Republican Congressional vote in the state. Five of the six Congressional districts in Philadelphia were underpopulated. Two of the five districts fell short of the district population ratio by more than 100,000 people. All six seats in the Philadelphia Congressional delegation were held by Democrats.

## THE LEGISLATURE WAITS ON CONGRESS

State legislatures seldom gain a reputation for brisk action, and the Pennsylvania General Assembly is no exception. But, given the obstacles to writing a new Congressional redistricting act in 1961, it is understandable that the legislature put off the task as long as it could. Moreover, a possibility existed that Congress might simplify matters by voting to enlarge the size of the House. If the House were increased only slightly, to 438 members, Pennsylvania would lose only two of its thirty seats. A House of 452 members would mean that Pennsylvania would lose only one seat, and a House of 469 members would eliminate Pennsylvania's losses altogether. Hence, so long as a chance remained that Congress might expand its membership, as it had often done in the distant past, party leaders in and out of the legislature chose to concentrate their energies on other matters. By early summer, however, hope had all but vanished that Congress would bail the state out, for by then Speaker Rayburn was adamantly opposed to expansion. The solution, then, had to be sought within the state and its political structure.

Complicating efforts to obtain an agreement were serious intraparty pressures. The Philadelphia delegation presented a special problem for the Democrats. Of the 109 Democratic votes in the lower house, thirty-eight were from Philadelphia; on crucial matters these votes were invariably cast in a bloc (at the command of City Chairman (Congressman) William J. Green, it is usually said). Eight of the twenty-five Democrats in the Senate were also Philadelphians, including the president *pro tem* and the majority leader. For good measure, the presiding officer, the lieutenant governor, was also a "Green man." In both houses, it is fair to say, Green had an extraordinarily prominent voice in the formulation of Democratic policy. If the Democratic Party was to be unified in the redistricting struggle, it was plain that the interests of Congressman Green and the Philadelphia delegation would have to be taken into account.

The Republicans had troubles of their own in the 1961 session. As an aftermath of the 1960 Democratic victories, a coalition of eastern and western urban and suburban Republicans wrested the leadership of the House away from rural Republicans. A young Allegheny County suburbanite, Willard F. Agnew, Jr., was elected minority leader. However, midway through the 1961 session, Representative Agnew died suddenly, and in the subsequent caucus the minority leadership reverted to the rural wing of the party by the election of a former minority leader, Albert W. Johnson, of McKean County.

## THE SEARCH FOR PARTY AND AREA
## ADVANTAGE IN REDISTRICTING BILLS

Only after the prospect of Congressional relief had faded did the parties set out in earnest to draft redistricting bills.[2] Numerous bills were introduced during the spring and summer months, but only two received much consideration. The principal Republican proposal was introduced in the House in mid-June. Brought out simply for bargaining purposes and weighted heavily on the Republican side, the bill had no chance of passage. It received but scant debate in the legislature and minimal attention in the press.

Following weeks of negotiations among party leaders, the Democratic redistricting bill was launched in the House on August 7. Even though the main outlines of the bill had been rumored well in advance of this date, its introduction had an explosive effect. The bill had been drafted in the party spirit, and it was wholly objectionable to the Republicans. Whereas the principal objective of the Republican plan had been to pare Philadelphia's Congressional delegation from six to five, the Democratic plan retained all six. Under the Democratic bill, two of Philadelphia's six Congressional districts would be expanded into adjacent suburban counties: four townships in Delaware County (Haverford, Radnor, Marple, and Newtown) would be added to the Second District in Philadelphia, and Bensalem Township in Bucks County would be linked to Philadelphia's Fifth District. By adding these suburban areas to Philadelphia districts and redistributing certain wards among the other city Congressional districts, the Democratic plan offered a better mathematical argument for retaining six seats "in" Philadelphia.[3]

Equally objectionable to the Republicans were the other features of the Democratic plan. In the east-central portion of the state two incumbent Republicans would be thrown into the same district, thus eliminating one Republican. Also in the east, another new district was fashioned which would square off an incumbent Democrat against an incumbent Republican, with the odds greatly favoring the Democrat. The same plan was pursued in western Pennsylvania, again placing a

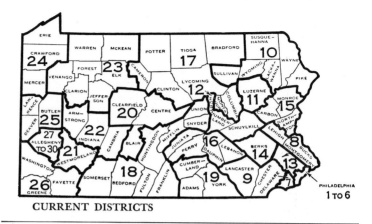

CURRENT DISTRICTS

NEW DISTRICTS

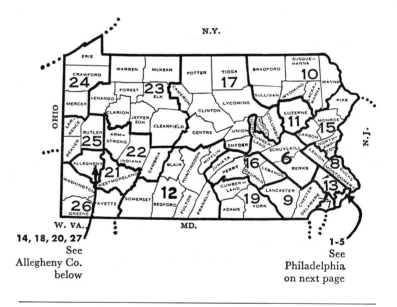

14, 18, 20, 27
See
Allegheny Co.
below

1-5
See
Philadelphia
on next page

ALLEGHENY COUNTY

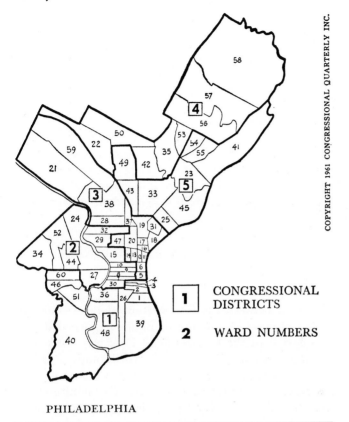

**1** CONGRESSIONAL DISTRICTS

**2** WARD NUMBERS

PHILADELPHIA

Democratic incumbent and a Republican incumbent in a district designed to elect a Democrat. In addition, the Democratic bill rearranged the four districts in Allegheny County (Pittsburgh) in such a way that three Democrats would supplant the two-and-two formula that had persisted since the county was last redistricted by a Republican legislature. All in all, only seven of the state's thirty Congressional districts would retain their pristine purity, were the Democratic bill enacted.

Among the first to comment on the Democratic bill following its formal introduction was George I. Bloom, Republican state chairman. In his view, the bill was "absurd," a "fraud," nothing less than a "legislative monstrosity." The Democratic reapportionment plan, he contended, would eliminate six Republicans and no Democrats, and he went on to point out:

> Significantly, two districts which would have the fewest number of voters are located in Philadelphia (First and Fourth) which squirms under the heavy hand of Congressman William J. Green, Democratic

ruler in Pennsylvania. The plan advanced by Democrats is an attempt
to extend their spending-and-tax philosophy by an instrument of absolute political immorality since it does not give recognition to Republican influence and responsibility. The Democrats are intent on
forcing their brand of scandal-ridden Philadelphia government into
the Republican suburbs adjacent to the city [in order to] annex portions of those counties to Philadelphia.[4]

In a similar vein, the Republican floor leader in the House remarked
that not a single Republican vote would be forthcoming for a bill that
retained the Philadelphia delegation at six. "We expect Philadelphia to
give up a congressman, we are willing to give up one and then sit down
with Democrats and figure out as fairly as possible where the other seat
can be cut." This was the initial Republican demand; it proved eventually to be the formula for settlement.

## AUGUST TO NOVEMBER 7: IMPASSE, HEIGHTENED
## ARGUMENT, AND A CAMPAIGN ISSUE

Three months elapsed between the introduction of the Democratic
bill and the November election. A number of things happened during
this interval, but resolution of the Congressional issue was not among
them. Three other developments are, however, worth noting. In the
first place, the legislature's control over redistricting, which had been
tenuous at best, slipped away when the governor and other nonlegislative
party leaders entered the fray actively and publicly. Second, Republican
strategy came to focus on the Democratic bill as a campaign issue, notably
on its provisions concerning Philadelphia and its suburbs. Third, prolonged stalemate produced increasing anxiety over the possibility that
all twenty-seven congressmen would be elected at-large. Incumbent congressmen, who seem sensitive to things of this sort, worried most of all.

Well before the legislature adjourned in early September, the governor's office had become the center for redistricting negotiations between
the parties. In a press release of August 14, Gov. David L. Lawrence
acknowledged the difficulty of bringing about a redistricting bill that
would satisfy both parties:

A Republican bill has been introduced and a Democratic proposal has
been advanced, and it is apparent that each is objectionable to the
other side. There has been much hue and cry from both sides, but
little effort to arrive at a solution which we must have if people of
Pennsylvania are to be properly represented in the Congress. . . . To
be properly represented, of course, demands that every attempt be made
to have the new districts equal in population. . . . If we are to [achieve
this], it is clear that intra-State political boundaries would have to be
crossed as they are in many states, including New York, New Jersey,

Ohio and Maryland, to mention just those which adjoin us. . . . Accordingly, I am inviting the Chairmen and Secretaries of both political parties, together with three Congressmen selected by each party, and the floor leaders of both parties in the Legislature, to meet with me in the Governor's Office to seek areas of agreement.

Shortly after this announcement, leaders of both parties met in the Governor's office to search for "areas of agreement," a compromise plan that would satisfy both parties. Very little was achieved at this initial meeting. None of the six congressmen who had been invited were able to attend, since a foreign aid bill was under consideration in Congress; moreover, no representatives from Philadelphia were present. In a statement to the press following the meeting, the Republican state chairman remarked, "I don't think we made any particular progress. But they certainly understand our position and we understand theirs." The sticky issue had been Philadelphia; Republican spokesmen, backed by solid caucus votes in the Senate and House, insisted that Philadelphia must give up one congressman before an agreement could be reached. Nor would they accept any plan that extended Philadelphia Congressional districts into suburban counties.[5] The Democratic state chairman, Otis B. Morse, summed up the meeting with a lament that Mr. Bloom "thinks of Philadelphia as a small town. We think of it as a metropolitan area."

Several additional meetings of the bipartisan committee were held in succeeding weeks. Philadelphia continued to be the major cause of distress: "We won't put six seats in Philadelphia," Chairman Bloom said again and again. The only significant agreement reached by the parties in these meetings, and it was only tentative, provided that the four Allegheny County districts would remain relatively unchanged, apparently eliminating the peril to one of the two Republican seats.

The redistricting problem remained unsolved when the General Assembly adjourned in September, and legislators left Harrisburg bitter and disappointed. If new Congressional districts were to be drawn before the 1962 election, such action would have to be taken in a special session of the legislature, to be held either in November or December or to run concurrently with the "taxes-and-appropriations" session beginning in January. The only bright spot in a bleak picture appeared in the Governor's statement that he would call a special session if the parties could agree *in advance* on a redistricting plan. "To capriciously call a special session and have another go-around," he said, "doesn't appeal to me at all."

## A Campaign Issue: "The Green Grab"

Round one in the bout over redistricting ended in a draw. Round two, which was fought in southeastern Pennsylvania between late August and the November election, was won decisively by the Republicans, using a campaign issue handed them by the Democrats. Known variously as "the Green Grab," "the Billymander," and "the Green Kidnap Bill," the issue was manufactured out of the Democratic redistricting bill that would retain six congressmen in Philadelphia. By itself, according to the 1960 census, Philadelphia was entitled to 4.78 congressmen, but by linking five suburban townships to two city districts Philadelphia was able to strengthen its claim to six seats. Who had forged the "link"? To the Republican Party and most of the state's vigilant newspapers, at least, the culprit was Congressman William J. Green, Democratic city chairman of Philadelphia, referred to by both the tabloids and respectable papers as "Boss" Green.

Odd-year elections are held in Pennsylvania to fill local offices, but in 1961 one state-wide office, a twenty-one-year term on the Pennsylvania Supreme Court, was also voted upon. Voters in western, central, and northern Pennsylvania concentrated on selecting city council members, district attorneys, a variety of other local officials, and the Supreme Court justice. But in southeastern Pennsylvania—Philadelphia and its surrounding counties—election campaigns centered on "Boss" Green and his plan to "annex" suburban territory to Philadelphia. By now the redistricting plan offered by the Democrats in August had become "Green's Plan" for "suburb-snatching."

Very few, if any, election campaigns in Pennsylvania have been so dominated by a single issue as this one. "Annexation" was the issue, perhaps the *only* issue used by the Republican Party, as one political writer for a Philadelphia suburban paper contends.[6] An "Anti-Annexation Committee of Southeastern Pennsylvania" was formed to alert suburbanites to the new menace, and it carried the message to community after community in "antiannexation" rallies. Young Republicans distributed "Stop the Green Grab" bumper stickers throughout Delaware County, and in Upper Darby, for example, posters were plastered everywhere, imploring the citizens to "Stop the Green Grab, Vote Republican, Keep Philadelphia Out of Upper Darby." A Montgomery County Republican Anti-Annexation Committee warned in a pamphlet that the redistricting proposal was only a first step: "City spokesmen have advocated making the suburbs an actual part of the metropolitan city government. Such an eventuality would mean suburban citizens would be saddled with Philadelphia's staggering debt, soaring crime rates, machine politics and the other ills bred by big city political bossism." Petitions protesting "the Green Plan" were signed by 15,000 residents of Haverford Township, one of the communities to be joined to a Philadelphia Congressional district, and given to a local Republican state senator for forwarding to Governor Lawrence.

Whatever the ethics of the "annexation" argument, it, combined with other anxieties induced by "Billymandering" and "bossism," had a startling impact upon the voters in Philadelphia and the suburban counties. The Democratic candidate for the Supreme Court lost the state by 72,000 votes, carrying Philadelphia by only 85,000 votes. In 1960, it is worth recalling, Philadelphia had given John F. Kennedy a majority of 331,544, and in 1958 it had given the Democratic candidate for governor, David L. Lawrence, a majority of 177,000. Indeed, since 1952, when Philadelphia turned in a majority of 160,000 votes for Adlai Stevenson while the rest of the nation voted Republican, the city had been the stronghold of Pennsylvania's Democrats. In the suburban counties in 1961 the story was the same. Although the Democratic Party had been making steady gains over the years, it was routed in this election, with the Republican vote reaching heights that had not been enjoyed in years. And in the townships singled out for attachment to the city districts, Republican victories were overwhelming.

Not all of the Republican success in southeastern Pennsylvania, of course, could be attributed to the redistricting boomerang, but observers unanimously agreed that this factor far outweighed all others in influencing election results. So great was the Democratic drop in Philadelphia itself that Green's own Congressional district supported the Republican candidate for the Supreme Court.

## NOVEMBER THROUGH JANUARY: RISING

## EXPECTATIONS AND FINAL ACCOMMODATION

How much the election results were due to the issue of the "Green Grab" and how much to other factors, including popular resentment against the "machine," remains problematical. The blame for the fiasco, in any case, was laid squarely on Congressman Green. Suburban Democrats, not unexpectedly, traced their humiliating defeats to the "grab." And from two other quarters shortly after the election came other criticisms. Numerous speakers at a meeting of the Philadelphia AFL-CIO Council attributed the poor showing of Democrats to the redistricting issue, and Philadelphia Mayor Richardson Dilworth, who had up to then stayed aloof from the fray, charged that the issue had been "murderous" and urged the Philadelphia organization to adopt a more reasonable attitude toward redistricting. Another step in the party's reappraisal occurred at the Governor's first press conference following the election. It was a "cold fact," he said, that the Democratic Party and its candidate for the Supreme Court had been hurt by the redistricting squabble. Putting these things together, observers concluded that the election had generated new pressures within the Democratic Party for a settlement with the Republican Party.

The first break in the stalemate came on December 6 at a meeting in Harrisburg of Green and eight other Democratic congressmen with Governor Lawrence, State Chairman Morse, and State Party Secretary Genevieve Blatt. By all accounts, Green was now under heavy pressure from his non-Philadelphia colleagues, state leaders, and organized labor to accept five seats for Philadelphia. Newspaper stories from Washington intimated that the White House wanted Green to abandon a Philadelphia seat. Reluctantly, Green gave way. In addition, final agreement was reached that the district of Democratic Congressman George M. Rhodes (the Fourteenth) would become part of the new "swing district" —one that would be evenly balanced between the parties. The meeting adjourned with the understanding that Green would determine how Philadelphia was to be redistricted and that he would make the announcement.

Optimism prevailed in Harrisburg, and some leaders thought that a special session could be called before the Christmas holidays. But Green did not meet with his Philadelphia delegation until December 19; at this meeting he relayed the bad news and was authorized to devise a five-district plan. Another secret meeting was held on January 3, and the word was passed to Chairman Morse that Philadelphia was now ready. Morse immediately called his Republican counterpart, George Bloom, to arrange a meeting.

On Monday, January 8, Governor Lawrence met with Bloom and Morse and they agreed to hold a meeting that night, to be attended by the two state chairmen and their top aides. An understanding was reached that night that the Democrats would relinquish one seat in Philadelphia and that the Republicans would combine two existing districts in central Pennsylvania to form one district. Both sides also agreed that Green and the Philadelphia organization would have complete control over the city's redistricting and that the Republicans would have a free hand in fashioning their central Pennsylvania district. (Later, Wilbur H. Hamilton, Philadelphia Republican leader, was to call Green's plan "the worst kind of gerrymandering ever submitted to the General Assembly"; Lawrence's answer to this was that "Mr. Hamilton should have made his squawk a long time ago to Mr. Bloom.") Finally, the boundaries of the new "swing district" were discussed, but no agreement was reached. The timetable now called for a meeting of the parties' negotiators with the General Assembly's Select Committee on Reapportionment in order to obtain final agreement on the details.

The select committee, made up of party leaders in both houses plus several other senators and representatives, met with Bloom and his assistant Martin Brackbill, Morse, Blatt, and Joseph Lockard of Green's headquarters on January 10. The Democrats confirmed their plan to eliminate a Philadelphia district but gave no indication of how this would be done. The Republicans submitted their proposal to combine Congressmen Whalley's (Eighteenth) and Van Zandt's (Twentieth) districts. Both sides agreed that there would be no changes in the Allegheny County districts. The Van Zandt district was to be eliminated by assigning Clearfield County to the Twenty-Third District (Congressman Gavin, R.), Centre County to the Seventeenth District (Schneebeli, R.), and Blair County to the new Twelfth (Whalley-Van Zandt). Union and Snyder counties, formerly in Whalley's district, would be added to the Seventeenth. It was decided that Luzerne County would remain untouched, though its population would be some 17 per cent under the ratio. Each side submitted several plans for a "swing district" in eastern Pennsylvania. The Democrats hoped to combine the old Fourteenth District (Berks County) with part of the old Twelfth (Schuylkill County). This district would give the Democratic incumbent, Rhodes, a clear edge over his rival, Ivor D. Fenton. The Republican proposal, advanced by State Senator M. Harvey Taylor, venerable leader in Republican state politics, was to combine Fenton's old district of Northumberland and Schuylkill counties with Northampton and Carbon counties, the major portions of Francis E. Walter's old district. This arrangement would pit the two deans of the Pennsylvania delegations against each other. The meeting broke up without resolving the conflict over the swing district.

On Saturday, January 13, Lawrence criticized the Republican's proposed swing district as too large and unwieldy, and in Washington Congressman Fenton declared that he had no desire to run against Walter. On the following Monday, the committee again took up the problem. State Senator Taylor, who now appeared to be the Republican wagonmaster, pushed the Fenton-Walter district to a point where the Democrats abandoned the Berks-Schuylkill county arrangement and compromised with the addition of Northumberland County to Berks and Schuylkill.[7] The committee also agreed to move Bradford County, a Republican stronghold, into the Tenth District, thus making it more secure for Republican incumbent William Scranton. Walter's district, grossly underpopulated, was disturbed only slightly by the addition of Pike County, bringing it over the 300,000 mark. Although neither party was completely satisfied, Chairman Bloom reported that "there was a majority vote from members of the committee on each side."

On the following day, January 16, Republican and Democratic caucuses met in both houses to consider the compromise plan; they accepted it by substantial majorities. In Washington, Congressman Van

Zandt criticized the compromise, saying that he had never been consulted about reapportionment.[8] Congressman Fenton issued a statement labeling the proposed bill a "kiss of death" to his twenty-three-year political career.[9] On January 16, Governor Lawrence consulted with Democratic and Republican legislative leaders and then issued a call for a special session of the General Assembly to begin on January 22.

Although the select committee had first announced that no changes would be made in Allegheny County's four districts and subsequently reported the need for only minor changes, the final plan contained significant alterations to these districts. The Allegheny plan, attributed to the four incumbents but largely the work of Congressmen James G. Fulton (R.) and Elmer J. Holland (D.), strengthened the position of each of the incumbents by transferring opposition wards and municipalities to other districts. Why these changes were made is something of a mystery, and Governor Lawrence was quoted as being "furious" at the committee's acceptance of the congressmen's proposal.[10] In 1961, Governor Lawrence had rejected a similar plan advanced by the Greater Pittsburgh Chamber of Commerce in conjunction with the four congressmen. With a five-to-three registration edge in the county, Democratic leaders believed that the redistricting should have assured the party of a three-to-one advantage. The 1962 scheme is likely to perpetuate the two-to-two division for some time.

Although agreements were by now firm and arrangements were in order for convening of the special session, not even the Governor knew the details of Green's plan for Philadelphia. Late Thursday evening, January 18, Democratic state headquarters received the Philadelphia plan, barely in time to get it to the printer for introduction on Monday. Released to the Philadelphia press on Friday morning, the plan met a storm of protest. Instead of eliminating the district of Congressman James A. Byrne, on whom early speculation had settled,[11] the Green proposal called for Mrs. Kathryn E. Granahan to give up her seat. U.S. Senator Joseph S. Clark (D.), beginning his campaign for re-election, deplored Mrs. Granahan's removal, and Democratic leaders outside Philadelphia privately expressed disbelief. Republicans everywhere were quick to commiserate the victim, the lone woman in the entire Pennsylvania Congressional delegation.

Having lost the battle to retain six seats in Philadelphia, Democratic leaders resolved to make the remaining five as securely Democratic as possible. Indications are that headquarters started with the idea of eliminating Byrne's district but came to the conclusion that Mrs. Granahan's would represent a better choice in terms of party advantage. Their task was further complicated by the location of Negro districts. This problem could be minimized by eliminating Mrs. Granahan's district.

Finally, a maximum advantage to the incumbents as well as to the party could be realized by the sacrifice of Mrs. Granahan. Congressman Green's own district, for example, had voted Republican in the 1961 elections, and it seemed to require shoring-up. Early in the negotiations in 1961, a Philadelphia civic group, the Committee of Seventy, had publicized its own redistricting plan for the city which, if enacted, would very likely have resulted in a three-two party split.[12] The Republican threat to Democratic hegemony was thus sufficient to induce Congressman Green and aides to jettison Mrs. Granahan. A writer for the *Philadelphia Evening Bulletin,* John C. Calpin, viewed the Green formula in power terms: "Whether he intended it that way or not, Congressman William J. Green's personal plan for reapportioning the city's Congressional districts seems to have fixed it so that there can be no effective, cohesive opposition to his leadership."

After the Philadelphia fireworks, writing the political agreements into law was a formality. The redistricting bill was introduced in the House as a bipartisan measure on Monday, January 22, given a first reading, and referred to the Committee on Reapportionment. A brief debate took place on second reading the following day, and the bill passed easily, 182-20, on Wednesday morning, January 24. Seven Democrats and thirteen Republicans opposed its passage. The Senate took up the bill that afternoon, gave it a first reading and referred it to committee, and within four minutes the bill had been reported out favorably. On Thursday night, January 25, the Senate gave the bill a fast second reading, paused until after midnight, and passed it.

On January 29, a week from the day it was introduced, the redistricting bill was signed into law by the Governor. His remarks at the time caught the prevailing mood:

> It does not meet the standards of either fairness or equity. . . . Its only virtue is that it prevents the chaos which would result from having Pennsylvania's 27 congressmen running at large. . . . In signing it, I want to emphasize that no one should consider it to be a final solution to the reapportionment problem.

The Governor's signature did not put the matter to rest. On February 6, the Judiciary Committee of the U.S. House of Representatives approved a bill sponsored by Pennsylvania Congressman Francis Walter (D.) increasing the size of the House to 438 members. Under its terms, three states which had lost seats—Massachusetts, Missouri, and Pennsylvania—would each be awarded one seat. The official explanation for the bill was that none of the forty-eight states should be "victims" of the admission of the newest states, which had received three seats under the 1960 apportionment—Hawaii two and Alaska one. In fact, however, the expansionist bill appears to have been designed mainly to contribute to a compromise in Massachusetts where a Republican governor and a Democratic legislature were deadlocked over plans to eliminate two seats and, more importantly, to help avoid the possibility that the new speaker of the House, John McCormack, would have to run at-large.

Despite widespread predictions that the bill would pass handily, it was killed by recommittal to committee on March 8. Support for the bill disappeared when, after a remarkably confusing debate, an amendment by Congressman Walter was adopted which eliminated a provision that the states affected (in this case Missouri and Pennsylvania) could either draw up new redistricting laws *or* elect the additional member at-large. The amendment provided that Missouri, which had lost only one seat in the 1960 census and was now regaining it, could elect its eleven congressmen from the old districts. Congressman Walter had earlier arranged with leaders of both parties in Pennsylvania that another special session of the legislature would be called and that the Rhodes-Fenton swing district would be split into two districts, thus absorbing the new seat.

However, it was brought out in debate over the Walter amendment, that if the Pennsylvania legislature did not meet or, having met, failed to pass a new redistricting bill, then the provisions of the automatic apportionment act of 1929 would take effect, and all twenty-eight seats would be filled by an at-large election. After a considerable delay, brought about by the demand of a Pennsylvania Republican member that an engrossed copy of the bill be prepared before the vote on passage, the bill was again brought up for consideration. Pennsylvania congressmen, especially Republicans, were now convinced that the Walter amendment had increased the risk that all twenty-eight congressmen would have to run at-large. Remembering the frustrations of the past year, they were unwilling to take a chance on the legislature drafting a new law and were fearful that their nominating petitions would be declared void, since under existing law March 12 was the last day for filing petitions. Enough other congressmen came to their rescue to recommit the bill, and thus ended a year of negotiations over plans to increase the membership of the House.

## CONCLUSION

Estimates of party gains and losses in the redistricting outcome rest on intuition and assorted statistics. Each party, of course, lost a seat outright. The swing district is about as evenly balanced between the parties as it was possible to make it—only 1,478 registrations in the new district separated the parties in 1961, only 1,989 votes separated the candidates in 1960. The edge, such as it is, belongs to George M. Rhodes, the Democratic incumbent. The Democratic concession on Bradford County strengthened Republican Scranton's hold on the Tenth District, and the options given the Republicans in rearranging central Pennsylvania districts served to solidify their position in the Twelfth and Seventeenth districts. The decision on Allegheny County will undoubtedly help the Republicans to retain two of the four seats. The agreement to leave Luzerne County alone and not to tamper significantly with Congressman Walter's underpopulated district represented an advantage for the Democrats.

On the basis of past performance, the twenty-seven districts would divide as follows: eleven safe Republican, twelve safe Democratic, three marginal, and one even. A comparable breakdown for the 1952-1960 elections would be: fourteen safe Republican, thirteen safe Democratic, and three marginal. At first glance it may appear that the new act has aided the Democrats more than the Republicans. A detailed examination of voting patterns in the new districts, however, shows that the Democrats have reached a maximum in safe districts. Moreover, the three marginal districts tilt toward the Republican Party. A normal election year might be expected to result in the election of fourteen Republicans and twelve Democrats, with the new Sixth District a toss-up. A landslide election for either party could produce a 17-10 division. The new law will have a minimal impact upon the party composition of the Pennsylvania delegation.

Population parity was not given high priority, and the districts ranged from a high of 553,154 in the Seventh District to a low of 303,026 in the Fifteenth, though the 1962 act did reduce the number of districts significantly above and below the state mean. Suburbia continues to be sadly underrepresented. Pennsylvania Republican congressmen will represent an average of 47,000 more people per district than will Democratic congressmen because of the failure to cross county lines in the formation of districts. A comparison of the 1951 and 1962 acts in terms of population deviations from the state mean is given in Table 4.

### TABLE 4

|      | Republican +15% | Republican −15% | Marginal +15% | Marginal −15% | Democratic +15% | Democratic −15% |
|------|------|------|------|------|------|------|
| 1951 | 2 | 2 | 0 | 0 | 1 | 2 |
| 1962 | 4 | 0 | 1 | 0 | 0 | 1 |

|      | Rural +15% | Rural −15% | Semirural +15% | Semirural −15% | Suburban +15% | Suburban −15% | Urban-Industrial +15% | Urban-Industrial −15% |
|------|------|------|------|------|------|------|------|------|
| 1951 | 1 | 2 | 1 | 0 | 1 | 0 | 0 | 2 |
| 1962 | 0 | 0 | 1 | 0 | 3 | 0 | 1 | 1 |

In the main, the 1962 Congressional redistricting act was fashioned by a few leaders in each party. After a year's sparring over proposals designed in the party interest, they settled on a plan of unadorned expediency, one that temporarily solved "the problem." Pressure groups were neither especially active nor influential in the struggle, and one of them (the Greater Pittsburgh Chamber of Commerce) was told pointedly by the Governor that it should mind its own business and leave reapportionment to public officials.

State legislators introduced a variety of redistricting bills, several of which could only be called zany, but with perhaps the exception of that of Sen. M. Harvey Taylor (R.), their role was minimal in the total process. The scope of the conflict was, in fact, too wide for a legislature divided in party control. Moreover, since no state legislator's career was on the line, only a few members became greatly aroused when the legislature early lost control of the issue to the Governor, the state party chairmen, and the key congressmen. Limiting the range of legislative action was, of course, the adamant position of Philadelphia City Chairman Green. Eight votes in the Senate and thirty-eight in the House assured Green of a veto over any redistricting bill he opposed. On the Republican side, Senator Taylor and his leadership in a divided Senate had to be reckoned with before agreement could be obtained.

The parties' Congressional delegations were active in the protracted dispute, but their over-all impact seems not to have been substantial. Fearful of an at-large election, they sought to keep the issue before the public, the legislature, and the party chieftains. Representatives of the delegations also met on several occasions with state party leaders in Harrisburg and Washington to seek a way out of the impasse. Congressmen in both parties joined forces to press for passage of a bill that would enlarge the size of the House of Representatives and thereby diminish Pennsylvania's problem. Neither delegation, *qua* delegation, presented a redistricting plan to the state leaders, but some individual congressmen whose districts appeared to be in jeopardy submitted proposals. The final settlement on Allegheny County (Pittsburgh) was the handiwork of the county's two Democratic and two Republican congressmen, and it served the best interests of *both* incumbents. Republican congressmen, though echoing their state chairman's confidence in an at-large election, were privately apprehensive, especially as they viewed the 1962 primary. Several Democratic congressmen were openly fearful of an at-large free-for-all.

The most conspicuous congressman in either delegation was, of course, William J. Green, but his prominence was due to his position as leader of the Democratic Party in Philadelphia and the city's large delegation in the state legislature. It was Green who posed the crucial problem in the exasperating struggle, and it remained for Republican leaders and the newspapers to sharpen and elaborate it and an election to settle it.

One fact concerning the role of Pennsylvania congressmen in the redistricting process emerges most clearly. It concerns the single-minded devotion of each congressman to a basic principle: the most important political life that any congressman can save is his own. In this redistricting at least, Democratic incumbents were quite willing to see the districts of Republican incumbents made safer if, in the process, their own positions could be strengthened, and Republicans felt the same way. From the vantage point of an incumbent, the party interest in redistricting appears thin and insubstantial.

On the Republican side, the redistricting struggle was linked with the problem of selecting a state-wide ticket for the 1962 election. The decision of Republican leaders to eliminate Congressman James Van Zandt's district was apparently made with a view to slating him for governor or U.S. senator. Shortly after the bill was adopted, Van Zandt became an announced candidate for the Senate. His willingness to contest for a state-wide office conveniently settled the problem of choosing the district to abandon. By contrast, the Democratic choice was both painful and circumscribed. There was almost no leeway for maneuver, since Republican leaders, especially Chairman Bloom, had insisted from the outset that a Philadelphia seat be eliminated. Finally, following weeks of rumors in December and January, Congresswoman Kathryn Granahan's district was chosen, even though she had more seniority than two of the other Philadelphia congressmen.

With no more than occasional difficulty, the Governor wore two hats during the long battle. Publicly, the Governor stood above the squabbling of partisans, adopting at times a "plague-on-both-your-houses" position. Every now and then he spoke out against certain Republican redistricting proposals, and he also took pains to support Congressman Green's stand that there was nothing irregular in a plan to extend one or more of Philadelphia's districts into surrounding counties. Yet, throughout, his public tone was predominantly conciliatory. Privately, as a long-time Democratic leader, the Governor naturally desired a plan most favorable to his party, but to represent his interest in party advantage he delegated considerable power to Democratic State Chairman Otis Morse. In retrospect, it appears that the Governor's willingness to forsake the role of active party leader helped immeasurably to foster conditions under which a compromise was possible. His office became the instrument for winning an expedient settlement, the most that could be hoped for under the circumstances.

Despite the alterations made in Congressional districts (eleven were not affected in any way), their general layout will seem familiar upon inspection. Following two "rules"—that each party be given a free hand in cutting out a district (except that the Democrats were forced to limit their choice to Philadelphia) and that each party's safe districts might well be made safer—the parties' leaderships arrived at an uneasy accommodation. Both rules, of course, are ordinarily inimical to standards of fair apportionment. Nonetheless, the problem could be unraveled in no other way.

Delay in the passage of a redistricting act came close to immobilizing Pennsylvania state government for a year. The issue drove other news of the legislature off the front pages or otherwise submerged it. The controversy did nothing to put life back into the legislature; indeed, the legislature may have lost ground in its quest for public esteem, for it was unable to do anything by itself to break the impasse. The long delay produced waves of anxieties and a multitude of new hostilities within and between the parties. And the mind boggles at the thought of the hours consumed by congressmen, state legislators, and party leaders in mulling over the issue and developing plans for its resolution.

Perhaps out of all this the public, or some parts of it, got a sharpened sense of the perils that attend the resolution of issues when party control of government is divided. But the public did not secure an equitable rearrangement of districts. Hardly anyone, save congressmen from safe districts, is satisfied with the law. It goes without saying that the first party to control the governorship and both houses of the legislature will be strongly tempted to undo the 1962 act in favor of a new arrangement, and it may be that the bitterness of 1961-1962 will encourage the coming majority to adopt a redistricting formula weighted heavily in its interest.

# Notes

1 Act of 1931 (P.L. 1416); Act of 1942 (P.L. 7); Act of 1943 (P.L. 256); Act of 1951 (P.L. 1734).

2 Democratic state leaders had met with the Democratic Congressional delegation on April 13 and had placed responsibility on these incumbents for an appropriate redistricting plan. A July 1 deadline was suggested, and a committee of three—Green, Holland, and Rhodes—was set up. Neither the committee nor the delegation took action. On June 17, Governor Lawrence and State Chairman Morse hurried to Washington and again met with the Democratic delegation. Lawrence received a final "no" from Speaker Rayburn on the possibility of increasing the size of the House and attempted to impress upon the delegation the necessity for the congressmen to propose a plan.

3 On the basis of twenty-seven seats, the average population per district would be 419,236 people. Even with the addition of suburban territory, none of the six Philadelphia districts would have met the standard. The largest district of the six would have 382,919 people and the smallest 332,223. Another district would have 333,496. Both the small districts would have less than 80 per cent of a ratio.

4 *Philadelphia Evening Bulletin,* Aug. 7, 1961.

5 Republican strategy, it appears, was to confuse the Congressional redistricting picture by bringing into the debate the state constitutional ban on crossing county boundaries for senate districts. No legal barrier existed, and, in fact, in the 1942 act the Twenty-Fifth District included the whole of Washington County plus a part of Allegheny County. Republican Chairman Bloom had at one time suggested crossing county lines, but in such a way as to assure Republican majorities. Bloom did not push this plan because, first, the Democratic plan had become a campaign issue and, second, county leaders in suburban Philadelphia preferred one-county districts even if it meant underrepresentation.

6 Letter to the authors by a writer who prefers to remain anonymous.

7 Taylor's strategy was in part directed toward preserving the sixteenth, his home district, where he rules supreme. The Democratic plan would have attached Northumberland to this district. Taylor was also playing gubernatorial politics at this point.

8 Underlying the selection of Van Zandt's district for consolidation was the feeling held by many Republican leaders, including Bloom, that Van Zandt would become the Republican U.S. senatorial candidate.

9 Bloom never met formally with the entire Republican Congressional delegation, though he communicated with individual congressmen. Moreover, a special subcommittee of Republican state legislators had been set up to work with Bloom on redistricting. On this subcommittee were Van Zandt's county representative (also county chair-

man) and Fenton's state senator. Both Representative Holiday and Senator Wagner were members of the Select Committee on Reapportionment which negotiated the final settlement.

[10] Governor Lawrence suggested, but without much supporting evidence, that the Allegheny County changes were part of a deal to compensate the Republicans for giving Green a free hand in the Philadelphia redistricting.

[11] The basis for the speculation was that the other five congressmen had firmer support: Green was the party leader; Granahan, the only female representative; Nix, a Negro; Toll, Jewish; and Barrett had seniority and power in his own right.

[12] Philadelphia's lone Republican state legislator, Austin M. Lee, offered an amendment in the House which was almost the same as the Committee of Seventy's plan.

# 9

# Apportionment and Districting in Ohio
## COMPONENTS OF DEADLOCK *

*HERBERT WALTZER*
*Miami University*

In many ways Ohio is a microcosm of politics in the United States, and it offers an interesting case study in American politics.[1] In recent years the distribution of the popular vote in Ohio presidential elections has closely approximated that of the total national vote. Since 1900 the Buckeye State has cast its electoral votes for the national victor in fourteen of sixteen presidential elections.[2]

Ohio does not fit the stereotype of a Midwestern state under Republican domination. In both state and national elections it has strong two-party competition. To be sure, the Republicans enjoy a slight advantage, but it is an edge that is slim and frequently upset. Illustrative of the closely competitive party politics in Ohio are its presidential elections. Since 1900 the Republicans have won ten presidential elections to six for the Democrats. The Republicans have averaged 53.7 per cent of the popular vote, and the Democrats 46.3 per cent.[3] However, the election of 1932 and the Roosevelt New Deal marked the emergence of a new and broadened Democratic coalition and the tightening of two-party competition in Ohio. Since 1932 each major party has won four presidential elections, the Republicans with an average popular vote of 51.4 per cent and the Democrats with an average of 48.6 per cent.

Ohio's Republicans have controlled the state's Congressional delegations by a more than a two-to-one ratio, even though the Democrats closely contest these elections. Since 1940 the Democrats have only once

* A note of special appreciation must be extended to Rep. Robert F. Groneman of the Ohio General Assembly and Prof. Howard White of the Department of Government, Miami University, for their assistance and counsel in the preparation of this study.

(1948) won a majority of Ohio seats in the Congress. However, in gubernatorial elections the Democrats have won nine of fourteen contests since 1932, although the average Democratic vote in these elections was 50.1 per cent to 49.9 per cent for the Republican contenders. Although the Democrats have demonstrated the capacity to mold state-wide majorities in presidential and gubernatorial elections, the Republicans have dominated the state legislature. The Democrats closely contest them in terms of the aggregate state-wide vote for representative and senator in the Ohio General Assembly, but the Republicans have enjoyed more and larger majorities in both chambers of the legislature. This has frequently produced divided government. In six of the eleven legislative bienniums since 1940 one or both houses of the General Assembly have been controlled by the party *not* in the governor's mansion.

Divided state government partly explains the difficulty of coping with the politically explosive issues of apportionment and districting in Ohio and is itself in large measure explained by the nature of the state's system of legislative representation. In Ohio, divided government usually means a Democratic governor and a Republican legislature. Although the Democrats are traditionally strong in some rural counties, their greatest strength is in metropolitan counties, where there has been a marked increase in Democratic voting since 1920. The Republicans frequently win majorities in a few metropolitan counties, but they are predominately strong, and growing stronger, in the rural counties. The apportionment system in the lower house gives a clear advantage to the rural areas of the state and consequently to the Republican party. This handicaps the Democrats in the House; but it does not, as in some states, guarantee their defeat. In strong Democratic years (such as 1948 and 1958), they can win a majority in the House, in part because with a heavy Democratic vote they can profit from the at-large feature of legislative elections in metropolitan counties.

Ohio is typical of the many states of the Union in which the democratic principle of "one person, one vote" is diluted if not nullified by apportionment and districting mechanisms that produce disproportionate representation. In Ohio, and in other states, this issue is the focus of partisan, sectional, and interest-group battles. Therefore Ohio offers an illuminating case study of the problems of apportionment and districting and of the political struggles over what has become the Holy Trinity of the state's underrepresented: (1) *reapportionment* of representation in the state legislature to bring it more in accordance with population; (2) *subdistricting* of multiple-member legislative districts to eliminate the "bed-sheet ballot" and the discrimination against the minority party that such at-large elections often involve; and (3) *redistricting* of the state's Congressional constituencies to accommodate decennial changes in Congressional apportionment and/or equalize Congressional districts in accordance with population.

## REAPPORTIONMENT

The history of apportionment in Ohio begins with the Northwest Ordinance which provided for a territorial legislature composed of one representative for every 500 free male inhabitants. The first state constitution of 1802 established a bicameral legislature (General Assembly) of a House of Representatives and a Senate. The thirty seats in the House and the fifteen in the Senate were to be apportioned among the state's nine counties in accordance with population.

In 1851 a more populous and complex Ohio adopted a new constitution which established the basic system of legislative apportionment that is in effect today.[4] The effort was made to devise a mechanism that would: (1) distribute legislative representation in accordance with population; (2) provide a nonpolitical and self-operating mathematical formula to avoid or reduce partisan wrangling; (3) accommodate population changes more easily by *not* fixing any limits to the size of either house of the General Assembly; and (4) exclude the legislature from exercising any voice in the determination of its own apportionment.

The system is based on the decennial federal census or any similar population count that might be substituted. The unit of representation for the Ohio House of Representatives, the more numerous branch, is the county, of which there are eighty-eight. After each census a ratio of representation for the House is established by dividing the state's population (9,706,397 in 1960) by 100 (a ratio of 97,064). A county with at least a one-half ratio is entitled to one representative; with at least a one and three-quarters ratio, two seats; with three ratios, three seats; four ratios, four seats; and so on. A system of fractions adds to a county's representation during the decennial period, which embraces five General Assemblies. When a county has a population fraction above its full ratios that equals one-fifth a ratio, it receives an additional seat in the fifth General Assembly of that decennial period; a fraction of a two-fifths ratio entitles a county to an additional seat in the fourth and third bienniums; a fraction of a three-fifths ratio earns an extra seat in the third, second, and first bienniums; and so on. The system of distribution of fractional representation spreads the resulting additional membership in the House over the five bienniums of the decennial period.

Apportionment of the Ohio Senate is accomplished in a similar manner. The ratio of representation is determined by dividing the state's population by thirty-five (a ratio of 277,326). The state is divided into thirty-five senatorial districts composed of several counties or a single county if it has a population equal to at least a full Senate ratio and is therefore entitled to separate representation. There are only four counties that qualify to stand alone as senatorial districts—Cuyahoga (Cleveland), Hamilton (Cincinnati), Lucas (Toledo), and Summit (Akron). Moreover, disproportionate population increases have resulted in twenty-six of the multiple-county senatorial districts falling below the minimum ratio for one senator and being combined into multiple-district election units. The largest includes four senatorial districts incorporating nine counties. A fractional representation system provides for additional part-time seats to senatorial districts in a manner similar to that employed in the House.

Finally, the administration of the legislative apportionment system is placed in the hands of a board composed of the governor, auditor, and secretary of state. The board is required to "ascertain and determine the ratio(s) of representation" six months prior to the election following a federal census. This is done for the five bienniums of the ten-year census period. The action of the board is not subject to legislative or judicial review, except that recourse to the courts is available if the board fails to perform its responsibilities.

Although a county receives one representative if it has a population of one-half to one and three-fourths a ratio, this apportionment system does make an effort to base representation on population. What, then, is the problem? In 1850 Ohio had a population approaching 2,000,-000 that was 12.2 per cent urban and 87.8 per cent rural. With this population distribution, the apportionment formula did injustice to only a few. In 1900 the state had more than 4,000,000 people, 48 per cent of whom lived in urban areas and 52 per cent of whom lived in rural areas. Only 35 per cent of the people lived on farms, and only one-third of the labor force worked directly in agriculture. Moreover, the population additions were concentrating in a few industrial centers, and the number of counties that could meet the minimum one-half ratio requirement for separate representation in the House continued to decrease. These counties were rural and largely Republican. A continuation of the "numbers game" would have soon meant that the power as well as the population scale would tip in the direction of the urbanite and the Democratic Party. In 1903 Mark Hanna, with typical political astuteness, realized the consequences of this population trend as it would affect the urban-rural and Democratic-Republican balances in the House. He was also interested in winning the support of the rural Republicans in his bid for nomination and election to the United States Senate. Hanna lead the movement for the adoption of a constitutional amendment which adds the simple but shattering proviso that "each county shall have one representative" in the House regardless of its population.

The "Hanna Amendment" in effect eliminates the minimum requirement of at least one-half a ratio for a county to earn the separate representation of its own seat in the House. This provision and recent population changes have combined to help make Ohio a model of disproportionate representation. Ohio's population today is 70 per cent urban and 30 per cent rural. The state's rate of population growth is above the national average, and the new population is almost entirely urban. Less than 9 per cent of the people live on farms, and only 1.7 per cent of Ohio's gross personal income is earned in farming. In terms of representation in the House of Representatives, forty-eight of the eighty-eight counties (55 per cent) do not have populations equal to the one-half ratio formerly required as a minimum for separate representation. Moreover, seventy-one of the eighty-eight counties (81 per cent) do not have populations equal to a full ratio. These seventy-one counties have 31 per cent of the state's population and 52 per cent of the seats in the House. The seventeen most populous counties have 69 per cent of the population but just 48 per cent of the representation in the House. One voter in the state's smallest county (Vinton, 10,247) casts a ballot equal to ten votes in the largest (Cuyahoga, 1,647,895 and seventeen House seats). The state's representation problem is obviously complicated by a great unevenness in population growth and distribution. The more uniform the distribution of a state's population density, the more pleasantly manageable is its task of legislative apportionment and districting. Few states have this comfort. Only eight of Ohio's counties, each with one large city, are classified as metropolitan in character. Moreover, only Cuyahoga County, with its city of Cleveland, appears to have a population conscious of being the victim of gross underrepresentation.

Any alteration of this apportionment system must be accomplished by the laborious process of constitutional revision. Political scientists, politicians, and reformers would agree that the avenue of constitutional amendment is a difficult one, strewn with obstacles. The question of a constitutional convention arose in 1932 and 1952 in Ohio. In both instances the issue of disproportionate representation was raised in support of the call. In both instances the voters chose not to convene a convention. Resort to the initiative petition method of placing a proposed amendment on the ballot for ratification by popular vote has thus far proven equally unsuccessful. In 1929 George Bender, then a Republican state senator from Cleveland, launched a campaign to obtain 250,000 signatures on such a petition. Business interests in the state persuaded the Republican Party and Bender to call off his initiative drive. In 1940 a similar campaign was opened by an official of the Cleveland Carpenters' Union. It terminated when he was convicted for accepting a bribe and sent to the penitentiary. The third method of initiating constitutional

revision is by legislative proposal. As might be expected, many proposals have been made, but none have been passed by the legislature.

The first order of business presented to the 1961 session of the
Ohio House of Representatives was a resolution introduced by four
Cuyahoga Democrats which provided for the repeal of the Hanna Amendment. What little support appeared for this proposal to eliminate the
guarantee of one representative to every county came entirely from Cleveland. *The Cleveland Press,* a Scripps-Howard newspaper enjoying the
editorship of Louis Seltzer, gave the proposal full news coverage and
editorial support. The Republican-oriented *Cleveland Plain Dealer* was
not interested in having more Democrats than necessary sent to the
House from Cuyahoga County. The resolution received little attention in
the rest of the state.

The Cleveland Federation of Labor endorsed the proposal to end
the guarantee of one representative per county. Its support prompted
one of the sponsors of the proposed amendment to say: "We only hope,
now that this forward looking group of civic-minded citizens has acted,
that others—such as the [Cleveland] League of Women Voters, the
Women's City Club, the Chamber of Commerce, and the Citizens League
—will see fit to join in this crusade to give just representation to those
areas now deprived of fair and equitable representation." [5] These organizations called to the colors of reapportionment are groups with allegiance to the party which would not benefit from more equitable representation for Cleveland. Moreover, the sponsors of the proposal hoped
that, if legislative action would not put the question on the ballot, the
Ohio AFL-CIO would provide the manpower to obtain the 400,000
signatures required for an initiative petition. Although organized labor
in Cleveland had endorsed the proposed amendment in principle, support by action was not provided by Ohio labor generally.

The Democrats of Cuyahoga County could not move the state's
Democratic governor, Michael V. DiSalle, to come to their aid. Repeal
of the Hanna Amendment would certainly add to Democratic representation in the House, especially from Democratic Cuyahoga County.
But DiSalle was feuding with and trying to break the political power
of Sen. Ray Miller, leader of Cuyahoga's Democrats. Senator Miller had
refused to support the "favorite-son" slate of delegates to the 1960 Democratic national convention that was pledged to DiSalle. Neither a treaty
nor a truce was negotiated between DiSalle and the Cuyahoga Democrats, and the Governor sat the resolution out. Moreover, the Governor
had other and tactically more important issues to contest with the
Republican majorities he faced in both houses of the General Assembly.
Even with DiSalle's support, it is questionable whether the resolution

would even have obtained a hearing. Republican Speaker of the House Roger Cloud, when asked about the proposed amendment, replied:

> I don't think we need it. I'm not speaking now from a purely rural viewpoint. I think it is of some advantage to have every segment of the State represented geographically. I can't see that this is wholly unjust.
>
> After all, the rural legislators don't control. I would say 65% to 75% of the legislators are chosen on a population basis. I have no objection, however, to holding hearings. But I don't think they can get it out of committee.[6]

Speaker Cloud proved to be correct in his prediction. Hearings were not held, and the resolution died in committee. The issue of disproportionate representation in the Ohio House of Representatives has thus far failed to generate any interest or concern in the state as a whole or among interest groups or civic organizations. It is not expected that the Republicans will take up the gauntlet of changing an apportionment system that makes them the majority party in the legislature more often than not. Even the Democrats must tread lightly in this area. They still depend on several traditionally Democratic rural counties for a margin of their state-wide majority. Until they can rely more completely on their urban vote, they will move with caution on reapportionment. The propensity toward divided government in Ohio, in large part a product of the apportionment system, will serve in turn as an obstacle to any alteration of the apportionment system.

The issue of disproportionate representation in the House remains with Ohioans. As the size of the metropolitan and urban vote continues to increase, concern with this question will grow. The Democrats will make political campaign capital of the inequities of the system of representation. However, it will undoubtedly require a Democratic sweep of the state—Democratic control of the governor's mansion and both chambers of the General Assembly—and a major campaign to mold popular support for the needed constitutional revision. If this ever comes to pass, it will no doubt precipitate a glorious and bitter political battle.

Finally, repeal of the Hanna Amendment would not transform the Buckeye State into a utopia of political equality and representation based purely on population. It would significantly reduce existing unfairness and inequality of representation in the House. But the Ohio Constitution would still grant one representative to counties with between half a ratio and a full ratio. Under the present ratio of representation, 26 per cent of the counties with less than one ratio but at least half a ratio would be overrepresented, and more and more counties will fit into this category with future population changes. The answer to the question of equitable representation in the Ohio General Assembly is not to be found simply in the repeal of the Hanna Amendment. It is to be found in complete revision of the apportionment system or, more simply and indirectly, in the consolidation of counties to eliminate the smaller and less populous ones. Political soothsaying reveals neither in Ohio's near future.

## SUBDISTRICTING

The counties and senatorial districts in Ohio with multiple representation in the General Assembly select their representatives and senators in at-large elections. In 1960 the voters of Cuyahoga County cast ballots for seventeen representatives and six senators in an at-large election. The other urban counties and senatorial districts, though they do not approach the population and legislative representation of Cuyahoga, use a similar system. The advocates of subdistricting urge that these large multiple-member counties and senatorial districts be divided into smaller units for election and representation purposes. Some propose that subdistricting be mandatory, others that it be permissive and left to the judgment of the voters in the areas affected. Some advocate subdistricting into single-member constituencies, others that the smaller units elect a few representatives or senators on an at-large basis. The proponents of subdistricting argue that the "bed-sheet ballot" created by the present system imposes an unnecessary and intolerable burden on the voters, produces nonvoting or "blind" voting, and denies fair representation to the minority party.

Although a proposal to subdistrict large constituencies into smaller election units might appear to be simple, understandable, and technically desirable, this is a delicate political question that the parties have handled with caution and an acute sensitivity to their partisan interests. There is a strong tendency in these at-large elections for the majority party to sweep all or almost all the seats of the constituency. In 1960 the Republicans of Cuyahoga County sent only one representative to the General Assembly. Democratic Summit County (Akron) sent a completely Democratic delegation to the state capital. Hamilton County (Cincinnati) elected three Republican senators, eight Republican representatives, and one Democratic representative. Therefore, both parties benefit in their sections of strength from the system of at-large elections.

The Republicans are eager to have subdistricting in Cuyahoga County, where they are the minority party. Their pockets of strength, now smothered by the Democratic majority in at-large, county-wide elections, would probably provide them with several more seats if they were made into separate smaller constituencies. The Democrats are equally eager to extend subdistricting to the Republican strongholds of Hamilton and Franklin (Columbus) counties, and for the same political reasons.

In 1961 the platform of the Ohio Republican Party advocated subdistricting for counties with five or more senators and fifteen or more representatives in the General Assembly. To put it more directly, it urged subdistricting for Cuyahoga, the only county with the required amount of representation. The Democrats responded by suggesting a more general subdistricting system that would include the other populous counties. At the opening of the 1961 session of the General Assembly, Rep. William Taft, the lone Republican in the Cuyahoga delegation, introduced a proposal for the subdistricting of counties with twelve or more seats in the House. The county second to Cuyahoga in representation in the House is Hamilton, with nine seats. He did not suggest senatorial subdistricting, and his plan was permissive. An initiative petition signed by 3 per cent of the voters in a county would put the question of subdistricting to the voters on a referendum. If a majority of those voting cast affirmative ballots, the county board of elections was to divide the county into not less than three nor more than five districts. These districts were to be approximately equal in population, compact in shape and boundary, and to conform as nearly as possible to existing natural and political boundaries. The Democrats parried by proposing subdistricting for all counties that by themselves constitute senatorial districts: Cuyahoga, Hamilton, Lucas (Toledo), and Summit.

Cleveland provided the only support for these subdistricting proposals. The *Cleveland Plain Dealer,* silent on reapportionment, supported the Taft proposal. Hearings were held by the House Committee on Elections and Federal Relations. The chief witness on behalf of the Taft plan was Harry Broder, a humanities instructor at Case Institute of Technology and chairman of the Citizens for a Shorter Ballot, a Cleveland organization. Other supporting witnesses represented the League of Women Voters, Women's City Club, Citizens League, and the NAACP. With the exception of the last-named group, all are Cleveland organizations which failed to answer the call to support the repeal of the Hanna Amendment.

The subdistricting proposals never left committee. The Republican majority in the General Assembly was not anxious to ram the Taft proposal, which would have permitted subdistricting in Cuyahoga County, through the legislature only to have it vetoed with an accompanying and appropriately biting broadside by Governor DiSalle condemning the partisan nature of the scheme. Moreover, while it might be in the interest of Cuyahoga Republicans to win subdistricting, it might not be in the interest of the state Republican Party to accept a general subdistricting

plan that would undercut the Republican advantage in Hamilton and
Franklin counties and possibly involve a loss of seats equal to or greater
than the gains that might be made in Cleveland. The Republican
majorities in these urban counties have made it well known that they are
firmly opposed to any subdistricting plan that would involve them and
affect their advantage. Indeed, they are cautious about subdistricting for
Cuyahoga in fear that it might establish a precedent that would later
return to haunt them.

The Democrats will not accept subdistricting that does not include
the urban counties other than Cuyahoga. Again, subdistricting may be
to the advantage of Democrats in Cincinnati and Columbus, but it is not
in the interest of their fellow partisans in Cleveland, Akron, and Toledo
and might in total impact involve no gains or possible losses of representation in the General Assembly. Moreover, Ohio politicians of both parties
are hesitant to burden themselves with the headache of partisan wrangling
over boundaries and the threat of gerrymandering that would probably
be the result of the required subdistricting. There is no evidence that
sufficient public enthusiasm can be mustered in behalf of subdistricting
to prompt legislative action or accomplishment of a subdistricting plan
by initiative petition. If there is to be subdistricting, it will have to come
as part of a general revision of the system of apportionment and districting of the General Assembly. Both parties have vested interests in elements of the existing system. It would be contrary to experience and the
evidence to expect or hope for either complete or compromise revision
in the near future.

### REDISTRICTING

In its 160 years as a state, Ohio has made eighteen changes in its Congressional districting. Rarely have these alterations had anything to do
with basing of representation on population. Indeed, from 1880 to 1892,
as control of the General Assembly shifted from one party to the other,
each celebrated victory by redrawing the state's Congressional map along
partisan lines. In the early part of the twentieth century, the Prohibition-
ists blocked redistricting because it would have added strength to the
Wets of the "big cities." Ohio had its first congressman-at-large in 1913
and has sent congressmen-at-large to eleven sessions of Congress in this
century, an indication of the difficulty in handling this question and the
tendency to avoid it through the temporary expedient of a congressman-
at-large.

The 1960 federal census and the resulting national reapportionment
among the states of House seats rewarded Ohio with a twenty-fourth seat
because its population increase was above average. The Democrats

promptly demanded general redistricting of the state to equalize districts in accordance with population. Governor DiSalle urged the empaneling of a bipartisan commission to develop a new and fair map of twenty-four Congressional districts. Its recommendations were to be submitted to the General Assembly for action. The newspapers in Cuyahoga and Montgomery (Dayton) counties picked up the battle cry and advocated total redistricting. It was pointed out that Ohio's Congressional districts range from 57 to 178 per cent of what the average population of the state's districts should be (422,017). Ohio boasts the sixth largest Congressional district in the United States—the Third District, which includes Montgomery and Butler counties and 726,156 people. Republican State Chairman Ray Bliss refused to serve on the proposed commission, arguing that redistricting should be left to the state legislature. In the absence of Republican cooperation, the idea of a bipartisan commission was abandoned.

The focus of attention shifted to the Republican-controlled General Assembly, and the question narrowed to whether Ohio would elect a congressman-at-large in 1962 or would find a twenty-fourth district for him —and where. Journalists and others offered the Republicans friendly and often unsolicited advice. They warned that, unless the Republicans were sure of maintaining their majorities in the 1963 General Assembly, they ought to create a twenty-fourth district. Otherwise, the Democrats would use their failure to do so as an excuse to redistrict the whole state, and to Democratic advantage. The Democrats knew that any redistricting plan that took into account the question of numbers of people would benefit them. They prepared to enjoy the spectacle of the opposition party trying to redistrict against itself. More than a dozen separate redistricting plans were introduced in the House of Representatives. A Subcommittee on Congressional Redistricting was organized in the House Committee on Elections and Federal Relations to review them. In its report, the subcommittee stated that, in evaluating the various proposals for redistricting, it considered the factors of equalization of district population, the geographical area of districts, the similarity of constituencies in individual districts, and the residence and district of incumbent congressmen. The subcommittee acknowledged that "it has been pointed out that unless there is a substantial equality of population in the various districts, the end result may be a disinfranchisement [*sic*] of the voter in the overpopulated districts." However, it asserted that "the factor of equality of population should not be the sole criterion for the committee in making its final determination in this matter" and singled out the factor of "equalization of interest" as having equal importance. The subcommittee stated its opposition to redistricting which would combine a sparsely populated rural area with a populous urban area. Finally, the report stated that it is not "desirable to pit two incumbent congressmen against each other when both of them have been previously elected by the people of their respective districts." [7]

The Democrats in the House introduced several measures calling for general redistricting. Rep. Jesse Yoder (Democrat; Montgomery County) presented a plan drafted by Prof. David King of the University of Akron. It included changes in twelve of the twenty-three existing Congressional districts and would have established a pattern in which the greatest variance from the average district population would have been 20 per cent. However, the Republicans were not interested in general redistricting. The subcommittee had as its goal the reporting out of a plan which would create a twenty-fourth district with the least change in existing districts.

All eyes turned to Ohio's largest Congressional district (the Third) and the dismantling of it as the least painful alternative. This would terminate gross underrepresentation and stand as evidence of positive Republican concern with the issue of fair representation. The change would affect only a few counties and districts and would not involve the political interests of great numbers of persons. It would not affect the party balance in the area or the prospects of the incumbent congressman for re-election. If the two counties of the Third District, Butler and Montgomery, had been of nearly equal population, each could have been made a separate Congressional district. Montgomery County, with a population of 527,080, could stand by itself as the Third Congressional District. But Butler County has a population of 199,076 and necessarily had to be combined with neighboring counties detached from other Congressional districts. Three separate plans were offered to break up the Third District and create the twenty-fourth district with Butler County as its base and most populous county. These proposals were offered by the Republican representatives of Butler County. Two of them detached one county from each of three Congressional districts to form a twenty-fourth district of three counties.[8] The third plan detached one county from each of four districts to create a twenty-fourth district of four counties. The four-county plan was found less desirable because the added county unnecessarily involved another congressman and constituency in the matter while adding only a small population to the proposed new district. Moreover, the fourth county has only a minor interest in, or geographical relationship to, the other three.

The proposed new Congressional district would have a below-average population. The Democrats, particularly in the populous and underrepresented northeast part of the state, howled at the failure of the Republicans to produce genuine redistricting. *The Cleveland Press* in an editorial entitled "This is Redistricting?" condemned the proposal for a twenty-fourth district as "a feeble gesture, an easy way out." It said: "If any redistricting is to be done it should be a thorough job of modernizing the districts, assuring equal representation of all areas of the state." [9] The newspapers of Butler and Montgomery counties endorsed the subcommittee's recommendation. That was the extent of the interest and excitement the question stirred. There was little public concern, and none of the pressure groups or civic organizations that would be expected to have an interest in redistricting manifested it.

The controversy over the proposed redistricting was primarily over personal politics and ambition. First, the issue was complicated by the conflicting ambitions of several Republicans. The effect to make Butler County the base of a new district was spearheaded by the county's two Republican representatives. Both men had expressed interest in running for Congress, but neither had the political wherewithal to successfully challenge the incumbent Republican in the Third District. A new district with Butler County as its base would provide them with their opportunity. It is generally agreed that the candidate from the more populous county of a Congressional district has a significant advantage. But they were neither powers nor close friends of powers in the Republican Party. Moreover, there were several prominent Republicans interested in running for congressman-at-large to fulfill long-standing political ambitions or as a means of testing and demonstrating their state-wide voter appeal. Speaker Cloud, a constituent of Ohio's senior congressman, Clarence J. Brown, had found his ambition to go to Washington thwarted by Brown's unfulfilled promise to retire. Perhaps he might be Ohio's congressman-at-large. A twenty-fourth Congressional district might close his door to Congress. Rep. Robert Taft, Jr., majority leader of the Ohio House, had not concealed his desire to serve in the United States Senate or the governor's mansion. He had never faced the test of a state-wide election. An at-large election might test and prove his voter appeal, especially in the absence of any equally prominent name or candidate available to the other party.[10] Other Republicans had publicly or privately made known their interest in running for congressman-at-large.

Second, the state Republican leadership considered the opportunity of an election for a congressman-at-large more to the party's advantage than the creation of a twenty-fourth district. The chances for victory in an at-large election were excellent, and it would provide the party with a new star in its constellation of candidates.

Third, Ohio's incumbent congressmen, particularly the Republicans in the affected districts, were opposed to redistricting. Representative Paul F. Schenck of the Third District said, "It has been a high honor and a great privilege to represent all the folks in Butler and Montgomery counties since 1957. I hope there will be no change in the Third District." Rep. William H. Harsha, Jr., who would lose Clermont County from his Sixth District, stated: "I regret it very much. I'd like to keep enjoying representing all my nine counties. I'm opposed to breaking up my district." The real power of Congressional opposition rested in the indomitable Representative Brown. He commented: "My district fits better as it is. I don't want to lose a county out of my district. I'm opposed to it. My people have grown to trust me." [11] But Representative Brown had to do more than comment to keep Warren County in his Seventh District. He informed the Republican members of the Ohio General Assembly that he thought it to their best interest and to the advantage of their party to defeat the redistricting proposal. Both in committee and on the floor of the House the effort was made to revise the bill to render it unacceptable by altering the boundaries of many Congressional districts without materially affecting district populations. Similarly, some tried to amend the bill to make it obnoxious to the Democrats and their governor. This would force DiSalle to veto the bill and bear the onus for the failure to redistrict. However, these efforts were to no avail. The bill was reported out of committee in its original form and passed the House of Representatives.

The measure then went to the Senate and its Committee on State Government, chaired by Sen. Theodore Gray, of Piqua County. About half of Gray's senatorial district is in Congressman Brown's Congressional district. The bill was not given a hearing until the day the General Assembly had selected for recessing. It was then reported out in a "new" form. The simple plan to create a twenty-fourth district of Butler, Clermont, and Warren counties was complicated by the addition of Preble County. Moreover, the bill was amended to include minor changes in thirteen of the twenty-three existing Congressional districts. The Republican caucus in the Senate voted thirteen-to-seven against the redistricting bill, and it never came to a final vote on the floor of that chamber. Although the 104th General Assembly later reconvened in special session, the issue of Congressional redistricting was not reconsidered.

The Republican leadership wanted an at-large election to select the state's twenty-fourth congressman; however, they suffered an attack of fright. The unpredictable Cleveland Republican, George Bender, a constant source of embarrassment to his party, obtained petitions for a place on the primary ballot for nomination as his party's candidate for congressman-at-large. A serious bid for the nomination by Bender and his name on the ballot might have led the Republican Party to create a twenty-fourth district to avoid having the Republican cause identified with him or the possibility of having him as the party's candidate. At the same time, Republican Congressman Gordon H. Scherer, who represented Taft's district in Congress, announced his retirement. This would have permitted Taft to run for Congress in his own safely Republican district. But Bender died suddenly, and perhaps the last political reason to create a twenty-fourth district disappeared. "Young Bob" Taft later announced his candidacy for the Republican nomination for congressman-at-large.

Thus Ohio turned for the twelfth time in the twentieth century to the expedient of a congressman-at-large. During the battle over the twenty-fourth district, Governor DiSalle quipped, "Hell hath no fury like a congressman whose district is being tampered with." The Republicans controlled the state legislature, but the influence of the incumbent and affected Republican congressmen, the Republicans with ambitions that were best served by an at-large election and office, and the partisan interests and calculations of the Republican Party combined to defeat the redistricting proposal. In a similar set of circumstances, it is difficult to imagine that the Democrats would not have done the same.

However, Ohio will have its twenty-fourth district. The Democrats will no doubt make a campaign issue of the Republican failure to redistrict and emphasize the partisan motives of this inaction. Before the Congressional election of 1964, a Republican-controlled General Assembly will probably carve out the twenty-fourth district that was rejected in 1961. For them to do otherwise would be an open invitation to the Democrats, should they win control of the legislature, to redraw Ohio's Congressional map to Democratic advantage. Ohio may have general Congressional redistricting and reapportionment and subdistricting of the General Assembly, but one cannot pretend to predict when, by whom, and how.[12]

# Notes

1 For a brief but comprehensive survey of contemporary politics in Ohio see: Thomas A. Flinn, "Outline of Ohio Politics," *Western Political Quarterly,* XIII (1960), 702-721. Other useful works include Francis R. Aumann, "Rural Ohio Hangs On," *National Municipal Review,* XLVI (1957), 189-194, 222; Aumann and Harvey Walker, *The Government and Administration of Ohio* (New York: Thomas Y. Crowell, 1956); Heinz Eulau, "The Ecological Basis of Party Systems: The Case of Ohio," *Midwest Journal of Political Science,* I (1957), 125-136; and National Municipal League, *Compendium on Legislative Apportionment* (New York, 1960).

2 In presidential elections since 1936 the deviation of the popular vote of the winning (majority) party in Ohio from that of the nation as a whole has been less than 2 per cent. Ohio cast its electoral votes for Dewey over Roosevelt in 1944 and for Nixon over Kennedy in 1960.

3 The votes cast for minor parties and candidates are omitted.

4 Article XI of the *Constitution of the State of Ohio* deals with apportionment. The constitutional convention of 1851 curiously tried to bind the people of Ohio in perpetuity to the system of apportionment it established by providing that "no change shall ever be made in the principles of representation as herein established . . . ." However, the 1903 "Hanna Amendment" violated this section.

5 *The Cleveland Press,* March 10, 1961, p. 1.

6 *Ibid.,* April 24, 1961, p. 12.

7 *Congressional Redistricting* (Subcommittee on Congressional Redistricting, House Committee on Elections and Federal Relations, 104th General Assembly of Ohio, Regular Session, 1961-1962), p. 1.

8 One plan proposed a district composed of Butler, Clermont, and Warren counties, with a population of 345,317. The other included Butler, Preble, and Warren counties, with a population of 297,236. Because of its smaller population, the second proposed district was rejected.

9 June 1, 1961, p. 12.

10 It must be noted that Representative Taft supported the proposal to create a twenty-fourth district during the House consideration of the measure.

11 *The Cleveland Plain Dealer,* May 31, 1961, p. 1.

12 Two suits have been filed in federal court challenging the constitutionality of the Hanna Amendment.

# PART FOUR

# Congressional Reapportionment
# Under One-Party Control

*INTRODUCTION*

Where a single party controls state government, it is easier to accomplish a comprehensive revision of Congressional districts. Yet vested interests—regional, local, personal —remain, and the resulting reapportionment may be a minimal one leaving serious inequalities.

North Carolina, West Virginia, and Maryland are states that, at least most recently, have been under firm Democratic control and have predominantly Democratic Congressional delegations. In each case, one object of the Congressional reapportionment was to maximize the Democratic proportion of seats. In none of these states were the Republicans strong enough to challenge this objective.

189

In both North Carolina and West Virginia, where the single Republican district was combined with a Democratic one, there was considerable doubt that the resulting district would be Democratic. In Maryland, the new apportionment plan, which gave only limited recognition to the growth of suburban and often Republican counties, was at least temporarily blocked by a successful petition campaign for a referendum.

In none of these states was political advantage the only consideration. There were sharp regional conflicts in North Carolina that nearly overshadowed the partisan factor. In all three states there was a strong incentive to maintain existing district boundaries whenever possible, to avoid disturbing incumbent congressmen. Given this motive, the factors of geography and population distribution and rigid county boundaries left the legislature with relatively little choice in its apportionment, particularly in West Virginia and Maryland. The resulting inequalities in district population were large, particularly in North Carolina and Maryland.

The Congressional reapportionments of 1961 and 1962 produced a number of similar examples of minimal reapportionment in states under one-party control. In Kentucky, two of the smallest districts were combined, and in the remaining districts a few changes were made that did not upset existing political patterns. In that state, no effort was made by the Democrats to crack the one solidly Republican district nor to guarantee Democratic control of the marginal Louisville district by splitting off the Republican suburbs. In Mississippi, two districts were combined, leaving the other four untouched, although the combined district is more than twice as large as one of the others. In Arkansas, the loss of two seats was accommodated by combining four districts into two and leaving the other two largely unchanged. In both Mississippi and Arkansas, the controversy in the legislature and its solution centered on the political attributes and strength of the congressmen involved.

# 10

## North Carolina

"THIS BILL OR NOTHING" *

*PRESTON W. EDSALL*
*North Carolina State College*

The air-conditioned Senate Chamber in North Carolina's classic old capitol rang with the words: "Gentlemen, it's this bill or nothing." Thus warned, the upper house on May 26, 1961, reached an hour of decision. National law had long before decreed that under the 1960 census North Carolina must make eleven districts where twelve had been. Knowledgeable legislators realized that, in accomplishing this, they would be setting a geopolitical pattern for years to come.

Ever since the General Assembly convened in February, it had been evident that redistricting decisions would be made by Democrats and that the Republican minority of two senators and fifteen representatives would be freely disregarded. Indeed, before the convening, Lt. Gov. H. Cloyd Philpott and Speaker-to-be Joseph M. Hunt, Jr., residents of adjoining industrial piedmont counties, had agreed that the Congressional district problem should be handled in each house by a committee consisting of twelve carefully chosen Democrats, one from each existing district. The Republicans, contrary to previous practice, were to be unrepresented on these committees. To chair the House group, Hunt selected his Guilford County colleague, third-termer Ed Kemp, and Philpott settled on Robert F. Morgan of Shelby, in Cleveland County, former president pro tempore of the Senate. In view of these appointments, it is interesting that none of the six redistricting bills subsequently introduced suggested any change in the four-county, definitely urban Sixth District, which includes Guilford, and that neither of the bills proposing to pit the Democrat representing Senator Morgan's Congressional district

---

* See introductory note on p. 98.

against the state's one Republican ever received more than fleeting committee consideration. The apparent piedmont leadership of the committees was offset by the presence of two eastern leaders, Sen. Lindsay C. Warren, a former congressman and United States comptroller general, and Rep. John H. Kerr, Jr., a former speaker of the House, determined that their section should not lose a congressman.

## ALTERNATIVES BEFORE THE LEGISLATURE

On the opening day, the as-yet-unidentified chairmen introduced in their respective houses identical resolutions declaring it to be the sense of the General Assembly that the committees should begin work immediately and hold public hearings. In the House, Representative Kerr successfully opposed Kemp's effort to force his resolution through under a suspension of the rules, terming the move "pure demagoguery." Meanwhile, the Morgan resolution cleared the Senate and, on the following day, slipped through the House without opposition. The resemblance of these resolutions to that introduced by Sen. Claude Currie concerning the activities of the committee responsible for redistricting the Senate indicates close collaboration of Democratic leaders in approaching their problems.

At early meetings of the committees, hope was expressed that Congress might yet increase the membership of its lower house and thus make redistricting unnecessary. The suggestion that the congressmen themselves appear before the committees to make their own views known received little support. Two months of the session were to pass before the introduction of the first redistricting bill, but it soon became known that the major issue was this: Shall consolidation take place in the east, with its smaller population, or in the rapidly growing piedmont and the mountains? [1] There existed but one wholly mountain district, the Twelfth; ever since 1901 the rest of the mountain counties, in all of which the Republican Party was strong, had been combined with piedmont counties into districts that ran diagonally across the state to or toward the South Carolina line. The four Congressional districts lying in the tidewater and coastal plains area of the state, stretching 100 to 180 miles westward from Cape Hatteras and the Outer Banks, constituted sure Democratic country. Wilmington, the state's largest city in 1900 but eighth in 1960, had a bare 44,000 population, and only seven of the region's thirty-eight counties showed population gains above the state-wide average (12.17 per cent) since 1950, whereas sixteen counties showed losses. [2] The eight eastern members of the two committees on Congressional districts were determined not to give up a congressman. In a sense, the case became one of the east against the field, and it was soon apparent that three basic partisan questions called for answers:

1. Assuming that all incumbent congressmen were to seek reelection, should two Democrats be pitted against each other in the 1962 primaries or should one of the Democrats be obliged to face incumbent Republican Charles Raper Jonas in November?

2. Which specific Democrats should be placed in the same district, and which one should share a district with Jonas?

3. Did any particular plan being considered improve the Democratic chances in close districts?

Other criteria, urged in the House committee by one of its members and later incorporated into a joint resolution to create a Congressional district study commission, included population, population trends, nature and extent of geographic areas, similarity of interests of the inhabitants, and personalities and seniority of incumbent congressmen.[3] The degree to which attention was paid to some of these points is perhaps debatable; in the opinion of opponents of the bill finally enacted, inadequate attention was given to most of them.

In the months that followed their appointment, the committees resisted suggestions that they meet jointly. Neither drafted its own bill, leaving this task to individuals and groups, in and out of the General Assembly. At last, on April 17, Senator Morgan and Representative Kemp introduced their own proposals,[4] and matters began to come into focus. Both bills subtracted four eastern counties from Rep. Harold D. Cooley's Fourth District and added him and them to L. H. Fountain's Second District. The rest of the Cooley district, including Wake County, went into a new Seventh District whose resident (and vulnerable) congressman is A. Paul Kitchin. These two bills differed in the area assigned to Congressman Jonas, but neither matched him against a Democratic incumbent, and neither deprived him of paper majorities. In 1958 Republican Congressional candidates had carried the area in the Kemp bill by 184 votes and that in the Morgan bill by 140 votes; 1960 Republican Congressional majorities in these same areas had been 22,812 and 22,059, respectively. These margins were well below the 4,181 and 28,377 majorities given Jonas by the old Tenth District in these years.

Four other bills subsequently made their appearance. One, introduced by Sen. J. Max Thomas and nine piedmont colleagues, left nine districts untouched, but combined three eastern districts into two and proposed placing fifth-termer L. H. Fountain and first-termer David Henderson in the same district.[5] Its supporters relied on its appeal to the *status quo* and do not appear to have pressed their measure with vigor; in any event, theirs was the last Democrat-versus-Democrat plan. Another

bill introduced in the House by Herbert Hardy, an easterner, added only
three counties and less than 75,000 population to the districts east of the
"fall line" (separating the geographical piedmont from the coastal
plain), making its consolidations in the balance of the state.[6] None of the
sponsors of the Hardy bill were on the House Congressional District Committee, but the measure revealed much careful work. In presenting it,
Hardy promised that a companion bill with some variations would soon
be introduced in the Senate, and, on May 9, Sen. W. M. Eubank, with
thirteen cosponsors (three of them members of the Senate Congressional
District Committee), introduced the first of his two redistricting bills.[7]
All the introducers were easterners, and their bill left the four eastern
districts (1, 2, 3, and 7) virtually intact. Though they differed considerably
in detail, the Hardy and Eubank bills both put Democratic Congressman
Basil L. Whitener and Jonas into the same district, but Hardy's bill made
this an eight-county district in which Democratic Congressional candidates showed a 5,326-vote margin in 1960, whereas the Eubank bill provided a four-county district (including populous Mecklenburg), with a
9,430-vote Republican margin. On the surface, it appeared that a
Whitener-Jonas contest was in the making. This appearance was strengthened by the fact that each Congressional district committee indicated
at this stage strong preference for the Democrat-versus-Republican formula.

## THE CHOICE

Behind the scenes, however, Senator Eubank and a powerful group
of legislators, including Sen. Lindsay Warren, were busy with a new
proposal to remodel the Eighth District so as to bring Representative
Jonas and A. Paul Kitchin, a Democrat, into the same territory. When
Senator Eubank introduced his second bill on May 24, his seven cosigners, including this time six members of the Senate committee, represented Congressional districts reaching from the coast to the Tennessee-
Georgia border.[8] Cut off from the old Eighth in laying out the new district were two small Democratic counties at its southeastern tip and
three Republican counties and a politically doubtful county stretching
from a very narrow base toward the northwest. Added were Mecklenburg, where Jonas had great strength, and Lincoln, where he resides.
Other important changes involved additions to the old Ninth, a general revision of Congressman Whitener's district (now renamed Tenth),
and the enlargement of the old Twelfth, which became the new Eleventh.
Reaction was mixed, but Governor Sanford, in one of his rare public
comments on specific redistricting measures, termed the bill fair in that
it left Jonas his Mecklenburg stronghold.

On the next day, the Senate committee gave the bill a favorable report by an 8-to-2 vote and sped it to the Senate floor, where, forty-eight hours after its introduction, the second Eubank bill passed second reading. As in committee, so in the Senate itself, debate had been heated, but the vote was 35-to-11. Opposition, save for the two Republican senators and one from the western edge of the coastal plain, was concentrated in the piedmont. Senator Morgan reluctantly voted for the bill because of his commitment to support what his committee desired, but he made clear his conviction that the bill was a political mistake. "I don't believe in disregarding population and in pitting the state's lone Republican against a Democrat." Sen. John R. Jordan defended the bill as a fair compromise and demanded to know "by what right is the Republican congressman entitled to immunity." Every urban senator in that area except John R. Jordan voted No, as did all four senators resident in the Jonas-Kitchin Congressional district. Opponents were successful in blocking a determined effort to complete Senate action immediately, and the bill went over to Monday, May 29, when it passed third reading on a voice vote.[9]

Rushed to the House by special messenger, the Eubank bill came upon harder going. Chairman Kemp announced that all who wished to be heard by his committee would have a chance. At the same time, twenty-two Democrats, including Rep. H. P. Taylor, Jr., committee member and Kitchin's law partner, and all fifteen Republicans sponsored the previously mentioned joint resolution calling for a study commission to analyze the redistricting problem and report to the governor, who could then call a special session of the legislature. After holding three public hearings, the committee voted down the study-commission resolution 6-to-4 and approved the bill 7-to-4. Decisive were two piedmont votes and the vote of the representative of the mountainous Twelfth District.[10]

Chairman Kemp, true to repeated promises to his committee, endeavored on June 14 to present the Eubank bill to the House "as fairly and equitably as possible." Debate was heated; efforts of individual members at amendment proved futile. Roll call on second reading, with every member accounted for, produced a 74-to-41 victory for the measure. Every Republican voted No, as did all representatives from every county in the Eighth District, old and new. Otherwise, opposition tended to concentrate in the urbanized portions of the piedmont, although Wake and Forsyth counties were divided, and Durham, like mountainous Buncombe, was solid for the bill. Three "black-belt" easterners representing counties bordering Virginia opposed it. So did one Democratic representative from the Twelfth District. Chairman Kemp voted No because the bill gave "certain sections an inordinate voice" and failed "to

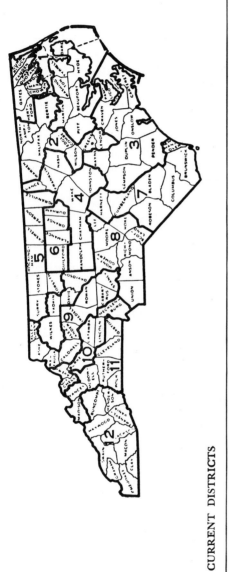

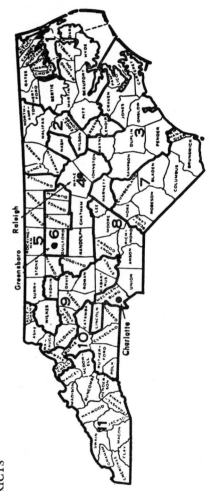

CURRENT DISTRICTS

NEW DISTRICTS

give proper consideration to population . . . or community of interest." He believed the bill would "do serious and irreparable damage to the Democratic Party, particularly in the Piedmont and Western sections" of the state.[11] The next day, after one last attempt at amendment, the Congressional redistricting bill passed third reading. On June 16 it was ratified into law.

Supporters of the bill argued that the Democratic strongholds were in the east, that to redistrict there would be to make the reliably Democratic areas less influential, and that there was no need to seek greater equality in population because national law had dropped this requirement, a point repeatedly emphasized by Sen. Lindsay Warren, who as a congressman had voted for the Automatic Reapportionment Act of 1929. Warren also repeatedly declared that it was the Eubank bill or nothing. The bill was, he told the Senate, "a Democratic bill and a Democratic answer to the trust imposed in us. It is entitled to the support of every Democrat in this body—those who sit at the Democratic table and eat its bread and those who are now seeking favors from the Democratic party." [12]

The most vocal supporters of the new law had been chiefly legislators; its outspoken Democratic opposition included members of the General Assembly, county chairmen, local officials, and influential political leaders, including one former legislator who had twice failed to defeat Jonas. Their argument charged that, in revising the Congressional map, too little attention had been paid to population concentration and rates of growth, to community of interests, and to practical politics. Too much attention had been given to personalities—especially to one personality. If Jonas were defeated in a gerrymandered district, he would be a martyr; if he won, he would be a hero. Either outcome would increase his potential drawing power as a gubernatorial candidate in 1964. Shifts in three other districts rendered Democratic margins too thin for comfort, and the whole operation could be expected to stimulate the growth of Republicanism in the piedmont. "Let's lay the blame down east, where it belongs," said one irate Democratic county chairman. "Folks down east don't think the state extends west of Raleigh." So argued the Democrats in committee and on the floor. Republicans were equally critical. Displeased at the outset by the decision not to place a Republican on either of the Congressional district committees, they refrained from introducing a redistricting bill and assumed no responsibility for the legislative result, which they unanimously opposed. Their position was stated clearly, if somewhat optimistically, by their state chairman, William E. Cobb, at the final House committee hearing: "In a purely partisan sense, we are delighted with the Eubank proposal. We feel that it will not unfavorably affect the tenure of our present one seat in Con-

gress, and that it will make possible the winning of three others. However, as advocates of good government, we cannot sit idly by and allow
the present proposal to be enacted without formal protest." It would
have been possible to establish eleven Congressional districts with a maximum variation of 5 per cent in population. "Our proposals have not
been presented because, by our complete exclusion from this Committee,
it is obvious that [the Republican] 46 or 47 per cent of the voting population is not going to be considered in the final action." [13]

## REASONS FOR THE CHOICE

Four questions remain to be answered: Why was the Democrat-
versus-Republican formula finally selected? Why was Representative
Kitchin's district picked as the area to be disputed? What are the relative
partisan positions as a result of the new law? Finally, how fair is the 1961
law if population is the standard?

Given the inflexible will of eastern legislators to accept no reduction
in their representation in Congress, it was inevitable that the Democratic
incumbents would not confront each other. Sen. Lindsay Warren, the
eastern leader, repeatedly revealed his own intention to protect Herbert
Bonner, who had succeeded him in the First District.[14] Cooley and Fountain had special safeguards. Both men had strong supporters in the General Assembly. Cooley, the Congressional delegation's senior member, had
been chairman of the House Committee on Agriculture since 1949, except
for the first two Eisenhower years. His value to predominantly agricultural North Carolina does not require demonstration. Fountain, who
had acquired seniority and some prominence, could possibly have defeated Cooley in the identical Second districts of the Kemp and Morgan
bills. It seemed best, then, to keep them apart. The move to oppose
Fountain and Henderson, coming at a stage when other proposals were
being pushed forward, never got under way.

Selecting a specific Democratic rival for Jonas (Tenth District) did
not allow a wide field of choice. Only congressmen Whitener (Eleventh
District), Kitchin (Eighth District), and Hugh Q. Alexander (Ninth District) were geographically available. A Jonas-Alexander district would
have involved a serious hazard to the latter, and there is no evidence that
the idea was much considered. Whitener, if confronted by Jonas, would
need "all the help we can give him," as one House committee member
put it. Had it been the decision to throw the two against each other, the
experienced Senator Morgan would surely have been supported in com-
posing the district. On final consideration, however, Kitchin seemed the
most likely victor over Jonas, especially if his district were modified to
rid it of its Republican extension to the northwest. With a voting record

in Congress scarcely distinguishable from that of Jonas, he might be able to cut into the latter's Mecklenburg majority and at the same time hold the rest of his district. On the other hand, it was suggested that Kitchin was the most expendable Democrat. This view was attributed to Speaker Rayburn but subsequently denied by him.

On two or three points, there is much agreement. Individual members of the North Carolina Congressional delegation, while they were kept informed of legislative developments, did little or no lobbying in their own behalf. Congressman Herbert Bonner was reported to have urged Senator Warren to accomplish a transfer of Yadkin, one of Representative Alexander's newly acquired Republican counties, to the Fifth District; if Bonner did so, the request was futile. There were occasional rumors concerning the reactions of the Washington administration to news accounts of North Carolina's course, but no evidence of White House involvement has come to light. Certainly, close relations existed between the White House and Governor Sanford, and one of the governor's closest political allies, former General Assembly member Henry Hall Wilson, a resident of Kitchin's district, was (and is) a member of the White House staff assigned to liaison work with the House of Representatives.

As to Sanford's own position, not much appears on the official record. His contacts with the presiding officers of the two houses were close, and, in accordance with custom, he was consulted by them in making the committee appointments. He was kept informed by his own staff and by legislative leaders regarding developments in this as in other legislative areas and consulted with legislators as negotiations progressed. Three of his "contact people," including J. William Copeland, his legislative counsel, came from the Bonner, Fountain, and Cooley districts, and one of them attended some Congressional District Committee meetings at which the author was present. The Governor evidently looked with favor on the Cooley-Fountain consolidation at one stage; he was fully aware of the political risks in gerrymandering Jonas out of Congress and opposed this type of solution. As the problem developed, however, he accepted the Democrat-versus-Republican formula. His prompt public endorsement of the second Eubank bill as fair to Jonas undoubtedly influenced the position of some undecided legislators. Congressional redistricting was, however, only one of the major problems the Governor faced; its priority therefore varied as the season advanced. He was determined that the redistricting should take place at the regular session and consequently opposed all efforts to delay action. One thing must be remembered: because the governor of North Carolina has no veto, the achievements and the errors of the General Assembly are peculiarly its own.

## THE RESULTS

Does the new political geography strengthen or weaken the Democratic Party? First, using 1958 and 1960 figures as a guide, all eleven new districts are Democratic, but several of them are narrowly so, as the following table shows:

TABLE 1

DEMOCRATIC MARGINS

| District No. | 1958 Total vote | Majority | 1960 Total vote | Majority |
|---|---|---|---|---|
| 8 | 79,927 | 11,457 | 150,191 | 6,877 |
| 9 | 98,010 | 28,596 | 159,737 | 4,027 |
| 10 | 71,097* | 17,511 | 142,419 | 5,513 |
| 11 | 100,835* | 37,787 | 149,008 | 8,024 |
| Total majorities | | 95,351 | | 24,441 |

* No Republican candidate in three populous Tenth-District counties and four small Eleventh-District counties.

When it is recalled that 1958 was both an "off year" and a bad year for the Republican Party in North Carolina as in the nation and that 1960 was a good year in that state, the 1958 majorities are not necessarily impressive. Much of the territory is dominated by "presidential Republicans," large numbers of whom are registered Democrats. Should these voters decide to become also "Congressional Republicans," the above-noted Democratic margins could melt away swiftly. Democratic paper margins in the Ninth District have been narrow: 50 votes in 1952, 3,326 in 1954, and 6,701 in 1956. Locally strong Republican candidates —something rarely seen in the past—backed by effective organization and adequate financing might win any one of these districts. This combination is exactly what occurred in the old Tenth District when Jonas upset a hitherto-successful elongation gerrymander in 1952.

Lastly, how well does the 1961 law represent population? Each of the twelve districts created by the 1941 law increased in population in 1950 and 1960. Under the new law, the Sixth District was unchanged. Every other basically old district except the Seventh grew over its 1960 census figure. Table 2 reveals this situation in detail. Five districts— 1, 2, 9, 10, and 11—fell below the ideal 414,196 by figures ranging from 10,103 to 136,335. The other districts exceeded the average by amounts varying from 16,164 to 77,265. Smallest in population but largest in area was Herbert Bonner's First District, with 6,299 square miles. Largest in population was the controversial Eighth District, with 491,961 people

## TABLE 2

### POPULATION AND RELATIVE REPRESENTATION

| District No. | Population | | | | Relative representation | | | |
|---|---|---|---|---|---|---|---|---|
| | 1943 | 1950 | 1960 | 1963 | 1943 | 1950 | 1960 | 1963 |
| 1 | 239,040 | 247,894 | 253,511 | 277,861 | 1.24 | 1.37 | 1.49 | 1.49 |
| 2 | 293,297 | 306,904 | 313,728 | 350,135 | 1.01 | 1.10 | 1.21 | 1.18 |
| 3 | 251,370 | 308,470 | 382,124 | 430,360 | 1.18 | 1.10 | .99 | .96 |
| 4 | 358,573 | 401,913 | 442,059 | 460,795 | .83 | .84 | .85 | .89 |
| 5 | 323,217 | 355,088 | 408,992 | 454,261 | .92 | .95 | .92 | .91 |
| 6 | 314,659 | 398,351 | 487,159 | 487,159 | .94 | .85 | .77 | .85 |
| 7 | 318,298 | 394,214 | 455,630 | 448,933 | .93 | .86 | .83 | .92 |
| 8 | 340,457 | 369,455 | 396,369 | 491,461 | .87 | .92 | .95 | .84 |
| 9 | 310,225 | 338,907 | 364,561 | 404,093 | .95 | 1.00 | 1.04 | 1.02 |
| 10 | 295,822 | 360,318 | 452,732 | 390,020 | 1.00 | .94 | .83 | 1.06 |
| 11 | 265,757 | 295,724 | 307,575 | 361,077 | 1.11 | 1.14 | 1.23 | 1.11 |
| 12 | 260,908 | 284,691 | 291,715 | — | 1.13 | 1.19 | 1.30 | — |
| Total | 3,571,623 | 4,061,929 | 4,556,155 | 4,556,155 | | | | |
| Average | 297,635 | 338,494 | 379,623 | 414,196 | | | | |

—over 4,000 more than the unchanged Sixth, which was smallest in area. Critics emphasize that Mecklenburg County, in the Jonas-Kitchin district, had 272,111 people, only 5,000 less than the entire fifteen-county First District. The maximum population spread—213,600—was between these two districts. Relative representation figures reveal a somewhat greater deviation from 1.00 than was the case in 1940 and 1950, but, except for the carefully protected First District, overrepresentation is not extreme. Five districts are within .09 of the ideal 1.00.

Although it would have been quite possible to have constructed at least two districts with potential Republican majorities, it cannot be charged that the paper margins provided for Democrats constitute aggravated gerrymandering. The 1962 results will show whether the "elimination" gerrymander has been successful in the new Eighth District. This district, formerly a striking example of elongated dispersal (as were also the old Ninth, Tenth, and Eleventh districts), is somewhat less so now. Districts 4, 5, 9, and 10 now fall in this category. In order to bring Jonas into the Eighth District and keep Cooley in the Fourth, map drawers had to provide one-county jut-outs at the extremes of both districts.

To the argument that the piedmont is underrepresented, it may be responded that only one congressman lives in the mountain area of the state, whereas today four live close together in the south-central piedmont, and three are likely to do so after the next election. Add to these the representatives of the Fifth and Sixth districts, and there are no less than five piedmont representatives. Add Cooley's Fourth, which includes the capital city and several smaller piedmont industrial communities, and the claim of underrepresentation seems scarcely tenable. The industry-conscious urbanizing areas of the state have only to show determination at the ballot box to have nonrural congressmen. Of the North Carolina congressmen now in office, over half come from predominantly rural counties, and only three reside in counties of over 100,000 population; but this does not necessarily mean that they are insensitive to urban and industrial problems.

In this period when the struggle of the Negro for equal treatment characterizes the whole South, the question naturally arises whether the redistricting had any relationship to this problem. There is nothing to show that it did. To take a simple piece of evidence: in 1956, Congressman Kitchin won his seat by defeating one of the two North Carolinians who had refused to sign the "Southern Manifesto," yet it was Kitchin who was forced to accept Jonas. On the other hand, Representative Cooley, who survived a similar 1956 apostasy, was saved from doing battle against his near-neighbor, Fountain.

The Kemp and Morgan bills would have made Cooley vulnerable

to a signer of the manifesto, but this aspect was furthest from the authors' consideration.

The decision of the General Assembly to keep the eleven Democratic congressmen in separate districts did not protect them against other Democratic rivals. As this is written, the representatives from the Fifth and Eighth districts face hard primary battles against attractive, young state legislators from Winston-Salem and Charlotte, and less strenuous contests are in progress in the Third and Sixth districts.[15] Matching the Democratic primaries are similar rivalries for Republican nominations in the Fifth, Sixth, Ninth, and Eleventh districts which portend real contests in November 1962. All except Herbert Bonner and L. H. Fountain will face Republican opposition at that time.

Republicans do not, however, constitute the only threat. There is now the action of the United States Supreme Court in *Baker* v. *Carr*. When a state legislature deliberately creates eight of eleven Congressional districts exceeding by 112,159 to 213,600 the population of its least-inhabited district, it only invites some disgruntled citizen to ask the courts what the equal protection clause of the Fourteenth Amendment means in this context. Senator Warren's assertion that population does not count would contribute to the litigant's brief. Many lawyers in the General Assembly recognized this risk to Senator Eubank's winning plan. Since the Supreme Court ruling, Assistant Attorney General Ralph Moody, a specialist in constitutional problems, has said that, "if the Court can reach into the reapportionment formulas of the states, it will have no trouble reaching into their schemes and methods of redistricting Congress. . . . We're fast approaching a scheme in which every vote must be weighted in proportion to population." [16]

# Notes

[1] For a discussion of the geopolitical sections of North Carolina, see "North Carolina: People or Pine Trees," pp. 99 f., *supra*.

[2] Congressional districts 1, 2, 3, and 7 alone are considered here. District 4 contains three rural eastern counties but is predominantly piedmont in population and area.

[3] HR 999, introduced May 31, by Reps. J. Paul Wallace, H. P. Taylor, Jr., and others.

[4] SB 205; HB 478.

[5] SB 275, introduced on May 8; cosigners included Sen. R. F. Van Landingham of the Congressional District Committee.

[6] HB 601, introduced on April 28.

[7] SB 279, introduced on May 9. Cointroducers included Con. Dist. Comm. members Lindsay Warren, Stewart Warren, and Henry G. Shelton.

[8] SB 353.

[9] For Senate votes, see *Senate Journal,* pp. 396 f., 405.

[10] HR 999.

[11] Kemp's statement for inclusion in *House Journal.*

[12] Quoted in *Charlotte Observer,* May 27.

[13] Mimeographed statement read to committee by Chairman Cobb.

[14] Early in the session, there was speculation that Representative Bonner's pro-administration vote in the Rules Committee expansion fight would protect him. All other North Carolina congressmen voted against the Rayburn position. Governor Sanford expressed the opinion on February 1 that the Rules Committee vote would not affect redistricting.

[15] All incumbents won in the primaries, however.

[16] *Charlotte Observer,* April 6.

# 11

## West Virginia

### TRADITION AND PARTISAN ADVANTAGE

*VICTOR K. HEYMAN ***

For the first time since 1910, West Virginia has had a change in the number of congressmen to which it is entitled—a reduction from six to five. The event evoked little interest in most areas of the state, for the partisan situation dictated the district most likely to be eliminated, and politicogeographic and historical factors dictated most of the shifts in counties that were made by the West Virginia Legislature's Congressional Reapportionment Act of 1961.

### THE DEMOCRATIC OBJECTIVE

The state of West Virginia, created in 1863 as a product of the Civil War, has oscillated politically in much the same fashion as the nation as a whole. Until the Southern elements of this border state regained full political rights in 1870, West Virginia was in the Republican column. The Republicans regained control in 1895, and, with few exceptions, 1895-1933 was a period of Republican dominance. Since then, the Democrats have controlled the Legislature continuously and have lost the governor's chair only as a result of periodic scandals. One indication of the strength of these political cycles can be obtained from noting that, of the sixteen Congresses between 1901 and 1933, in only two did Democrats control the state's delegation to the U.S. House of Representatives; in the fifteen since then, the Republicans controlled only one. At the state level, since 1931 the speaker of the House of Delegates has been a Democrat, as has the president of the Senate since 1933.

With the 1961 state Legislature dominated by Democrats (25-to-7 in

---

* Dr. Heyman, formerly with Marshall University, Huntington, W. Va., is now a Defense Analyst in the Department of Defense.

the Senate, 82-to-18 in the House of Delegates), a Democratic governor, and a Congressional delegation weighted five-to-one Democratic, the news that West Virginia was to lose one seat in 1962 meant only one thing to most observers—Republican Congressman Arch A. Moore, Jr., would be subjected to an "elimination gerrymander." The questions that created real interest were how to get rid of Moore and who was to take him on.

When a state loses a seat, the simplest reshuffling of counties often takes place, leaving the incumbent to be eliminated without a district. Arch Moore's district (the First) is so shaped, however, that something more needed to be done. Two possibilities were widely discussed, one to combine Congressman Ken Hechler's Fourth District with Moore's First District and the other to push Rep. Cleveland Bailey's Third District together with Moore's. Hechler and Moore resemble each other in their political styles, and many people suggested that it might be interesting to watch two wildcats go after each other. In addition, Bailey, as dean of the state's delegation to the House of Representatives, an old man, and a powerful figure on the House Education and Labor Committee, was thought to be entitled to consideration.

Population and geography probably more than "power politics" dictated no Hechler-Moore match.

TABLE 1

WEST VIRGINIA CONGRESSIONAL DISTRICT POPULATION,
1950-1960

| District | Representative | 1950 | 1960 | Change |
|---|---|---|---|---|
| 1 | Moore (R.) | 279,954 | 273,107 | −6,847 |
| 2 | Staggers (D.) | 302,297 | 276,874 | −25,423 |
| 3 | Bailey (D.) | 315,479 | 268,334 | −47,145 |
| 4 | Hechler (D.) | 330,906 | 345,208 | +14,302 |
| 5 | Kee (D.) | 330,450 | 275,813 | −54,637 |
| 6 | Slack (D.) | 446,466 | 421,085 | −25,381 |
| | | 2,005,552 | 1,860,421 | −145,131 |

Hechler's district was already within 28,000 of the 1960 West Virginia apportionment ratio of 372,084, it was the only one to show growth, and it had the brightest future in an otherwise badly distressed state. A shoestring district, one county wide, along the Ohio Valley would have contained 441,000 people. To have combined the two old districts directly would have meant a new district of more than 600,000. Perhaps of greater significance, either action would have meant a probable Republican victory: the shoestring district would have been about 55 per cent Republan, and Hechler's district was less Democratic than Moore's was Republican. In the last eight Congresses, since World War II, both the First and Fourth Congressional districts have been won four times by Republicans and four times by Democrats, but Moore's 1960 margin was almost 28,000 votes, and Hechler's less than 10,000.

## THE REDISTRICTING PROCESS

The process by which redistricting took place in 1961 was marked by close cooperation between the Democratic state legislators immediately involved and the Democratic congressmen. Moore played no part in the proceedings. The most fascinating aspect of the process was, however, the role played by a professor of political science in the Bureau for Government Research of West Virginia University. In December, 1960, Prof. Claude J. Davis prepared a monograph containing fourteen alternative redistricting plans for the 1961 session of the Legislature to consider. Hechler and Moore were not placed in the same district in any of the fourteen plans, but Moore and Bailey were paired in six.

Early in February the chairman of the House redistricting committee announced that he had asked the six incumbents to submit their redistricting proposals for consideration by the committee, but only Staggers and Bailey replied. With the end of the session set for March 11 and neither the Senate nor the House redistricting committees having made any decision, the end of February arrived with no redistricting action appearing likely.

The log jam was broken on the last day on which bills could be introduced—Wednesday, March 1—when two redistricting bills were introduced in the House: Davis' Plan Thirteen (a "least-change" alternative) and a plan created by the chairman of the House redistricting committee. Both plans put Moore and Bailey in the same district. Plan Thirteen removed seven of Bailey's twelve counties and one of Moore's, leaving a Democratic majority, according to registration, of 60 per cent. A Republican victory in the district was nevertheless likely, since, according to the 1960 Congressional vote, the Republicans would have a majority of 54 per cent. The principal difference between the two bills was that the latter removed two more of Bailey's old counties, virtually assuring a Moore victory, and enlarged Slack's Third District from 371,000 to 443,000. In terms of political practicalities, the professor did better than the chairman, and the House committee reported out Plan Thirteen without change on March 3. The committee, however, working under the pressure of time, made no recommendation.

On Saturday, March 4, a meeting was held between the legislative leaders, the Democratic congressmen, the governor (a Democrat), and the

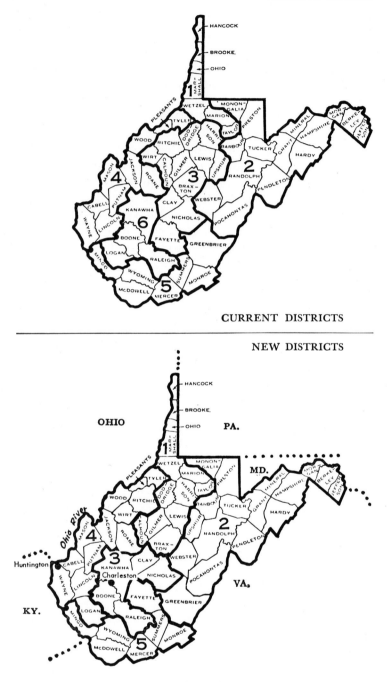

CURRENT DISTRICTS

NEW DISTRICTS

Democratic state party chairman. If the congressmen preferred to run at-large, hoping to defeat Moore in a state-wide contest in 1962 and then have new districts drawn, this course might have been followed. However, with Bailey ill and not in attendance, there was no one to urge this action, and Hechler and Staggers argued against it. The party chairman urged, among other things, that the ultimate bill be "fair" and that no obvious gerrymandering take place that might redound to the state-wide disadvantage of the party in 1962.

The following Wednesday, March 8, the House took up Plan Thirteen. One of Bailey's old counties and one of Moore's were put into the new First District for a net Moore gain of 1,500 votes (based on 1960). Hechler was helped greatly by the addition of coal-rich Mingo County, which had delivered a 7,300-vote Democratic plurality in 1960, more than offsetting the 1,700-vote Republican plurality of Wirt and Ritchie counties added to his district by Plan Thirteen. The Democratic Mingo County delegation objected strongly, but as the Democratic floor leader explained, "We want to move Mingo into the Fourth to strengthen it for the Democrats."

Party loyalty notwithstanding, the Kanawha County (Charleston) delegation, large and powerful since it was both united and had the floor leader among its members, managed to have Nicholas County (2,800 Democratic plurality) moved to Slack's new Third District, even though both Staggers in the Second District and Bailey needed it more. In addition, a side fight developed when the Raleigh County delegation tried to get Logan County moved back into the new Third District. Logan and Raleigh had teamed for years to give Raleigh dominance in the old Sixth District, but Kanawha had finally won with Slack in 1958. Neither Kanawha nor Logan desired to have Logan moved back, and it stayed in Mrs. Kee's Fifth District. The House then passed the bill 78-19, with fourteen Republicans and five Democrats opposed. Two Democrats from Bailey's home county of Harrison opposed the bill, along with both Democrats from Greenbrier County, who opposed the shifting of their county from the Fifth to the Second District.

Three days later the Senate moved Mingo back to the Fifth District, but gave Hechler Logan County, with its 9,700 Democratic plurality. The Senate then did a double gyration when it first moved Greenbrier County on the southeastern edge of the state from the new Second District where it had been shifted by Plan Thirteen to the Fifth (where it had been located since 1951) and then moved it back on a second vote. Mrs. Kee was obviously trying to maintain her old district intact (first regaining Mingo and then trying to regain Greenbrier). The move of Greenbrier to her district would also have brought this declining district 34,000 people closer to the West Virginia apportionment ratio, but senators from the Second District protested so vigorously that this would make the Second a Republican district that the Senate revoked its action. (In fact, the 1960 vote was 59 per cent Democratic in the new Second District with or without Greenbrier, but on the last day of the session, no one was ready to dispute the point.) The Senate passed the bill, and the House concurred that night (March 11).

The governor allowed the bill to become law on March 17 without his signature, perhaps out of respect for Bailey and Bailey's supporters, who were quite angry.

Republican Moore said he felt the redistricting plan was "essentially fair," that he had "a fighting chance" to keep his seat, and, "considering that both houses of the Legislature were overwhelmingly in control of the opposition, I couldn't have asked for any fairer treatment." Bailey, on the other hand, complained that his district was "virtually dismembered," that he had been put in "an almost certain Republican district." The Legislature, he said, "evidently intended from the beginning to use me to run against Moore." Mrs. Kee said that she was "terribly saddened" by the loss of Greenbrier County because "I'm terribly close to the people up there." Hechler was happy, and Slack and Staggers had no comment.

Over-all, it is obvious that one of the most important considerations in the 1961 reapportionment was continuity with the past. This is of great importance in understanding past apportionments. (The 1934 apportionment shifted only seven of the fifty-five counties from their 1915 districts, and the 1951 reapportionment moved only one county.) Of thirty-six counties outside the old First and Third districts, only two were moved in 1961. Professor Davis himself labeled Plan Thirteen "an attempt to leave the present districts as they are as much as possible, with the exception of the first district." The rule in West Virginia appears to be as in most other states that the least change is the best change.

## THE RESULTS

How well did the Legislature do its job? From the point of view of compact, contiguous, equipopulous districts, the answer must be: Not very well. Table 2 shows that the variation in districts is from 13.42 per cent over the quota in Hechler's district to 18.54 per cent below it in Mrs. Kee's Fifth Congressional District. Considering that a mass emigration from the heartland of the West Virginia soft-coal area in the Fifth District has occurred, that it is almost certain to continue, and that the growth of the Ohio Valley industrial area in Hechler's Fourth is equally likely to continue, it would not be surprising to see a 1970 population of 440,000 in the Fourth Congressional District and 255,000 in the Fifth

TABLE 2

DISTRICT POPULATION AND RELATIVE DEVIATION FROM
1960 WEST VIRGINIA APPORTIONMENT RATIO OF 372,084
IN FIVE NEW DISTRICTS

| District Number | 1960 Population | Number over (+) or under (−) ratio | Per cent over (+) or under (−) ratio |
|---|---|---|---|
| 1 | 408,794 | +36,710 | +9.87 |
| 2 | 329,612 | −42,472 | −11.41 |
| 3 | 396,871 | +24,787 | +6.66 |
| 4 | 422,046 | +49,962 | +13.42 |
| 5 | 303,098 | −68,986 | −18.54 |

TABLE 3

DEMOCRATIC REGISTRATION AND CONGRESSIONAL
VOTE (1960) IN FIVE NEW WEST VIRGINIA DISTRICTS

| | Democratic 1960 registration | | Democratic 1960 Congressional vote | |
|---|---|---|---|---|
| | Plurality | Per cent of total registration | Plurality | Per cent of total vote |
| 1 | 50,842 | 60.2 | −16,507 | 45.9 |
| 2 | 34,403 | 58.9 | 27,517 | 59.5 |
| 3 | 61,026 | 64.4 | 35,365 | 60.6 |
| 4 | 41,050 | 58.3 | 17,823 | 54.8 |
| 5 | 86,087 | 73.7 | 51,577 | 71.2 |

Congressional District. The underpopulated Second Congressional District will probably also show a decline, and the overpopulated Third Congressional District (containing the state capital of Charleston) will probably grow. In short, the population shifts of the past ten years have not been accommodated, and future shifts are likely to accentuate the disparity.

As for the effectiveness of the "elimination gerrymander," only the 1962 election will tell for certain. However, Table 3 indicates that Bailey rather than Moore will be eliminated. Although Bailey has the nominal advantage of a 60.2 per cent Democratic registration, the 1960 Congressional vote in the new district was 54.1 per cent Republican. However, Moore's old district remained intact, while Bailey brought with him only six of his former twelve counties.

Hechler, incidentally, received a small but important boost. His 1960 victory margin was only 9,845 votes (53.2 per cent), the second largest Democratic margin in the history of the district, which dates back to 1882. The reapportionment, based on the 1960 Congressional vote, would appear to increase his margin to about 17,000, or 54.8 per cent of the total vote. However, a stronger Republican candidate in 1962 might make this margin evaporate. The old Fourth District supported Nixon in 1960 with a 19,000-vote plurality.

Is there any economic sense in the new, very oddly shaped districts? Putting the question differently, are the new districts defensible in any terms other than historical, partisan, and personal? A case can be made that they are, at least in part. The homogeneity of the agricultural and mountainous Second Congressional District, coal-mining Fifth Congressional District, and Ohio Valley, industrialized Fourth Congressional District is reasonably clear. A major conflict would have been stirred by the placing of the two largest West Virginia cities of Charleston and Huntington in the same district, so the existence of the Third and Fourth Congressional districts can be easily explained. However, it must be admitted that the new First Congressional District includes the quite disparate areas around Wheeling in the panhandle and the glassmaking, chemical, and agricultural areas in the rest of the district. Much more compact districts would have been both possible and economically homogeneous.

The 1970 census will probably cause West Virginia to lose at least one more seat; if this occurs, a major redistribution will be unavoidable. Until that time, however, West Virginia will be able to enjoy its proudest possession—tradition.

# 12

## Maryland
### FRUSTRATION OF ONE-PARTY CONTROL

*DWYNAL B. PETTENGILL*
*College of William and Mary*

The additional seat in the House of Representatives awarded Maryland as a result of the 1960 census was not an unmixed blessing. With the aid of a constitutional provision calling for a surprisingly small number of signatures, irate citizens of Maryland in 1961 were able to derail the "Tawesamander Special" creating the state's eighth Congressional district. Because of an antiquated constitutional provision, voters numbering only 10,000 (29,520 signatures were finally validated) have been able to cause a two-year delay in the drawing of new district boundaries. As a result, the eighth congressman must now be nominated and elected at-large, according to the procedures of the unusual unit-rule requirements of the state law for state-wide candidates. He will serve a full term, since no bill creating a district can be drawn before 1963.

The war years and normal population growth patterns of a highly industrialized state had probably produced as much imbalance in the ratios of the several districts as could be found in any other part of the nation. Other factors bear on Congressional districting matters. These include the importance of county lines, based on tradition and on the considerable degree of local autonomy granted by the state government. Moreover, geography had endowed Maryland with sharp regional divisions, creating areas of political "togetherness" not to be lightly disregarded. Western Maryland, the eastern shore, and southern Maryland are all in an often-intense competition for political spoils. Finally, the two "bedroom suburbs" surrounding Baltimore and Washington are of a continuous sort which can be fractioned only by disrupting the existence of the county as a county. No such division has ever been undertaken for purposes of Congressional districting.

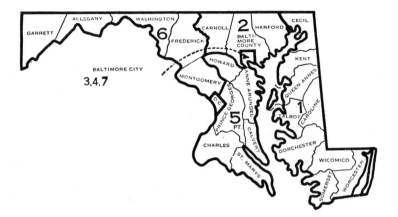

CURRENT DISTRICTS

NEW DISTRICTS

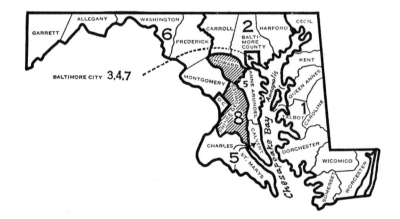

The most widely acclaimed and long practiced rule in redistricting is that that set of boundary lines is best which disturbs the existing arrangement least. Since the Baltimore and Washington suburban areas had experienced the greatest amount of growth from 1950 to 1960, it would have seemed only logical to leave the Baltimore city district lines alone. The eastern shore, plus or minus one or two counties at the head of Chesapeake Bay, comprises a well-defined area, whereas the four or five western Maryland counties would almost certainly be included in one district because they are in an unbroken line across the northern boundary of the state. Only southern Maryland and the four large suburban counties, therefore, remained as possibilities for juggling to form a new district. And as can be seen from the population figures in Table 1, these counties are too large to be arranged in a great number of alternative combinations. Thus, only a few choices were available to the group which bore the responsibility for drawing the boundaries of the Maryland Eighth Congressional District.

For example, it is widely assumed that the governor and the six Democratic members of the Maryland delegation to the House of Representatives would have left Baltimore County as the nucleus of one district, as indeed it now is. Likewise, it would have been impracticable to include Montgomery County with any area except western Maryland, unless it were to have formed a single district by itself. And Richard Lankford, whose Fifth was the largest of the districts, justifiably wished to have his home county of Anne Arundel included in his district. Prince George's, therefore, would have had to be the pivotal county for any new plan, and whichever southern Maryland counties were not included in the new district built around Prince George's County would have to be assigned to that constructed around Anne Arundel County.

The legislature, docile on this issue because it was embroiled in so many other controversies, offered little or no opposition. The only exception was the attempt by diminutive Howard County's delegate in the House to amend the proposed statute in committee by putting his county in the Fifth instead of with Prince George's County in the new Eighth District. This stratagem was overrruled by the full weight of the governor's influence when the bill was reported to the floor.

Less than one month later, a referendum campaign was underway, led by the Montgomery County League of Women Voters. The ease of the campaign is explained by the precise requirements of the referendum provisions in the Maryland constitution and in Article 33 of the Code of Laws. The constitution requires a mere 10,000 signatures to put an act of the General Assembly on the state-wide ballot, the only further stipulation being that no more than half the required signatures come from one county. A complication in Article 33 of the code is the lack of

TABLE 1

POPULATION OF MARYLAND COUNTIES

| County | Population (1960) |
|--------|------------------|
| Allegany | 84,169 |
| Anne Arundel | 206,634 |
| Baltimore City | 939,024 |
| Baltimore | 492,428 |
| Calvert | 15,826 |
| Caroline | 19,462 |
| Carroll | 52,785 |
| Cecil | 48,408 |
| Charles | 32,572 |
| Dorchester | 29,666 |
| Frederick | 71,930 |
| Garrett | 20,420 |
| Harford | 76,422 |
| Howard | 36,152 |
| Kent | 15,481 |
| Montgomery | 340,928 |
| Prince George's | 357,395 |
| Queen Anne's | 16,569 |
| St. Mary's | 38,915 |
| Somerset | 19,623 |
| Talbot | 21,578 |
| Washington | 91,219 |
| Wicomico | 49,050 |
| Worcester | 23,733 |

a section dealing with special elections, except for United States senators, so that election of a congressman-at-large was assured once the 1961 petitions calling for a referendum were submitted and validated. The argument of the League of Women Voters stressed the lack of relief to Sixth-District population pressures and to the inequity arising from leaving Second-District boundaries intact. The League was joined by many elements of the Republican Party and by the Maryland Committee for Fair Representation. Republican support was concentrated in the suburban counties; the state party showed little interest in the referendum campaign. It must be pointed out, however, that there was little public attention to the administration's districting scheme. About two-thirds of the nearly 30,000 signatures were obtained from Montgomery County; some 3,000 came from Howard County, which had been combined with the much-larger Prince George's County in the proposed Eighth District; and the remainder came from other counties.

Newspaper analysts and political observers assumed that the seat had been created by the Tawes administration for the Speaker of the House, who lives in Prince George's County and had long been a staunch supporter of Tawes. It therefore occasioned little surprise when Speaker Perry Wilkinson was selected to fill the at-large Congressional spot in the 1962 primary campaign on the administration's state-wide ticket.

Governor Tawes and the Democratic members of the House of Representatives from Maryland, following age-old intuitive patterns in drawing lines for a new Congressional district, had to choose between satisfying Montgomery County or Prince George's County. The decision was certain to alienate people living in one of the two counties.

# PART FIVE

## Reapportionment as a Means of Political Control

*INTRODUCTION*

Rural control over legislative bodies is normally maintained by preserving the *status quo*. Congressional reapportionment is frequently carried out on a minimal basis in order to preserve the dominance of rural areas or of a ruling party or to avoid disturbing the vested interests of incumbent congressmen. In the states where two-party competition is strongest, one party is seldom capable of tailoring far-reaching changes in the apportionment system to its interests. The party may be blocked by divided government, frustrated by the difficulty of amending a state constitution, or inhibited by the necessity of protecting the political future of its congressmen or legislators. The situation is different, however, in New York and California.

These are examples of states where a single party has most recently held full governmental control. In New York, the Republicans used this opportunity and the necessity of reducing Congressional districts to carry out a carefully conceived gerrymander, particularly in New York City. In California, the addition of eight Congressional seats gave the Democratic Party a chance to create both Congressional and Assembly districts that were politically the most advantageous. In both states minority protests, though loud, were ineffective.

In New York, the Republicans have also been able to use the legislative apportionment system to serve their political purposes and to assure Republican majorities in both houses even during the frequent periods of Democratic governorships. They have preserved in the constitution a complicated apportionment formula that overrepresents the normally Republican small cities and rural upstate areas. At the same time, to take advantage of growing—and normally Republican—suburbs, the Republicans have carried out periodic reapportionments under this formula at the expense of normally Democratic New York City. As the suburban and urban wing of the Republican Party grows more important, however, this successful formula seems likely to come under increasing attack within Republican ranks. In California, where the urban-rural (or metropolitan-versus-nonmetropolitan) polarization of the parties has not yet clearly developed, neither party, as such, has as much to gain from preserving or attacking the antipopulation bias in the constitutional formula for Senate apportionment.

# 13

## New York

"CONSTITUTIONALLY REPUBLICAN"

---

GUS TYLER, Director
DAVID I. WELLS, Assistant Director
Political Department, International Ladies'
Garment Workers' Union

Politically, New York is a "swing" state. In presidential elections during the past half-century, the state has given its electoral votes to the Democrats six times and to the Republicans seven. Over the same period, the governorship has been won by Democrats in twelve elections and by Republicans in seven. Democrats have won eleven elections for U.S. Senate seats; Republicans have won seven.

A very different situation has prevailed in the New York State Legislature. In only two elections in the past fifty years have the Democrats been able to win control of the Legislature. Since 1938 the Republicans have held *uninterrupted* control with at least 55 per cent of the seats in both houses. New York is, then, a two-party state with a one-party Legislature.

This record does not indicate that the voters of the Empire State are politically schizophrenic, voting one way for governor and another for the Legislature. The illness is embedded in the structure of the state government, with Republican control built into the very constitution of the state. Gov. Alfred E. Smith used to refer to the New York Legislature as "constitutionally Republican."

The constitutional provisions which produce the schizoid state are those which establish New York's legislative apportionment. Republican control of the lower house (the Assembly) is perpetuated by a system of representation based on area—namely, the county. In the Senate, GOP dominance is based on the state's population pattern, not as it exists today but as it was sixty-eight years ago. In both houses, one-party control is maintained by involved constitutional formulas which guarantee that the sparsely populated counties will be overrepresented and that the heavily populated ones (whether urban or suburban) will be underrepresented.

While Republican control of the state Legislature is based on mathematical formulas established by the state constitution, GOP overrepresentation in the state's Congressional delegation is the product of skillful gerrymandering.

The almost unanimous action of the Republican leadership in New York in maintaining this artificial power system at the legislative level tends to obscure real ideological differences within the New York Republican Party.

The Republican Party of New York is not an exclusively rural party, although it is strongest in the rural areas. While Democratic strength has been growing steadily in the suburban counties around New York City (Nassau, Suffolk, Westchester, Rockland) in recent years, these counties still lean toward the Republicans. The suburban communities fringing the larger upstate cities are also basically Republican. Among the cities themselves, while New York City and Albany are normally strongly Democratic, a number of the state's major urban centers tend to be Republican. Syracuse, for example, votes Republican rather consistently, and Rochester does so almost as regularly. Other such large cities as Buffalo and Yonkers are politically marginal, leaning one way or the other with almost equal frequency. Even within Democratic New York City there are sizable areas of Republican strength.

The social diversity of the Republican Party expresses itself in the typical urban-rural, liberal-conservative clashes of program and personalities. There have been battles over nominations for state-wide offices. There is a vast ideological gulf between the state's Republican senators of the past decade (Ives, Javits, and Keating) and most of the state's Republican congressmen, the bulk of whom represent rural constituencies. There have been conflicts between Republican governors of the liberal wing (Dewey and Rockefeller) and the Republican Legislature, which has been dominated by the conservatives.

Nevertheless, despite these far-from-inconsequential divisions, there is little or no division within the GOP over districting and apportionment. The party unites to maintain and use its control for strictly partisan purposes. The most recent case was the Congressional redistricting of 1961, necessitated by the loss of two seats and intended to convert a Democratic majority of one in the state's delegation to the House of Representatives into a Republican majority of nine—without any change in the popular vote.

## THE 1961 CONGRESSIONAL REDISTRICTING

On November 10, 1961, at a special session called by Gov. Nelson Rockefeller, the New York Legislature enacted a Congressional redistricting law to provide the Republican Party with a substantial "head start" in electing the state's Congressional delegation in every election from 1962 through 1970.

Though the nature of the redistricting was shocking to many, it did not surprise those who understood the political situation in which it occurred. Although the actual district-by-district details had been kept secret until the day before passage, it was perfectly predictable that, in the absence of any federal or state standards for the establishment of Congressional districts, the Republican Party, in control of both the Legislature and the governorship, would do exactly as it did under the same circumstances a decade ago—it would gerrymander the districts.

Gerrymandering in the drawing of Congressional lines was used more extensively in 1961 (as in 1951) in New York than in any other state. In most states, partisan advantage at the Congressional level is secured by creating some districts several times more populous than others. Though there are population variations among the new New York districts, the chief method used to achieve Republican advantage is contour contortion—the drawing of boundaries.

### Background—the 1951 Redistricting

New York's 1961 Congressional redistricting was cast in the same mold as the redistricting of ten years earlier. For several decades prior to 1951, the threat of gubernatorial veto-power in Democratic hands inhibited the Republican urge to gerrymander. There had, in fact, been no state-wide redistricting at all for almost forty years. In 1951, however, a loss of two seats necessitated some redistricting. Moreover, in that year Republican Thomas E. Dewey was governor, and his party, now in control of both the second and third floors of the State Capitol Building (the Albany equivalent of controlling both ends of Pennsylvania Avenue), was free to indulge in unrestrained assault on congressional contours.

By detaching a portion of Rochester from one upstate district and replacing it with an adjacent rural county, a new safely Republican district was established. In the Bronx, a district to elect one Republican representative in a Democratic citadel was designed. Democratic Rockaway, a part of Queens County, was attached to a strongly Democratic Brooklyn district, thus making it possible to set up a new Republican-leaning district in Queens. Other changes in the state converted formerly Democratic districts into doubtful ones and doubtful districts into Republican ones. The most notable of the 1951 gerrymanders—now over-shadowed by several of the even more striking 1961 models—was the Twelfth Congressional District in Brooklyn, designed to include in one district several small, widely scattered pockets of Republican strength in order to make probable the election of at least one Republican representative in the heart of an overwhelmingly Democratic area. It began in the northwest corner of the county and then tortuously wended its way southward and eastward to the opposite side of Brooklyn, forming a serpentine shape sprawling from one end of the borough to the other. This gerrymander worked so well that the district elected a Republican in four of the five elections held during its existence. It fell to the Democrats only in the Kennedy sweep of 1960.

The 1951 redistricting was quite effective in inflating Republican strength in Congressional elections. In 1954, when GOP candidates received 51 per cent of the state-wide vote, the district lines tilted the balance in enough districts to give the party 61 per cent of the Congressional seats. In 1960, when the GOP share of the popular vote fell to 47 per cent, they were still able to hold 49 per cent of the seats. In 1958 a Democratic majority at the polls was actually converted into a Republican majority in the Congressional delegation; with only 49 per cent of the votes, Republicans won 56 per cent of the districts. (See Table 4.)

### 1961: Updating the Gerrymanders

The 1961 redistricting was an attempt to improve the work of 1951 by redrawing lines to add to Republican advantages obtained a decade earlier and exploiting new population shifts and changing political patterns. Its objectives were: (1) to reduce the number of up-state Democratic congressmen from three to two; (2) to secure the party's hold on the Bronx Republican district set up a decade earlier—a move necessitated by increasing Democratic strength in several parts of the district caused by altered ethnic and income characteristics; (3) to reduce the number of Manhattan Congressional districts from six to four without jeopardizing the seat of the borough's one Republican representative; (4) to make it easier for the Republicans to recapture a Queens district which had shifted to the Democrats in 1960; (5) to eliminate a Brooklyn Democratic district, to set up a new Brooklyn GOP district which would be even safer than the old Twelfth (which the 1960 election had shown to be not quite safe enough) and still to leave enough Brooklyn Republican strength outside this new district so that by attaching Staten Island to a part of Brooklyn another Republican-leaning district could be established; (6) to increase the number of Long Island districts from three to five while shaping the boundaries in such a way as not only to defeat the island's one Democratic congressman but also, despite the area's rapidly growing Democratic strength, to keep all its districts as safely Republican as possible.

These were exacting objectives. The indications are that to meet these specifications experts worked over the political maps for many months, fitting areas together in jigsaw-puzzle fashion until the most politically advantageous shapes had been devised. *The New York Times* reported as early as February 21, 1961, that Republican leaders were near agreement on the objectives. Following the redistricting, *The Times* indicated that, although the legislation "was technically drafted by a joint legislative committee headed by Senator Robert C. McEwen of Ogdensburg . . . most of the vital political decisions were made by Republican party officials. The committee and its staff translated the decisions into geographical boundaries."

Through the spring, summer, and early fall, Chairman McEwen steadfastly ignored Democratic requests for public hearings on redistricting. In May he said, "I don't see what could be brought out at public hearings that we don't already know." In the same month, State Republican Chairman L. Judson Morhouse said that "the new redistricting . . . will be as equitable as practically possible." In October, McEwen described redistricting as "strictly a technical subject" and stated that "no argument offered at a public hearing, no matter how emotional, political or impassioned it might be, can change a census statistic."

The November date for the special session appears to have been chosen so that any outcry over the bill's contents would come after the municipal elections held in various communities of the state. The Legislature was summoned to meet on the Thursday following Election Tuesday.

When the creatures of the 1961 Congressional gerrymander were exposed to public view, there was a wave of protest. The attached maps explain why.

In up-state New York, the primary aim, elimination of a Democratic representative, was achieved by the dismemberment of the district of Schenectady Congressman Samuel Stratton, who had won two successive terms in a formerly safe Republican district. The district consisted of the city of Schenectady and vicinity—Stratton's strongest area—and several nearby, essentially rural counties. In the dismemberment, Schenectady was joined to the adjacent district of one of the two other up-state Democratic congressmen, Leo O'Brien, whose heavily Democratic constituency needs no added Democratic votes. The remaining counties of the Stratton district were parceled out among adjoining Republican districts. The resultant new Thirty-Fifth District extends al-

**4-25**
New York City

## CURRENT DISTRICTS

## NEW DISTRICTS

**6-24**
See
New York City

NEW YORK CITY DISTRICTS

most two-thirds of the way across the state from the outskirts of Schenectady to the outskirts of Rochester. It is some 200 miles long, but only a few miles wide at points.

To tighten the Republican hold on the Bronx district of Republican Congressman Paul A. Fino, all of increasingly Democratic Riverdale was sliced off and tacked onto a neighboring district which the Republicans have no hopes of winning. Six of the old district's seven low-income housing projects (which tend to be strongly Democratic) were removed from the Fino district. Most startling of all, a Democratic pocket in the very heart of the district was simply cut out by the extension of a long, narrow, winding protrusion of the adjacent Democratic district into Fino's territory resembling a badly twisted knife blade.

In Brooklyn, the Republicans created a new safe district—the Fifteenth District. It begins in Bay Ridge, a GOP stronghold in the southwest corner of the borough, jumps across a cemetery and park to pick up additional Republican pockets in central Brooklyn, and then makes a 90-degree turn directly into a high-income neighborhood near Brooklyn's northwest corner. This northwest extension of the Fifteenth is responsible for the fact that the adjacent strongly Democratic Fourteenth is composed of two segments connected only by a nine-block long, one-block wide, completely unpopulated corridor running along the waterfront.

The most geographically (as distinguished from geometrically) illogical district in the state is the Sixteenth. Its existence is explained, however, by carefully thought-out political logic. The Sixteenth includes all of Staten Island, which lies to the west of Brooklyn, and a small enclave on the opposite (southeastern) side of Brooklyn. Underlying this unique connection of two areas separated by many miles of land and water is the fact that Staten Island is politically marginal. It gives a small edge to the Democrats in some years and to the Republicans in others. The Brooklyn portion of the Sixteenth is intended to add enough additional GOP votes to the new district so that it can be won in most years. (The Brooklyn segment is not heavily Republican, but the GOP leaders apparently felt the party's strength there was enough to make its attachment to Staten Island worthwhile.)

The districts described above are the most glaring but not the only instances of gerrymandering in the 1961 redistricting. The changes in several other areas were less sensational, the gerrymandering less apparent, but the lines were just as carefully tailored to Republican specifications.

In Queens County, a few seemingly minor border revisions were enough to alter the political picture. Before the changes, there were two districts which were rather safely Democratic, one rather safely Republican, and one (currently held by a Democrat) doubtful. The changes are illustrated by the diagram on page 229.

First, a predominantly Republican neighborhood was taken out of one of the normally Democratic districts (which the Republicans had little hope of winning) and placed in the doubtful district to add to GOP strength there. Then, a Democratic section of the doubtful district was removed and incorporated into the normally Republican district. Finally, to make certain that this additional Democratic strength in the Republican district did not place the GOP seat there in jeopardy, a Democratic neighborhood within the Republican district was cut out and tacked onto the other Democratic district. Thus, by virtue of just three relatively minor boundary revisions, the Republicans increased their chances in the doubtful district and maintained their strength in the district they already held. The only price paid was the further reduction of Republican strength in two already-Democratic districts.

Similar small changes in district lines in the Buffalo area were designed to add to Republican strength in two districts they had been

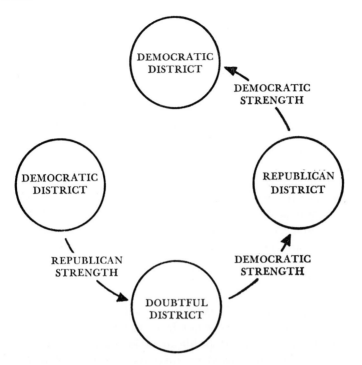

winning by relatively narrow margins. To accomplish this, a marginally Democratic area had to be made more strongly Democratic. These changes indicate that, rather than risk the loss of one or both of the districts they already held, the Republicans preferred to freeze the existing two-to-one political division.

Examination of the district boundaries does not, however, reveal the full political impact of the new setup. There are, in addition, significant differences in district populations. Defenders of the redistricting point out that the average population of the up-state districts is the same as the average within New York City. This is true, but it ignores the sizeable variations in population which exist, not between rural and urban districts, but between Democratic and Republican ones. The Republican districts are consistently less heavily populated. The populations range from 349,000 (a Bronx Republican district) to 470,000 (a Brooklyn Democratic district).

In the state as a whole, the average population of districts expected to elect Republicans is 398,000; for those expected to go Democratic, the average is 424,000. Within New York City, the average of Republican-leaning districts is 384,000; the Democratic average is 421,000. The average of Republican districts outside the city is 406,000; for Democratic districts it is 445,000. Manhattan's one Republican district has a population of 382,000; the average of the three Democratic districts is 439,000. Among the Brooklyn districts, the average population of the two expected to elect Republicans is 351,000; for the five expected to go Democratic, it is 444,000.

## The Special Session and Its Aftermath

The session of the Legislature which enacted the 1961 redistricting lasted for just two days. The legislation embodying the new districts was introduced on November 9 and debated and passed the following day.

Aside from the redistricting itself, perhaps the most interesting feature of the session was the role of Governor Rockefeller. The Governor, widely thought of as the nation's leading liberal Republican, never openly identified himself with the redistricting. His only official actions were to call the session and put his signature to the bill. (Indeed, the Governor pointedly refused to be photographed at the signing.) Nevertheless, it was apparent that Rockefeller was not simply acquiescing in the action of the Legislature.

The only point at which the bill seemed to be in jeopardy was in the Assembly. The threat came not from the Democratic minority but from defections within the Republican majority. (The bulk of Republican defections were not based on qualms regarding the bill's over-all purposes but rather, according to *The New York Times'* report, on a belief that certain up-state districts had not been made *safe enough*.) The state constitution provides that, to be passed in the Assembly, a bill must be approved by a constitutional majority of at least seventy-six assemblymen. The dissatisfaction of a number of Republicans over certain details of the bill made it less than certain that the required seventy-six votes could be mustered. In a caucus on November 9, Assembly Speaker Joseph F. Carlino, a close associate of the Governor, had been able to obtain assurances from only seventy-three Republicans that they would vote for passage. On the morning of November 10, the Governor made a most unusual appearance in Carlino's office, where he reportedly conferred with several of the balking legislators. "At the time," reported the *New York Herald-Tribune,* "it was said [Assemblyman] Lewis H. Folmer of Cortland County, still a hold-out, was summoned and Governor Rockefeller persuaded him to change his mind and vote for the bill." (Folmer subsequently admitted having gone to Carlino's office, but denied that it was pressure by the Governor that had caused him to change his mind.) When the voting came a few hours later, enough of the reluctant Republicans voted for the bill to give it the required seventy-six votes. Five Republicans remained adamant and voted with the Democrats.

Following the session, Democratic fire was concentrated on the new districts themselves, on the role played by Rockefeller, and on the secrecy which had cloaked the drafting of the bill and had been maintained until the day the session convened. Perhaps the bitterest comment was that of Democratic National Chairman John Bailey, who referred to the redistricting as "political larceny in the robber baron tradition" and added: "Your granddad would have been proud of you, Nelson."

Many other Democrats joined in the public attack on the measure. Congressman Emanuel Celler announced that he would renew his drive in Congress to enact standards for fair Congressional districting so the New York act could be voided. Mayor Robert F. Wagner went on television to describe several of the most outrageously carved districts. He called the act a form of discrimination against Democratic voters and pinned the blame on Rockefeller, saying: "The Legislature and the Governor did the job. . . . They hid the maps—literally hid the maps—until the legislators were in their seats to vote on the bill. The members of the minority in the Legislature—the Democrats, even though they are a majority of the voters in the state, were never called for a meeting of the committee which drafted the plan." Wagner also announced that he would file suit to have the act invalidated on the grounds that it constituted a denial of equal protection of the law. To date, the only suit filed has been by a group of Democrats.

The protest against the gerrymander was not limited to the Democratic Party. A number of newspapers vigorously denounced the action. *The New York Times* ran a series of editorial attacks on the redistricting.

One odd, though certainly not deliberate, result of the redistricting was the elimination of the districts of two Democratic congressmen of Italian origin (Alfred E. Santangelo and Victor L. Anfuso) and the jeopardizing of the seat of a third (Joseph P. Addabbo). Some Italian-American leaders charged discrimination.

New York City Reform Democrats charged that the new lines in Manhattan represented "an undercover alliance between the Republicans, Tammany Hall and Governor Rockefeller." The reference was to the elimination of a district held by reform Congressman William F. Ryan, who had won the Democratic nomination in a primary battle against the organization. Ryan's west side district was split in half; the segments were tacked onto the districts of Congressmen Herbert Zelenko and Leonard Farbstein—both organization Democrats.

The Republican argument for the districting act is: the variation in district populations is not as great as in many other states; the average populations of the districts in New York City and the rest of the state are almost the same; the Democrats would do the same thing if they could; the Democrats do do the same thing in other states where the political situation is reversed.

Among the Republican comments were those of Speaker Carlino, who accused Mayor Wagner of "whining and crying" over the disparities among the districts and said that Democratic attacks could imperil "the cooperation, understanding and constructive work" at Albany that the New York City administration would require to meet the city's needs. Three days later, however, in an unusually frank remark on what had occurred, Carlino said that any legislature would be "very peculiar" if it did not draw lines to favor the party in control. "The only way to handle [redistricting] is for the majority party to get together and do what has to be done," he added.

The GOP argument that the Democrats would do the same thing if they were able is as convincing as it is unprovable, since the Democrats never *are* able. Barring political miracles, the best they can hope for is a Democratic governor to exercise a check on the Republican Legislature.

## UNEQUAL REPRESENTATION IN THE

## STATE LEGISLATURE

Republican manipulation of Congressional districting rests, of course, on Republican control of the Legislature, where the extent of minority rule can be gauged by simply weighting the votes. For instance, the seventy-six assemblymen who voted in favor of the 1961 Congressional redistricting bill represented some 6,200,000 citizens; the seventy-one who voted against it represented 7,900,000. In the upper house, the thirty-three senators who favored the measure represented 6,900,000 citizens; the twenty-five who opposed it represented 7,400,000. These artificial legislative majorities are the product of New York State's nineteenth-century constitution.

In the New York Legislature, rural overrepresentation is automatically produced by a sensitive mechanism designed at the Constitutional Convention of 1894 to perpetuate rural virtue over urban vice. One of the delegates expressed the attitude that appeared to dominate the convention: "The lower strata of society in the great cities is such that . . . [the city citizen] is not . . . so well worthy of confidence as the average citizen in the rural districts." Proclaimed one delegate, "Your government will be . . . safer in [the rural citizens'] hands than in the hands of the average citizen of the great cities." Conjuring up pictures of city radicals menacing life and property, he warned: "Then you will cry for help. And to whom? You will then turn your eyes to the green fields of Oneida and Herkimer and Jefferson and Saint Lawrence. . . ."

An opposition delegate said: ". . . it is openly stated by the majority of the committee that [its] purpose was to prevent the cities from getting the apportionment to which they were entitled and to give it to the country districts, and this work does it beautifully."

The effectiveness of the nineteenth-century constitution in perpetuating and even furthering inequities in the twentieth century may be seen in the reapportionment required by the constitution. (By applying the constitutional apportionment formulas to the 1960 citizen-population figures, the number of seats the various counties will receive can be readily determined.) The following would be among the resultant inequities:

1. Under the new apportionment, there would be an assemblyman representing more than 190,000 citizens and another representing fewer than 15,000—a thirteen-to-one ratio.

2. The average number of citizens per Assembly seat in New York City would be 133,000. In the suburban counties (Nassau, Westchester, Suffolk, and Rockland), the figure would be 129,000. For the populous up-state counties it would be 119,000. For the remaining, primarily rural, counties, there would be a seat for every 51,000 citizens.

3. New York City and Erie County (Buffalo) would have a Senate seat for every 353,000 citizens. Nassau County would have one for every 425,000. The average ratio for the rest of the state would be one to 217,000.

4. New York City, with 46 per cent of the state's citizen-population, would have only 37 per cent of the Senate and Assembly seats.

5. Under the present apportionment, 39 per cent of the citizens elect a majority of the assemblymen; 40 per cent elect a majority in the Senate. After reapportionment, these figures would drop to 37 and 38 per cent, respectively.

6. In the 1961-1962 Legislature, Democratic assemblymen represent an average of 114,000 citizens each; the Republican average is 80,000. The average for Democratic senators is 282,000; for Republican senators it is 216,000.

7. In 1958 and again in 1960, sizable Republican margins were retained in both houses despite Democratic majorities of the votes cast. (See Table 4.)

## The Assembly Apportionment Formula

The state constitution fixes the membership of the Assembly at 150. The seats are distributed as follows:

First, every county except one is given one seat. Next, every county with at least one per cent of the state's citizen-population is given an additional seat. Finally, the remaining seats are distributed among counties with at least one and one-third per cent of the citizen-population. This process establishes three classes of counties. The inequality arises from the fact that so many seats are "used up" in the first step that not enough remain to permit the larger counties to obtain an equitable share. The inequalities thus produced may be gauged from the way the seats will be distributed in the forthcoming reapportionment:

In the one-assemblyman counties, there will be 63,000 citizens per seat. The two-assemblymen counties will have 110,000 citizens per seat. In the remaining (populous urban and suburban) counties, there will be 130,000 citizens per seat. The counties in the first group have 17 per cent of the state's citizen-population and will receive 29 per cent of the seats. Those in the third, with 74 per cent of the citizens, will get 61 per cent of the seats.

If Assembly seats were distributed in direct proportion to citizen-population, the counties in the third group would receive nineteen additional seats, New York City thirteen, the suburban counties four, and Erie County two.

Tables 1 and 2 indicate the inequities produced by the Assembly apportionment formula.

## The Senate Apportionment Formula

New York's Senate apportionment formula is a graphic illustration of the use of apportionment to resist the passage of time. It attempts to impose on the present the political pattern of three generations ago—to maintain the *status quo* of the year 1894.

The system separates the counties into two categories: those which have more than six per cent of the state's citizen-population and those which have less. Different procedures determine the number of seats apportioned to each group.

Whereas the number of assemblymen is fixed, the size of the Senate varies. There is a minimum of fifty seats, but no specified maximum. (There are now fifty-eight senators; after reapportionment there will be fifty-seven.) This flexibility in size acts as a shock-absorber in the apportionment machinery to protect the rural counties against the impact of metropolitan growth.

The seats are apportioned as follows:

First, the state's citizen-population is divided by 50. The resulting number is called the "first ratio." All counties with citizen-populations at least three times this ratio (that is, at least 6 per cent of the citizen-

## TABLE 1

### INEQUITIES IN ASSEMBLY REPRESENTATION UNDER NEW APPORTIONMENT

EXTREMES

Highest Assembly district citizen-population: 190,343
(a Monroe County district)
Lowest Assembly district citizen-population:   14,974

INEQUITIES BETWEEN THE THREE GROUPS OF COUNTIES

| Group | No. of seats | Total citizen-population | Average citizen-population per Assembly district |
|---|---|---|---|
| Counties with three or more seats* | 92 | 11,937,406 | 129,754 |
| Counties with two seats** | 14 | 1,541,724 | 110,123 |
| Counties with one seat*** | 44 | 2,761,656 | 62,765 |

* Kings, Queens, New York, Bronx, Nassau, Erie, Westchester, Suffolk, Monroe, Onondaga
** Albany, Oneida, Niagara, Richmond, Broome, Orange, Dutchess
*** All others (Hamilton and Fulton considered as single county)

INEQUITIES BETWEEN TYPES OF COUNTIES

| Group | No. of seats | Total citizen-population | Average citizen-population per Assembly district |
|---|---|---|---|
| Five counties of New York City | 56 | 7,420,631 | 132,511 |
| Suburban counties outside New York City (Nassau, Suffolk, Rockland, Westchester) | 22 | 2,839,926 | 129,088 |
| Populous upstate counties (pop. of 100,000 or more) | 34 | 4,034,512 | 118,662 |
| Remaining upstate counties | 38 | 1,945,717 | 51,203 |

TABLE 2

PERCENTAGE OF CITIZEN-POPULATION COMPARED TO PERCENTAGE OF SEATS UNDER NEW APPORTIONMENT

| Counties | Per cent of state citizen-population | Per cent of seats | No. of seats if seats were distributed in direct proportion to citizen-population of each county | Actual number of seats | Difference |
|---|---|---|---|---|---|
| ASSEMBLY | | | | | |
| Ten most heavily populated counties (those with three or more Assembly seats) | 73.5 | 61.3 | 111 | 92 | −19 |
| Seven "in-between" counties (those with two Assembly seats) | 9.5 | 9.3 | 15 | 14 | −1 |
| Forty-five least populous counties (those with one Assembly seat) | 17.0 | 29.3 | 24 | 44 | +20 |
| SENATE | | | | | |
| Six most populated counties ("first-ratio" counties) | 58.6 | 45.6 | 34 | 26 | −8 |
| Remaining counties ("second-ratio" counties) | 41.4 | 54.4 | 23 | 31 | +8 |

population) are assigned seats by comparing their citizen-populations to the first ratio. (These are referred to as "first-ratio counties.") Counties with citizen-populations between three and four times the ratio receive three seats; those with populations between four and five times the ratio receive four seats; those with populations between five and six times the ratio get five seats; and so on.

Next, the number of seats given each first-ratio county is compared to the number it had in 1894. If any of these counties has more seats than it had in 1894, the total Senate membership is increased by the same number of additional seats. (Thus, if a county that had two seats in 1894 were given seven under a new apportionment, Senate membership would increase by five seats over the basic fifty.)

After this process is completed, the remaining seats are divided among the counties which have less than 6 per cent of the citizen-population. To apportion these seats, a "second ratio" is used—obtained by dividing the combined citizen-population of all the under-six-per-cent counties by the remaining number of seats (including the newly created ones). These seats are then distributed on the basis of this second ratio.

Under the coming reapportionment, this process will operate as follows:

Six counties—Kings, Queens, New York, Bronx, Nassau, and Erie—have citizen-populations of more than 974,448 (6 per cent of the state total). In comparing the number of seats these counties qualify for to the number they had in 1894, New York and Bronx are considered as one county, since they comprised a single county in 1894. For the same reason, Queens and Nassau counties are considered together. Kings and Erie will have the same number of seats as in 1894—seven and three, respectively. Neither, therefore, will affect the total number of senators.

New York and Bronx together had twelve seats in 1894 and will receive four each under the new apportionment. Decreases do not change the total number of senators, so neither county will affect the size of the Senate.

In 1894, Queens, which then included Nassau, had one seat. Under the new apportionment, Queens will get five, and Nassau three. This is an increase of seven over 1894. Consequently, seven seats will be added to the basic fifty to produce a fifty-seven-member Senate.

The first-ratio counties will receive a total of twenty-six seats, leaving thirty-one for the other counties. The twenty-six first-ratio county senators will represent 59 per cent of the state's citizens; the thirty-one from the second-ratio counties will represent 41 per cent of the citizens. (See Table 2.) There will be 366,000 citizens per senator in the first-ratio counties; in the second-ratio counties there will be 217,000 per senator. If the two-ratio system did not exist, there would not be thirty-one seats

left for the less populous counties, but only twenty-four. Each time a
first-ratio county becomes entitled to a greater share of the original fifty
seats than it had in 1894, the number available for the other counties
would be reduced if the constitutional machinery did not create extra
seats. As a result, the comparative power of voters in the smaller counties
actually increases as those counties' proportionate share of the population
decreases. (See Table 3.)

The two-ratio system is not the only inequity in Senate apportionment. Another stems from a requirement that, to qualify for additional
seats beyond three, counties must have additional full first ratios. There
is no similar requirement for second-ratio seats. Thus, in the coming

TABLE 3

INCREASING SEVERITY OF UNDERREPRESENTATION OF "FIRST-
RATIO" (POPULOUS) COUNTIES IN SENATE ELECTIONS
SINCE ADOPTION OF 1894 CONSTITUTION

| Year of apportionment | Per cent of state's citizen-population in first-ratio counties | Per cent of Senate seats apportioned to first-ratio counties | Difference (per cent) |
|---|---|---|---|
| 1894 | 39.5 | 38.0 | 1.5 |
| 1907 | 48.4 | 45.1 | 3.3 |
| 1917 | 48.6 | 45.1 | 3.5 |
| 1943 | 58.3 | 48.2 | 10.1 |
| 1953 | 57.3 | 46.6 | 10.7 |
| New apportionment | 58.7 | 45.6 | 13.1 |

| Year of apportionment | Average citizen-population of Senate districts in first-ratio counties | Average citizen-population of Senate districts in second-ratio counties | Number of voters in second-ratio counties with same power as 100 voters in first-ratio counties |
|---|---|---|---|
| 1894 | 118,076 | 114,420 | 97 |
| 1907 | 148,594 | 130,189 | 88 |
| 1917 | 170,288 | 147,994 | 87 |
| 1943 | 267,909 | 178,299 | 67 |
| 1953 | 301,178 | 195,859 | 65 |
| New apportionment | 366,128 | 216,822 | 59 |

reapportionment, Nassau, with 3.93 first ratios, can get no more than three seats, but in the last apportionment Onondaga, with only 1.71 second ratios, was given two seats.

If seats were distributed in direct proportion to citizen-population, the first-ratio counties would receive, not twenty-six, but thirty-four seats in a fifty-seven member Senate. (New York City would get an additional six, and Nassau and Erie one each.)

### Districting

While the Legislature exercises almost no discretion in apportioning seats (aside from making some relatively minor decisions on the distribution of second-ratio Senate seats), it does draw Senate district lines. This gives the Legislature a chance to gerrymander, but there is far less gerrymandering at this level than in the formation of Congressional districts. The apportionment formulas provide so big a rural (and, consequently, Republican) advantage that there is much less *need* to gerrymander.

In counties with two or more Assembly seats, local governing bodies draw Assembly district lines, but the gerrymandering opportunity thus sometimes afforded the Democratic opposition is limited by a constitutional requirement that, in counties with two or more Senate seats, Assembly lines must be drawn within the Senate boundaries established by the Legislature.

### The Forthcoming Reapportionment

Barring unforeseen and unlikely developments, Senate and Assembly seats will be reapportioned in the near future. Reapportionment could be postponed, but this is most improbable, for Republicans stand to benefit from it unless the constitutional method is changed. Therefore it appears likely that reapportionment will be enacted during the Legislature's 1963 session.

Although there is some doubt about the date of reapportionment, there is none about its geographic effects if the present constitutional formula is retained. New York City would lose seats in both houses. The chief gainers would be the suburbs and, to a lesser extent, the metropolitan up-state counties.

New York City would lose nine Assembly seats (Manhattan four, Brooklyn three, the Bronx two). Suburban Nassau and Suffolk would gain four and two, respectively; Monroe and Onondaga (the Rochester and Syracuse areas) and still largely rural Dutchess would each gain one. New York City would lose four Senate seats (Manhattan and Brooklyn two each); Suffolk would gain two, Monroe one, and one would be eliminated because of the one-seat reduction in Senate membership.

The Senate changes should add to the Republican edge there. The counties that would lose seats, New York and Kings, are both heavily Democratic; Democrats currently hold thirteen of their fifteen Senate seats. Since the Legislature will draw the new Senate lines, it is likely that these counties' two Republican districts would not be jeopardized, and the Democratic margin in the two counties would thus probably be reduced by four seats. On the other hand, the Republicans now hold all three Senate seats in Suffolk and Monroe, the counties scheduled to pick up seats. Unless the Democrats can break through to take at least two of the total of six seats these counties would have after reapportionment, the combined Republican edge in the two counties would increase. In over-all effect, then, the best the Democrats could hope for is not to be too badly hurt by the shifts in Senate seats. They would not be helped.

The Assembly picture is not substantially different. Here, again, the counties losing seats—New York, Kings, and Bronx—are Democratic strongholds, and the gainers—Nassau, Suffolk, Monroe, Onondaga, and Dutchess—are Republican in varying degrees. Democrats now hold forty-six of fifty seats in the former group of counties and only two of the seventeen in the latter. Even if the Democrats could draw the Assembly lines so as to hold onto *all* the remaining Kings, New York, and Bronx seats, their current margin in the three counties would decrease by one. To reduce the current combined thirteen-seat margin the Republican Party now holds in the counties which gain seats, the Democrats would have to win a minimum of seven of the twenty-six Assembly seats these counties will have. Such gains are not likely—at least for some years.

## The Effects of Inequitable Representation

As a result of its one-party Legislature, the state is subject to frequent periods of "divided government." Because New York is a two-party state and because the governor is elected by a state-wide constituency, control of the governorship shifts back and forth between the two parties. Over the last half-century, Democrats have held it during twenty-eight years, Republicans during twenty-two. Of the twenty-eight years of Democratic governors, however, the governor's party has controlled the Legislature in only three. Thus, during twenty-five of the last fifty years there has been a partisan division between the executive and legislative branches. This almost invariably produces governmental stalemate; political paralysis becomes the rule, and meaningful action by state government to solve public problems becomes the exception. Such stalemates are all but inevitable under Democratic governors. Barring such rare exceptions as the 1934 landslide, the best the Democrats can hope for is to "break even," for the apportionment system puts the GOP in a "heads-I-win-tails-it's-a-tie" position. However, even when Republicans occupy the governor's chair, some of the problems of divided government continue, for, as we have seen, the apportionment formulas create advantages for the rural areas of the state. Republicans who seek the governorship, on the other hand, must appeal to a state-wide electorate, an increasing majority of which is metropolitan. To do so successfully, the GOP has, in recent decades, chosen its gubernatorial candidates from its "left" wing. Once elected, these governors have often had to contend with the extreme conservatism of rural Republican legislators.

Inequitable representation not only affects the two parties in their contests with each other; it also has important effects within both parties. Gerrymandering has increased the number of safe districts, Democratic as well as Republican. (To gain advantages in some districts, the dominant party must often "concede" others to the opposition.) As a result, the number of genuinely contestable districts is reduced. This is particularly true of the Congressional districts, but it is found to a lesser degree at the state level, too. In the safe districts, real contests, if any, take place in the primary, not in the general election. Fewer voters participate in primaries than in general elections. The smaller turnout makes it far easier for party machines to nominate (and thus, in effect, elect) their candidates.

This may explain why some Democrats appear unconcerned about the representational inequities. Such lack of concern is most apparent where there *are* safe Democratic districts. That the party is in a permanent minority in the Legislature is often less important to Democrats in such areas than that they have little to fear from the *local* Republican opposition.

The inequalities have effects within the Republican Party, too. They stem from the increasingly metropolitan character of the state. Because the party's hold on the Legislature results from rural overrepresentation and because the rural areas are losing population while the suburban areas are gaining it, the party's continued hold on the Legislature is dependent on an ever-shrinking segment of the population at the same time that its chances in state-wide elections depend to an ever-greater degree on its appeal to suburbanites. Therefore, the widening dissimilarities between the interests of the rural and suburban areas set up increasing strains within the Republican Party.

As noted earlier, Republican unity has been strong to date on the issue of apportionment and districting, but continued maintenance of that unity will become more difficult as suburban Republican officeholders are forced to contend with progressively stronger Democratic opposition. For example, Nassau County Democrats have for some years been calling public attention to the apportionment issue and particularly

## TABLE 4

### DIVISION OF STATE-WIDE VOTE BETWEEN PARTIES AND DIVISION OF CONGRESSIONAL AND LEGISLATIVE SEATS

| Year | Vote for Democratic candidates* | Vote for Republican candidates* | Democratic seats | Republican seats | Republican per cent of votes* | Republican per cent of seats* |
|---|---|---|---|---|---|---|
| Congressional contests during period when 1951 redistricting was in effect | | | | | | |
| Congress | | | | | | |
| 1952 | 2,521,736 | 3,853,934 | 16 | 27 | 60.4 | 62.8 |
| 1954 | 2,398,556 | 2,505,228 | 17 | 26 | 51.1 | 60.5 |
| 1956 | 3,072,860 | 3,745,059 | 17 | 26 | 54.9 | 60.5 |
| 1958 | 2,763,883 | 2,686,818 | 19 | 24 | 49.3 | 55.8 |
| 1960 | 3,514,951 | 3,167,717 | 22 | 21 | 47.4 | 48.8 |
| Legislative contests during period since 1953 apportionment has been in effect | | | | | | |
| State Senate | | | | | | |
| 1954 | 2,396,377 | 2,467,725 | 24 | 34 | 50.8 | 58.6 |
| 1956 | 3,042,016 | 3,737,368 | 20 | 38 | 55.1 | 65.5 |
| 1958 | 2,732,471 | 2,703,309 | 24 | 34 | 49.7 | 58.6 |
| 1960 | 3,525,787 | 3,277,503 | 25 | 33 | 48.9 | 56.9 |
| Assembly | | | | | | |
| 1954 | 2,305,022 | 2,452,892 | 60 | 90 | 51.6 | 60.0 |
| 1956 | 2,976,869 | 3,707,994 | 54 | 96 | 55.5 | 64.0 |
| 1958 | 2,735,360 | 2,712,456 | 58 | 92 | 49.8 | 61.3 |
| 1960 | 3,557,043 | 3,309,830 | 66 | 84 | 48.2 | 56.0 |

* Vote figures for Democratic and Republican candidates include votes cast on Liberal line for Liberal-endorsed Democrats and Republicans.

to the severe underrepresentation Nassau will suffer after reapportionment. Early in 1961, the Republican-controlled Nassau Board of Supervisors rejected a Democratic resolution calling on the county's state legislators to press for revision of the apportionment system. In November, Nassau Democrats won their first county-wide victory, electing the county executive. Then, in February 1962, the Republican supervisors, under the leadership of Speaker Carlino, who is the Republican county chairman, voted unanimously in favor of a Democratic resolution almost identical to the one they had turned down a year earlier.

The adverse effect of unequal representation on the welfare of the state's urban and suburban citizens is undoubtedly its most far-reaching consequence. For many years, the politics both of New York City and of the state as a whole seemed to boil down to a constant battle between the City and the Legislature (allied at times with Republican governors). The most publicized aspect of this struggle has been over state aid for the city's school system. The city complains of being "short-changed." It points out that in 1960-1961, for instance, it received $197 in aid per pupil while communities elsewhere in the state received an average of $325. The city also charges discriminatory treatment in numerous other respects. Among the most important complaints are that the Legislature places arbitrary and unfair limits on the city's taxing powers.

From 1950 to 1960, the number of citizens in the major suburban counties (Nassau, Westchester, Suffolk, and Rockland) grew from 1,600,-000 to 2,800,000—an increase of over 75 per cent. They had less than 11 per cent of the state's 1950 population; by 1960 they had almost 18 per cent. The burgeoning of the suburbs has given rise to increasingly critical problems as the influx of new residents continues unabated. The governments of villages with swollen populations, of communities sprung up where only months before there were potato fields, of entire counties engulfed in a tide of people, find themselves unable to meet the sudden need for more schools, hospitals, water, sewage facilities, streets, mass transportation. State action to help deal with these problems requires increased expenditures, but frugal rural conservatives, so heavily overrepresented in the Legislature, are noted for reluctance in this regard. For this and other reasons, an increasing number of suburbanites are becoming increasingly aware that New York City is not the only part of the state not fairly represented in Albany. (Active suburban Democrats do their best, of course, to promote this awareness. The Nassau Democratic organization has made unequal representation its "number-one issue" in recent years.)

Although the suburbs would gain seats in a reapportionment under the present constitutional provisions, they would actually become more severely underrepresented. The four counties' Assembly representation would jump from sixteen to twenty-two, but if seats were apportioned strictly on a population basis they would get twenty-six. (Nassau would get two more and Westchester and Suffolk one each.) In the Senate, Nassau would become the most severely underrepresented county in the state. From 1950 to 1960 its population doubled (656,000 to 1,276,000), yet it will receive no additional Senate seats. It would continue to have only three senators—one for every 425,000 citizens, in contrast to a state average of one for 285,000. This would mark the first time the Senate apportionment formula, which heretofore has victimized only the New York City and Buffalo areas, would operate against a suburban county. In sharp contrast to Nassau, neighboring Suffolk, still a second-ratio county, has just half Nassau's population but would have an equal number of senators.

Democrats have steadily increased their percentage of the suburban vote and have already won some victories in counties which only a decade or so ago were overwhelmingly Republican. Within the last three years they elected the Nassau and Suffolk county executives, won a Congressional district embracing all of Suffolk and part of Nassau, took control of Rockland's Board of Supervisors, and won control of several Westchester communities for the first time. With these counties becoming contestable two-party territory, their underrepresentation in the Legislature is bound to receive increasing public attention.

### Efforts to Change the Apportionment System

New Yorkers seeking to reform the apportionment system have channeled their efforts in three directions: (1) attempts to amend the state constitution, (2) court action to overturn the system, and (3) public education to acquaint the people with the existence and consequences of the inequalities.

The New York constitution can be amended in two ways: by the voters' ratification of an amendment drafted by a constitutional convention or by the voters' ratification of an amendment passed by two successive Legislatures. Because the Legislature has been in the firm grip of the beneficiaries of the existing system, the latter method of amendment has offered almost no hope of success. (In 1935, the only time in recent history when the Democrats controlled the Legislature and had an opportunity to change the system, an alliance of upstate Republicans and Tammany [Manhattan] Democrats who feared losing their seats reportedly prevented any action.)

The constitution provides that every twenty years the voters shall decide whether a constitutional convention should be held. The last time the question came up was 1957. The referendum that year was the most recent opportunity the voters had to take steps which might have led to a reform of the system; the opportunity was lost. Half the voters failed to vote on the convention question; 48 per cent of those who did vote favored a convention; 52 per cent did not. The next opportunity will come in 1977.

Even if a convention had been held, the odds were against corrective action on apportionment, for the conventions themselves are constitutionally "stacked": each Senate district elects three delegates; fifteen are elected at-large.

Although a number of Republicans actively favored a convention in 1957 and were among the leaders of a "Committee for a Constitutional Convention," the state's most prominent Republicans were opposed. Former Governor Dewey, Party Chairman Morhouse, J. Russell Sprague (then the Nassau chairman and most powerful Republican in the state), Senate Majority Leader Walter J. Mahoney and the late Assembly Speaker Oswald D. Heck all lined up in opposition. The following excerpt from a *New York World-Telegram and Sun* story (Oct. 31, 1957) listing Dewey's reasons for opposing a convention is instructive: "Some persons who favor the Convention—Mr. Dewey did not specify who— want to use it to push for annexation of Nassau and Westchester Counties by New York City." The former governor also warned that a convention might raise existing limits on real estate taxes. These arguments were recalled when Nassau and Westchester votes were decisive in defeating the convention proposal. (New York City voted 61 per cent in favor; Nassau and Westchester voted 56 per cent against; the rest of the state voted 64 per cent against.)

Following the defeat of the convention proposal, a new possibility for reforming the apportionment system presented itself. In 1956, in anticipation of a convention, a "Temporary State Commission on the Constitutional Convention" had been set up to study issues and make recommendations. The Democratic governor, Averell Harriman, and the Republican Senate and Assembly leaders each appointed five members of the commission. (Politically, it was composed of eight Republicans, six Democrats, and one Liberal.) The commissioners chose Nelson Rockefeller as their chairman and held hearings on various subjects during 1957. There was more testimony on apportionment than on any other subject.

After the defeat of the convention proposal, Harriman, reportedly apprehensive over Rockefeller's rising prominence, opposed a 1958 Republican proposal that the commission be kept in existence to study constitutional revision and simplification. In opposing a convention, a number of Republicans had promised to press instead for continued study of the need for revision. When Harriman vetoed a bill to this effect, the Legislature simply changed the commission's title so as to make gubernatorial approval unnecessary. Instead of a "state commission," it became a "legislative committee" and later a "temporary commission." After Rockefeller was elected governor, a prominent jurist, David Peck, became chairman.

Late in 1958, the commission engaged a prominent out-of-state political scientist, Prof. Ruth Silva of Pennsylvania State University, to make a study of the apportionment problem. Her two-volume report, completed early in 1960, contained extensive criticism of the existing system and detailed suggestions for reforming it. Following its submission, some 200 copies of the report were reproduced, but these were never released and were apparently later "lost." Even the State Library was unable to secure one until Professor Silva turned her own copy over to it. She has never learned the fate of the other copies.

It is widely believed that the Silva report led directly to the final demise of the commission. As a "temporary" body, its continued existence depended on annual authorization by the Legislature. There was no controversy over this in 1959 or 1960, but in 1961, at the first session following completion of the apportionment report, the Republican leadership decided not to renew the authorization. Senate Minority Leader Joseph Zaretzki charged that "the Republican majority did not want the commission to continue its study of the controversial reapportionment section of the Constitution."

Although, for reasons cited above, the prospects for meaningful reform through action of the Legislature have seemed remote, recent developments may have made such action a real possibility. The Supreme Court's decision in *Baker v. Carr*, empowering federal courts to determine whether a state representation system violated the federal Constitution, may well impel the Legislature to act. Even before the decision, there had been indications that the New York system was being restudied by the Rockefeller administration. On March 29, 1962, three days after the Tennessee decision, the Governor announced that he had ordered a staff study of the question in the light of the opinion. He declined, however, to speculate on when the study would be completed or whether it would result in recommendations for changing the system.

Both before and since the March 26 decision, Democrats in the Legislature have been stressing the issue with increasing frequency. In the 1962 legislative session, the Senate and Assembly minority leaders introduced an amendment which would establish a bipartisan apportionment commission, a sixty-member Senate, a 180-member Assembly, and guarantee that Senate districts could not vary from one another in population by more than 7 per cent. There would still be an Assembly seat for each county, but the addition of thirty seats for the populous counties would considerably lessen the existing inequities. A *New York Times'* report

(Feb. 23, 1962), noting that the proposal's chances were minimal, said it could nevertheless "call attention to what the Democrats regard as 'a scandalous and discriminatory' reapportionment system" and that "it can also furnish Democrats with ammunition for the state election this year." The Legislature did not approve the proposed amendment.

Because of the Supreme Court decision, it now appears that at least some of the evils in the existing representation system may be vulnerable to attack through legal action. A federal court suit challenging the New York system of apportionment was initiated in 1961 by a New York radio station (WMCA) and five individual citizens, with the subsequent support of the New York City government. The plaintiffs contended that the state's apportionment formulas result in a grossly unfair weighting of both legislative houses in favor of the rural areas and that consequently the residents of the densely populated areas are denied the equal protection of the state's laws. The state's attorney general replied that no federal question was involved and that the federal courts therefore lacked jurisdiction. A three-judge federal court ruled in January 1962 that the plaintiffs had failed to establish a case upon which relief could be granted. In April, however, following the Tennessee decision, the case was appealed to the Supreme Court.

On June 11, in a 7-1 decision, the Supreme Court set aside the ruling of the three-judge court in a brief order. (Justice Harlan dissented, criticizing the Court for not setting guide-lines for the lower court.) The case was returned to the three-judge court for a hearing on its merits. Though neither the date nor the nature of that court's decision can be anticipated, there is serious doubt whether the state constitutional provisions, particularly those on Senate apportionment, can successfully withstand a challenge in the light of *Baker* v. *Carr*.

Since March 26, and particularly following the June 11 court directive, there has been much pressure on the Governor to call the Legislature into special session in order to make the apportionment system more equitable in advance of a possible court ruling. Demands for such a session have come not only from Democratic and Liberal Party sources but from several influential nonpartisan civic organizations.

In addition, at least one nationally prominent Republican has joined in the demand for a special session. J. Lee Rankin, solicitor general in the Eisenhower administration and now a resident of New York state, not only voiced such a demand but at the same time pointed out that the Justice Department's decision to act in support of the plaintiffs in the Tennessee case was made under a Republican administration. The reference was made in a letter to Governor Rockefeller urging that Republicans join in the attempts to achieve fairer systems of representation in state legislatures.

To date, the Governor has refused to call the Legislature into session, claiming that the matter is "too political" to be handled in a gubernatorial election year. As a result, the subject promises to become a major campaign issue in the fall elections.

Though it cannot be said that the recent Supreme Court decisions mark the beginning of the end of the fight for fairer representation in New York (or in most states), there is general agreement that they at least mark the end of the beginning.

# 14

## California
### "BRUTAL BUTCHERY OF THE TWO-PARTY SYSTEM"?

*H. FRANK WAY*
*University of California—Riverside*

Until 1958, California had long been a Republican bailiwick. Except for Culbert Olson, elected governor in 1938, no Democrat had lived in the governor's mansion since 1898. In 1958 Edmund G. Brown was elected as a Democratic governor, and the Democrats won all state-wide offices except that of Secretary of State. The new Congressional delegation was sixteen Democrats and fourteen Republicans, and the new state Legislature had solid Democratic majorities.[1] Democratic registration had long exceeded Republican in the state,[2] but this advantage in registration had meant little in the face of a weak and divided party and successful Republican gerrymandering.[3] However, the successes of the Democratic Party in the 1958 elections did not mean that the Republican Party was dead in California. In face of an overwhelming Democratic registration in the 1960 elections, the Republicans maintained their fourteen seats in the Congressional delegation and carried the state for Nixon in the presidential race.[4] It must also be remembered that the thumping success of the Democrats in 1958 was at least partially influenced by fortuitous circumstances, namely, two referendum issues which turned out voters with traditional Democratic loyalties—Catholics and labor-union members.[5] Fortune might not be so kind in the future. But the fact remains that in the decade of the 1950's the lot of the Republican Party in California had not been a happy one. The 1961 Assembly, which dominated the reapportionment process, was controlled by the Democrats in exactly the same ratio, forty-seven to thirty-three, as that by which the Republicans had controlled this body in 1951. Also in 1951 the Republicans had twenty-eight members in the Senate against twelve Democrats; now it was thirty Democrats against ten Republicans. Thus, when a

Democratic state Legislature was faced in early 1961 with the reapportionment of Assembly and Congressional districts, it appeared to be an opportunity to give a long-term Democratic cast to legislative elections in California. The stakes were not small; eighty Assembly districts were to be recast and eight new Congressional seats added. California gained 48.5 per cent in population from 1950 to 1960, from 10,586,223 to 15,717,204, and as a result was entitled to an increase in the House of Representatives from thirty to thirty-eight. This was one of the largest gains of any state in a single decade since the Civil War.[6]

## LEGAL RESTRICTIONS ON DISTRICTING

The opportunity which the Democrats had in 1961 to reapportion the Assembly and the Congressional districts had to be realized within the restrictions imposed by the state constitution. These restrictions are partially responsible for the gerrymandered face of California. However, both the Republicans and the Democrats have used the constitutional provisions to facilitate a gerrymander. The constitution, Article IV, Section 27, places the following limitations on the Legislature when it redraws Congressional district lines:

1. Counties in a Congressional district must be contiguous;

2. No county may be divided to make a Congressional district unless it has more than the ratio of population required for one or more Congressional districts; if it does have, then a residue Assembly district may be attached to compact adjoining Assembly districts in another county; and

3. Within a county, no Assembly district may be divided to form a Congressional district, and each Congressional district must be composed of compact, contiguous, whole Assembly districts.

Point Three tends to place the work of redistricting in a legal strait jacket, since it precludes making up Congressional districts of parts of Assembly districts. With the number of Assembly districts set at eighty, it is inevitable that in multidistrict counties, such as Los Angeles and San Francisco, but particularly the former, there will be some distortion of population.[7]

In the one place in the state where there is any large-scale opportunity for partisan redistricting, Los Angeles County, the constitutional limitations provide the means to that end. As Professor Hardy has stated of the 1951 reapportionment, "politicians took advantage of the constitutional requirements. . . . An assemblyman's support was obtained for a concentrated district in his favor; then the Assembly districts could be organized into Congressional districts to accomplish other purposes. A legislator bound himself to a Congressional bill, which in many cases was of only minor interest to him, in order to achieve his own personal interests in the Assembly reapportionment." [8]

The following limitations are placed on the Legislature when it redraws Assembly seats:

1. Assembly seats must be composed of contiguous territory;

2. No part of a county may be united with another county to form an assembly district;

3. No county may be divided to form Assembly districts unless it contains enough population to form two or more districts within itself;

4. Assembly districts must be as "nearly equal in population as may be." [9]

It is interesting to note that points Two and Three tend to contradict Point Four.

## THE LEGISLATIVE PROCESS IN 1961

Reapportionment is basically a legislative matter, and in California in 1961, since the Senate was not being reapportioned, reapportionment was the principal concern of the Assembly. Of course, reapportionment is also a broad political matter, and it would be misleading to maintain that the political issues here were determined and solved exclusively by the Assembly. Governor Brown did play a role, although its exact nature is difficult to state. At only one point was his name prominently associated with reapportionment, and that was when the Assembly leaders, Robert Crown and Jesse Unruh, requested that the compromises to which they had agreed with the Republicans be placed in the bill as it went through the Senate. Democratic Senator Richard Richards of Los Angeles County objected to these compromises, and Brown acted as a mediator between Richards and Crown. The result was an acceptance by the Senate of the agreed-upon compromises. Although Brown consistently denied being involved in the details of reapportionment, there were constant rumors throughout the late spring that the Governor was injecting his influence to bring about concessions demanded by local groups. For example, it was rumored that Brown's influence caused the legislative committee to alter its plans to include a part of Los Angeles County in the Santa Barbara-Ventura Congressional district. Nevertheless, the Governor's role was far from decisive. If there was a single guiding hand, it was probably that of Assemblyman Unruh, known throughout the state as "Big Daddy." It was widely rumored at the time of apportionment that Unruh was using reapportionment as a means of ensuring his election as speaker. Unruh, then chairman of the Ways and Means Committee, and Assemblyman Crown, chairman of the Committee on Elections and Apportionment, directed and controlled the strategy of the Democratic reapportionment. Unruh was later elected speaker of the Assembly, and Crown became the new chairman of the powerful Ways and Means Committee.

The Assembly Committee on Elections and Apportionment began its work in great secret in 1959.

The committee report was unveiled in May 1961. Most political observers agreed that the proposal was heavily weighted to favor the Democratic Party, practically insuring it seven new Congressional seats and five new Assembly seats. The report immediately met loud protests from various Republican Party leaders. Republican State Chairman John Krehbiel said the plan was the handiwork of selfish politicians who were more interested in perpetuating power than in the welfare of the state. In general, the Republicans called the plan a basic attack on the two-party system in California, predicting that it would cut down the Republican Party to token representation. The *Los Angeles Times* said of the plan: "This exceeds honest gerrymandering; it approaches grand larceny." [10]

The Republicans were particularly incensed to discover that a number of incumbent Republican assemblymen and congressmen had been thrown into the same districts. The Democratic strategy seemed simple enough. Protection of incumbency is one of the principal factors in reapportionment; therefore threaten enough Republican incumbents with defeat and induce a spirit of compromise among them. This is basically what happened. Many Republican leaders, particularly those outside the Legislature, wanted to take the issue to the people through a referendum. Their plan seemed to be to hold their lines against the proposals, make no compromises, and then attempt to win the voters over to the Republican position through a referendum. The strategy seemed plausible, but it did not work, for two reasons. First, the Republican lines were already cracked by Republicans who had compromised with the Democrats prior to May; and, second, referendums are costly, and referendums on reapportionment are particularly hazardous because of the complex nature of the issue which would face the voters.

Shortly after the proposal was unveiled, three Republican assemblymen agreed with the Democratic leadership to work out compromises which would save some incumbents. There were two groups of Republican assemblymen who helped to work out the compromises with the

Democratic leadership. The members of the first group, headed by assemblymen John Collier, James Holmes, and Glenn Coolidge, were either faced with tough Republican situations in their own districts or were interested in certain other advantages which might accrue to them if they were cooperative. For example, Assemblyman Coolidge was reported to have been interested in the new Twelfth Congressional District seat. This group was thus initially cooperative for personal reasons, mainly the protection of their incumbency. The second group, consisting of seven younger Republican assemblymen, was not involved in the initial consultations between the Democratic leadership and the Republicans prior to May. But, once the bill was unveiled and they saw no possibility of holding the Republican ranks together, they decided to support the Democratic bill in return for certain concessions, namely to reduce the Democratic registration by changing assemblymen Chet Wolfrum's and Clark Bradley's districts. The Democrats were interested in forestalling the possibility of a referendum by securing a majority vote of the Republican assemblymen in support of their bill.[11] The concessions were agreed upon, and the registration was lowered to 56 per cent Democratic. In California, such a registration will usually assure a Republican incumbent of victory.

These compromises, together with some modifications demanded by incumbent Democrats in the House of Representatives and the state Assembly, were agreed to by both the Assembly and the Senate, with more than a majority of the Republicans in the Assembly voting for the bill. Thereafter, Republican opposition outside the Legislature tapered off, with a few perfunctory threats of a court battle against the bill and some further talk about a referendum fight. Newspaper accounts seemed to indicate that Republicans, particularly those outside the Legislature, were placing high hopes in a referendum battle. But the Republican legislators knew that such a battle had little real possibility of success. The state chairman publicly talked of a referendum, but he apparently never anticipated such a battle and only talked about it to placate die-hard elements in the party and in the process to demonstrate to them the impossibility of such a struggle. Thus, from the point of view of Republican strategy, the referendum was always a thought, but not a very serious one. Though the compromises did protect incumbent Republicans in both the Assembly and the House of Representatives, it is certain that a few Republican legislators are marked for extinction in the Assembly and the U.S. House.

For a short time it appeared that the Republicans would get support from the Democratic Negro and Mexican groups in Los Angeles, who felt that the bill did not give their groups sufficient advantage. At the time of reapportionment there were two Negro assemblymen, both

Democrats, and no Negro congressmen. Negro groups in the Los Angeles area were demanding that the committee draw districts so as to ensure the election of four Negro assemblymen and two Negro congressmen. The bill as finally adopted appears to ensure the election of one Negro congressman and two assemblymen from the Los Angeles area, but the one Negro assemblyman from the north, William Rumford (D. Alameda County), if he seeks re-election, will be running in a district which no longer has a substantial Negro population. (It was rumored at the time of reapportionment that Assemblyman Rumford was slated for a federal appointment.) This opposition, vocal for a few weeks after the committee announced its plan, disappeared by the late summer.

A variety of local interests were influential in the shaping of the 1961 reapportionment. Major governmental, political, and economic pressure groups consulted informally with the Democratic Assembly leadership throughout 1959 and 1960. The committee also sought out public opinion in a series of public hearings held throughout the state in the fall of 1959 and the spring of 1960.[12] Most of the delegations were interested in securing or maintaining local advantages in reapportionment. Since California has a high ratio of military and naval installations and since the state is one of the largest recipients of federal contracts, there were many vested interests to be protected, particularly in Congressional reapportionment. However, the reapportionment process in 1961 was essentially a closed-door affair, and it is difficult to measure the impact of these local representations on the committee. That they were made and that they had some impact is undoubted. Certainly in those cases where the committee failed to protect strong local interests in the framing of its proposed legislation opposition was raised. For example, when the committee released its legislation in early May it had placed Republicans H. Allen Smith and G. P. Lipscomb in the same district. This brought a protest from the Republican state chairman: "If we lose H. Allen Smith, California will lose vital rules committee seniority in Congress, thereby affecting our defense contracts and federal aid."[13] The committee subsequently agreed to boundary changes which placed these incumbents in separate and safe Republican districts. In the final analysis, it is difficult to distinguish the protection of local interests from the protection of incumbency. In a weak party system, the incumbent is frequently the protector of local interests, and thus most students of reapportionment see incumbency as the central factor.

The one final issue which might have influenced reapportionment, the north-south struggle, appears to have had little if any influence in the current reapportionment. Southern California, with its exploding population, received five of the eight new seats. Of these five, Los Angeles received three, and Orange and San Diego each got an additional seat.

The southern half of California [14] has approximately 60 per cent of the state's population and 60 per cent of the new Assembly seats. The south now has forty-seven of the eighty seats, whereas under the 1951 bill it had only forty-five of the eighty. Thus, the south controls the Assembly, and the real north-south struggle will come in the reapportionment of the Senate, where the south has only ten seats out of forty districts.[15]

## RESULTS OF THE 1951 APPORTIONMENT

The Republicans were successful in four elections from 1952 to 1958 in maintaining a partisan advantage in Congressional representation by reapportionment and were only slightly less successful in maintaining this advantage in Assembly representation.[16] Contrary to the conclusions of a recent study of this problem,[17] it can be quickly demonstrated that at least the 1951 reapportionment did not give the two parties seats in a ratio consistent with the proportion of votes received. In fact, the Republicans were so successful in maintaining a partisan advantage from gerrymandering that in 1956 they continued to control a majority of Assembly seats in face of a state-wide majority favoring the Democrats. Also in 1954 and 1956 the Republicans got well over a majority of the congressional seats, but the Democrats had a substantial state-wide majority in both elections.

However, by 1960 the advantages of the earlier apportionment had turned into a disadvantage in Assembly elections. In 1960 the Republicans increased their total state-wide Assembly vote proportionately by 5 per cent over 1958, and yet their delegation was reduced by one. The explanation is not difficult. In a state with a rapidly increasing and highly mobile population, the formerly safe and overrepresented Republican districts of 1952 became safe and underrepresented districts in 1960. This is particularly true in the metropolitan suburban areas. For example, the Seventy-Fourth Assembly District, in Orange County, in a contested 1952 election returned a Republican majority of 34,000, but this safe Republican majority was 72,000 by 1960.

Although by 1960 the Assembly apportionment had turned slightly against the Republicans, they continued to reap a small advantage from the Congressional apportionment. But even here the tide appeared to be turning against the 1951 apportionment. Had this Congressional apportionment continued, the Republicans might have faced severe underrepresentation. Again, the same general explanation applies as in the case of Assembly districts: formerly safe and overrepresented Republican districts were now safe and underrepresented. For example, the Twenty-Eighth Congressional District, comprising Orange County and part of San Diego County, returned a Republican majority of 106,000 in the

**CURRENT DISTRICTS**

**NEW DISTRICTS**

5-11, 14 →
See
San Francisco Area

17, 19-32
See
Los Angeles Area

34-37 →
See
San Diego Area

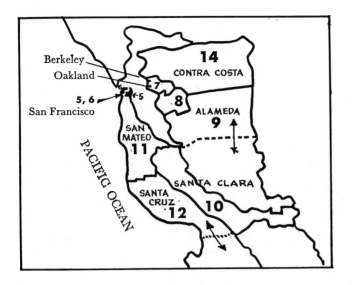

SAN FRANCISCO AREA

SAN DIEGO AREA

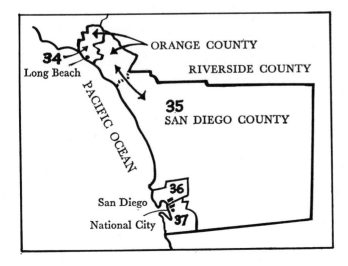

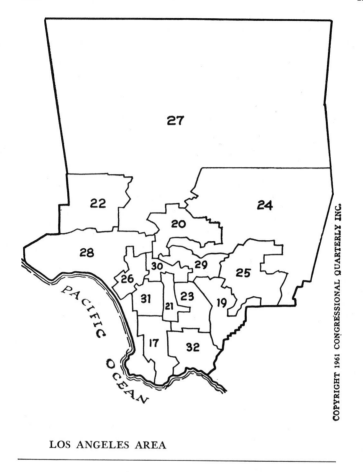

LOS ANGELES AREA

contested 1952 election. By 1960 this majority had grown to 241,000. The same development occurred in other districts, particularly the Tenth, Thirteenth, Twenty-First, and Thirtieth.

It would be easy to conclude, then, that reapportionment in California is a risky business and that a gerrymander can easily backfire. Though this is true, the risks are not great, and the rewards can be. To observe that the Republicans *might* have suffered in the 1960's if the 1951 apportionment had remained the law is not to conclude that the 1951 gerrymander backfired. The 1951 legislation was not framed for the 1960's and it certainly served a highly partisan end for a considerable period of its intended life. It did not reduce the Democratic Party to a nonentity, and the Democrats even regained power under it, but it did give the Republican Party an advantage in the face of a strengthening opponent.

## DID GERRYMANDERING OCCUR IN CALIFORNIA IN 1961?

Redistricting in California in 1961 had many of the traditional characteristics of gerrymandering: districts of unequal populations with contorted shapes and the usual combinations of heterogeneous population groups. The Republicans cried "brutal butchery," and the Democrats proclaimed a clean conscience. They claimed, with some justification, that at least their reapportionment was not as distorted as the gerrymandering of the Republicans in 1951.[18] On the basis of population deviations, the new districts are more nearly equal than were those designed by the Republicans in 1951. The Democrats pointed out that, whereas in 1951 there were forty-one (over half) Assembly districts and twenty (56 per cent) Congressional districts which exceeded a 10 per-cent population deviation, under their 1961 plan only thirty-one (38 per cent) Assembly districts and fifteen (40 per cent) Congressional districts exceeded this 10 per-cent deviation. But the new plan will give the Democrats a considerable edge over the Republicans by drawing the districts in such a way that the overwhelming majority of districts which are either safely Democratic or lean to that party are below the mean, whereas the majority of districts which are either safely or leaning Republican are above the mean population. In other words, the new plan concentrates the Republican strength throughout the state in as few districts as possible.[19] Finally, it is also important to realize that in California the greatest partisan advantages from reapportionment can be realized in the multidistrict counties, particularly Los Angeles County. Thus, under the 1961 Congressional reapportionment the Democrats have ten overrepresented districts and one underrepresented district, whereas the Republicans have two over- and one underrepresented districts.

Yet this explanation is relatively unconvincing in determining whether gerrymandering occurred on a large scale. What is important is not the percentage of Assembly or Congressional districts which deviate from the ideal or arithmetic mean, but rather the extent of the deviation and where and how it occurred. The highest percentage deviation in a Congressional district in 1951 was −35.2 (Sixteenth District), whereas the Democrats topped this in 1961 with a +43.1 population deviation in the new Twenty-Eighth Congressional District.[20] In the Republican reapportionment of the state Assembly in 1951, the highest percentage deviations were −52.8 (Seventy-Sixth District) and +51.5 (Twelfth District). Under the 1961 bill, the Democrats again topped the Republicans with a +55.9 (Seventy-Fourth District) and −63.3 (Seventy-Fifth District). The +55.9 deviation occurred in Riverside County, making it the most un-

## TABLE 1

### CONGRESSIONAL AND ASSEMBLY ELECTIONS 1952-1960 *

*1952*

*Assembly vote*

| | | | *Assemblymen elected* | | |
|---|---|---|---|---|---|
| Republican | 2,665,239 | (67%) | Republican | 56 | (70%) |
| Democrat | 1,306,659 | (33%) | Democrat | 24 | (30%) |

*Congressional vote* — *Congressmen elected*

| Republican | 2,382,921 | (54%) | Republican | 19 | (63.3%) |
| Democrat | 2,030,550 | (46%) | Democrat | 11 | (36.7%) |

*1954*

*Assembly vote* — *Assemblymen elected*

| Republican | 1,831,074 | (50.5%) | Republican | 48 | (60%) |
| Democrat | 1,793,860 | (49.5%) | Democrat | 32 | (40%) |

*Congressional vote* — *Congressmen elected*

| Republican | 1,876,626 | (48.5%) | Republican | 19 | (63.3%) |
| Democrat | 1,991,169 | (51.5%) | Democrat | 11 | (36.7%) |

*1956*

*Assembly vote* — *Assemblymen elected*

| Republican | 2,331,529 | (46.5%) | Republican | 42 | (52.5%) |
| Democrat | 2,664,873 | (53.5%) | Democrat | 38 | (47.5%) |

*Congressional vote* — *Congressmen elected*

| Republican | 2,466,620 | (47.6%) | Republican | 17 | (56.6%) |
| Democrat | 2,710,700 | (52.4%) | Democrat | 13 | (43.4%) |

*1958*

*Assembly vote* — *Assemblymen elected*

| Republican | 1,972,123 | (40.5%) | Republican | 34 | (42.5%) |
| Democrat | 2,897,358 | (59.5%) | Democrat | 46 | (57.5%) |

*Congressional vote* — *Congressmen elected*

| Republican | 1,981,356 | (40%) | Republican | 14 | (46.7%) |
| Democrat | 2,971,761 | (60%) | Democrat | 16 | (53.3%) |

*1960*

*Assembly vote* — *Assemblymen elected*

| Republican | 2,754,361 | (45%) | Republican | 33 | (41.2%) |
| Democrat | 3,358,750 | (55%) | Democrat | 47 | (58.8%) |

*Congressional vote* — *Congressmen elected*

| Republican | 2,855,114 | (46.1%) | Republican | 14 | (46.7%) |
| Democrat | 3,336,989 | (53.9%) | Democrat | 16 | (53.3%) |

* Contested as well as uncontested elections are reported here. If only contested elections were used, it would be possible to arrive at the startling conclusion that the Democrats were overrepresented in the middle 1950's because they were less successful in cross-filing and thus had to face more contested elections. Cross-filing was abolished in 1958, but the party label appeared on the ballot beginning in 1954.

derrepresented Assembly district in the state. This district now has a Republican assemblyman, and if it were given a new assemblyman it would probably elect another Republican. On the other hand, the most overrepresented district, the −63.3 district, is a Democratic one.

## CONCLUSIONS

1. Gerrymandering in California under the Democrats in 1961 was on a somewhat reduced scale in comparison to the Republican reapportionment of 1951, but it was nonetheless gerrymandering. The 1961 law caused the same types of contorted districts and population distortions as occurred in 1951.

2. The constitutional requirement that Congressional districts be made up of whole Assembly districts and the requirement that no part of a county may be united with another county to form an Assembly district make some inequalities necessary and provide excuses for further inequalities.

3. The willingness of the Republican assemblymen to compromise with the Democrats ruined any slight chance they had of winning a referendum vote against the new apportionment. However, these compromises did protect a number of incumbent Republicans in the Assembly and the House of Representatives. Still, it is certain that a few Republicans are marked for extinction in the Assembly and the House of Representatives simply because of the gerrymandered nature of the new apportionment. It is apparent that the factor of incumbency was the central factor inducing compromise, and incumbency is thus strong enough to break party lines, particularly the lines of an already-weakened minority party.

4. If the electorate in California continues to vote according to the trend of the last six years, the new apportionment will result in a new line-up of twenty-three Democrats and fifteen Republicans in the House delegation and fifty-two Democrats and twenty-eight Republicans in the Assembly. However, the Republicans are likely to retain the minimum twenty-seven Assembly seats necessary to kill a Democratic governor's budget or uphold a Republic governor's veto.

5. The Republican charges that the new apportionment is a basic assault on the two-party system in California seem less than justified. Gerrymandering in California will not give anything like a permanent cast to California legislative elections. Much as the Democrats were able in the late 1950's to wipe out the 1951 Republican gerrymander by increasing successes at the polls, so, too, would a revitalized Republican Party be able to do the same thing. In this respect, the reappearance of Richard Nixon in California politics is the big question mark. If Nixon can rid the

party of the taint of the radical right in California without alienating either traditional centers of financial support or the rank-and-file conservative party workers, then the Republican Party will be able to reassert its former power in Sacramento.

# Notes

[1] Dean E. McHenry, "The Pattern of California Politics," *Western Political Quarterly*, I (1948), 44-53; Winston W. Crouch *et al.*, *California Government and Politics* (2nd ed.; Englewood Cliffs, N.J.: Prentice-Hall, 1960), pp. 53-75.

[2] Crouch, *op. cit.*, p. 56.

[3] See Table 1 for results of 1951 Republican reapportionment.

[4] There are other reasons than those suggested above why Democratic registration in California is misleading: first, many Democrats are such in name only, their original attachment being based on their Southern origin, the Depression, or Dust-Bowl loyalty; second, Republicans are more apt to vote.

[5] The issues were two proposed amendments, one the so-called right-to-work law and the other a proposed taxation of Catholic parochial schools.

[6] "California—Eight Seat Gain," *Congressional Quarterly Weekly Report*, XIX (1961), 1280-1285.

[7] Robert J. Pitchell, "Reapportionment as a Control of Voting in California," *Western Political Quarterly*, XIV (1961), 214, 234. The requirement that Congressional districts be made up of whole Assembly districts appears to stem from pressure by the associations of county clerks and registrars of voters, who would find it more difficult to prepare ballots if Assembly districts were divided in making up Congressional districts.

[8] Leroy C. Hardy, "The California Reapportionment of 1951" (unpublished Ph.D. dissertation, University of California, Los Angeles, 1955), p. 403.

[9] California State Legislature, *Report of the Assembly Interim Committee on Elections and Reapportionment* (1951), pp. 23-26.

[10] May 17, 1961, part III, p. 4.

[11] On the first vote in the Assembly, on May 25, the two separate apportionment bills, Assembly and Congressional districts, were accepted fifty-five to twenty-five, with ten Republicans joining forty-five Democrats and two Democrats joining twenty-three Republicans. The Senate vote on June 10 was strictly along party lines, twenty-seven Democrats to ten Republicans. In the final passage in the Assembly, the Democrats picked up seven more Republican votes, thus giving them a majority of the Republican assemblymen.

[12] For a summary of these hearings see, *Assembly Interim Committee Reports, 1959-1961*, Vol. 7, No. 5, "Report of the Assembly Interim Committee on Elections and Reapportionment."

[13] *Sacramento Bee*, May 19, 1961, p. A 6. The Democrats claimed privately that placing Smith and Lipscomb in the same district was merely a technical error in drafting the law and that they had no intention of depriving either man of his seat.

14 Though there are several lines which have been used to divide the state, the most frequently used one is the straight line from northern San Luis Obispo County through northern San Bernardino County.

15 Since the new Twelfth Congressional District cuts across the north-south line, it is not possible to give an accurate percentage of the south's share of the Congressional seats, although it does not appear to be underrepresented.

16 See Table 1.

17 Pitchell, *op. cit.,* pp. 233-235.

18 See Table 1 for the results of the 1951 reapportionment.

19 On the basis of the forecast made by the *Congressional Quarterly Weekly Report, op. cit.,* p. 1280, the Democrats have nineteen of the twenty-four most overrepresented Congressional districts, and the Republicans have eight of the fourteen most underrepresented districts.

20 See the map, which shows this contorted district.

# PART SIX

## Bypassing the Legislature — An Urban Opportunity

*INTRODUCTION*     In states where urban interests are unable to win the majority in the legislature necessary to accomplish constitutional or statutory revision in apportionment, there are some routes open that bypass the legislature: the initiative, the constitutional convention, and the courts.

Only about one-fourth the states have provisions for constitutional change by initiative, and a few others permit the statutory initiative. The initiative has been used occasionally to overcome legislative inertia, to revise the constitutional formula for apportionment, and even to transfer the apportioning function out of legislative hands. It is, however, a weapon that can be, and has been, used by rural as well as urban forces. The best study of the initiative is the case study by Gordon E. Baker, *The Politics of Reapportionment in Washington State*. This study of the 1956 initiative campaign in that state demonstrates the difficulty of handling such a complex issue through the initiative and the pitfalls that can be created by legislators hostile to reapportionment. Although both parties were divided on the issue, the initiative was approved by the voters, but there was strong enough opposition in the legislature to bring about drastic amendment of the initiated measure.

The constitutional convention bypasses the legislature, but less completely. Except in states where there is a periodic referendum on a convention, the legislature must take the first step. Moreover, the convention is often apportioned on the same basis as the legislature. It is significant that in Michigan it was necessary to adopt a formula for representation in the convention less favorable to rural areas before urban and labor groups would support a convention. In past constitutional conventions, the apportionment issue has frequently been subordinated to other reforms, or even completely excluded. The controversy over constitutional reform in Michigan has centered on the apportionment issue. It is an issue that has divided both parties, particularly the Republicans, while providing the focus for interparty conflict over the convention. The success or failure of constitutional reform in Michigan hinges largely on the apportionment question. Michigan's experience may, in turn, determine whether the convention becomes a more promising method of apportionment reform for other states.

Proponents of judicial review of apportionment systems could hardly have found a better state than Tennessee for their test case. It is a state where population trends have been ignored for sixty years, with demonstrable effect on the political structure and legislative decision-making in the state. The decision in *Baker* v. *Carr* had just as prompt an impact in Maryland, where a case was already pending in the state courts. The situation in Maryland was different because the malapportionment resulted largely from the state constitution, whereas in Tennessee it resulted from ignoring constitutional provisions. But the case for judicial intervention was strong in Maryland because the apportionment system vitally affected the power structure and because the political routes to apportionment reform appeared virtually impassable.

Unlike the initiative and the constitutional convention, the courts offer a route to reapportionment in all states. But it is by no means certain that the courts will find that every apportionment system denying complete voting equality to urbanites and suburbanites is a denial of equal protection of the laws. The decision in *Baker* v. *Carr* has given a powerful but uncertain weapon to urban citizens; it has added a new dimension to the politics of reapportionment.

# 15

# Michigan Legislative Apportionment
## KEY TO CONSTITUTIONAL CHANGE *

*KARL A. LAMB*
*University of Michigan*

The state of Michigan presents a classic example of the effects of industrialization and urbanization on the pattern of legislative apportionment. All the usual elements of the drama are present—a single dominant urban area; the Democratic Party, with strength based in that area, capturing state-wide offices; Republicans maintaining control of the Legislature; and the leaders of each party blaming the other for governmental stalemate. There have even been constitutional provisions to divert state sales taxes collected largely in the cities to the support of government in rural areas. Yet there are factors to complicate the classic picture, for the least-populous counties (in Michigan's chronically depressed upper peninsula) are Democratic in their political allegiance, are generally the most overrepresented, and have been reluctant to join their city colleagues in the call for reapportionment. Furthermore, the most underrepresented districts are the burgeoning suburbs around Detroit, areas of potential Republican strength.

Michigan's parties are wedded to opposing ideologies more firmly than most U.S. political parties. The confrontation of Democratic governor and Republican Legislature has resulted in more than a decade of partisan bitterness and governmental frustration. But the issue of legislative apportionment caused such factional differences that neither party could agree within itself how to resolve the issue. Nonpartisan

* The author wishes to acknowledge the aid of Dr. Walter deVries of Calvin College, a delegate to the Constitutional Convention from Kent County, and of Prof. John P. White, University of Michigan, who acted as a research adviser to the Convention, though they bear no responsibility for the facts or interpretation here presented.

civic organizations were largely responsible for bringing about the Constitutional Convention of 1961-1962.

Thus, Michigan falls in the category of states where machinery is available to handle the problem of legislative apportionment. The Constitutional Convention dealt with a much broader range of issues, but reapportionment was the storm center around which all else revolved.

## CAUSE AND CONSEQUENCES OF DIVIDED GOVERNMENT

In 1908, when Michigan's present constitution was adopted, the automobile industry had yet to begin its explosive development. But the centralization of that industry in the next two decades, coupled with the closing of the exhausted mines of the upper peninsula, resulted in dramatic population shifts. Four counties in southeastern Michigan contained 24 per cent of the state's population in 1910, 49 per cent in 1930, and 54 per cent in 1960.[1]

The constitution of 1908 required the Legislature to rearrange the senatorial districts and reapportion the lower house every ten years, but the Legislature was understandably content with its own makeup and refused to take this responsibility very seriously. Prior to 1952, the Senate had last been apportioned in 1925, and the House in 1943. Initiative proposals calling for reapportionment were defeated by the voters in 1924, 1930, and 1932.

The present basis of Michigan's legislative apportionment was established by a constitutional amendment adopted in 1952. In that year, the Michigan Committee for Representative Government, supported largely by the CIO, initiated a petition providing for the use of population as the sole basis for representation in both houses. Due to the attitude of Democrats in the upper peninsula, the Democratic Party did not support the measure with unanimity. A counterproposal providing for a "balanced Legislature" was initiated by a group of conservative interests, including the Michigan Farm Bureau. Its chief spokesmen were Republican legislators. After a campaign marked by its vehemence, the counterproposal was adopted by a margin of 294,000 votes. The "population-only" proposal won a majority only in Macomb, Oakland, and Wayne counties, in southeastern Michigan.

The 1952 amendment specified the boundaries of the senatorial districts—with minor changes, the same boundaries that then existed—and froze them into the constitution. The senatorial districts were, therefore, based on the incomplete reapportionment of 1925, which, even then, provided substantial overrepresentation for areas which have since declined steadily in population. The House was to be reapportioned every ten years, if not by the Legislature, then by the State Board of

Canvassers. Apportionment of House seats in counties with more than one member was made the responsibility of the county boards of supervisors. At-large districts were permitted, resulting in a slight Republican edge in Kent County and a considerable Democratic advantage in Wayne County. The size of the House was fixed at 110 seats, a "moiety clause" provided that any county or group of counties with one-half of one per cent of the state's population would be granted a seat in the lower house. There were twenty-three moiety districts, including all those in the upper peninsula and others in the farming areas of the state. The result was that, compared to other states, the Michigan lower house ranked seventh in "representativeness" (that is, there were six states in which population distribution was better reflected in the apportionment of the lower house). In regard to the Senate, however, Michigan ranked twenty-ninth; there were twenty-eight states in which a larger proportion of the population controlled a majority of the seats. In 1961, 27 per cent of Michigan's population could elect 51 per cent of the Senate.[2]

Since 1952, Democrats have won nearly every state-wide office; Republicans have maintained a slender majority in the lower house. Most of the moiety districts are Republican, and the Republican vote for legislators has been minuscule in Wayne County. In 1958, 1,404,935 Democratic votes elected fifty-five representatives, while 776,999 Republican votes also elected fifty-five representatives. (The illness of a Democratic member allowed the Republicans to organize the House.) The Senate, on the other hand, has been since 1952 "Republican by constitutional design." In the 1958 election, twenty-two Republicans and twelve Democratic senators were elected. The Democrats together received 46,000 more votes than did the Republicans. Democratic Wayne County (Detroit), which contains 34.2 per cent of the state's population, elected but seven of the thirty-four members of the Senate.

The full impact of Michigan's apportionment system has been felt with the development of a genuine two-party system in the state. Since the Civil War, Michigan had been safely Republican territory. Democrats won state office only when factional divisions in the Republican Party splintered its clear majority. As with most one-party areas, the internal politics of the Michigan Republican Party was the politics of patronage and personal factionalism.[3] In 1948, G. Mennen Williams, a Democrat, was elected governor for the first of an unprecedented six terms. During that time, Williams developed a coalition based on the political activity and support of organized labor and led by a group of enthusiastic amateurs of liberal persuasion. The program of the Michigan party has been aggressively liberal in content, particularly after the United Automobile Workers defeated the Teamsters for influence in the party. The main weapon in Governor Williams' arsenal was a partisan attack on the Republican Legislature, which he pictured with considerable veracity as dominated by conservatism and hostile to the residents of urban areas, specifically Detroit.

The Republican Party felt effectively excluded from Wayne County because Republican neighborhoods were swallowed up in multimember districts. Turning their backs on Detroit, Republicans cemented the relationship between their rural and small-town adherents and the leaders of Michigan industry. The common conception of Michigan politics is that the Democratic Party is the creature of the United Automobile Workers, whereas the Republican party is dominated by the directors of General Motors and Ford. A study of campaign finances, however, reveals that this impression is certainly exaggerated and probably misleading. The interest-group coalitions supporting both parties are in fact much more complex, and certainly many rural Republican legislators would continue to occupy safe seats if the entire board of directors of General Motors should enlist in the Democratic Party.[4]

Michigan has suffered from the malady of divided government for fourteen years. The effects of this malady are considerably attenuated when an executive of one party is able to count on a large measure of cooperation from the legislative majority of the opposite party, as happened during the Eisenhower administration. Such cooperation has never existed in Michigan. Michigan's present parties are ideologically oriented; the party caucus is supreme in both houses of the Legislature; partisan passions burn at fever heat; and the state has a long record of bitter rivalry between the governor and the Legislature, which reached its peak in the tax crisis of 1959.[5] This incident, which resulted in a "payless payday" for state employees, was widely considered to have been engineered by Republican legislators to destroy the presidential aspirations of Governor Williams.

Conflict was renewed with the election of Democrat John B. Swainson as Williams' successor in 1960. A former senator and lieutenant governor, Swainson was hailed as a chief executive who could work with the Legislature. Faltering attempts on his part to achieve cooperation between the two branches of government were soundly rebuffed. Recent events—such as the refusal of the Legislature to pass enabling legislation which would have brought $20,000,000 in federal funds for aid to dependent children—reveal the deep-rooted conflict between the urban-centered Democratic Party and the rural-based Republican legislative party.

The leaders of the state Republican organization have clearly perceived that the Republican Party can win state-wide office only by appealing to the urban centers. In recent years, state chairmen have been elected by party conventions which provided adequate representation for urban areas. But the state Republican organization (exemplified by its central committee) has little influence over the action of the county organizations and none over the behavior of party members in the Legislature.

The divergence of views between the urban-oriented moderate Republicans and the rural-based conservative Republicans is very great, but the two wings are bound together at least by the party label. With Democratic strength concentrated in Wayne County, the Republican Party is the single institution with the potential ability of building a bridge of compromise between the Michigan of the Farm Bureau and the Michigan of the United Automobile Workers. The party proved unequal to that task during the years of Williams' governorship. The responsibility for accomplishing it became inescapable with the calling of the Constitutional Convention.

## THE ROAD TO CON-CON

Students of government had long proclaimed the flaws in Michigan's constitutional structure which hampered the adaptation of the government to the demands of an urban, industrial society. One of these was the debt limitation of $250,000; another was the long ballot. Michigan elected eight state officials, making the heads of administrative departments independent of the will of the governor. The earmarking of taxes limited the power of the Legislature to manage fiscal policy, and the structure of township and county government was specified by the Constitution. Among those groups which had long studied the possibility of constitutional revision, the most notable was the League of Women Voters.

The 1908 constitution provided that the question of calling a constitutional convention be proposed to the voters every sixteen years. This automatic submission date fell in 1958. The League of Women Voters campaigned vigorously for the call for a constitutional convention (or "Con-Con") and their efforts were endorsed by Paul Bagwell, the Republican nominee for governor. Major elements of Bagwell's party did not support his stand on this issue. The State Association of Supervisors opposed the scheme, for any examination of the constitution would challenge the system of township government and the constitutional status of their jobs. The Michigan Farm Bureau, happy with the influence exerted by its agents on rural senators, viewed Con-Con as a threat to the existing apportionment of the Legislature and thus of their power to block the programs of Democratic governors.

The Michigan AFL-CIO, which had met defeat in its campaign for the principle of "one man, one vote" in 1952, opposed the 1958 call for Con-Con because the constitution provided that three delegates would be chosen from each senatorial district. Such a convention, labor claimed, would be a continuation of the minority rule of the malapportioned Senate. It could easily write a worse constitution than that of 1908. With the Democrats of the upper peninsula opposing Con-Con because of a fear of reapportionment, the Democratic Party was almost unanimously opposed to the measure. The combination of the AFL-CIO with the Farm Bureau on the same side of an issue is as rare in Michigan as it is unbeatable.

A majority of those voting on the issue approved the Con-Con call, but the 1908 constitution required a majority voting in the election. This was not achieved, and the issue failed. Paul Bagwell's challenge to G. Mennen Williams was unsuccessful, with Wayne County piling up a large Democratic majority. Rural Republicans claimed that Bagwell's defeat was due to his courting the big-city vote; such antics, they held, kept nonmetropolitan Republicans away from the polls.

Election statistics do in fact reveal a gradual attrition of the Republican unanimity of many of Michigan's most rural counties. The Democratic vote for governor has risen more than 5 per cent since 1952 in eleven counties in the upper section of Michigan's lower peninsula. A typical county is Kalkaska, which voted 32.5 per cent for Democrat Williams in 1952. Democrat Swainson received 37.7 per cent of Kalkaska's vote in 1960. The state-wide Democratic percentage was practically identical in the two years, because Democratic gains in some areas were balanced by Republican gains in others. Bagwell's two campaigns brought significant increases in the Republican majorities in the heavily populated counties outside the Detroit metropolitan area—such counties as Muskegon (city of Muskegon), Kent (Grand Rapids), Ottawa (Grand Rapids suburbs and Holland), Calhoun (Battle Creek), and Kalamazoo (city of Kalamazoo). Bagwell's campaigns made little impact in the Detroit area, where the Democratic percentage rose throughout the period.[6]

Because the Democratic vote increase in nonmetropolitan Michigan is still far short of attaining majority proportions, the result has been to intensify the political division of the state. It is more than a party division between urban and rural areas. It is in fact a division between Detroit and the balance of the state, with the exception of a few Democrats elected from the upper peninsula. Because the overwhelming Democratic vote in the Detroit area provides the basis for a safe Democratic majority in most state-wide contests, the Democrats expect to elect the governor. They also expect his program to be frustrated by the Republican Legislature.

Legislative reapportionment seems the only way to end the stalemate. In 1959, August Scholle, president of the Michigan AFL-CIO, planned a new attack on the problem. He filed suit in the Michigan Supreme Court, charging that the "balanced-Legislature" amendment of 1952 violated the guarantees of due process and equal protection of the laws provided in the Fourteenth Amendment to the United States Constitution. Scholle asked the court to declare the 1952 amendment invalid; to enjoin the secretary of state from issuing 1960 election notices until the Senate reapportioned itself according to the requirements of the unamended 1908 Michigan constitution; and, failing reapportionment, to declare all elections to the state Senate to be at-large.

Three members of the court were willing to act; five were not. Five opinions were written. The one view common to the majority opinions was that there was no established federal principle by which the state provision could be judged and that the Michigan court must find the question nonjusticiable, following the precedent established by the United States Supreme Court.[7]

Notice of appeal to the U.S. Supreme Court was filed on December 12, 1960. The Michigan case joined that group of reapportionment cases headed by *Baker* v. *Carr,* the Tennessee dispute.

As the judicial process continued along its leisurely path, the 1959 session of the Legislature ground to its end in an atmosphere of intractable partisan bitterness. Economic recession had limited the receipts from the state sales tax, the state's principal source of income, and the Senate and the governor were unable to agree on a program of tax reform. The "payless payday" was a result. It seemed clear that Michigan's basic governmental structure was unable to deal with the fundamental problems of the state. The League of Women Voters renewed its interest in constitutional revision and was joined by the Junior Chamber of Commerce. A "gateway amendment" to the 1908 constitution was drafted, providing that one delegate to a future constitutional convention be chosen from each senatorial district and one from each district of the lower house. It further provided that a majority voting on the question would be sufficient to call a convention and that the question should be posed in April 1961.

Opinion among the public concerned with state politics was bitterly divided as the League of Women Voters and the Junior Chamber of Commerce began the initiative campaign to place the gateway amendment on the ballot. The AFL-CIO felt that this compromise on the selection of Con-Con delegates was unsatisfactory because it still provided substantial overrepresentation for rural areas. The Farm Bureau opposed the amendment, as did the Association of Supervisors, but the Michigan Chamber

of Commerce favored it. It was no small task to obtain signatures on petitions equal to 10 per cent of the total vote for governor at the previous
election.

Just when it seemed that the initiative campaign might fail, a new
"civic-reform" organization appeared on the scene. It was called Citizens
for Michigan and was headed by George Romney, president of American
Motors Company. Romney criticized the political activities of the other
automakers and launched the organization with overtones of hostility to
parties and the political process. At its peak, Citizens for Michigan
claimed about 2,000 members, centered largely in the urban areas. But
the organization provided money and technical knowledge that pushed
the initiative campaign over the top. The question won a place on the
ballot of November 1960.

Paul Bagwell again won the Republican nomination and campaigned strenuously for approval of the Con-Con amendment. Retiring
governor Williams also supported the scheme. Bagwell's opponent, John
Swainson, had been a surprise victor in the Democratic primary, which
he won through massive support from the AFL-CIO. Swainson at first
refused to support the Con-Con amendment, but, when it seemed clear
late in the campaign that passage of the measure was assured, the AFL-
CIO modified its opposition, and Swainson endorsed the proposal.

The center of attention in the election was, of course, the contest
between Nixon and Kennedy. Kennedy carried Michigan, while Swainson
and all other Democratic candidates for state-wide office were victorious.
The gateway amendment, which had been a main Bagwell campaign
theme, was adopted by a slender majority, while Bagwell was defeated
with a vote total leading Nixon's. Swainson's majority came from the
populous counties of southeastern Michigan; the Con-Con amendment
was adopted because of the vote in the same areas. The majority of voters
in the other seventy-nine counties were opposed to Con-Con. In the
Spring election of 1961, the regular time for electing the superintendent
of public instruction and the governing bodies of the three state universities, the call for a constitutional convention was placed on the ballot.
Fifty-one per cent of those voting on the issue approved the call. Substantial majorities were rolled up in southeastern Michigan—Wayne,
Oakland, and Macomb counties (Detroit metropolitan area) and Wash-
tenaw county (Ann Arbor). Seventy-nine counties were arrayed against
the measure. One-quarter of the state's eligible voters exercised their
franchise on the issue.

## The Contest for Delegates

Considerable discussion took place concerning the method of electing delegates to Con-Con, with some members of the League of Women

Voters favoring nonpartisan elections. Members of the Junior Chamber of Commerce drafting the gateway amendment decided to leave this matter to the Legislature. That body determined that delegates should be nominated in party primaries, elected on a partisan ticket, and receive a salary of $1,000 per month during the period of the convention.

Opportunity was provided for the injection of party responsibility into a situation that would otherwise have been chaotic. Party organizations were generally able to defeat "crackpot" candidates, such as those who would solve all Michigan's problems through the institution of a state-sponsored lottery. Both parties made a concerted effort to enlist distinguished citizens into Con-Con candidacy, and there was general agreement that the Con-Con nominees were of a generally higher caliber than those who would normally become candidates for the state Legislature.

But all was not smooth sailing for the parties. The Con-Con salary was intended to provide adequate compensation for capable delegates. It also seemed a windfall to party hacks. Faithful ward workers in Detroit who had built up the party organization during the Williams era saw the delegate position as a just reward. When the party leaders sought candidates elsewhere, the enthusiasm of the ward workers for the campaign was considerably lessened. The outcome of the election was considered by many commentators to be in part due to the failure of these Democratic organization workers to support the nominees of their party with enthusiasm, once the primary was concluded.

The Republicans also faced serious problems. The most important was the simple fact that a majority of the voters in the Republican counties had opposed the call for a constitutional convention and so had the Republican politicians. The outcome of a constitutional convention would be jeopardized if it were controlled by those who felt that the basic law of the state required no change. The newly elected Republican state chairman, George Van Puersem, had developed as speaker of the House of Representatives a political style accenting compromise and persuasion. The Republican State Central Committee made no serious attempt to impose a common platform stance on Republican candidates. Indeed, a theme common to the campaigns of several Republican candidates was the claim that the delegate would go to the Convention uncommitted, would weigh the evidence with care, and would make mature judgments in the best interests of the state. The Democrats were, as usual, portrayed as the willing tools of Walter Reuther and August Scholle. In outstate areas, however, the recurrent Republican slogan was some variation of "I won't let them take away our senator." Even the most conservative Republicans seemed to concede that the House should be apportioned strictly according to population, in order to "balance" a Senate based in part on area.

In the Detroit area, the Democrats talked of reapportionment. The "one man, one vote" argument, which has been the understandable preoccupation of Michigan Democrats, was presented again and again. Republican candidates complained that, in debates, the Democrats could speak of nothing else. Republican candidates in these areas began to invent formulas for reapportioning the Senate in order to assure voters that some increase in the representation of southeastern Michigan would be assured even by a Republican constitutional convention. As the summer wore on, however, voter apathy seemed to be the most marked characteristic of the election campaign.

Narrow Republican control of the Convention seemed certain. One hundred and forty-four delegates were to be elected, one for each seat in the two houses of the Legislature. If normal party affiliation ruled the outcome in every district, there would be seventy-eight Republicans and sixty-six Democrats, because of the weighting of the legislative districts in the favor of rural Republicans.

The special election of Con-Con delegates was held on September 12, 1961. Seventeen per cent of Michigan's voters went to the polls, a number only slightly higher than the turnout for the Con-Con primary of July 25.[8]

The results made national headlines. The Republican "sweep" gave ninety-nine seats to the Republicans, only forty-five to the Democrats. Republicans were elected from solidly Democratic areas in the upper peninsula; this was readily interpreted as a hostile reaction to the Democratic theme of reapportionment, which would of necessity reduce the representation of the sparsely settled upper peninsula. But Republicans also won in the Detroit area. Wayne County, which usually sends no Republicans to the Senate and only one to the House (from the swank residential area of Grosse Pointe), elected eight Republican Con-Con delegates. Republican victories were common in the Detroit suburban area, where rapid growth had resulted in the most marked underrepresentation.

Interpretations of this outcome were varied. The light turnout was cited as the major factor, because the voters with the most marked Democratic affiliation are those of lower socioeconomic and educational status and most likely to be uninformed concerning the nature of the Constitutional Convention and its potential impact on their interests. The presumed failure of Democratic workers to mobilize support behind party candidates has been mentioned above. And, in many districts, Republicans expanded their campaigns against the calling of the Convention into campaigns for election as delegates.

### The Republican Responsibility

With the Convention scheduled to open on October 3, the Republican Party was faced with the responsibility for positive action which it had avoided during the Williams years. With a two-thirds Republican majority, the Democrats could hardly be blamed for inadequacies in the final product. The document prepared by the Convention would bear a Republican label. If it were rejected by the voters, the state-wide fortunes of the party could go into eclipse for at least another decade.

The immediate question was that of organizing the Convention. The logic of partisan election required that the officers of the Convention be determined by the Republican caucus, but there was no obvious leader behind whom the Republican delegates could unite. One identifiable group, generally from the rural areas, was quite conservative in outlook and included several delegates who had opposed the call of the Convention. Included in this group was Stanley Powell, registered lobbyist for the Michigan Farm Bureau, who had led the Farm Bureau fight against the calling of the Convention. Best known of the group was D. Hale Brake, former state treasurer, now education director of the State Association of Supervisors, who enjoyed the title of "Mr. Republican" in rural areas and had opposed the campaign policies of the Bagwell group in the two preceding elections. This faction chose as its candidate Edward Hutchinson, of Fennville, a former state senator and unsuccessful contender for the 1960 nomination for lieutenant governor. *The Detroit News* opined that "Hutchinson is able and an expert on constitutional questions. In a political vacuum he would be a first-class con-con president. But con-con will not operate in such a vacuum. . . . Hutchinson would be no better a president than the obstructionist company he keeps." [9]

The second major faction included the delegates elected from the more urban areas of the state: Wayne, Oakland, and Macomb counties and Kent County in the western part of the state (Grand Rapids). The person with the greatest support among this group was George Romney. Romney was a newcomer to partisan politics, which alone disqualified him in the eyes of some aging professionals; others saw in him a potential candidate for governor, who, if elected, would pose a threat to the power of the rural-oriented wing of the party. Publicity as Con-Con president plus his own "charismatic" personality would give Romney a much better chance at election than Bagwell had ever enjoyed. Republicans in Romney's home county had long urged him to become a candidate for state-wide office. The previous year, he had refused to support a movement to enter his name in the Republican primary election for United States senator. Romney seemed primarily interested in achieving the objectives of constitutional revision formulated by his organization, Citizens for Michigan. He described himself as an "Oakland County Republican" when seeking the position of delegate to the Constitutional Convention. Thus, he modified his "plague-on-both-your-houses" stance regarding partisan politics. At this time, Romney had made no announcement of further interest in political office, but his supporters clearly wished to make him president of Con-Con in order to groom him for election as governor. Both his friends and enemies seemed convinced that he would decide to enter the gubernatorial contest.

The prospect of a deadlock in the Republican caucus between the Romney and Hutchinson forces led to the mention of possible compromise candidates. Most prominent of these were Prof. James K. Pollock of the University of Michigan Political Science Department and Pres. John A. Hannah of Michigan State University. Each had substantial support in the caucus, but neither could win a majority.

There had been much discussion during the campaign of the possibility of conducting an "open convention." Newspapers succeeded in obtaining commitments from most of the candidates that they would not approve executive sessions of the Con-Con committees, much less of the full Convention. When the Republican caucus met in Lansing the Saturday before the opening of the Convention, the death knell of the Hutchinson candidacy was sounded in the first vote, which opened the caucus to the public (that is, members of the press) against the opposition of the conservatives. The conservatives were defeated on other questions of Convention procedure as the liberals pressed for measures which would pave the way for bi-partisan compromise in writing the new document. In addition to all sessions being open, it was determined that there should be no party floor-leaders or whips; that the convention rules should not be determined by the majority-party caucus; that Democratic delegates should be elected to some of the offices of the Convention; and that staff recruitment should be on the basis of merit, rather than by patronage. In addition, Professor Pollock reminded the Republican conservatives—many of whom had considerable legislative experience—that "we are all freshmen. Seniority plays no part in our deliberations."

Lurking in the background was the fear that the Republican caucus would be so divided against itself that a Republican faction, combining with the Democratic minority, could control the election of the Convention officers. It was determined that, to be successful, the caucus designee for Convention president should receive seventy-three votes in caucus, a majority of all delegates elected to the convention. Balloting went on all day Friday, with neither Romney nor Hutchinson able to secure the required majority, or even a majority of those present. The caucus then recessed over the weekend, and on Monday morning three ballots demonstrated that there had been no substantial change. Romney attempted to shift his support to Hannah, but his followers were not agreed on Hannah as their second choice. The floor was then opened for further nominations. The name of Stephen Nisbet, retired Gerber Foods Company executive and former member of the State Board of Education, was presented to the caucus. Nisbet had opposed the Convention, preferring constitutional revision by amendment, but he was a respected senior figure who had not been a participant in the most strenuous interparty battles. No party faction had strong objections to his candidacy, and the caucus flocked to his standard with obvious relief.

It was next decided that Hutchinson and Romney should serve as vice-presidents, with a third vice-president designated by the Democrats. This "troika" scheme of organization was later extended into the Convention committee system, with each committee having Republican chairmen and vice-chairmen with Democratic second vice-chairmen. The latter designation was more a cooperative gesture than an award of influence.

Democratic leaders had been prepared to oppose the presidency of either Hutchinson or Romney—Hutchinson because of his association with the conservative Republicans, Romney because his potential gubernatorial candidacy posed a threat to Democratic hegemony in Michigan. But Nisbet had no further political ambitions, and Democratic leaders who had worked with him in public life claimed respect for Nisbet as "a real gentleman."

The Constitutional Convention opened the day following the Republican caucus. Stephen Nisbet's nomination as president was seconded by a Democratic leader and approved unanimously. The Convention opened in the most harmonious atmosphere that newsmen could recall in Michigan politics. Newspaper editors penned lyrics in favor of non-partisanship, and members of the citizens' groups which had brought the Convention into being found reason to rejoice.

There were signs that the harmony existed only on the surface. Members of the Democratic caucus questioned the "sweetness-and-light" attitude of their leaders, and Republican conservatives pointed out that "Republicans can do anything we want to. We have the votes."

## THE LENGTHENING SHADOW OF REAPPORTIONMENT

The Convention membership was divided into three procedural and nine substantive committees. Each of the substantive committees was assigned a section of the old constitution. Committees began the long process of public hearings, testimony, and discussion. The merits of proposals introduced by individual delegates were studied, and language was finally recommended to the full Convention for inclusion in the new document.

Discussion in the full Convention was brief, as the work pressed on in the committees. In public speeches, Democrats pointed out that their prime criterion for judging the new document would be the provisions for legislative apportionment. The "moderate" Republicans chided them for this obsession; they predicted many important improvements in other areas of the constitution. But the most conservative Republicans perceived apportionment as the key issue, as evidenced by their requests for assignment to that committee.

The Committee on Legislative Organization, assigned the task of reapportionment, was headed by John Hannah. Reflecting the two-thirds Republican majority in the Convention, fourteen of the twenty-one members of the committee were Republicans. Republicans were assigned to committees largely on the basis of personal choice. Twelve of the fourteen Republicans represented areas which had voted against the gateway amendment and the call to the Constitutional Convention. One of the seven Democrats came from the upper peninsula; the others came from areas favoring Con-Con and reapportionment.

As Hannah mobilized faculty research talent, the Legislative Organization Committee Room filled up with maps, graphs, and charts showing the outcome of various proposals for drawing new legislative district lines. At least forty proposals of this type were discussed by the committee, and the vocabulary of delegates became enriched by such terms as "equal proportions" and "major fractions." One proposal called for the allocation of basic Senate seats with equal numbers assigned to districts drawn in concentric circles around Detroit, with additional seats based on population.

George Romney introduced the notion of "sparsity." Large districts have sparse populations, he said; there is considerable wear and tear on the legislator who attempts to sample constituent opinion in a large district; the simple demands of geography and economics therefore require increased representation for sparsely populated areas. Romney claimed that the only possible interpretation of the mandate given the Republican Party in the election of delegates to the Constitutional Convention was that both houses of the Legislature should not be apportioned strictly by population. But Romney felt that a rational principle for determining apportionment was required. Population shifts should not be ignored by perpetuating existing districts.[10]

Romney's assessment of the mood of the Republican delegates to the Convention was substantially correct. Only a small number would retain the present apportionment system at all costs; most favored some change, with area represented in at least one house. The disagreement was over how to obtain a "rational standard" which would provide area representation and over how heavily the claims of area should be weighted. Romney's plan was criticized by Democratic delegates as providing a rationale for continuing the present districts with little alteration. Republican members of the Committee on Legislative Organization preferred their own schemes to Romney's. Indeed, none of the proposals made to the committee won its support.

In the closing hours of committee meetings, just prior to the deadline for submission of committee reports, Democratic members of the committee offered to support plans presented by two leading Republicans. If these two proposals were adopted, they promised to support the new constitution. Republican committee members rejected the Democratic offer.

Democratic committee members favored the proposal of Professor Pollock for the apportionment of the Senate and that of Chairman Hannah for apportionment of the House. Pollock's proposal called for the immediate addition of five Senate seats to the underrepresented counties of southeastern Michigan, followed by a "cooling-off period" lasting until the 1970 census. At that time, Senate seats would be apportioned so as to be as nearly equal in population as possible, with a maximum deviation in population of 30 per cent from the ratio of representation determined by dividing the state's population by the number of seats. The Hannah proposal called for apportionment of the House in single-member districts as nearly as possible on the basis of population following county lines. Democrats were willing to accept single-member House districts, which would result in the election of a few Republicans in Wayne County.

The proposal reported to the Convention by the Committee on Legislative Organization was written within the committee and was identified as in large part the handiwork of Delegate William Hanna of Muskegon. Its first provision was for a Reapportionment Commission appointed by the political parties on the basis of districts. Southeastern Michigan, with over half the state's population, would have only a quarter of the membership of the Reapportionment Commission. This transparent inequity loomed large in the early stages of the plan's development, but later changes defined the task of the commission so carefully as to permit it little discretion.

The committee report stated that "the House of Representatives shall consist of 110 members elected for a two-year term from single member districts apportioned on a basis of population as hereinafter provided." [11] The "population basis" in fact prescribed that a first seat in the House would be assigned to each district, conforming to county lines, which contained seven-tenths of one per cent of the state's population. Additional seats were to be assigned by the method of equal proportions. Convention staff members discovered that the retention of county lines for House districts prevented strict population apportionment. Although the change from five-tenths of one per cent (the old "moiety clause") to seven-tenths of one per cent as the basis for a first distribution of seats could be viewed as a minimal change and was so viewed by the official newspaper of the Democratic State Central Committee,[12] both parties agreed that the abandonment of county-line restrictions would create insurmountable problems of party reorganization. (An amendment sponsored by two Republican delegates to change the seven-tenths-of-one-per-cent figure to seventy-five hundredths of one per cent, which was as close to a strict population basis as county lines would allow, was later defeated by a vote of 81-to-37. Five Republicans joined thirty-two Democrats in favoring the measure.) [13]

Thus the campaign logic of a balanced Legislature with one house based on population gave way to the realities of geography and politics.

House apportionment was, of course, a secondary issue. The real contest concerned the apportionment of the Senate, which was the home of the "veto bloc" and the source of a decade of governmental frustration. The committee proposal in this regard was most ingenious. It began by immediately granting four new Senate seats—one each to the counties of Wayne, Oakland, Macomb, and Genesee. This would provide additional representation in the most grossly underrepresented areas of southeastern Michigan, but it would not necessarily provide for four new Democratic senators. Convention Vice-President Tom Downs later pointed out that the division into two senatorial districts each of Oakland, Macomb, and Genesee counties could, with ingenious gerrymandering, provide new Republican senators.[14]

After the 1970 census and each ten years thereafter the Reapportionment Commission would apply a formula which, the committee announced, was based 80 per cent on population and 20 per cent on area. The language defining the formula was very specific:

> . . . each county shall be assigned an apportionment factor according to the following formula: the percentage of the state's population as shown by the last regular federal decennial census computed to the nearest 1/100 of 1% shall be multiplied by 4 and there shall be added thereto the percentage of the state's area computed to the nearest 1/100 of 1% . . . counties with 13 or more apportionment factors shall be entitled to one senatorial district for each 13 apportionment factors. . . .[15]

Announced as an "80 per cent population-20 per cent area" formula, with no further clarification, the proposal had an undeniable ring of reasonableness. But the details of applying it provided the booby traps.

To begin with, existing senatorial districts were not to be tampered with, except under the most extreme circumstances. It happened that most of the present rural Senate districts would have about ten apportionment factors. The proposal next provided that each district should have "as nearly as possible 13 apportionment factors, but in no case less than 10 nor more than 16." In fact, few rural districts would have more than ten, and most urban districts would have nearly sixteen. Populous counties would have a district for each thirteen factors (two for twenty-six, three for thirty-nine; but Kent County, home of some of the most influential Republican delegates, would thus be deprived of its second Senator because of attaining only twenty factors when the formula was applied. Kent County has elected two Republican Senators for half a century. So a provision was added that counties with 19.5 factors should have a second senator. In allowing Republican Kent County to retain the second senator, the provision made certain the retention in 1970 by rapidly growing (and Democratic) Genesee County (Flint) of its newly provided second senator. Since the population of Genesee County in 1962 is somewhat greater than that of Kent, one of the most glaring inequities of the 1952 amendment (one of two counties with nearly equal population has twice the senatorial representation) was removed. But the gap between a two-senator and a three-senator county was twenty apportionment factors, the equivalent of two senators in rural areas.

Calculations based on 1970 population projections revealed that, after changing rural Osceola County from one district to the neighboring one, there would be no change in the 1960 boundaries of Republican senatorial districts.

Proposals of the Committee on Legislative Organization were placed halfway down the calendar of debate by the committee of the whole. But the content of the committee proposals became known to the delegates. An example of the impact of the apportionment plan on delegate attitudes was provided by the issue of county home rule. The growth of urbanized counties had rendered obsolete the rigid provisions for county government specified in the 1908 constitution. A self-executing provision for county home rule was proposed, but it was blocked in the Committee on Local Government by a coalition of Republican and Democratic delegates who were also county officeholders interested in protecting the constitutional status of their jobs. A compromise was reached which permitted, but did not require, the Legislature to adopt county home rule. Its language was identical to that which has permitted the development of highly regarded city home-rule plans in Michigan since 1908. But proponents of the self-executing measure claimed that this was no compromise at all. A Legislature unresponsive to urban needs would never approve county home rule. Opponents of county home rule seemed well satisfied with the prospects of delaying its coming almost indefinitely in the Legislature.

## THE ROMNEY CANDIDACY

Following his election as Convention vice-president, George Romney receded somewhat into the background during opening months of the Convention. The business of American Motors caused him to ask for frequent leaves of absence, although these requests were no more frequent than those of several other delegates. During these same months, however, Romney was being launched by the national mass media into the political firmament as the brightest new Republican star. His accomplishments, religious convictions, and political opinions were depicted in nearly every national news magazine and paraded across the television screen. He was portrayed as the most likely Republican presidential nominee in 1964, a perfect compromise between the Goldwater and Rockefeller wings of the party, and the natural heir of the party following of Richard Nixon. Nixon had removed himself from the 1964 race as part of his campaign to capture the California Statehouse.

Most of these reports were written as though Romney had already been elected governor, whereas his candidacy for the office was yet to be announced. Michigan Democrats had no intention of deserting the field because of Romney's appearance. They were well aware of the fact that he was the single Republican candidate since the election of G. Mennen Williams most likely to turn the Democrats out of the governor's office. Approval of a new constitution might carry Romney into office. Democrats began to consider what their party position might be with Romney as governor. A strong temptation was created for Democratic delegates to take a short-range view of the problems of constitutional revision.

The pressures on Romney to decide on his candidacy mounted steadily. In mid-February, at the regular board meeting of American Motors, he submitted his resignation and announced that he would seek the gubernatorial office. He further announced that his first responsibility was to the Constitutional Convention and that he would undertake no campaigning until the Convention had finished its work.

At that time, the Convention was debating in committee of the whole the several proposals of the Committee on the Judicial Article, which had been unable to agree on a method of selecting judges for the Michigan Supreme Court. Under the provisions of the 1908 constitution, though candidates were nominated by party conventions, they appeared on the ballot without party designation and were in fact usually initially appointed by the governor. Michigan enjoyed a *de facto* appointive system surrounded by *de jure* confusion. The Convention considered a proposal for nonpartisan election of judges from nine specified districts, five of which were outside the Detroit metropolitan areas. This transparent attempt to end the influence of the city vote on the election of high-court judges (and alter the five-to-three Democratic majority) was violently opposed by delegates of both parties. For three weeks conservative Republicans introduced the district proposal in various forms, but it was voted down in each reincarnation.[16]

Much energy had been devoted to the district plan by the conservative Republicans. Its defeat left them disappointed and bitter. One source of their bitterness was that many Republicans had joined with Democrats to favor the state-wide election of judges.

Although such a classification grossly oversimplified the reality, the Convention delegates could be divided into three factions: (1) the conservative, or "Farm-Bureau," Republicans (many of whom lived in cities); (2) the "moderate," or more urban-oriented, Republicans; and (3) the Democrats. A coalition of any two factions could control the Convention. Having been beaten on the Supreme Court question, the conservative Republicans saw a chance to combine with the Democrats on the next issue due for committee of the whole debate. It concerned the recommendations of the Committee on the Executive Branch.

The 1908 constitution limits the powers of the governor in numerous ways, not the least of which is the provision for the independent election of all members of the Administrative Board, or cabinet. The flaw of such a system is most obvious when members of the governor's cabinet are not members of his own party. Former Governor Williams had experienced that situation and recommended to the Committee on the Executive Branch that the governor be given the power of appointing the Administrative Board. Even when all are members of the same party, the system weakens the governor's power, because of the practice of ticket-balancing among party factions. Some of the leading conservative Republicans had been elected to the Administrative Board and favored retention of this limit on the governor's power.

The Committee on the Executive Branch, chaired by a "moderate Republican," was prepared to recommend appointment of the Administrative Board by the governor, with the approval of the Senate. Most Democratic committee members gave initial support to the plan, but reversed their positions when the Democratic State Central Committee endorsed election of all members of the Administrative Board. Republicans were quick to point out that Democrats held all positions on the Board, that important political empires controlled by the Democratic secretary of state and highway commissioner were at stake, and that these officials were likely to be re-elected even if George Romney were elected governor. Democrats responded that, since Republican proposals for senatorial reapportionment provided for little change, they could not accept the imposition of the veto power of the Legislature on gubernatorial appointments; and they cited the bitter experience of governors Williams and Swainson, whose key appointees were rejected by the Republican Senate.

Conservative Republicans, committed to restricting the power of state officers as part of a general theory of strictly limited government, joined with the Democrats in opposing the appointment of the Administrative Board. George Romney, with his executive experience in business, felt strongly that the powers of the governor should be increased to be somewhat commensurate with his authority. Faced with a coalition of Democrats and conservative Republicans which would protect the *status quo* on this question, Romney made perhaps the most fateful decision of the Convention. After extensive conferences between Romney and the leaders of the conservative wing, the majority of those present at a series of Republican caucuses agreed on solutions to three crucial questions of the Convention: the method of selecting members of the Administrative Board, taxation, and legislative apportionment.

Complete details of the agreement were never published, but its main features seemed to include a complicated compromise on the selection of Administrative Board members (four to be elected, three appointed by independent commissions, one appointed by the governor); reinstatement of the fifteen-mill tax limitation on local governmental units which had been rejected by the Constitutional Convention on first reading, and the retention of constitutionally earmarked tax funds; and adoption of the committee proposals concerning legislative apportionment without substantial change.

Perhaps the Romney "package-deal" compromise merely made formal the inevitable trend of the Convention, predestined once Romney's candidacy was announced. Democratic fears of contributing any glow of success to the Romney political image prevented a working coalition with the moderate Republican faction. This reaction by the Democrats drove the Republicans together. But the conservative Republicans, with decades of collective legislative experience, drove a hard bargain; the door so carefully left open by the moderates to allow bipartisan cooperation was banged shut, and the new constitution took on a conservative cast.

Democrats greeted news of the Romney compromise with cries of outrage. Democratic delegates threatened to walk out of the Convention, charging that the "sudden intrusion" of partisanship had left no role for an opposition party. On the Convention floor, Romney defended the agreement as necessary to save any progressive change from defeat by the threatened Democratic-conservative Republican alliance. Democrats interpreted the action as Romney pandering to the conservatives in order to assure his own election as governor. The Democratic Party newspaper announced in black headlines, "ROMNEY SELLS OUT." [17]

In succeeding days, the Republican caucus agreement passed its first test, as its provisions for the selection of members of the Administrative Board were accepted on first reading by the Convention.

## DECISION IN WASHINGTON

On March 26, 1962, the United States Supreme Court rendered its decision in *Baker* v. *Carr*. The Court majority held that the Tennessee legislature had failed to obey the reapportionment provisions of the state constitution and that the people of Tennessee, having no other source of relief, should be encouraged to turn to the courts. For the first time, the federal judiciary claimed authority to influence the organization of state legislatures.

Opinion was divided in Lansing. Democrats hailed the decision as a historic milestone and called for an end to Republican obstructionism on the issue of Michigan legislative apportionment. Republicans pointed out the clear differences between the cases. The people of Michigan, through the provision for initiated amendments to the constitution, have the power to remold that document at will. The district lines of the state Senate were in fact determined by an amendment to the constitution by majority vote in 1952. Requiring the Tennessee legislature to obey the Tennessee constitution was rather a different matter than invalidating a constitutional amendment adopted by the people of Michigan.

One hundred and fifty copies of the Supreme Court decision were air-mailed to Lansing at the request of John Hannah, who, in addition to his other duties, was chairman of the President's Commission on Civil Rights. After the initial flurry of publicity concerning *Baker* v. *Carr,* it became clear that it would change few attitudes toward the committee proposal on reapportionment. But it may have convinced some wavering delegates that some plan was needed which would provide the semblance of a reasonable standard by which to reapportion the upper house. Some substitute for the 1952 amendment—which froze the districts basically determined in 1925 into perpetual existence—seemed desirable. A proposal to transfer the precise language of the 1952 amendment into the new constitution was defeated by a vote of 111 to 20.[18]

One expert on reapportionment who paid considerable attention to the Baker decision was William Hanna, author of the committee proposal. After studying the decision, he began to doubt that all parts of his plan would prove acceptable to the Supreme Court and began to consider alternatives.

Professor Pollock, meanwhile, made ready to present the fruits of several weeks' work on amendments to the committee proposal. His amendments were intended to remove the built-in inequities and permit uniform application of the advertised "80 per cent population-20 per cent area" formula.

On the morning of April 4, Pollock introduced his "perfecting amendments," and, one by one, they were adopted by a coalition of liberal Republicans and Democrats. The most significant action of the morning was the modification of the "Kent-County provision," which guaranteed two senators to that district (and, almost inadvertently, to Genesee County). Pollock's plan gave a second senator to Kent but, providing an extra seat for any remainder of six and five-tenths apportionment factors, also bestowed an extra seat on Wayne and Oakland counties. The Convention thereupon recessed for lunch.

After lunch, every amendment introduced by Pollock was defeated. The purpose of the amendments had not changed, but the minds of the delegates had changed. In the Republican caucus during the lunch hour, Republican conservatives invoked the package compromise. Decisions should not be made, they insisted, through collusion with the Democrats. The word went out, and Pollock's effort was finished. Caucus leaders reported legal advice to the effect that the disparity between two-senator counties and three-senator counties—a substantial overrepresentation based on no reasonable principle—was clearly unconstitutional under *Baker* v. *Carr*. Instead of retaining the Pollock amendment adopted earlier which would have given extra seats to four urban counties, the Convention voted to eliminate the provision altogether, thus eliminating Kent County's second senator. Chairman Hannah of the Committee on Legislative Organization promised to submit an amendment on second reading which would rectify the situation. The balance of the committee proposals were adopted without change.[19]

At the next meeting of the Democratic State Central Committee, the state chairman blasted the actions of Republicans in the Constitutional Convention and gave the strongest hint yet that Democrats were determined to oppose the new constitution. A more thoughtful talk was given by Melvin Nord, Detroit attorney and leading Democratic member of the Committee on Legislative Organization. Nord announced that hopes for satisfactory apportionment by the Constitutional Convention were dead. The people of Michigan hereafter would have to look to the courts for aid in their quest for fair apportionment of the Legislature.[20]

The Convention proceeded to consider proposed constitutional language and made plans for adjourning before its appropriation—and delegate salaries—should be exhausted. The Legislature was not prepared to supply further funds, either for the continuation of the Convention or for a commission of its delegates to oversee the presentation of the new document to the voters. Democratic legislators charged that this was a device for paying the campaign expenses of George Romney from state funds, and Republican legislators were distressed by the plans of a number of Con-Con delegates seeking election to the Legislature. The Convention therefore decided to complete its final consideration of the new document on May 11 and then to adjourn until August 1. On that date they would budget any funds remaining and approve the "Address to the People," which would be the basis of explaining their work to the electorate.

Democratic hopes for a judicial resolution of the apportionment problem were bolstered by the United States Supreme Court. A few weeks after rendering the decision in *Baker* v. *Carr,* the Court remanded the case of *Scholle* v. *Hare* to the Supreme Court of Michigan, directing a new decision in light of the Baker case. Since the central finding of the Michigan court had been that apportionment is not a justiciable matter, intriguing possibilities were opened. If the arguments of the original case were adhered to and no cognizance was taken of the action of the Constitutional Convention, the Court could invalidate the 1952 "balanced-legislature" amendment and decree that elections to the state Senate in 1962 would be at-large unless the Legislature first fulfilled the requirement of the 1908 constitution for apportionment according to population. Even if the Court recognized the proposals of the Constitutional Convention, it could easily decide that the inequities of the situation were sufficiently grave to prohibit delay until 1970 of the application of the apportionment formula.

When the proposal for legislative apportionment came up for second reading, a Democratic delegate moved that action on the matter be postponed until the final meeting of the Convention on August 1, so that the Convention might have the benefit of the Court's decision on the Scholle case and that a committee appointed by President Nisbet might assist in bringing the matter before the Court. The motion was defeated on a party-line vote.[21]

The Committee on Legislative Organization then proposed an amendment that can be explained only by the impact of the judicial decisions. With its authorship attributed to Delegate William Hanna, the amendment was introduced by Chairman John Hannah. It had the blessing of the committee and, more important, of the Republican caucus.

The new measure tightened up the application of the "80-20" formula in 1970 until it would be more nearly tied to population than even the apportionment proposal of Professor Pollock which had been earlier defeated. The first provision separated metropolitan counties as a class from rural counties. A metropolitan county having more than thirteen apportionment factors would be entitled to more than one senator. Additional senators would be allocated to these counties on the basis of equal proportions applied to their remaining apportionment factors. The rural districts (one or more counties with a single senator), placed in a separate category, could vary in composition from ten to sixteen apportionment factors.[22] The importance of this provision was that it would prevent rural areas from retaining representation at the expense of growing urban areas. A rural district could be overrepresented only if a neighboring rural district were underrepresented.

The accuracy of predictions concerning the operation of the formula depends on the accuracy of population projections for 1970. With this reservation, it can be predicted that the application of the formula in that year would result in the five metropolitan counties (Wayne, Oakland, Macomb, Genessee, and Kent), with 57 or 58 per cent of the population, being represented by eighteen senators. The balance of the state would elect twenty senators. The new senators would not necessarily be Democrats, and, even if they were, the Senate would almost certainly have a Republican majority. But the presently underrepresented suburban areas would wield new power, and the rural Republican veto bloc would be nearly destroyed. The apportionment would be much more nearly on the basis of population. One of the few Democratic delegates voting for the Convention's proposed document stated that:

> The per cent of the state's population which can elect a majority of the Senate goes up from the present 29 per cent to 43 per cent. . . . Under the new Constitution Michigan would rank fourth among all the fifty states as to the importance of population in the legislative apportionment.[23]

Thus the Constitutional Convention at last produced a system which provided for significant change in the apportionment of the state Senate. It provided a statistically equitable system of weighting the claims of area as well as of population, provided that any representation of area can be labeled "fair." On the basis of the experience of previous initiative votes, including one as recently as 1952, delegates believed that the voters of Michigan would approve the principle of area representation. Once approved by the voters, the formula would, they felt, be upheld in the courts. The acceptance by rural Republicans of a formula which, at least by 1970, would destroy the power of the rural veto bloc in the Senate is explicable only in the light of the action of the United States Supreme Court in making legislative apportionment, specifically in Michigan, a justiciable matter. The committee proposal suddenly seemed a "reasonable compromise" short of the strict population apportionment long demanded by labor leaders. But that compromise was unacceptable to Democratic delegates for the very reason that, if adopted, it might withstand a court test. This would preclude further attempts to win "one man, one vote" through judicial action.

## THE BATTLE LINES ARE DRAWN

The role of the Michigan Supreme Court was not limited to the anticipated decision of *Scholle* v. *Hare*. The adoption of the new constitution may itself depend on action by that body. Republicans hope the court will place the new constitution on the ballot in the November election. An earlier interpretation by the attorney general, based on a literal reading of the 1908 constitution, held that the Convention should have adjourned *sine die* before April 1 if the new document were to be voted on in November. Republicans argue that the 1908 delegates intended that the product of any future convention be voted on at the next succeeding general election, provided that ninety days for study intervened; and this rule would be satisfied by *sine die* adjournment in August. Governor Swainson has ruled that the question is not of sufficient importance for him to exercise his right of requesting an advisory opinion from the state Supreme Court. At the present writing, Republicans have initiated action in a district court hoping for an early determination by the supreme state tribunal.

The only possible interpretation of these actions is that Republicans want the new constitution to be adopted; most Democrats want it defeated. Voting turnout will be greater in November, when a governor is to be elected, particularly in those urban areas which approved the original call of the Convention. Politicians have the impression that the Convention has, on balance, created a positive image and that chances for approval of the document are best while that image is fresh. Democrats oppose the document, as noted above, in large part because of their hope of obtaining through judicial action an apportionment system more to their liking. With a light turnout in the spring election, particularly in urban areas, the chances of the document will be substantially reduced. A more important strategic consideration may be the Republican hope that approval of the new constitution will carry with it the election of George Romney to the governor's office, because of his identification with the writing of the document. Democrats seem to be motivated by the fear that this will indeed be the case.

As the Constitutional Convention drew to a close, Democrats became concerned with the projection of a negative party image. After long deliberation, Republicans were proposing changes in the 1908 document; Democrats were opposing the changes. This did not fit the picture of the Democrats as the party of progressive reform, yet the Democrats clearly did not wish to support in the Convention language which they would attack in a possible campaign against adoption of the new document.

As each section of the proposed constitution was presented to the Convention for third reading, Democrats proposed substitutes which were, almost ritually, rejected by the Republican majority. Then, when the entire document was presented for a final vote, the Democrats presented an entire substitute constitution. It accepted much of the language of the Convention proposal without change, but on controversial matters it presented the pure Democratic position, unsullied by accommodation to the wishes of the majority. These provisions ranged from lowering the voting age to eighteen to the prohibition of the death penalty. All members of the Administrative Board were to be elected, including an auditor general, though a legislative auditor was also permitted. Self-executing home rule for counties was provided, and the article on taxation was substantially rewritten.[24]

The Democratic provisions for apportionment are of considerable interest. To begin with, an addition was made to Article I of the proposed constitution, the Declaration of Rights:

> Equality of political power being necessary to equality of right, the people shall be entitled to proportionate representation in the legislature.[25]

No definition of the phrase "proportionate representation" was offered. Its definition could only be sought in those sections dealing with the apportionment of the two houses of the Legislature and Congressional districts. In each case, apportionment was to be accomplished by the Legislature at its first session in 1963, or, should the Legislature fail to act, by the State Board of Canvassers. Districts of each house and Congressional districts were to contain "as nearly as may be, an equal number of persons, but in no case shall the districts vary in number of persons more than 15 per cent above or below the ratio" determined by dividing the population of the state by the number of seats. County lines would apparently be followed in all cases, and counties entitled to more than one seat in the lower house of the state Legislature could be divided into multimember districts by the County Board of Supervisors.[26] This would reinstitute the present system by which Republican areas in the city of Detroit are prevented from electing members to the Michigan House of Representatives. It constitutes a curious definition of "proportionate representation."

The Democratic substitute was defeated, 100 to 43. The proposed document of the Convention was then adopted by a vote of 99 to 44. Five Democrats voted with Republicans for the Convention proposal; two Republicans joined Democrats in opposing it, on the grounds that it was too radical; and one Republican abstained.[27] The minority party had thus achieved nearly unanimous disapproval of the product of the Convention deliberations. There were reports that the Democratic substitute constitution would be placed on the ballot as an alternative to the official proposal. This could only be done by use of the initiative provisions of the 1908 constitution, and the task of obtaining the requisite number of valid signatures would be a staggering one. But Democrats and labor spokesmen made clear their intent to battle against the new document.

## CONCLUSIONS

The Constitutional Convention of 1961-1962 was brought into being through the efforts of citizen reform groups disgusted by the failure of Michigan's political parties to resolve a decade of governmental stalemate. Since that stalemate was produced by the contest between a Democratic governor and a rural Republican veto bloc in the state Senate, legislative reapportionment was the key to successful revision of the constitution.

Legislative-executive conflict is based on real divisions in Michigan society. The conflict is more than an urban-rural contest; it in fact pits the single metropolitan area of Detroit against the balance of the state because of differences in economic enterprise, ethnic make-up, and social organization. Michigan's political parties did not create this conflict, but they reflect it all too well. The Detroit area is Democratic, and the balance of the state is Republican, with the exception of Democratic districts in the upper peninsula and a few Republican neighborhoods in and near Detroit. The conflict is much greater than that normally provided by the separation of governmental powers. Both the governor and the Senate veto bloc represent separate and warring constituencies, and there is a limit to the amelioration of social conflict that can be brought about by the reform of governmental institutions. Michigan politics were partisan, bitter, and ideologically polarized before the Constitutional Convention; after the convention, those characteristics remain in evidence.

When the citizens' organizations succeeded in calling the Constitutional Convention into being, the Michigan Legislature provided it with funds for seven months of operation. But the Legislature appropriated no money for preparation for the work of the Convention[28] and permitted the Convention no funds to advertise its product to the voters. This hostility on the part of the Legislature is clear indication of the fact that a constitutional convention provides a method of by-passing the Legislature to achieve reapportionment and other reforms.

If the device of a constitutional convention is to be labeled an "urban opportunity," however, it must be pointed out that the opportunity is limited by the nature of constitutional conventions, and the opportunity in Michigan was not very completely realized. To begin with, constitutional conventions are representative institutions, and their delegates are likely to be elected by districts, rather than from the state at-large. The apportionment of the convention is, therefore, a crucial question. In Michigan, the apportionment of the two houses of the Legislature taken together was duplicated in the apportionment of the Convention. This provided an initial weighting in favor of rural areas and also in favor of the Republican Party.

Furthermore, the very urban majorities which are underrepresented in state legislatures may constitute that group of voters least interested in state government generally and unexcited by the problems of constitutional revision in particular. In the normal election, many voters may not exercise their franchise on constitutional issues. In Michigan, the Democratic Party was unable to mobilize its normal urban majority in the special election of delegates to the Constitutional Convention. The result was a two-thirds Republican majority in the Convention, although the Democrats are the normal majority party in the state.

Republicans were under no illusion that their victory in the special election presaged a return by the voters of Michigan to the bosom of the party of Lincoln (or even the party of Eisenhower and Romney). Both parties expected the pattern of party affiliation to continue, and this fact, rather than some abstract principle of sound government, explains the actions of both parties. Democrats insisted that the governor's cabinet should be elected, rather than appointed. Republicans sought to maintain their veto power in the state Senate, but the impact of the U.S. Supreme Court decisions in *Baker* v. *Carr* and *Scholle* v. *Hare* led them to accept a formula providing substantial change in the direction of population representation. Frustrated by their minority position and worried by the political ascendency of George Romney, Democratic delegates chose a negative role instead of cooperating with the liberal wing of the Republican party to outvote the conservative Republicans. The liberal Republicans were hampered in seeking such a coalition by the necessity of establishing Romney's image as a partisan. Romney could hardly deal with the Democrats one month and castigate them the next.

The result was Republican unity. Republican delegates from areas which had opposed calling the Convention became advocates of constitutional revision, and Republicans were nearly unanimously agreed to recommend the Convention product to their constituents. The support of conservative Republicans was, of course, purchased by substantial concessions to their viewpoint. The task of the Republican Party in Michigan is analogous to that of the national Democratic Party. Just as the Democrats attempt to bind together the urban North and the conservative South, so must Michigan Republicans attempt to build a bridge of understanding between rural Michigan and industrial Detroit. Michigan Republicans have not accomplished this task so far, and large portions of the party would not even accept it as a duty.

There is no indication that George Romney, as governor, could enact a reform program with the aid of either the present Legislature or the one that the new constitution would establish. But the party has achieved large-scale support for the new constitution. The Michigan Farm Bureau, the most vociferous interest-group opponent of constitutional revision, has announced its support of the new document. The Michigan League of Women Voters, a leader in the battle for constitutional revision, has also endorsed the proposed document. And the Republican organization, hoping for a long-delayed return to state-wide office, seems prepared to do battle for the constitution and for George Romney, although perhaps not in that order.

Michigan's proposed constitution is not a model document. If the standard of judgment is apportionment of the legislature strictly by population, then the Convention has been a failure. But the constitution recognizes problems which were not present when the 1908 constitution was adopted, and in its legislative article it provides a tentative and gradual shift of the balance of political power away from rural Michigan and toward the urban centers. It seems now that many residents of rural Michigan will accept the new document as an aspect of that inevitable and necessary change. If the new constitution thus accomplishes political change in a manner which prevents the alienation from the system of these groups whose power will be lessened, the new document may foreshadow a more satisfactory political climate in Michigan.

---

*See note, p. 297.*

# Notes

1 John W. Lederle, "The Legislative Article," in Robert H. Pealy, ed., *The Voter and the Michigan Constitution* (Ann Arbor: Institute of Public Administration, The University of Michigan, 1960), pp. 39 f.

2 Herbert Garfinkel and L. J. Fein, *Fair Representation: A Citizen's Guide to Legislative Apportionment in Michigan* (East Lansing: Bureau of Social and Political Research, Michigan State University, 1960), p. 11.

3 The advent of the New Deal shattered Republican unanimity in Michigan and made Wayne County basically Democratic in its party affiliation. But the two-party system was on a very precarious footing before the election of Gov. G. Mennen Williams. For a history of Michigan's party system see Stephen B. and Vera H. Sarasohn, *Political Party Patterns in Michigan* (Detroit: Wayne State University Press, 1957). The success of the Democrats in building an issue-oriented party organization under Governor Williams and State Chairman Neil Staebler is analyzed by Robert Lee Sawyer, *The Democratic State Central Committee in Michigan, 1949-1959* (Ann Arbor: Institute of Public Administration, University of Michigan, 1960).

4 John P. White and John R. Owens, *Parties, Group Interests, and Campaign Finance: Michigan 1956* (Princeton: Citizens' Research Foundation, 1960), *passim*.

5 Michigan's disciplined and programmatic parties in fact approach the ideal nature of political parties envisioned by many American political scientists. Michigan's experience shows that "responsible" parties in a divided government lead only to stalemate. See Norman C. Thomas, Neil Staebler, and Arnold J. Levin, *Parties and Politics in Michigan* (Ann Arbor: Michigan Citizenship Clearing House, 1960), *passim*.

6 Basic election data for Michigan are provided by John P. White, *Michigan Votes: Election Statistics 1928-1956* (Ann Arbor: Institute of Public Administration, The University of Michigan, 1958), and in the 1958 and 1960 *Supplements* to that volume (published in 1959 and 1961). The shifts in party strength are analyzed in the 1960 *Supplement*, pp. vi f.

7 *Scholle* v. *Hare*, 360 Michigan 1-125.

8 700,000 of Michigan's 4,000,000 registered voters cast ballots in the Con-Con election. Less than 600,000, or 15 per cent of the eligible electorate, participated in the Con-Con primary. *Ann Arbor News*, July 26, 1961; *Detroit News*, September 13, 1961.

9 *The Detroit News*, October 3, 1961.

10 George Romney, speech at Central Michigan University, Mt. Pleasant, December 2, 1961.

11 *Journal of the Constitutional Convention*, 112 (April 2, 1962), 855. Cited hereafter as *Journal*.

12 *The Michigan Democrat*, March 1962, p. 1.

13 *Journal*, 114 (April 4, 1962), 870.

14 Speech at Ann Arbor, May 23, 1962. Mr. Downs is an attorney for the Michigan AFL-CIO.

15 *Journal*, 112 (April 2, 1962), 854 f.

16 The final provision pleased nobody. Its only logic was that of compromise. Nominations are to be made by party conventions, followed by state-wide nonpartisan election. Incumbent judges are to be able to renominate themselves without seeking party endorsement simply by filing a notice of intent. Attorneys unable to attain a party nomination can win a place on the ballot by filing nominating petitions signed by a number of qualified electors equal to 3 per cent of the vote cast for governor in the previous election. Vacancies are to be filled by special election, thus taking from the governor his *de facto* power of determining the makeup of the court. *Journal*, 98 (March 13, 1962), 753.

17 *The Michigan Democrat, op. cit.*

18 *Journal*, 114 (April 4, 1962), 866-868.

19 *Loc. cit.* and *ibid.*, 115 (April 5, 1962), 864-882.

20 *The Detroit News*, April 15, 1962.

21 *Journal*, 128 (April 25, 1962), 1126 f.

22 *Ibid.*, p. 1128.

23 Katherine Moore Cushman, letter to the editor, *The Detroit News*, May 27, 1962, p. 14B. Mrs. Cushman is a leader of the Michigan League of Women Voters, and her husband is a vice-president of American Motors.

24 *Journal*, 136 (May 11, 1962), 1309-1321.

25 *Ibid.*, p. 1308.

26 *Ibid.*, pp. 1311 and 1313.

27 *Ibid.*, p. 1322. At the close of the Convention, there were ninety-seven Republicans and forty-seven Democrats. Two Democrats were appointed by the governor to replace resigning Republican delegates elected to vacant seats in the legislature.

28 The Constitutional Convention Preparatory Commission was financed by a grant from the Kellogg Foundation of Battle Creek.

## NOTE

Ruling for the second time on *Scholle* v. *Hare,* the Michigan Supreme Court in mid-July ruled the 1952 "balanced-legislature" amendment unconstitutional, citing *Baker* v. *Carr,* and ordered the Legislature to reapportion the Senate on the basis of the 1908 constitution before August 20. The justices were divided four-to-three along party lines (with one disqualifying himself). The Democratic majority gave the legislature thirty-three days to reduce the Senate by two members (it had been increased in 1952) and apportion it in an acceptable manner. If it failed, at-large elections would be held. On July 27, 1962, however, Justice Potter Stewart of the U.S. Supreme Court granted a stay of execution of the Michigan court's order, noting the decree that both houses of the Legislature must be apportioned on a population standard. This question was not presented to the U.S. Supreme Court. The Michigan court's decision implied that the Con-Con Senate apportionment formula must be judged unconstitutional. Meeting for a final session on August 1 (after recess since mid-May), Republican Con-Con delegates took cognizance of the judicial action to the extent of eliminating the "cooling-off" period. If the new document were approved in April, the Senate would be redistricted according to the 80-20 formula in 1964.

# 16

## Maryland

### JUDICIAL CHALLENGE TO RURAL CONTROL

*DWYNAL B. PETTENGILL*
*College of William and Mary*

A not-unexpected revelation of the 1960 census placed Maryland near the top of a list of the worst-apportioned states in the nation. It has been suggested that the decennial census exposures trigger the periodic and, until now, ineffective protests against the prevailing scheme, since the protests have usually been separated by a decade. Just as after the 1950 census, there is now another ground-swell of opinion among the "outs" against the apportionment of the Maryland General Assembly.

For the beginnings of this story, one should examine the convolutions of the Maryland constitution; the state's unique law providing for county-unit nomination of state-wide candidates; the unmistakably border-state ideology; extraordinary population changes in the suburban counties; the political autonomy enjoyed by Baltimore city; and finally the condition of the party system itself, a vehicle quite unfit to bear the burdens it must carry.

But with all these factors taken into consideration, there still remains the eleven-to-one ratio of apportionment between Baltimore County's representation in the General Assembly and that of Kent and other small counties. Furthermore, Maryland probably has a greater proportion of underrepresented suburbanites than any other state. At last count, these numbered slightly less than 45 per cent of the state's entire population.

### CONSTITUTIONAL FRAMEWORK

The Free State's present constitution is the fourth since 1776. The 1776 and 1851 documents included some built-in underrepresentation for the people of Baltimore city; the 1864 constitution was short-lived. The constitution adopted at the end of the Civil War, a much-amended and sometimes incoherent outline of government, still forms the basis for apportionment of legislative districts. With a mathematical formula considered in 1867 extremely flexible, each county's seat total in the lower house was determined by its plateau of population up to a maximum of 55,000 and six delegates. The minimum number of seats for any county or the three legislative districts of Baltimore city was fixed at two. Baltimore city, according to a provision in the 1867 constitution, was to have as many seats in each legislative district as the most heavily populated county. Three more districts were added to Baltimore city by subsequent amendments in 1901 and 1922.

No flexibility whatsoever attended Senate representation, which was early established as one single-member district for each county and each of the legislative districts of Baltimore city. For purposes of legislative representation, including the patronage attached to the office, each district of Baltimore city is treated as a county, the only exceptions being appropriations for bond issues and certain other bills which are considered by the entire Baltimore city delegation as a select committee of the House and by the city's members in the Senate.

The House of Delegates grew progressively larger, until a ceiling was established by a constitutional amendment proposed in 1949 and ratified at the 1950 general election. With the results of the 1950 census casting a long shadow of rapid population growth and change, the Maryland legislators that year sought to prevent an additional increase in the size of the House resulting from the burgeoning suburban populations of Baltimore County and the metropolitan Washington counties. The amendment to the constitution not only set a permanent limit on the size of the House of Delegates, but "froze" the existing apportionment scheme by naming each county and fixing its number of delegates. This arrangement was carried over by an omnibus amendment in 1956 which deleted obsolete sections. It is interesting to note that the basis for apportioning House seats has been completely discarded, since there are now eight counties with populations in excess of 55,000. Three more are nearing that magic figure set almost 100 years ago.

Amendment of the Maryland constitution requires a three-fifths majority of the members of each house, followed by a referendum at the next general election. It has been observed that the most careful planning could not have created the ossified apportionment scheme under which Marylanders labor.

Section Two of the amending article, however, invests the General Assembly with a direct mandate for ascertaining "the sense of the people" on calling a constitutional convention every twenty years. Such a pro-

vision would seem to offer substantial and periodic relief from the current
ills; but, when the requisite referendum was offered in 1950, the legislature refused to act because it was held that "majority of voters" in the
constitution meant the majority of those who voted in the election. Maryland voters are not unique in their dislike of balloting on constitutional
questions, particularly on the long ballot in a gubernatorial year. Those
who voted in favor of the referendum were in the large majority over
those against, but the total vote on the referendum was not a sufficiently
large proportion of the total vote in the election. The attorney general
dutifully upheld the validity of the General Assembly's justification for
inaction, and the referendum will not be presented again until the 1970
general election. Should the referendum for a constitutional convention
be adopted, even by a majority of the voters in the election, legislative
discretion still governs the calling of a convention. Nonetheless, it is
felt that some relief would be afforded by a convention, since it would
meet as one body and require a simple majority vote.

Furthermore, in the unlikely event that a constitutional convention
were called, the representation would be according to the same formula
as that of the state legislature. Although Maryland long ago adopted
a constitutional amendment providing for referendum, it has no initiative
procedure.

There is some historical basis for speculation that a majority of the
members of the General Assembly could call a constitutional convention
and provide it with sufficient legality to amend or rewrite the entire
document. Regardless of the narrow legal procedures required by Article
XIV, Section 2 of the present constitution, the 1867 convention appears
to have been irregularly called, thus establishing a rather firm precedent.

## COUNTY-UNIT SYSTEM OF NOMINATION

Only slightly less important than the constitutional bars to reapportionment in Maryland is the fact that representation is tied to an un-
democratic process of state-wide nomination. The reader unfamiliar with
Maryland political history will require some background information
to sort out this aspect of the rural-urban conflict as it has developed in
past years.

Baltimore city (as distinguished from Baltimore County) became a
separate entity with county status under the state government in 1851;
even before that it had been for some years more populous than other
municipalities in the state. Shortly after the turn of the century there
was great fear that the metropolitan colossus at the mouth of the Patapsco
River would dominate state affairs.

At least in part because of these fears of Baltimore's numerical preeminence and presumably in deference to the democratic feelings which resulted in a mechanical theory of government, the state of Maryland produced an election law in 1910 which provided for state-wide nominations by party state conventions, with each candidate receiving all the vote of the county (or legislative district of Baltimore city) where he had won a majority of the popular vote in the primary election. Unit vote totals in convention comprised the number of members of the state legislature from each subdivision, both House and Senate. Democracy could thus be served, but well within the framework of small-county autonomy. Each county or district elects, in the party primary, delegates to the state convention who must, by law, vote for the candidate with the highest popular vote in their county or district. In 1939, an amendment anticipating a tie in the unit vote made it mandatory in such cases to nominate the state-wide candidate with the highest popular vote total across the state. A tie unit vote did occur in 1956, when the late Millard E. Tydings, in a strong come-back effort, was equalled in unit votes (seventy-six) by George P. Mahoney.

This Gordian knot binds the composition of the state convention to the number of representatives in the General Assembly prescribed by the constitution. The maze of interlacing laws and constitutional provisions is obsolete and frustrating. The candidate for state-wide office with the highest popular vote in the primary has five times been deprived of the nomination. In outline the system somewhat resembles the process by which presidents and vice-presidents are elected in the national government, but with the vastly greater discrepancies in representation accorded each subdivision.

That the channels of legislative representation are clogged by the present constitutional and legal provisions is obvious. In order for a candidate to win the unit vote of the counties with the proportionately larger voice in nominations, he must be unappealing to those in the populous suburban counties who will have the power to elect him in the general election. Conversely, a candidate attractive to the 1,450,000 suburbanites normally has few charms for the residents of fishing and farming areas. This was never better illustrated than in 1954, when H. C. Byrd, an organization-backed, segregationist ex-president of the University of Maryland, won over paving contractor George P. Mahoney on the strength of small-county support in the Democratic primary for governor, only to be decisively overcome in November by the appeals of Theodore R. McKeldin to the masses of urban and suburban voters. Mahoney has himself been twice beaten by Republicans in general elections (1952 and 1956), principally because he was unable to compete for suburban votes.

## POLITICS OF THE *STATUS QUO*

Politically, the *status quo* in Maryland embraces a curious ambivalence marked on the one hand by a predisposition toward the Democratic Party in a border-state context (that is to say, the rural elements are Southern in outlook, whereas urban and suburban dwellers are definitely Northern) and on the other hand by a degree of urbanization and industrialization which marks a Northeastern seaboard state.

Maryland has within its boundaries manufacturing plants of many kinds, is the headquarters of one of the nation's largest railroad systems, and is generally considered one of the most heavily industrialized states. In contrast, the people who are most influential under the system of malapportionment and the unit vote for state-wide nominations are tidewater fishermen, truck farmers, fruit growers, and tobacco farmers. Almost five-sixths of Maryland's 3,100,000 people are industrial, white-collar, or government employees in the Baltimore-Washington metropolitan areas, yet the important men in the legislature are often from the least populous counties. Maryland is a border state par excellence, political dominance having long since accrued to the Bourbon majorities of the General Assembly.

Sen. John Marshall Butler is, at this writing, the only state-wide official from Baltimore city, and he has announced his decision to retire at the end of the present term; Governor J. Millard Tawes is from Somerset County (population 19,623); Senator J. Glenn Beall and Attorney General Thomas B. Finan are from Allegany County (84,169), and the latter succeeded C. Ferdinand Sybert of Howard County (36,152); Comptroller Louis L. Goldstein is from Calvert County (15,826). Ex-Mayor Thomas D'Alessandro, of Baltimore city, who was defeated by Beall in the general election of 1958, has been the city's only state-wide nominee since 1954; Theodore McKeldin, of Baltimore, of course, served as governor of Maryland from 1951 through 1958.

The apportionment system and the county-unit method of nomination affect the status of organized labor, which must be content with legislative crumbs from the small-county table; cause heavier proportional taxation in the larger counties with less benefits than the smaller counties receive (although real-estate tax assessments were previously more uneven than they are now); and contribute to the constant lack of attention to the needs of an increasingly larger Negro minority (now one-sixth of the total population, with three members of the General Assembly and no major appointive offices in the state's administrative hierarchy).

It is precisely the Democratic Party which has the largest stake in the *status quo*. When the majority Democratic Party is split, the Republicans, by tapping the strength unavailable in primary elections, can carry the suburban sections and the state. If the state were to be apportioned according to a more equitable formula, a viable two-party system would seem a distinct possibility.

Residents of Baltimore County, in particular, suffer from extreme underrepresentation; half a million people are equal in House voting strength to two of the smaller counties and in the Senate to one other county of any size. Yet, precisely because Maryland is so heavily Democratic, at least in state elections, the Baltimore County delegation is probably anxious to keep apportionment at the present levels. This is so because the functioning of the unit system has crystallized the "border" elements of Maryland's political life into permanence. The people who have become Marylanders in the past twenty years realize their impotence in primary elections for state-wide officials, a collective state of mind which is manifested in registration and election statistics. The vote for president in 1960, just over one million, still missed even the low mark of 50 per cent of total eligible voters. In the suburban counties, other than Montgomery, the suburban majorities are either not registered or are apathetic in all except presidential elections. Maryland ranks just above the Deep Southern states in percentage of turnout. Thus, the public posture of large-county legislators can be one of chagrin and helplessness, but behind the legislative scenes many of them are content with the existing conservative state government because they are able to perpetuate themselves more easily under the unit system.

Likewise, those in control of the Baltimore city delegation have no incentive to favor apportionment strictly by population, because Baltimore city is not now experiencing any underrepresentation. The Republicans have two U.S. senators and one member of the House of Representatives, but only ten members in the legislature (1961-1962). Baltimore city leaders know full well that there is little chance they will lose control of the city to the Republicans; whichever faction of the Democratic Party gets control wishes to perpetuate itself in the easiest way, and that way does not presently involve reapportionment.

No matter what the political complexion of the governor, small-county power is so deeply ingrained on the political map of Maryland that little can be done by altering the structure at the top. The small-county delegations, from overwhelmingly overrepresented areas, naturally want to keep it that way. The high points of Republicanism for the House of Delegates and the Senate have been thirty-six and eleven, respectively, following the 1946 general election, neither figure being close to a blocking minority vote. It follows that rural representatives can by and large do as they wish, as long as they control the faction within their counties.

The results may be catalogued in a few short statements. For years the small-county men in the legislature have used their concentrated power in the Senate, for example to maintain strict guardianship over university scholarships for county students; each senator, regardless of the size of his constituency, has the same amount of scholarship money available for distribution to the faithful who can pass the entrance examination. Members of the General Assembly receive hefty legal fees from the State Roads Commission for acquisition of rights of way by condemnation proceedings, and they write insurance business for the state by the millions of dollars. In the case of gubernatorial appointments to boards and commissions, which must be approved by the Senate, a very strict rule of courtesy exists. The rule is particularly effective in a body with only twenty-nine members.

There is no combined legislative opposition to these practices from the majority side of the House. Small-county delegations in fact run their counties through the state legislature, local bills being shunted through by the hundreds. The two large counties which have adopted home rule under a constitutional amendment are in somewhat better condition, and, of course, Baltimore city has its own municipal government. For the rest, the rules of courtesy which prevail easily permit a delegation of two or three persons from a small county to be the *de facto* governing body of their subdivision by functioning a few weeks a year in the legislature.

Republicans, who might be said to have the most to gain from reapportionment, have always seemed to be in favor of the idea, but the party has not been overly aggressive in pursuit of the objective. Sentiment in the party was not united on the issue following the 1950 census, and all Republicans in the House of Delegates during the 1961 session of the General Assembly voted against passage of a proposed constitutional amendment to apportion the state. It should be added that the seven gentlemen in question were all from small counties.

It must be remembered that the Republican Party is also controlled to a great extent by the functioning of the ubiquitous unit system. The potential Republican vote in the suburbs, as in other parts of the state, is still an untapped source of power, because the state-wide leadership is happy to have the unit system and its easier method of directing nominations. Few of the extremely underrepresented suburban Republicans take advantage of an almost meaningless franchise in primary elections, realizing where the power resides. There is no incentive for a registration drive in Baltimore County, the latent Republican strength of which could be expected to exercise an immense influence in a direct primary. Republican state-wide nominations depend on the unit system in exactly the same way as do the Democratic nominations. Despite its success in national elections, the Republican Party is not well-organized in the suburbs other than Montgomery County.

There is no record, for instance, that Governor McKeldin promoted the cause of reapportionment while in office, except as a side issue. The Republican City Committee of Baltimore is at present campaigning strenuously for a redistricting of the legislative district boundaries of the city. Influential opinion in the large Baltimore city Negro community is opposed to redistricting on the grounds that the cards are so heavily stacked against them now in the legislature that it would be better to maintain the *status quo,* which gives an entree of sorts to the present leadership. The Republican State Central Committee adopted a resolution in February 1961 in favor of equitable Congressional districts as well as of reapportionment of the General Assembly. In the area of legislative apportionment, however, efforts have been slight. At the 1958 Republican state convention, there was no mention of apportionment.

## RECENT BATTLES OVER REAPPORTIONMENT

Elements not evident in the early 1950's seem to have emerged in the current Maryland apportionment struggle. Following the success of efforts to enlist the courts in behalf of racial equality, a group of Maryland citizens with some financial support embarked on a campaign for equality of the franchise through reapportionment of the General Assembly. The chronicle of that group's public activities, as well as the steps and positions taken by other prominent interest groups in the state, is the focal point of this section, together with an assessment of the 1961 General Assembly's struggle over the issue.

It is not entirely true, first of all, to say that the issue of apportionment was quiescent from 1950 to 1960. The League of Women Voters, a group to be reckoned with on civic questions in any state, has had apportionment as one of its "must" items over the years. Great stress was not placed on action in this area, however, until the fall of 1959. For at least ten years, the program of the league has included calling a constitutional convention, and drastic changes in representation are inherent in that idea.

Members of the League of Women Voters and other civic-minded persons from Baltimore city and the four urban counties have combined to carry the fight into the courts, which seem to them to hold much promise for rectifying the existing situation. Headed by an academician and a politician, the Committee for Fair Representation has, through propaganda and litigation, inspired some soul-searching about the problem of reapportionment in Maryland and has served as a reference source for interested citizens. The committee, a "holding company" of a few dedicated individuals and some civic organizations, appears much stronger than it actually is. Names of labor leaders, Negroes, and public figures, with which the committee's letterhead is well-stocked, were obtained by simply asking for them, and they do not represent a solid phalanx of interest-group support. As with the petitions for a referendum on the bill creating Maryland's Eighth Congressional District, Montgomery County leads in support and in financing the committee. Legal services have been in large part donated, according to members of the group; there is little or no sustaining support from the other suburban counties; and the group has no allies or sympathizers in the legislature.

A chronology of recent happenings must begin with the Democratic state convention in the spring of 1958, where the party promised to do something about reapportionment if the ticket were successful in the general election of that year. The Democrats won, and Governor-elect Tawes appointed a group of distinguished citizens to draw up a new scheme of apportionment for the state. The Walsh Commission, so named after the former attorney general and judge who headed the study, submitted its findings in 1959, in time to have its recommendation roundly defeated by the interim committee of the General Assembly.

The twelve-to-five vote in the Maryland Legislative Council refusing to approve the Walsh Commission plan did not occasion great surprise. Apportionment was not a particularly significant element in the 1958 election, even in the large suburban counties most emasculated by the present system. Neither candidate occupied himself with the problem, Tawes having mentioned to a women's group that he would stick to the terms of the platform and "try to do something about it." One editorial on apportionment of negligible importance appeared in the *Baltimore Sun* two days before the election.

Refusal of the Legislative Council to consider the Walsh plan did, however, have one effect of a lasting nature. The Maryland Committee for Fair Representation immediately filed suit in the Anne Arundel County Circuit Court for a five-count judgment against Governor Tawes and the State Board of Canvassers. In the petition, MCFR requested:

1. A declaratory judgment holding that the Maryland Constitution violates the Fourteenth Amendment and the Civil Rights acts of 1957 and 1960.

2. A rule that failure of the General Assembly to apportion violates the above and Maryland law.

3. A declaration of the failure of the General Assembly to call for a constitutional convention.

4. Enjoinment of the Anne Arundel County Board of Supervisors of Elections from certifying the candidates in 1962.

5. The court to retain jurisdiction until reapportionment would be accomplished.

The MCFR plan of attack on the constitutionally based system of apportionment emphasized the judicial bar to election of legislators under the present formula until the General Assembly had been reapportioned. The courts were not asked to establish a particular formula of representation or to develop one of their own, but only to prod the legislature itself into action by electing all the membership at-large. The fact that the petition constituted a last legal resort was cited by the MCFR brief. It was also pointed out that ten bills concerning apportionment had failed of passage in recent years, as well as six attempts at resolutions calling for a constitutional convention.

MCFR's suit was dismissed in the Anne Arundel County Court on February 21, 1961 by Judge O. Bowie Duckett. A lack of judicial remedy was the principal basis for the fourteen-page opinion. Attorneys for MCFR persevered in an appeal to the highest court in the state, where arguments were heard in December 1961. Expressing its reluctance to move in the judicially beclouded reapportionment area, the Court of Appeals let the matter rest through the winter. Predictably, the court delayed consideration until the constitutional questions raised in *Baker* v. *Carr* were decided by the Supreme Court. In the meantime, a federal case seeking relief was brought in the District Court of Maryland by leaders of the largest suburban county immediately following the Supreme Court's initial action.

In the legislature itself, following the vote against the Walsh plan prior to the 1960 session, no action was taken on this specific item during the so-called short session. It should be pointed out here that the Maryland General Assembly passes local bills only every other year during the long, or ninety-day, session, while bills during the even-numbered session must be state fiscal bills, emergency, or general welfare legislation.

A moderately aroused daily press added its voice to that of the MCFR for an equitable distribution of legislative seats during the 1961 session. And, although the issue was not the most discussed or the most controversial of the 1961 session, it had some share of consideration and was as fully debated as the framework of representation in the General Assembly would permit.

In terms of the prevailing legislative mood, even the compromise bill finally voted on was unable to get the hearing it deserved in a small-county body whose members had scarcely thought of the system as something which ought to be altered. Small-county legislators in Maryland never appear shocked or surprised that someone is questioning the system of representation—they answer only that it is "working all right." A constitutional convention resolution received the same treatment as similar resolutions over the past several Assembly sessions, being summarily shelved in committee.

Before the 1961 session convened, several developments were to take place concerning reapportionment. Despite disapproval by the Legislative Council, there was a continued consideration in high circles of the Walsh Commission plan, a stopgap proposal which provided for an additional delegate in each county with a population in excess of 50,000, up to a maximum of 200,000, beginning at the present levels, and then one delegate for each 100,000 up to a maximum of ten. Table 1 reveals the implications for both small and large counties. In essence, the Walsh plan followed a line-of-least-resistance approach, disturbing the small counties only by increasing their chance of being outvoted at some future time. In spite of Governor Tawes' statement in January 1960 that he would "fight" for the Walsh proposals, the bill was never introduced in the form in which the commission had made the original recommendations to the Legislative Council the previous year.

One bill, that proposed by the MCFR, treated apportionment as a fundamental problem of Maryland government. By calling for the creation of twenty-seven additional seats in the House and twenty-one seats in the Senate, the committee felt that the quibbling about relationship of population to representation should be disposed of once and for all by adherence to a recognized principle. Testimony before the House Judiciary Committee revealed that the MCFR proposal had little or no support in the legislature.

The struggle evolved over the provisions of a bill introduced in the Senate as the Pine-Northrop bill and in the House of Delegates as HB 604. SB 76 carried the names of two large-county senators in the upper house and was reported by a Senate committee after the final defeat of HB 604. The favorable report on SB 76 (Pine-Northrop) was adopted by the Senate, but it was never finally passed. Had the House acted favorably on HB 604, a conference would have been necessary to adjust a difference of one seat which had been added in the House version. The only difference in the two bills as introduced was that between the 55,000 population level in the Senate bill for four delegates and the 45,000 population level in the House for the same number of seats.

Embodying the method, if not the exact arithmetic, of the Governor's Commission on More Equitable Representation, the House and Senate measures received some support from the administration, though it was

## TABLE 1

APPORTIONMENT OF MARYLAND HOUSE UNDER EXISTING
AND PROPOSED PLANS

| County | Population (1960) | By population | 1961 | Walsh plan | HB 604 | HB 23 |
|---|---|---|---|---|---|---|
| Allegany | 84,169 | 3 | 6 | 6 | 6 | 4 |
| Anne Arundel | 206,634 | 8 | 6 | 7 | 8 | 7 |
| Baltimore City | 939,024 | 36 | 36 | 36 | 40 | 36 |
| Baltimore | 492,428 | 19 | 6 | 9 | 4 | 11 |
| Calvert | 15,826 | 1 | 2 | 2 | 2 | 2 |
| Caroline | 19,462 | 1 | 2 | 2 | 2 | 2 |
| Carroll | 52,785 | 2 | 4 | 4 | 4 | 3 |
| Cecil | 48,408 | 2 | 3 | 3 | 4 | 3 |
| Charles | 32,572 | 2 | 2 | 2 | 3 | 2 |
| Dorchester | 29,666 | 1 | 4 | 4 | 4 | 2 |
| Frederick | 71,930 | 3 | 6 | 6 | 6 | 4 |
| Garrett | 20,420 | 1 | 3 | 3 | 3 | 2 |
| Harford | 76,422 | 2 | 4 | 4 | 5 | 4 |
| Howard | 36,152 | 1 | 2 | 2 | 3 | 2 |
| Kent | 15,481 | 1 | 2 | 2 | 2 | 2 |
| Montgomery | 340,928 | 13 | 6 | 8 | 9 | 9 |
| Prince George's | 357,395 | 14 | 6 | 8 | 9 | 9 |
| Queen Anne's | 16,569 | 1 | 2 | 2 | 2 | 2 |
| St. Mary's | 38,915 | 2 | 2 | 2 | 3 | 3 |
| Somerset | 19,623 | 1 | 3 | 3 | 3 | 2 |
| Talbot | 21,578 | 1 | 3 | 3 | 3 | 2 |
| Washington | 91,219 | 4 | 6 | 6 | 6 | 5 |
| Wicomico | 49,050 | 2 | 4 | 4 | 4 | 3 |
| Worcester | 23,733 | 1 | 3 | 3 | 3 | 2 |
| | | 122 | 123 | 131 | 138 | 123 |

not at the top of the list of legislative priorities. Under its terms, only the House of Delegates would be increased in size, by a total of twenty-one seats, spread through the areas of greatest population growth since 1950. Before the bill was introduced, however, a series of moves forced a compromise with the earlier compromises sufficient to add several of the smaller but growing counties to the list of large suburban subdivisions. Thus, for example, St. Mary's County, as well as Harford and two or three other of the smaller population centers, numbering at best not over 50,000 but having had their representation frozen since 1950, would have received one additional delegate, while the Third and Fifth districts of Baltimore, each over 200,000, would have received two each. At the time it was finally considered, the bill consisted of a rather watered-down version of equitable representation, its backers having embraced many small-county men in order to get better consideration for the proposal.

When the final vote was taken, the bill failed. One absent vote was that of a small-county truck-farmer–legislator who was unable to be in Annapolis that day because, it was reported, he had received a shipment of very delicate tomato plants requiring his immediate and prolonged personal attention. A second small-county man did not vote, and a third member was reportedly ill. An affirmative vote by any of these three would have assured final passage. The House vote was 73-47, with the division based strictly on small-versus-large–county constituencies. A three-fifths majority of the entire House was needed for a constitutional amendment, under the terms of the constitution.

One of the last acts of the state Senate during the regular 1962 legislative session was intended to prolong the system of legislative apportionment for at least five years. By a vote of sixteen to twelve, with one member abstaining, HB 23 failed by two votes to get the three-fifths majority of the membership required for a constitutional amendment. The House of Delegates had previously voted to put a constitutional amendment on the general election ballot for November 1962. In effect, Senate disapproval of a compromise plan to reapportion the 123-member House reflected the conservatism inherent in a ratio of representation which makes the senator from Baltimore County, with its half a million people, equal to the senator from Calvert County, with a population of 15,000. Had the Senate passed HB 23 by the necessary majority, no reapportionment would have taken place until 1965 or 1966, in accordance with the terms of the bill. But if a similar bill is passed in the 1963 session, there will then be no general election, as required for a referendum vote, until 1964; promulgation will doubtless consume more time, and chances are that 1966 will have come and gone before concrete action is taken.

HB 23—acceptable to the civic groups interested in apportionment because the House Judiciary Committee added an amendment giving the power to apportion the House to the governor following each decennial census—was an amalgamation of three or four measures submitted to the short legislative meeting of the Maryland General Assembly in February 1962. Under its terms, the House would retain its over-all membership of 123, with each county or legislative district entitled to a minimum of two delegates. The other sixty-five seats would be apportioned according to a formula of basic units of population and remainders which would in effect have taken thirteen seats from the overrepresented counties and given them to the large suburban counties. The biggest gainer would have been Baltimore County, to the extent of five extra seats. Baltimore city would have been required to redraw its district lines in order to maintain the six delegates per district to which it is now entitled. This would normally be done by the Baltimore city delegation in the House.

The bill, proposed in the fall of 1961 as a compromise by a small-county man, was adopted by Governor Tawes as one of his six priority legislative items before the 1962 session began. A group of large-county men with increasing determination, supported by effective pressure from the Governor's office, succeeded in passing the bill in the House with one vote to spare on a 75-47 roll call. In the smaller Senate, which was faced with its first serious consideration of the issue in an actual bill, provincial autonomy triumphed, and reapportionment was defeated. Most of the negative votes there can be explained by the fact that three-fourths of the state's population is represented by only one-third of the Senate. But the measure was opposed by two urban senators, from the First District of Baltimore city and from Anne Arundel County, the latter vote cast despite the fact that Anne Arundel would have *gained* seats under the proposed reapportionment.

## THE IMPACT OF *BAKER* V. *CARR*

As federal and state courts across the country began to flex their injunctive muscles over the issue of reapportionment, the Maryland Court of Appeals on April 25 remanded the case brought by the Maryland Committee for Fair Representation to Judge O. Bowie Duckett of the Anne Arundel County Circuit Court. In a 5-2 decision, the court held that the judiciary could and must decide whether states are apportioned in accord with the equal-protection clause of the Fourteenth Amendment cited by the U.S. Supreme Court. Judge Duckett was directed to assess the merits of a controversy which he had not even recognized as justiciable in his dismissal opinion of February 1961.

Two dissenters on the court held that no Supreme Court decision had yet faced the issue squarely and that even the Michigan case did not "foreclose" discretionary action by state courts. Furthermore, it was stated in the dissenting opinion, the Supreme Court cannot confer jurisdiction on state courts "even to enforce the Federal Constitution," should that power not be a part of the constitution and laws of Maryland.

The substance of the majority opinion went so far as to prescribe the remedies which the lower courts could offer, should the decision go in favor of the plaintiffs. First would be a declaration invalidating the constitutional sections providing for distribution of legislative seats. Since there is no provision for election of the General Assembly at-large, the legislature could, as a second possibility, sit in special session, if so called by the governor, to enact a reapportionment bill for the 1962 election. This might be accomplished by adjusting the voting strength of the members of the legislature or by an increase or decrease in the number of seats in the respective subdivisions. Third, the lower court order could also assign the legislature power to propose an amendment to the constitution making the temporary apportionment permanent.

In its entirety, the opinion bespoke an urgency which seemed to impel immediate action. Judge Duckett was admonished not to enjoin or offer injunctive relief. The Court of Appeals obviously wanted the governor and the legislature to cooperate in order to preserve the degree of political autonomy Maryland could still exercise. An outspoken warning that federal courts might take an active part in the intimate details of Maryland reapportionment was included in the opinion.

Governor Tawes, engaged in a bitterly contested party primary for which he had little stomach, sensed the need for the small-county support afforded him by the county-unit system of nominations. Yet, three weeks before Election Day a federal court in Georgia unhesitatingly threw out the only other similar nominating device, one which in some ways discriminated less against urban residents than did the Maryland law. The decision on Georgia's county-unit system, together with the Maryland Court of Appeals decision, prompted the Governor to promise to call a special session *after* the primary election. In the unprecedented situation confronting them, the Governor and the attorney general felt they should have the benefit of the lower court's opinion before the legislature met. At no point did the state argue that representation in the General Assembly was fair; it merely denied the capacity of the courts to judge basically political questions. The administration, which had worked for an evolutionary change in the apportionment system during the regular 1962 legislative session, sought—by the promise of a special session—to avoid the label of political hypocrisy placed on it by opponents in the primary.

The second fundamental force on the Maryland scene was the General Assembly, just beginning to realize that the day of reckoning was approaching. The leadership in the House of Delegates, which had been persuaded in the 1962 regular session to attempt enactment of a reapportionment amendment in the hope of postponing any direct consequences until at least 1967, now saw little chance for such a long delay.

A third major force, the Maryland Committee for Fair Representation and its allied civic organizations, assumed a more "reasonable" attitude in its public statements. The committee expanded its original argument before the Anne Arundel Circuit Court to include the county-unit system, and then used its good offices to sound out the administration and the legislators on salient features of any proposed new system of apportionment. Buttressed by the decision in *Baker* v. *Carr* and by the strong references made by the Maryland court to "invidious discrimination" in apportionment, the MCFR suddenly found itself in a commanding position.

A rapid-fire series of actions by all three branches of the Maryland government produced, in May 1962, a temporary measure designed to increase the representation of the population-swollen suburbs. Amid threats of gubernatorial retribution, insults and recriminations hurled at officials of the Committee for Fair Representation by small-county legislators, and unprecedented confusion in the legislative halls, a total of nineteen seats in the lower house was added to two districts of Baltimore city and four suburban counties in the Baltimore-Washington metropolitan areas. Maryland thus became the first state to reapportion under the pressure of the *Baker* v. *Carr* decision.

On May 24, Judge O. Bowie Duckett had ruled in *MCFR* v. *Tawes et al.* that the state constitutional requirements for distribution of seats in the House of Delegates were invalid. A special session of the legislature was convened in the last week of May pursuant to Judge Duckett's decision. That its measures were only temporary seemed of no great moment to suburban forces. A subsequent regular session would face the difficult task of drawing a permanent plan. The emergency statute was a necessity in view of the constitutional requirement for a larger majority for bills passed after June 1, and this was also one reason for the chaos that exceeded anything the nation's oldest state capitol building had ever seen. A suit to challenge the formula of Senate seating was pending, but the decades-long grip of small-county legislators seemed irrevocably broken.

# 17

## Tennessee

### INERTIA AND THE COURTS

*WILDER CRANE*
*University of Wisconsin—Milwaukee*

In March 1962, the United States Supreme Court made the unprecedented decision that a U.S. District Court had jurisdiction in a suit brought by urban taxpayers to challenge the apportionment of a state legislature. This paper is an account of the developments in Tennessee that led to a decision which is expected to have nation-wide consequences.

### THE PROBLEM

The Tennessee General Assembly, a Senate of thirty-three members and a House of Representatives of ninety-nine members, was not reapportioned between 1901 and 1962. The state constitution adopted in 1870 requires that the General Assembly reapportion its two houses the year following each national census, but the requirement was ignored by the legislators for sixty years.[1] The constitution does not, moreover, contain the common provisions guaranteeing small counties a minimum representation or restricting populous counties to a maximum. It restricts the House of Representatives to ninety-nine members and the Senate to one-third that number. Though it provides that counties having only two-thirds of the ratio shall be entitled to one member in the House of Representatives, it contains other provisions which allow compensation for fractional inequities in apportioning the Senate.[2] Thus, the constitution's only provision which might complicate reapportionment is its use of the terms "qualified voters"[3] and "qualified electors"[4] rather than population as the basis for apportionment. All parties to the court hearing in June 1962 used the adult population statistics.

The other distinctive institutional facts about the Tennessee legisla-

314

ture concern the basis of apportionment. Tennessee does not have a uniform system of single-member districts. All of the four metropolitan counties which have several representatives elect them all on a county-at-large basis; these metropolitan counties are Shelby (Memphis), Davidson (Nashville), Hamilton (Chattanooga), and Knox (Knoxville). A more distinctive Tennessee institution is the "floterial" district. In addition to their direct representatives, some counties share an extra representative with adjacent counties; some counties have no direct representative. Twenty-two of the ninety-nine districts in the House of Representatives under the 1901 apportionment were floterial. The seats are rotated among the counties in accordance with party agreements which are made with little regard to their respective populations, and sometimes with votes cast only in the candidates' county. This arrangement has required Davidson County (population 399,000) to allow neighboring Wilson County (population 27,000) to nominate this representative periodically and similarly requires Knox County (population 250,000) to defer to Loudon County (population 24,000).[5] Similar rotation agreements apply to some senatorial districts.

The failure of the legislature to reapportion from 1901 to 1962 resulted in the obvious underrepresentation of urban areas and over-representation of rural areas. In broadest terms, one-third of Tennessee's voters elected two-thirds of the legislators. The four metropolitan counties were most seriously underrepresented; as Table 1 indicates, these counties had over 40 per cent of the population but less than 20 per cent of the representatives.

TABLE 1

COMPARISON OF POPULATION AND LEGISLATIVE
REPRESENTATION OF FOUR METROPOLITAN
COUNTIES IN TENNESSEE

|  | Legislative seats (1961 session) | Population (1960 census) |
|---|---|---|
| House of Representatives | 20 per cent | 42 per cent |
| Senate | 18 per cent | 42 per cent |

However, the malapportionment was not as simple as mere discrimination against the four metropolitan counties. Tennessee, like Gaul, is divided into three parts, known as "grand divisions": mountainous east Tennessee, centering on Knoxville; bluegrass middle Tennessee, centering on Nashville; and what is virtually a northern extension of Mississippi, centering on Memphis.[6] The geographic, economic, and cultural differences among these divisions are probably greater than such differences among neighboring states in the North. For example, all the Midwestern states would have much more in common with one another than the three grand divisions of Tennessee have. The greatest contrasts exist between east and west Tennessee. East Tennessee was loyal to the Union during the Civil War, remains overwhelmingly Republican, is developing its industries at a rapid rate, and is growing in population. West Tennessee (with the single exception of Memphis) is a declining Southern rural area which is losing population at a rapid rate and whose segregationist policies (especially in Haywood and Fayette counties) have recently attracted nation-wide concern.

Malapportionment in Tennessee was most striking when one compared west and east Tennessee. Every county in west Tennessee except Shelby (Memphis) was overrepresented. Here one found counties such as Chester and Lake, which have less than 10,000 population but had a direct representative. In contrast, in east Tennessee one found non-metropolitan counties such as Sullivan (population 114,000) and Washington (population 64,000), which had only one representative.[7]

## THE INTERESTS

This overrepresentation of the stagnant and declining sections of the state has some cultural effects which may be as serious as the more obvious discrimination against metropolitan centers in the distribution of state aid. Overrepresentation of west Tennessee may be one of the explanations why the Tennessee legislature adopted resolutions condemning the Supreme Court decision on school segregation, whereas such Tennessee cities as Nashville have been cited as models for their effective and constructive steps toward school integration. Similar examples are the refusal of the 1961 legislature to repeal the prohibition of the teaching of evolution, for which Scopes was tried, and its refusal to allow bars and only grudging legalization of package liquor stores (with restrictive price controls) in five counties.

The consequences of malapportionment are more obvious in the distribution of state aid. The brief filed by the appellants in the Tennessee apportionment case before the Supreme Court summarizes the problem as follows:

> In the 1957-58 apportionment of the county aid funds, the General Assembly permitted 23 counties to receive 57.9% more state aid than would be the case on a basis of state aid per capita, and it turns out that these counties had 23 more direct representatives than permitted under the state constitution. Ten counties, having 25 less direct representatives than permitted under the Tennessee Constitution, among them Shelby, Knox, Hamilton, and Davidson, received 136.9% less state aid than on a per capita basis. Expressed another way, a voter

in Moore County (with a voting population in 1950 of 2,340) has 17 times as much representation in the Lower House as does a voter in Davidson County (1950 voting population 211,930), and Moore County receives 17 times the apportionment per vehicle of state gasoline taxes as does Davidson county.[8]

Accordingly, officials of the four metropolitan centers have taken the initiative in attempts to achieve reapportionment. Mayor Ben West of Nashville has been particularly active in this effort, but the other three metropolitan cities have also provided funds and legal assistance in efforts to achieve apportionment.

Nonetheless, it is not possible to assert that the reapportionment controversy is a simple rural-versus-urban conflict, because metropolitan area government officials have not been successful in mustering support from those other urban interests which might have been expected to support reapportionment. With the exception of the League of Women Voters, which has campaigned for reapportionment and cooperated in the attempts to achieve it by court action, other urban interests have given metropolitan city officials little assistance. Representatives of such clearly urban interests as labor, liquor, and the Tennessee Municipal League have on occasion stated that they did not favor reapportionment because it would merely increase the number of poor-quality metropolitan legislators. Even a state official of so clearly an urban interest as the AFL-CIO maintained that he found more sympathetic cooperation with the problems of labor from intelligent rural legislators than from the "bums" who reach the legislature from the county-at-large electoral lotteries in the metropolitan centers.

Partisan interests are probably as important in Tennessee as rural-versus-urban interests in the apportionment controversy. In contrast with most of the Northern states, however, the Republicans have most to gain from a reapportionment more accurately reflecting population. Thus, the few Republican legislators (partly because they are more competent than the Democratic metropolitan legislators) have taken the lead in fighting for reapportionment.

On a partisan basis, the apportionment of 1901 was not proportional, and recent trends have accelerated this discrepancy. In 1901, ten Republican counties with the requisite population were denied a representative, whereas thirteen Democratic counties without the requisite population were awarded a full representative.[9] Though there have been some partisan changes among the counties subsequently, east Tennessee remains solidly Republican, and its two Congressional districts are among the most safely Republican in the nation.[10] The Republicans have carried Tennessee in the last three presidential elections, with Nixon carrying the state by a 75,000-vote margin. In state-wide elections, the Repub-

licans can be certain of a minimum of 40 per cent of the votes.[11] Nonetheless, in the 1961 General Assembly, the Republicans had merely 19
per cent of the total: six of the thirty-three senators and nineteen of the
ninety-nine representatives. Although their leader, Sen. Robert Peters
(Kingsport), was the only member to enliven a legislature completely
dominated by the governor, the Republicans cannot really compete under
the present apportionment.

Senator Peters has regularly introduced reapportionment bills and
resolutions. Republicans and metropolitan Democrats have supported
him unanimously, but this combination can at best result in fourteen
of the thirty-three votes in the Senate and thirty-six of the ninety-nine
votes in the House of Representatives. East Tennessee Republicans also
took the initiative in court actions and subsequently enlisted the aid of
city officials and the League of Women Voters in the metropolitan
counties.

In 1961, after the U.S. Supreme Court had agreed to hear the Tennessee case, some observers had hoped that the Minnesota precedent [12]
would be followed, and that the Tennessee General Assembly would act
on its own initiative with some minimal reapportionment. However,
Senator Peters, although waging a series of verbal battles on the floor,
failed in his efforts to have his reapportionment bill taken from committee.[13] The most Peters could achieve was to join the Senate speaker
in cosponsoring measures to have the qualified voters enumerated and
the problem studied. The Legislative Council began another study after
the General Assembly adjourned in 1961 but announced it had nothing
to report even after the Supreme Court decision in 1962.

It has been customary for Tennessee governors to include a few
remarks in their messages to the General Assembly about the constitutional requirement of reapportionment. There is no indication that any
of the recent governors has done anything more. The incumbent governor,
Buford Ellington, a farm boy from Mississippi, squeezed through to
victory in an eight-way race in which he failed to win a plurality in any
metropolitan county. The *Nashville Tennessean* suggested that it was not
simply lack of intelligence which led him to state, when questioned on
the issue, that he was "not smart enough" to know how to achieve reapportionment.[14]

Tennessee governors are so powerful—with their four-year terms,
complete control over their administrations, and vast patronage—that
they have little trouble dominating their amateurish seventy-five-day-
maximum biennial legislatures, the majority of whose members are first-
termers. Thus, Governor Ellington pushed through his budget and complete administrative program this year in the first two weeks of the session.

Several techniques for reapportionment available in other states are not available in Tennessee. There are no constitutional provisions for initiative or referendum. The governor has no authority to call a constitutional convention. The General Assembly, which can call a convention by majority vote in two successive sessions, has consistently refused to do so.[15] Even if a convention were called, it would be chosen according to the present legislative apportionment.

The General Assembly itself may initiate amendments to the constitution by action in two successive sessions, but this device would hardly be a means of reapportioning. As a matter of fact, during the reapportionment controversies the only proposals for constitutional amendments came from the rural legislators, who proposed amending the constitution to give every county one representative in the event that the federal courts found that the violation of the Tennessee constitution also violated federal law.

## THE COURTS AND REAPPORTIONMENT

With all other routes barred, proponents of reapportionment began court action in 1955. The initiative was taken by persons in east Tennessee, primarily a group of Knoxville attorneys. Subsequently, city officials and members of the League of Women Voters contributed their support to these efforts.

In 1955, proponents of reapportionment brought an action in Chancery Court in Davidson County. As taxpayers, they alleged that the General Assembly was violating the state constitution. The Chancery Court accepted this allegation, but the Tennessee Supreme Court overruled; it held that to declare the 1901 act unconstitutional would deprive the state of a legislature.[16]

This decision closed the last door to state relief and thus led proponents of reapportionment to the federal courts. Money was obtained from city governments, more parties were enlisted, and a suit was brought in the U.S. District Court for the Middle District of Tennessee. The suit sought a declaratory judgment as well as an interlocutory and permanent injunction restraining state election officials from the execution of the apportionment act of 1901. Without taking testimony, a three-judge district court in 1959 granted a motion of attorneys from the Tennessee attorney general's office to dismiss on the ground that the court lacked jurisdiction.[17] Notice of appeal was filed with the U.S. Supreme Court in March 1960, and the Court noted probable jurisdiction in November 1960. Thus, the 1961 Tennessee legislature met with the threat of U.S. Supreme Court action hanging over it, but nonetheless did not act.

The Supreme Court heard arguments in April 1961 and heard further arguments at the beginning of the fall term in October. The appellants, as taxpayers and voters, brought their action under the U.S. Civil Rights acts, as amended in 1957 and 1960, to invalidate the 1901 Tennessee statute, which, they alleged, denied them equality of voting rights guaranteed by the constitution of Tennessee and by the equal-protection clause of the Fourteenth Amendment to the U.S. Constitution. They argued that the Tennessee case was distinguished from *Colegrove* v. *Green* in that, unlike *Colegrove,* there was no alternative to judicial assistance if relief were to be obtained; they also pointed out that in *Colegrove* there was no constitutional requirement for apportionment. Instead, they relied on *Gomillion* v. *Lightfoot,* in which state legislative action in setting local boundaries was found to be a deprivation of constitutional rights.[18]

The U.S. solicitor general entered the case in an *amicus* capacity to argue that U.S. courts should assume jurisdiction.[19] Remedies suggested by the appellants included remanding the case to the district court to allow state officials to present an acceptable apportionment plan, an injunction against further elections under the 1901 apportionment, an order to conduct state legislative elections at-large, or the direct application by the Court of the mathematical formula of the state constitution for reapportionment. Appellants stressed that the district court should be asked to attempt the first or least drastic of these remedies and move to the other remedies only in the event that the state legislature failed to act.

Attorneys for Tennessee argued merely that apportionment was an exclusively state matter, and that the federal courts had no jurisdiction. They did not attempt to defend the apportionment as equitable or constitutional and thus found themselves defending a violation of the state constitution.

On March 26, 1962, the Supreme Court announced its decision.[20] Although the justices disagreed on the implications of their six-to-two holding, the majority agreed as a minimum that U.S. courts had jurisdiction, that the case was justiciable, and that the plaintiffs had standing to bring the action. The two dissents and the three separate concurring opinions created some ambiguity. More important, however, was the failure of the Supreme Court to provide any guidance to the district court to which the case was remanded.

The immediate reaction of Tennessee officials to the Supreme Court decision gave little promise that they would assume the initiative for reapportionment. Governor Ellington was hesitant to call a special session of the legislature in the last months of his term. On reading the decision, the Governor declared that he was "more confused than ever," but he did apparently understand the implications of having received five hundred letters and calls urging him to defend the present apportionment, as contrasted with only three requests to call a special session of the legislature. Instead of immediately taking the initiative, the Governor blithely suggested that the state remain neutral to allow the urban and rural groups to fight the issue out in court. His attorney general immediately declared that this course of action was impossible, since his office had an obligation to defend the state against the plaintiffs' challenge.

The announced candidates for governor publicly expressed relief that the reapportionment question was in the courts and thus removed from campaign controversy. Similarly, legislative leaders adopted a wait-and-see attitude. The administration leader in the House of Representatives, long a leader of the rural faction, announced that the Court would have to order a specific plan of reapportionment, because the legislature was unable to do so. The Legislative Council, to which the problem had been assigned in the 1961 session, met a few days after the Supreme Court decision and announced that it had nothing to report and would have nothing to report until after the fall elections of 1962.

Following the Supreme Court decision, the only concrete proposal by rural legislative leaders was one to amend the constitution to give legal validity to rural overrepresentation in at least one house of the legislature. This proposal, which has been held in reserve for many years as a counterthreat to other reapportionment proposals, would give each of ninety-five counties one representative and each of the four metropolitan counties two representatives in the lower house. Paradoxically, therefore, the only rural legislators proposing to act before the district court made a decision suggested a reduction in urban representation.

A month after the Supreme Court announced its decision, Governor Ellington, observing the swift and decisive action by courts in Alabama, Georgia, and Maryland, changed his mind and began attempts at compromise. On May 2, the Governor announced that, though he had been unable to get advance legislative agreement on a reapportionment plan, he was calling a special session of the legislature. He warned that the federal courts might reapportion the state if the legislature failed to do so. In the meantime, the attorney general asked the court to delay hearing the case until the legislature had had an opportunity to act.

The Tennessee legislature met in special session on May 29, 1962. On June 7, Governor Ellington signed Tennessee's first reapportionment measure in sixty-one years. The new apportionment was the work of the Governor's legislative leaders, particularly House Speaker James Bomar and Senate Speaker William D. Baird, who skillfully steered the bills through both houses. The Governor stayed in the background, though he made some efforts to get a compromise acceptable to urban interests. He described the final bills as "good bills" that "went farther than I had expected." Reapportionment was accomplished through separate bills for each house, each of which increased representation for metropolitan and eastern Tennessee counties but neither of which conformed fully to population requirements in the state constitution. The four metropolitan counties, which have 43 per cent of the adult population, increased their Senate seats from six to ten out of thirty-three and lost one of the two Senate floterial seats. They increased their House seats from twenty to thirty-two out of ninety-nine and lost both floterial seats there. The eastern Tennessee counties, with 27 per cent of the adult population, continued to receive seven Senate seats but increased their number in the House from twenty to twenty-six. The Baird measure allotted the Senate seats somewhat equally among the nine Congressional districts with little regard for population equities. The Bomar measure for the House was based more closely on the state constitution, except that the principle of allotting a representative to counties with only two-thirds of a ratio was extended to the floterial districts.

Almost all metropolitan legislators opposed both bills in the roll calls. Two-thirds of the Republicans opposed the Senate bill, but a large majority of them (outside Knoxville) voted for the House measure, which had been amended by the leadership to grant concessions to Republican eastern Tennessee. Thus, the unusual coalition of metropolitan and eastern Tennessee legislators, formed with some difficulty at the start of the special session, failed to hold together. The coalition did propose a measure which was based completely on the voting-population standards in the state constitution, but it won only fifteen votes in the Senate and twenty-nine in the House.

The special session also voted to propose to the voters a limited constitutional convention pertaining to certain legislative articles, including apportionment. Metropolitan and Republican legislators generally voted against the proposed convention, not only because it might open the way to diluting the population principle set forth in the constitution, but also because the bill prescribed that representation at the convention would be the same as that prevailing for the lower house *before* reapportionment. Sponsors of the proposal for a convention, which could not meet until 1965, obviously hoped that judicial decisions before that time would clearly permit a modification of the population principle for one house.

After passage of the reapportionment legislation, the three-judge federal court held a hearing, on June 11, to consider whether the new law met constitutional standards. The plaintiffs argued that the new apportionment set no rational standards and made arbitrary distinctions even among urban counties and among rural counties. They argued that the court could and should draw up its own apportionment plan, and they offered several plans described as adhering to the state constitution. The court did not appear to welcome the invitation to accept one of these or devise its own. The defense position, argued most effectively by an attorney for the Farm Bureau, was that the House apportionment adhered quite closely to the state constitution, with most of the population inequalities resulting from the provision of a seat to counties with two-thirds of a ratio, as required by the constitution. There was a less vigorous defense of the Senate plan, which admittedly was based in part on the political necessity of winning votes in the legislature. The defense argued that, if there were inequities in either plan, the legislature should be given an opportunity to correct them in 1963.

On June 22 the three-judge court held that "at least one house should be based fully on population," and it said that neither house met that standard under the new apportionment. The reapportionment was judged to have removed glaring inequities in the House but to have retained enough inequality to cause serious doubts about its constitutionality, while the Senate reapportionment was said to be "devoid of any standard or rational plan or classification." Though accepting most of the plaintiff's arguments, the court accepted the remedy suggested by the defense. It said that the legislature could be elected in 1962 on the basis of the new apportionment and that the 1963 legislature should have an opportunity to make revisions in the apportionment. The case might be reopened in June 1963.[21] The *Baker* v. *Carr* decision, so significant for the rest of the nation, was beginning to have tangible effects on the politics of Tennessee.

# Notes

[1] Tennessee Constitution, Art. II, Sec. 4.

[2] *Loc. cit.*, 5 and 6.

[3] *Loc. cit.*, 4 and 5.

[4] *Loc. cit.*, 6.

[5] These statistics are taken from the 1960 census and are based on: *Memorandum on Legislative Reapportionment in Tennessee* (Knoxville: Bureau of Public Administration, University of Tennessee, 1961).

[6] The political geography of Tennessee is well explained by William Goodman, *Inherited Domain: Political Parties in Tennessee* (Knoxville: Bureau of Public Administration, University of Tennessee, 1954).

[7] *Memorandum on Legislative Apportionment in Tennessee, op. cit.* See also Tennessee State Planning Commission, *Population Projections and Apportionment of Representatives and Senators* (Nashville: 1953), and Sherlock Hope, *Statistical Key to Legislative Reapportionment* (Knoxville: n.d.).

[8] *Charles W. Baker, et al.* v. *Joe C. Carr, et al.,* Brief for Appellants, U.S. Supreme Court, No. 103, October Term, 1960, p. 13.

[9] Robert H. White, *Historical Background of Legislative Reapportionment in Tennessee* (Mimeographed; Nashville: State Library, 1959), p. 14.

[10] Congressional districts are malapportioned in accordance with this same pattern of underrepresentation of east Tennessee Republican districts and overrepresentation of west Tennessee Democratic districts. East Tennessee's First and Second districts have, respectively, 255,000 and 269,000 registered voters, whereas west Tennessee's Seventh and Eighth districts have 116,000 and 111,000 registered voters, respectively. Office of the Secretary of State, *Tennessee Voter Statistics* (Mimeographed; Nashville: 1960).

[11] For voting statistics, see *Tennessee Blue Book, 1960* (Nashville: 1960), pp. 174-200.

[12] *Magraw* v. *Donovan,* 159 F. Supp. 901, 163 F. Supp. 184 (1958), and 177 F. Supp. 803 (1959).

[13] Although the brief for appellants in the current apportionment case asserts that the maximum number of votes for reapportionment in the Senate is thirteen (*Baker* v. *Carr,* p. 14), Peters received fourteen votes in his attempts to bring his measure to the floor; one nonmetropolitan Democrat from a county with a population of 71,000 joined the Republicans and metropolitan Democrats in this 1961 roll call.

[14] *Nashville Tennessean,* June 4, 1961.

[15] Tennessee Constitution, Art. XI, Sec. 3.

[16] *Kidd* v. *McCanless,* 200 Tenn. 282, 292 S.W. 2d 40 (1956); appeal dismissed 352 U.S. 920.

[17] 179 F. Supp. 824 (M.D. Tenn. 1959).

[18] *Baker* v. *Carr* Brief, esp. pp. 31-34.

[19] *Congressional Quarterly,* XIX (1961), 531 f.

[20] *Baker* v. *Carr,* 369 U.S. 186 (1962).

[21] *Baker* v. *Carr,* 31 *U.S. Law Week* 2003.

# Bibliographic Note

One of the most comprehensive treatments of Congressional and legislative apportionment is "Legislative Reapportionment," *Law and Contemporary Problems*, XVII (Spring, 1952), 253-469. This series of articles, covering the legal, statistical, and political aspects of apportionment, includes a wealth of detail. The National Municipal League has published a *Compendium on Legislative Apportionment* (2nd ed.; New York: National Municipal League, 1962), containing brief reports on the status of apportionment in each state. The second edition (January 1962) includes 1960 census figures and legislative developments through May 1961, and this loose-leaf volume is designed to be kept up-to-date through periodic revision. The National Municipal League's periodical, *The National Civic Review*, regularly reports current developments in state legislative apportionment. The *Congressional Quarterly Weekly Reports* during 1961 and 1962 reported in detail the Congressional redistricting legislation in each state.

Two of the best brief treatments of the legislative apportionment question are the short volumes by Gordon E. Baker: *Rural Versus Urban Political Power* (New York: Random House, 1955) and *State Constitutions: Reapportionment* (New York: National Municipal League, 1960). A detailed statistical analysis of the value of the vote in state legislatures, based on the 1960 census, is to be found in Paul T. David and Ralph Eisenberg, *Devaluation of the Urban and Suburban Vote* (Charlottesville: Bureau of Public Administration, University of Virginia, 1961). Maurice Klain examined the labyrinth of single- and multimember districts in "A New Look at the Constituencies: The Need for a Recount and a Reappraisal," *American Political Science Review*, XLIX (1955), 1105-1119. For an analysis of the variety of constitutional provisions on apportionment, see Malcolm E. Jewell, "Constitutional Provisions for State

Legislative Apportionment," *Western Political Quarterly,* VIII (1955), 271-279. An excellent analysis of the judicial aspects of apportionment prior to the *Baker* v. *Carr* decision is to be found in Anthony Lewis, "Legislative Apportionment and the Federal Courts," *Harvard Law Review,* LXXI (1958), 1057-1098. A detailed bibliography of articles on apportionment is included in Belle Zeller, ed., *American State Legislatures* (New York: Thomas Y. Crowell Co., 1954).

There are many studies of apportionment in individual states, often published by bureaus of government research or public administration in the state universities. Among the best studies available are Gilbert Y. Steiner and Samuel K. Gove, *Legislative Politics in Illinois* (Urbana: University of Illinois Press, 1960), chs. 4 and 5; Thomas Page, *Legislative Apportionment in Kansas* (Lawrence: Bureau of Government Research, University of Kansas, 1952); William C. Havard and Loren P. Beth, *Representative Government and Reapportionment: A Case Study of Florida* (Gainesville: Public Administration Clearing Service, University of Florida, 1960); Gordon E. Baker, *The Politics of Reapportionment in Washington State* (New York: Holt, Rinehart, and Winston, 1960); and Thomas S. Barclay, "The Reapportionment Struggle in California in 1948," *Western Political Quarterly,* IV (1951), 313-324.

# INDEX

# Index